A Social History of Hebrew

The Anchor Yale Bible Reference Library is a project of international and interfaith scope in which Protestant, Catholic, and Jewish scholars from many countries contribute individual volumes. The project is not sponsored by any ecclesiastical organization and is not intended to reflect any particular theological doctrine.

The series is committed to producing volumes in the tradition established half a century ago by the founders of the Anchor Bible, William Foxwell Albright and David Noel Freedman. It aims to present the best contemporary scholarship in a way that is accessible not only to scholars but also to the educated nonspecialist. It is committed to work of sound philological and historical scholarship, supplemented by insight from modern methods, such as sociological and literary criticism.

John J. Collins
General Editor

WILLIAM M. SCHNIEDEWIND

A Social History of Hebrew

ITS ORIGINS THROUGH THE RABBINIC PERIOD

YALE
AYBRL

THE ANCHOR YALE BIBLE REFERENCE LIBRARY

Yale UNIVERSITY PRESS
New Haven &
London

Published with assistance from the foundation established in memory of Amasa Stone Mather of the Class of 1907, Yale College.

Set in Sabon type by Newgen North America.
Printed in the United States of America.

Library of Congress Cataloging-in-Publication Data

Schniedewind, William M.
A social history of Hebrew : its origins through the Rabbinic period / William M. Schniedewind.
pages cm. — (The Anchor Yale Bible reference library)
Includes bibliographical references and index.
ISBN 978-0-300-17668-1 (cloth : alk. paper) 1. Hebrew language—History. 2. Hebrew language, Post-Biblical—History. I. Title.
PJ4545.S434 2013
492.4′09—dc23

2013011898

A catalogue record for this book is available from the British Library.

This paper meets the requirements of ANSI/NISO Z39.48-1992 (Permanence of Paper).

10 9 8 7 6 5 4 3 2 1

To Norma Kershaw, for
her interest, enthusiasm, and
support in many ways

Contents

Preface

This book has had a long journey to its destination. It has been assisted along the way by many people, was sidetracked by detours, and met fellow travelers. The journey is an important preamble for understanding its final destination.

I wish to begin by thanking my first teachers in Hebrew and Semitic languages. The fact that the writer of this book began studying both modern and ancient Hebrew at the same time in the land of Israel, in Jerusalem, and on Mount Zion is a critical bit of background information about this book. My first biblical teachers were Jerome Lund, William Williams, and Weston Fields at the American Institute of Holy Land Studies (now known as Jerusalem University College). I remember with especial fondness the courses by Chaim Rabin, who taught me Comparative Semitics and served as an advisor on my M.A. thesis. He is still the best language teacher that I ever had and was far ahead of his time in the social approach to studying ancient Hebrew. I am forever grateful for the rigor in Hebrew required for my doctoral studies at Brandeis University. I especially wish to thank Stephen Geller, Avi Hurvitz, and Daniel Sivan, who taught me in various courses in Hebrew, Aramaic, epigraphy, and Northwest Semitics. I also remember with fondness the late Anson Rainey, who was first my teacher and later my friend, and who bore with me as I learned about the Hebrew verbal system and Amarna Canaanite.

The research for this book began in earnest after I took up my position at UCLA in 1994, and later in 1996 when I took a sabbatical in Jerusalem as a visiting scholar at the Hebrew University working on Northern Hebrew. UCLA has been a rich environment to study languages, beginning with my first chair, then colleague and friend Antonio Loprieno. I wish to thank my colleagues who have contributed in small and large ways to this book, including Carol Bakhos, Ra'anan Boustan, Aaron Burke, Jacco Dieleman, Rahim Shayegan, and Yona Sabar. I am grateful for Sarah Shectman, who became a colleague and also a careful reviewer. I have been particularly fortunate while working on this book to have encountered some of the finest scholars of linguistic anthropology at UCLA, including Alessandro Duranti and Paul Kroskrity. UCLA has been a wonderful place to work, and I am forever grateful for my colleagues who have enriched my scholarly horizons.

Perhaps one of the understated joys of scholarship is the fellow travelers that you meet along the journey. I have particularly profited from David Carr, Frank Polak, and Seth Sanders, whom I met along the way to completing this book. Perhaps most influential are my students, especially Matt Suriano, Jeremy Smoak, Cale Johnson, Moise Isaac, Melissa Ramos, and Alice Mandell, who served as research assistants and dialogue partners along the way. I've learned perhaps more from them than I was able to teach them, and I and the book are both better for all my students and their contributions. One can never have enough careful readers, and I am particularly thankful to John Collins for his incisive reading of the manuscript and his support for the project. I apologize to him for being too thick or dull to take all of his advice. I am also grateful for the support of Norma Kershaw, who endowed my chair at UCLA and who has been a faithful supporter of my research and of the field of ancient eastern Mediterranean studies.

This book has met with considerable detours and obstacles. The first obstacle was my appointment as chair of the Department of Near Eastern Languages and Cultures in 2000. Administrative duties have certainly waylaid this book. In the course of writing, I also had the idea of writing a more general work on the role of writing in the formation of the Bible, which was published as *How the Bible Became a Book: The Textualization of Ancient Israel* in 2004. Although I began that book after I began this one, I completed *How the Bible Became a Book* first. Nevertheless, I think it was a useful detour. I was finally able to complete the initial manuscript for this book during a three-year hiatus from serving as department chair from 2007 to 2010.

I have endeavored to make this book accessible to a wide range of readers. Just as I have profited from interactions with a variety of scholars outside of historical Hebrew linguistics, I hope this book will be of interest to a wide variety of people with interest in language and Jewish history. In that respect, I have generally used romanized Hebrew transcriptions rather than the modern Hebrew alphabet. I have also preferred to use simplified transcriptions of the ancient Hebrew (that is, without the later Masoretic vowels), except in cases where the later vocalizations served to illustrate or advance the argument. In general, the translations of the Bible are my own; that said, I give translations that are close to standard scholarly ones, like the New Revised Standard or the New Jewish Publication Society versions. Likewise, I give my own translations of ancient inscriptions, unless otherwise indicated.

Finally, while working on this book, I have also witnessed the growth of my two daughters from toddlers to college age. I hope that I have written something that is worthy of their reading. Though last, it is certainly not least that I acknowledge my patient wife, who has immeasurably enriched not only this book but my life.

Abbreviations

ABD	*Anchor Bible Dictionary*, edited by D. N. Freedman. 6 vols. New York: Doubleday, 1992
ABH	Archaic Biblical Hebrew
ABL	*Assyrian and Babylonian Letters*, edited by R. Harper. Chicago: University of Chicago Press, 1914
b.	Babylonian Talmud
CAD	*Chicago Assyrian Dictionary*, edited by M. Roth. Chicago: Oriental Institute of the University of Chicago, 1956–2006
COS	*Context of Scripture*, edited by W. Hallo and K. L. Younger. 3 vols. Leiden: Brill, 2003
EA	El-Amarna. See *The Amarna Letters*, edited by W. Moran. Baltimore, MD: Johns Hopkins University, 2000
EH	Epigraphic Hebrew
EM	*Encyclopedia Miqra'it*. Jerusalem: Bialik, 1965–1988
EncJud	*Encyclopedia Judaica*. 16 vols. Philadelphia: Coronet, 1972
IH	Israelian Hebrew
KTU	*Keilschrift Texte aus Ugarit*, edited by M. Dietrich, O. Loretz, and J. Sanmartin. Translated as *The Cuneiform Alphabetic Texts from Ugarit, Ras Ibn Hani and Other Places*. 2nd ed. Münster, Germany: Ugarit-Verlag, 1995
LBH	Late Biblical Hebrew
m.	Mishnah

MH Mishnaic Hebrew
MT Masoretic Text
PRU *Le palais royal d'Ugarit*, edited by C. Virolleaud, J. Nougayrol, and C. Shaeffer. Mission archéologique de Ras Shamra. Paris: Imprimerie nationale, 1955–1970
Q Qumran Cave
QH Qumran Hebrew
RH Rabbinic Hebrew
RH_1 Tannaitic Hebrew, or early Rabbinic Hebrew
RH_2 Amoraic Hebrew, or late Rabbinic Hebrew
SAA State Archives of Assyria. Institute for Asian & African Studies, University of Helsinki, Finland, 1987–
SBH Standard Biblical Hebrew
t. Tosefta
y. Talmud Yerushalmi

A Social History of Hebrew

1

Language, Land, and People: Toward the History of Classical Hebrew

These are the descendants of Shem according to their families, their languages, their lands, and their nations.

—*Genesis 10:31*

As I finish this book, I recall a public lecture I attended one evening at a prestigious private university. After the lecture, a few students gathered around an eminent scholar of Semitic languages, who casually commented, "I am only interested in the languages, not the people who spoke them." I was a young graduate student back then, and I no longer recall either the lecture or the exact topic of the conversation that prompted the remark. But I still remember those words and my sense of stunned amazement. I had thought that the purpose of studying obscure ancient languages was to understand the people, their societies, and their cultures. Little did I know that I would eventually be writing this book arguing for a close relationship between the early history of the Jewish people and the Hebrew language. This book contends that language does not stand apart from the social history of its people. Language and writing are part of a cultural system, and the early history of the Hebrew language is closely tied to the early history of the Jewish people.

Of course, my sense of amazement about the separation between the study of languages and the people who speak them was really a function of my own ignorance. The well-known linguistic anthropologist Alessandro Duranti points out that this distinction is typical of the formal approach to linguistic analysis: "In general, phonologists, morphologists, and syntacticians are more interested in the relationship among different elements of the linguistic system (sounds, parts of words, phrases and sentences) than in the relationship between such elements and the 'world out there' that such a system is meant to represent."[1] This disjunction between languages and their speakers takes the study of language out of context. As Duranti observes, "It is hence a very abstract and removed *Homo sapiens* that is being studied by most formal grammarians, not the kids in a Philadelphia neighborhood or the orators of Ghana."[2] Likewise, it has often been a disembodied Hebrew that scholars have studied, as if the history of the Hebrew language were somehow unrelated to the social history of the prophets and poets, scribes and priests who penned the ancient Hebrew language.

This book has two propositions that guide it and give it a unique perspective on the history of the Hebrew language. First, it begins with the premise that the ancient Hebrew language was part of the social fabric of the people living in the ancient eastern Mediterranean. This hardly seems like a revolutionary statement. Language is constrained by its role as a communication device. We do not talk to ourselves—at least we are not supposed to. A language is conditioned by the movements of social life—the vicissitudes of war and peace, the inroads of nationalism and imperialism, the upheavals of urbanization and immigration, and the ebb and flow of economic tides. As such, the history of a language mirrors the history of the people who speak it—or, in our present case, the people who wrote our texts. Languages take their cues from the social life of peoples and nations. As Edward Sapir put it, "The history of language and the history of culture move along parallel lines."[3] They move along parallel lines because they are part of the same cultural system.[4] The history of Hebrew is no exception. Classical Hebrew was intimately connected to the life of the people. The ancient Hebrew language was both socially conditioned and socially constrained.

Second, this book is shaped by the linguistics of *writing*, that is, the record of Hebrew in textual artifacts, rather than by the linguistics of *speech*, that is, the piecing together of the phonology of ancient Hebrew speakers. The study of Semitic languages, including Hebrew, has had an extraordinary focus on phonology, in spite of the problematic relationship between writing and speech as well as the inability to speak with native informants (except perhaps in a séance, as Saul and the witch of Endor did with Samuel!). Thus, this book focuses on the early history of Hebrew as a written language.

The Scope of This Book

The scope of this book is limited in a variety of ways. First of all, it focuses upon the history of ancient Hebrew *as a writing system*. The early history of the Hebrew language is, in some respects, the history of a writing system. As such, it is interested in questions that arise from the linguistics of textual artifacts, such as spelling, script, schools, and language standardization. It also tackles the problem of the relationship of writing to speech, while discussing the formidable problems encountered when trying to relate written artifacts to vernacular language. We can only guess how ancient Hebrew actually sounded, and scholars have tended to have rather romantic notions about the relationship between ancient writing systems and the sounds of these ancient languages. As the linguist Florian Coulmas has pointed out, "All phonographic writing systems, however refined and concerned with language-specific phonetic detail, omit great numbers of phonetic distinctions."[5] This book, then, will focus on the changes in the writing system and not on the phonetics of Hebrew.

At the same time, this book is concerned with the history of Hebrew as a vernacular. To be sure, there is no direct evidence for vernacular Hebrew. Obviously, there are no live informants. The written text is only indirect evidence for spoken Hebrew. But we can reconstruct aspects of the social life of the ancient Israelites who spoke Hebrew, what linguistic anthropologists call the "speech community."[6] Observations about the history of the speech community can lend great insight to the social history of the language, even if they do not tell us the exact pronunciation of the letter ש (is it *sh* or *s* or some variant thereof?) or exactly when the Canaanite shift (that is, /ā/ > /ō/) took place. This book will adapt the linguistic idea of the speech community to the type of evidence that we have, namely, written texts that were generated by a scribal community. The history of early Hebrew thus must be shaped first of all by understanding the history of the Hebrew scribal community (or communities) and secondarily by the history of the Hebrew speech community.

It should now be clear that this book will not be a traditional history of the Hebrew language. That is, this is not a history of the Hebrew language focusing primarily on the traditional linguistic categories of speech (for example, phonology, morphology). That has been done before, most recently by Angel Sáenz-Badillos, by Mireille Hadas-Lebel, and by E. Y. Kutscher's important, though incomplete, *History of the Hebrew Language*.[7] Several older works also cover aspects of the history of Hebrew. Bauer and Leander, Sperber, and several others have contributed historical grammars of biblical Hebrew. Those looking for a more complete description of phonetic and morphological developments in the Hebrew language must consult these other works. The present work aims more at understanding the relationship between the social life of the people in Canaan and the evolution of the Hebrew language. My approach is perhaps most influenced by my teacher Chaim Rabin. In his brief but brilliant little book *A Short History of the Hebrew Language*,[8] he describes the sociology of the Hebrew language, introducing us to the interplay between the Hebrew language and the history of the Jewish people. Rabin's work is now out of print and out of date, and it is so brief that it only tantalizes. There have been many attempts to popularize the history of the Hebrew language for a more general audience. The best examples of this are Edward Horowitz's old classic *How the Hebrew Language Grew* and Joel Hoffman's more recent book *In the Beginning: A Short History of the Hebrew Language*.[9] Yet, these works do not offer the broad historical survey of the Hebrew language as part of a cultural system, which I seek to reconstruct here.

Chronologically, this book is a social history of Hebrew from its emergence as a language in ancient Canaan until its disappearance as a regularly spoken language in Roman Palestine in about 200 C.E. Rabbinic Hebrew (RH) is the last gasp of Hebrew as a living language in Palestine.[10] Though Hebrew itself had ceased to be spoken by 200 C.E., the Mishnah was codified about 230 C.E. The term *Mishnaic Hebrew* (MH) is sometimes used as an alternative to *Rabbinic Hebrew*, but this term also has its deficiencies. Usually Mishnaic Hebrew privileges the Mishnah, even though the corpus of early rabbinic texts is much larger; furthermore, it focuses on textual artifacts rather than the cultural context with which I am trying to connect the Hebrew language. Indeed, scholars have described the two stages of Rabbinic Hebrew (that is, RH_1 and RH_2) as comprising an earlier period (RH_1, or Tannaitic Hebrew), continuing through the second century C.E. when Hebrew was still regularly spoken, and a later period (RH_2, or Amoraic Hebrew), at which stage Hebrew was essentially a literary language. Judging by the Bar Kokhba letters (132–135 C.E.), it would seem that the daily use of spoken Hebrew was already in sharp decline during the first centuries of the Common Era. Ultimately, Hebrew was uprooted from Palestine and accompanied the Jewish people throughout their wanderings until it found its way back to the Promised Land in the late nineteenth century C.E. As Sáenz-Badillos recognized, medieval Hebrew (as this stage is broadly termed) is much less clearly defined than are earlier stages.[11] This results from medieval Hebrew's eclectic dependence on various earlier stages of the language, the use of Hebrew primarily as a literary language, and the great variety of geographic and historical settings in which Hebrew was employed (for example, France, Spain, North Africa, Persia). These later stages in the social history of Hebrew have already been the subject of some sociolinguistic scrutiny and are beyond the scope of the present work.[12]

Inasmuch as this book is concerned with the nexus between language, land, and people, it has struggled with terminology. The terms that we use, like *Israel* or *Palestine*, are often loaded with modern political or religious baggage that is really outside the scope and interests of this book. I endeavor to use terms apolitically. One particularly interesting problem is the word for "people": What shall we call the people living in Judah/Yehud/Palestine from the Iron Age through the Roman period? There is only one Hebrew term, *yhwdy* /yᵉhûḏî/, which might be translated as "Yehudite," "Judean," or "Jew," reflecting the different eras of the people in the land. Typically, scholars might use the term *Jew* to refer to the Jewish people after the Bar Kokhba revolt (that is, after 135 C.E.). Some scholars might extend the use of the term to the people in the late Second Temple period, but would resist using *Jew* to refer to the Iron Age people living in and around Jerusalem. The distinctions make some historical sense, but they do not accord with the fact that there is just one Hebrew term. Moreover, one might question what makes the use of the term *Jew* acceptable for both 200 C.E. and 2000 C.E., but not for 200 C.E. and 200 B.C.E. Are "Jews" in 2000 and 200 C.E. more similar than in 200 C.E. and 200 B.C.E.? Moreover, the use of the same term by the ancient speech community created a sense of identity between the ancient "Jews" living in the Iron Age, the "Jews" living in the Second Temple period, and the "Jews" of late antiquity. A social anthropologist might even call this sense of identity "fictive kinship,"[13] but it is nevertheless reinforced by language and metalanguage (that is, the use of one Hebrew term, *yhwdy* /yᵉhûḏî/). For the purposes of this book, I wish to emphasize the linguistic connection between *yhwdy*, *yhwdh*, and *yhwdyt*—that is, the terms used for people, land, and language. It is not a coincidence that the linguistic nexus between people and language is broken after the Bar Kokhba revolt, when the Jews no longer lived in "Judah/Judea" and began using the term *ʿbryt*, "Hebrew," to refer to their language. In other words, the metalanguage for Hebrew closely follows the social history.

I call the language discussed in this book *classical* Hebrew. This is a much broader description than *biblical* Hebrew, which refers to the Hebrew represented in biblical texts. By classical Hebrew, I mean to refer to the Hebrew used during the classical period of history in Canaan, from the origins of the Jewish people until the dispersions of the early centuries of the Common Era. Thus, classical Hebrew subsumes several other Hebrew dialects, including biblical Hebrew, Qumran Hebrew, Epigraphic Hebrew, and early Rabbinic Hebrew. I will also utilize the standard chronological distinction within biblical Hebrew, namely, Archaic Biblical Hebrew (ABH), Standard Biblical Hebrew (SBH), and Late Biblical Hebrew (LBH).

The use of *classical* to refer to the entire scope of written Hebrew from biblical through Rabbinic Hebrew certainly broadens classical Hebrew out of its traditional constraints. I think, however, that it is important to recognize the aspects of continuity in spoken and written Hebrew over this time span, even though the Babylonian exile resulted in a major disjunction in the scribal institutions that produced Hebrew texts as well as the speech community that used Hebrew in ancient Judah. It is the continuity of Hebrew as a spoken and evolving language, in spite of the social and demographic disjunctions resulting from the Babylonian invasions and deportations, that justifies a more inclusive definition of classical Hebrew. Indeed, a broader definition of classical Hebrew has already been employed, for example, by *The Dictionary of Classical Hebrew*. This dictionary, however, does not include Rabbinic Hebrew—apparently for practical considerations. Its editor nevertheless boasts that his dictionary "does not restrict itself to, or privilege in any way, those ancient Hebrew texts found in the Bible."[14] Although a broader definition of classical Hebrew is commendable, the exclusion of the Mishnaic texts is given no linguistic rationale. The definition of classical Hebrew as spanning the period when Hebrew was a living, spoken language in a defined locale is a defensible linguistic definition that must include the first stage of Rabbinic Hebrew. More specifically, I will narrow the geographic region of this social history of Hebrew to the region of Judah/Yehud/Palestine. These three terms—*Judah*, *Yehud*, and *Palestine*—are the historical terms used in antiquity by the Jews themselves, the Persians, and the Romans for the territory centered around Jerusalem. The use of classical Hebrew arises in the kingdom of Judah at the end of the second millennium B.C.E. and declines in the province of Roman Palestina (Palestine) by 200 C.E.

It is worth reflecting on the question of *who* defines the scope of a language. How are languages classified and categorized? Languages are usually defined by politics, historical circumstance, or deeply held ideologies.[15] Thus, a language like "Chinese" is defined as one language by politics (as well as a unifying script that is promulgated by a government), in spite of the fact that the dialects of Mandarin and Cantonese are mutually unintelligible. On the other hand, a language like Serbo-Croatian has been redefined as two languages—Serbian and Croatian—as a result of historical and political events. One may ask whether Flemish and Dutch are one language or two. Here, it is important to recognize that all language classification is shaped by linguistic ideologies. For example, the description of Chinese as one language with several dialects, and of Norwegian, Danish, and Swedish as three languages is more a reflex of nationalism and borders than the conclusion of descriptive linguistics. As the sociolinguists Judith Irvine and Susan Gal observe, "Linguistic ideologies are held not only by the immediate participants in a local sociolinguistic system. They are also held by other observers, such as the linguists and ethnographers who have mapped the boundaries of languages and peoples, and provided descriptive accounts of them."[16]

We return now to our specific topic: Who has defined "classical Hebrew" as it has been understood in scholarship? Classical Hebrew has usually been synonymous with biblical Hebrew. This narrow definition of classical Hebrew has emerged, at least in part, as a result of the work of Christian theologians, who organized the rubric of *classical* Hebrew according to the *classical* period of Jewish history as they defined it. Thus, classical Hebrew has usually excluded Rabbinic or Mishnaic Hebrew, which belonged to the next era of history—the period after Christianity's decisive break with Judaism. Many medieval Jewish grammarians, in contrast, emphasized the continuity of the Hebrew language. No doubt this reflected, in part, the Jewish sense of historical continuity that is evident from ancient times. Consider, for example, a central social institution like the Passover commemoration or the oral tradition (see Exod. 13:14; *m. Avot* 1:1). Even though Hebrew itself ceased to be spoken as an everyday language by sometime in the third or fourth century C.E., Hebrew continued to be used as the language of sacred literature and even served as a trade language among Jews throughout the Diaspora. To be fair, the categories of classical and Rabbinic Hebrew were also shaped by the configuration of our sources. Until relatively recently, the main corpora of ancient Hebrew literature were the Hebrew Bible (or Old Testament) and rabbinic literature, with a considerable chronological gap between them. The discovery of a growing corpus of ancient Hebrew inscriptions as well as the Dead Sea Scrolls now invites us to redefine classical Hebrew in much broader terms.

Finally, it should be noted that the term *Hebrew* (עברית /ʿiḇrîṯ/) itself is not a biblical term for the Hebrew language. Although we now call the language of ancient Israel and Judah "Hebrew," this term first appears for the language in the Mishnah (*m. Gittin* 9:6, 8; *m. Yadayim* 4:5), which was edited around 230 C.E. That is, the metalinguistic term *Hebrew* emerged precisely when the speech community in Palestine was disappearing. Furthermore, it appeared when the traditional linguistic identification of people, language, and land had disappeared with the changed sociopolitical situation of the Jewish community. This new term also formally recognized the difference between Hebrew and Aramaic as two Jewish languages, in contrast to the New Testament's use of the Greek word *hebraisti* (Ἑβραϊστι) to refer to the vernacular Jewish language, without making clear whether this term refers to Hebrew or Aramaic.[17] The term for the Hebrew language that would have been used by the prophet Isaiah in 700 B.C.E. or the priest Ezra in 400 B.C.E. is *Yehudite* (יהודית /y^{e}hûḏîṯ/), which is derived from the word for the territory of Judah (יהודה /y^{e}hûḏâ/) and is also generally used for the ethnic group Judean/Jew (יהודי /y^{e}hûḏî/) in postexilic biblical literature, Qumran literature, and rabbinic literature. It is quite typical of languages to be called after territories and ethnicities: thus, German and Germany, English and England, or Chinese and China. This fact actually highlights changes in the Hebrew language as it related to *Jewish* identity in different periods. The Jews/Judeans who lived in Judah/Judea always spoke the Judean/Jewish language. It is only when the Jews were expelled from Judea that the Judean language ceased to be a living vernacular. In fact, it is only at this time that the Jewish language became "Hebrew." When the terminology for the language of the Jews is separated from that of the territory, it marks a profound shift in the history of the language itself. For the purposes of this book, I shall use the conventional (and later) term *Hebrew*.

In order to make this book more useful as a reference work to a variety of readers, I have attempted to compile short descriptions of the salient features of the various stages and dialects of written Hebrew. At the end of chapters 2–5 and 7–9, I provide a brief description of early West Semitic, Archaic Biblical Hebrew (ABH), Israelian Hebrew (IH), Epigraphic Hebrew (EH), Standard Biblical Hebrew (SBH), Late Biblical Hebrew (LBH), Qumran Hebrew (QH), and early Rabbinic Hebrew (RH_1).

The Linguistics of Writing Systems: Classical Hebrew

To further answer our question of what constitutes classical Hebrew, we should point to the exact object of our study—namely, textual artifacts. The ancient Hebrew language is embodied in a series of texts. Thus, whereas the ancient Hebrew language, as we know it, is a corpus of written texts, linguistics as a discipline has been fundamentally the study of *speech*. The question of the relationship between textual artifacts and speech raises the important question of linguistic consciousness. Namely, to what extent did ancient Judeans identify their vernacular with written texts? Or, put differently, would the term *Judahite*, which was used for the spoken language, also have referred to the writing system? These questions become even more interesting when we realize the limited nature of literacy in antiquity. Although we tend to equate writing with language, this is not an axiomatic connection. Thus, by posing the seemingly innocent question "What is classical Hebrew?" we also raise not only the issue of the intrinsic relationship between writing and speech but also the specific question about the relationship between the Hebrew writing system and the ancient speech community. Written artifacts are the products of a *scribal community*, not a *speech community*.

No writing system duplicates speech, and the gap between writing and speech varies from language to language. A strictly phonemic writing system would be a writing system with a one-to-one relationship between graphemes (that is, letters) and phonemes (that is, sounds).[18] Such writing systems are usually described as alphabetic writing. Languages like Spanish and Finnish have quite close relationships between graphemes and phonemes. English, on the other hand, exhibits a high degree of complexity in the relationship between graphemes and phonemes. Modern Hebrew lies somewhere between these extremes. *There are no pure phonemic writing systems*, and classical Hebrew is no exception. And it is not simply that writing imperfectly records speech. As Saussure notably pointed out, "Language and writing are two distinct systems of signs." Florian Coulmas goes further in his *Writing Systems: An Introduction to their Linguistic Analysis*, stating that "writing follows its own logic which is not that of speech."[19] In addition to the problematic relationship between writing and speech, there is also often an intentional distinction between certain aspects of writing systems and speech. The term *diglossia* is often used to describe the tension between writing conventions and speech.[20]

We know some of the ways in which classical Hebrew as a writing system was an imprecise representation of the phonemes of speech. Most notably, classical Hebrew writing originally lacked vowel letters, and for this reason it has been labeled an *abjad*, that is, an alphabetic writing system that generally represents only consonants.[21] Hebrew did begin to incorporate some vowels by the eighth century B.C.E., but a systematic representation of vowels did not develop until the sixth or seventh century C.E. In addition, we know that several Hebrew letters served for multiple phonemes, such as <ש> for /ś, š/; <ח> for /ḫ, ḥ/; and <ע> for /ʿ, ǵ/. Given that the Proto-Canaanite alphabetic inscriptions have a much richer inventory of graphemes—Ugaritic has twenty-eight consonantal graphemes, and the Serabit el-Khadem and Wadi el-Hôl inscriptions suggest at least forty-four graphemes—we cannot be certain about the precise degree to which the twenty-two-letter classical Hebrew alphabet represents its consonantal phonemes. For example, how was the Hebrew word *ʾrṣ* (ארץ), "land," pronounced in antiquity? We know that Arabic preserves the spelling *ʾrḍ*, and ancient Aramaic first wrote the word as *ʾrq* (ארק), then later as *ʾrʿ* (ארע). To what degree were hypothetical Proto-Semitic phonemes like /*ḍ/ preserved in the speech of ancient Israelites? Were they preserved in some places and not others? The shibboleth story in Judges 12:5–6 is instructive here:

> Then the Gileadites took the fords of the Jordan against the Ephraimites. Whenever one of the fugitives of Ephraim said, "Let me go over," the men of Gilead would say to him, "Are you an Ephraimite?" When he said, "No," they said to him, "Then say Shibboleth," and he said, "Sibboleth," for he could not pronounce it right. Then they seized him and killed him at the fords of the Jordan. Forty-two thousand of the Ephraimites fell at that time.

The difference here between *shibboleth* and *sibboleth* is a *graphemic* convention in the writing of the story, but scholars have only guesses about the pronunciations of this word.[22] The shibboleth-sibboleth story provides just a hint of the dialectal variation that must have existed and the limits of writing systems for conveying the precise nature of these differences. Without direct evidence from native speakers, we should be quite sanguine about reconstructing the phonology of ancient Hebrew.

The problem of reconstructing phonology is not simply the lack of native informants for ancient Hebrew but also the inadequacy of the written sources. Edward Ullendorff, for example, questioned the adequacy of the Bible as a source for Hebrew in his classic essay "Is Biblical Hebrew a Language?" Ullendorff began his critique by pointing out that the standard linguistic definition of language deals with sound, not text. Without native speakers, biblical Hebrew has no sounds. Ultimately, Ullendorff was more consumed by the inadequacy of the biblical Hebrew lexicon, namely, the fact that its limited vocabulary would not be adequate "to serve as the basis for the ordinary day-to-day requirements of a normal speech community."[23] The Hebrew Bible, for example, contains between seven thousand and eight thousand distinct words, as compared to a typical modern Hebrew dictionary, which contains upward of forty thousand words. But the problem is more than simply a reflex of the limited corpus of biblical Hebrew. Writing is simply not a surrogate for speech; thus, we must study the linguistics of a *writing system*, which has its own rules and logic quite apart from speech.

Spelling itself is not usually an attempt at graphic transcription of speech. *Spelling* might be defined as the phonographic segmentation of language, yet alphabetic spelling is problematic from a linguistic perspective. It has been pointed out, for example, that "illiterate adults find it difficult to divide the stream of speech into segments."[24] As a result, phonologists have increasingly moved away from the idea that the alphabet represents segments of speech, because individual letters are difficult to discern in speech.[25] Moreover, although speech may be represented as sequences of letters on an abstract level, letters never constitute a precise representation of speech. Compounding the problem of the relationship between speech and writing is the fact that spelling is a social convention. As Florian Coulmas has observed, "As a general rule, spelling conventions, once established, are more resistant to change than speech, which is another way of saying that written words tend to have an autonomous existence and phonetic interpretations are adjusted."[26] Conventional ways of spelling often override their straightforward phonetic reading. In a parody often attributed to Mark Twain, spelling has little to do with transcription and everything to do with convention. The author suggested some logical spelling reforms for English:

> For example, in Year 1 that useless letter *c* would be dropped to be replased either by *k* or *s*, and likewise *x* would no longer be part of the alphabet. The only kase in which *c* would be retained would be the *ch* formation, which will be dealt with later.
>
> Year 2 might reform *w* spelling, so that which and one would take the same konsonant, wile Year 3 might well abolish *y* replasing it with *i* and Iear 4 might fiks the *g/j* anomali wonse and for all.
>
> Jenerally, then, the improvement would kontinue iear bai iear with Iear 5 doing awai with useless double konsonants, and Iears 6–12 or so modifaiing vowlz and the rimeining voist and unvoist konsonants.
>
> Bai Iear 15 or sou, it wud fainali bi posibl tu meik ius ov thi ridandant letez *c*, *y* and *x*—bai now jast a memori in the maindz ov ould doderez—tu riplais *ch*, *sh*, and *th* rispektivli.
>
> Fainali, xen, aafte sam 20 iers ov orxogrefkl riform, wi wud hev a lojikl, kohirnt speling in ius xrewawt xe Ingliy-spiking werld.

English in particular is replete with irregularities and historical spellings, but this parody does highlight the fact that spelling is not transcription of speech.

Spelling can also have an ideological component. As an example, it is worth recalling Noah Webster's justification for spelling reform in American English in 1789: "As an independent nation, our honor requires us to have a system of our own, in language as well as government."[27] Somehow the spelling *honor*, as against the British *honour*, would help achieve a sense of national identity! Ironically, the differences in American and British spelling of words like *center/centre* or *color/colour* tell us very little about the differences in pronunciation. We can spell words like *schedule* or *about* exactly the same, but pronounce them quite differently.

Like spelling, script choice is also motivated by underlying ideologies.[28] Such ideological undercurrents can already be inferred in ancient Ugarit (ca. 1200 B.C.E.), where two writing systems—alphabetic cuneiform and standard cuneiform—are used and distinguish between national literature and correspondence and international matters. Another obvious example is the use of Paleo-Hebrew script on the coins used by fledgling Jewish kingdoms like the Hasmoneans and Bar Kokhba, as well as the modern state of Israel. When they established new and independent polities, they were careful to employ the Paleo-Hebrew script on the coins minted by the new government, even though the script was hopelessly anachronistic.

Orthography can also be a means of indicating language choice and group identity. Several scholars have discussed the "foreign factor" in the Hebrew Bible, that is, the tendency of biblical authors to introduce linguistic variation to indicate a foreign speaker or setting.[29] Scholars have noted a number of interesting examples of this phenomenon. Perhaps the most obvious is the use of an Aramaic sentence in Genesis 31:47, where Laban (who is described as an Aramaean and who lives in northern Syria) speaks one short sentence in Aramaic. Another notable example of this phenomenon is the word *mlh*, "word," in the book of Job. The story is set "in the east," and scholars have long noted the use of many linguistic elements colored with Aramaic and even Arabian "to indicate the foreign nature of the characters."[30] Perhaps the most telling example, however, is the variety of forms of the word *mlh*, "word," which itself is a metalinguistic term. In the book of Job, the word is interchangeably spelled with its Aramaic form *mlyn*, "words" (thirteen times), and its SBH form *mlym*, "words" (ten times). More telling, however, is the fact that this metalinguistic term is the only word in the entire book that interchanges between the Aramaic afformative *-yn* and the Hebrew afformative *-ym*. The scribes were thus quite aware of language and used it intentionally to indicate the identity of the characters in the narrative.

The field of linguistics has, in fact, emphasized speech as the proper focus for the study of language. One of Leonard Bloomfield's students went so far as to say that "language is basically speech, and writing is of no theoretical interest."[31] The reason for the virtual exclusion of writing from the field of linguistics is fundamentally biological. From a biological viewpoint, speech is perceived as "natural," whereas writing is contrived.[32] Speech—not writing—is one of the things that separate man from the animals. Speech exists in all human societies and appeared long before writing. For this reason, the French critic Jacques Derrida called writing "the wandering outcast" that has haunted the field of linguistics, even as the field tries to ignore it.[33] However, in the study of ancient Hebrew, we cannot ignore the written aspect of language.

Writing is not a simple correlate of language. The social setting for learning to read and write is formal. This social context is not conducive to radical changes, nor does it necessitate a close correspondence between writing and speech. In the words of Leonard Bloomfield, "The inadequacy of the actual [writing] systems is due largely to the conservatism of the people who write."[34] Writing is portrayed as an inadequate or inaccurate reflection of language. The conventions of writing often remain unchanged even after speech forms have undergone profound linguistic changes. As a result, writing is much more than a complement to speech. It is socially defined by scribal training. For example, the colloquial future in English is "going to," as in "I'm going to go on vacation next week," yet this colloquial future tense is not considered correct for formal written correspondence. Likewise, spelling is especially habitual, remaining long after speech forms have changed, as we readily observe in English words like *knight*, *gnat*, or *name*. In fact, Bloomfield points out that "once a system of spelling has become antiquated in relation to the spoken sounds, learned scribes are likely to invent pseudo-archaic spellings."[35] So, for example, the spelling with *b* in loanwords like *debt*, *doubt*, and *subtle* does not derive from Old French but rather was created by learned scribes who knew the Latin antecedents *debitum*, *dubito*, and *subtilis*. The changes in spelling, lexicon, and even grammar tend to be instigated by historical and ideological developments and not simply by the constant change in speech forms.

The problem of *writing* as a surrogate for *language* begins with the inadequacy of writing itself, namely, the problem of representing *sounds* with *letters*. Or, to use technical jargon, the graphemic inventory (that is, the letters) of Hebrew are an imprecise representation of the phonemic inventory (that is, the sounds) of the classical Hebrew language. The twenty-two-letter Hebrew alphabet was borrowed from Phoenician, which seems to have had a more limited inventory of phonemes than Hebrew. Furthermore, the Phoenician alphabet did not represent vowels, and this creates its own problems. As far as the consonantal graphemes are concerned, we know that Hebrew had at least twenty-five consonantal phonemes (that is, sounds) and that certain graphemes had to serve for multiple phonemes. So, for example, the letter *ʿayin* (ע) in the Phoenician alphabet had to serve double duty for both /ʿ/ and /ǵ/, and the letter *chet* (ח) serves for both /ḥ/ and /ḫ/. Likewise, the letter *shin* (ש) served for both /š/ and /ś/, and many centuries passed before the Masoretic system introduced a dot to distinguish between the two, שׁ and שׂ. Even these twenty-five consonants had to be an oversimplification of the phonemes of classical Hebrew. Spoken language naturally reflects a more fluid development between sounds, whereas the written language tends to be more static in its development. Often a significant gap develops between the written text that is prescribed by tradition, schools, and government and the spoken vernacular.

In his critique of biblical Hebrew as a language, Ullendorff further noted the deficiency of the consonantal skeleton of the Bible.[36] The system of writing ancient Hebrew is largely consonantal, even though vowel letters were introduced by the late eighth century B.C.E. The elaborate system of sublinear vowel letters (as well as accents) was only introduced by the Masoretes around the seventh century C.E. Although an increasingly developed use of vowel letters was introduced in ancient Israel and flourished in the Dead Sea Scrolls as well as rabbinic manuscripts, these vowel letters were still limited notations of the spoken language. Indeed, the Masoretic vocalizations of the book of Isaiah certainly did not represent the way the prophet Isaiah would have spoken Hebrew; rather, they represented a stylized liturgical tradition of reading that developed within the Jewish community.

Ferdinand de Saussure (1857–1913), the acknowledged Father of Modern Linguistics, called attention to *the arbitrariness of linguistic signs* (that is, written language). Saussure also called attention to the primary nature of the oral speech that underpins all verbal communication, criticizing the tendency to approach language primarily through its written manifestation. According to Saussure, writing is the complement to oral speech. Along the guidelines set forth by Saussure, linguistics developed primarily according to oral categories as a study of phonemics. To some extent, Saussure may be indirectly responsible for the focus in classical Hebrew studies on phonology and morphology.[37] For Hebrew, we would say that its writing was arbitrarily created and perpetuated in scribal schools. We should be clear, however, what we mean by "schools." The system of scribal training was largely an apprentice system, which was not open to all classes of society. The early history of Hebrew, then, would be a history of the scribal schools and the institutions that supported them.

In ancient societies, especially those without alphabetic writing (for example, Egyptian hieroglyphs or Mesopotamian cuneiform), the relationship between speech and written symbols was at best approximate. Even after the invention of the alphabet, the invention of only consonants without vowels makes the relationship between speech and writing imprecise.[38] The situation is much more complicated among other Levantine cultures that adopted the Phoenician consonantal alphabet, even though they had different and fuller phonetic inventories. This is somewhat analogous to cuneiform writing, where the writing system was invented by the Sumerians and borrowed for the Akkadian language even though Sumerian is an Indo-European language and Akkadian is Semitic. This observation does not even begin to take into consideration the conservative nature of the *written* linguistic code in representing the more fluid *oral* linguistic code.[39] This problem is amply illustrated for anyone who has tried to explain to a six-year-old why the English word spelled *knight* is pronounced /naɪt/. In short, letters greatly oversimplify sounds. This observation makes us quite sanguine about the nature of our investigation of the Hebrew language.

A Sociolinguistic Approach

The present study takes a sociolinguistic approach to the history of the Hebrew language. Simply put, sociolinguistics is the study of the relationship between language and society. It utilizes the tools and methods of the fields of linguistics and social theory. The discipline of sociolinguistics has grown immensely over the past few decades, and this has included the development of the field of anthropological linguistics. Although anthropological linguistics is sometimes separated from sociolinguistics, I regard them as related fields and would use the terms interchangeably.[40] There seems to be a general tendency for American scholars to prefer the term *anthropological linguistics*, whereas European scholars use the term *sociolinguistics*.

A critical premise of sociolinguistics is that language is part of a cultural system. Language does not exist in a vacuum. For example, sociolinguists argue that "*attitudes* to language clearly play an important role in preserving or removing dialect differences."[41] The noted linguist William Labov actually objected to the term *sociolinguistics* because he argued that language is a social behavior, thus rendering the term *sociolinguistics* redundant and misleading.[42] Language is used in social contexts for communicating needs, ideas, and emotions. Labov argued that the study of languages can never be conducted separately from their social contexts. He suggested that a different phrase, "the sociology of language," be used to refer to the interaction of large-scale social factors like dialect and language interaction, language planning, nationalism and language, or standardization of language. The present study will be more concerned with what Labov called the "sociology of language." In spite of Labov's objections, however, the term *sociolinguistics* has come to be used to describe a wide variety of the social aspects of language.

Though the discipline of sociolinguistics has developed especially in the last few decades, the social aspect of language has long been acknowledged in the academic study of linguistics. For example, Ferdinand de Saussure began his *Course in General Linguistics* with the premise that language is a social institution.[43] Saussure argued that language has both an individual and a social aspect and that one is not conceivable without the other.[44] It was not entirely novel for Saussure to claim that language is a social phenomenon. This view was influenced by Enlightenment thinkers such as the English philosophers Thomas Hobbes and John Locke, the German philosopher Johann Gottfried von Herder, and the French sociologist Émile Durkheim (to name only a few). Their influence was particularly strong in Saussure's understanding of language as a social institution.

The studies of Franz Boas, Edward Sapir, and Benjamin Whorf added an anthropological approach to the study of language.[45] Coming from the field of anthropology, they studied Native American peoples and their languages, and they argued that the grammar of a particular language shapes the way we think about reality. Indeed, this approach received a boost from the remarkable diversity of Native American languages. Boas, for instance, suggested that languages classify experience and that these linguistic classifications *reflect* rather than *dictate* culture. Sapir defined language as "*a purely human* and non-instinctive method of communicating ideas, emotions, and desires by means of *a system of voluntarily produced symbols*."[46] Whorf, although he acknowledged that culture might influence language, emphasized that it was through individuals and their habitual worlds that "language exerts pressure on the culture as a whole."[47] Although the stronger, deterministic version of the Sapir-Whorf "linguistic relativity hypothesis," namely, that language determines thought, is no longer acceptable, scholars acknowledge that language and culture do move along parallel lines, even if the exact relationship is difficult to prove.[48]

The modern study of language has also been shaped by the neogrammarian revolution in the late nineteenth century.[49] Neogrammarians argued that the principles or laws of language change could be analyzed accurately and completely once all the assembled facts were known. Laws regarding the regularity of sound change, such as Grimm's Law,[50] would then apply in all cases. The lure of the immutable neogrammarian "scientific" laws has exerted continuing influence. It is noteworthy that neogrammarian rules theoretically applied to spoken language, not to written language. Equally important has been the descriptive approach associated with Leonard Bloomfield.[51] Bloomfield himself was trained in the neogrammarian tradition, but his methodology was particularly influenced by his own fieldwork describing Native American languages. Though Bloomfield recognized the importance of the historical, or diachronic, aspect of language study, his own work focused on the synchronic description of language. Bloomfield argued that all historical study of language change or comparative study of languages was grounded in descriptive data. He allowed for no influence of society upon language, in part because his view was predominantly synchronic and contemporary. Nevertheless, the historical aspect of language, or language change, plays a minor role in his seminal work on language. Indeed, William Labov argued that "one cannot make any major advance towards understanding the mechanism of linguistic change without serious study of the social factors which motivate linguistic evolution."[52]

Recent trends in linguistics have emphasized the social function of language. This has developed into a field of its own—functional linguistics, which has blossomed over the past decades in an almost bewildering display of color and variety.[53] Socio- and functional linguistics have in common the premise that language arises from the human need to communicate (as opposed to the notion that language arises from man's need to express himself). Most linguists do not deal with social life at all.[54] The linguistic anthropologist Paul Kroskrity points to two neglected forces: "the linguistic 'awareness' of speakers and the (nonreferential) functions of language. Both of these forces were prematurely marginalized by the dominant and disciplinarily institutionalized approaches to language, which denied the relevance—to linguistics, certainly—of a speaker's own linguistic analysis and valorized the referential functions of language *to the exclusion of others*. In effect, this surgical removal of language from context produced an amputated 'language' that was the preferred object of the language sciences for most of the twentieth century."[55] As the British sociolinguist Suzanne Romaine notes, "Modern linguistics has generally taken for granted that grammars are unrelated to the social lives of their speakers"; at the same time, sociologists "have tended to treat society as if it could be constituted without language."[56] The term *sociolinguistics*—referring to the study of the relationship between language and society—was only coined in the 1950s, and the discipline is still young. It can hardly be surprising that sociolinguistics has yet to have an impact on the study of classical Hebrew.

Even in ancient Israel, language was a social marker linked with identity. The sociolinguist Andrée Tabouret-Keller notes, "The language spoken by somebody and his or her identity as a speaker of this language are inseparable.

This is surely a piece of knowledge as old as human speech itself."[57] This truism can be readily illustrated by an example that we have already discussed, namely, the shibboleth-sibboleth episode in Judges 12:5–6. Although the problem of how exactly the Gileadite and Ephraimite dialects differed is still a matter of debate (in part because of the imprecision of the graphemes), the commonplace sociolinguistic observation that language and linguistic forms can index social groups is played out. Traditional linguistic approaches to this text have endlessly debated the precise pronunciation of the sibilants, yet the real linguistic import of the text is sociolinguistic. It tells us, for instance, that language is a social boundary. Even among the Israelite tribes, linguistic distinctions were recognized and served as social markers. Seth Schwartz has observed that stories like the book of Ruth assume that "Judahites and Moabites spoke mutually comprehensible languages."[58] Yet just because languages or dialects are mutually intelligible does not mean that they do not index group identity. For example, a Canadian can distinguish himself from an American by the pronunciation of a few words, such as *about* or *schedule*, or by the use of "eh?" as the marker of a question. These are small but important markers of linguistic identity that are not merely modern, as we see in a story such as Judges 12. On the basis of language, we distinguish homelands and national and political affiliations, as well as social class. In the words of the fictional character Henry Higgins, "An Englishman's way of speaking absolutely classifies him."[59] To change our identity, we try to change the way we speak. This is to say, language change can be socially loaded.

The Study of Classical Hebrew

It should hardly be surprising that the diachronic study of classical Hebrew in its social context is relatively undeveloped territory. Indeed, a little more than two decades ago, Labov described the study of language change in its social context as a virgin field.[60] Since then, some scholars have begun to plow this field, but little work has been done to cultivate it specifically for classical Hebrew. The tradition of the field of Semitic linguistics and Hebrew in particular has followed a descriptive and neogrammarian orientation, with its emphasis on morphology and phonology. This is perhaps best illustrated by the fact that the classic grammar of Hebrew, by Gesenius, Kautzsch, and Cowley, gives almost no attention to syntax. The grammars of Joüon and Brockelmann are only slightly better.[61] The recent grammar by Waltke and O'Connor also focuses primarily on morphology and phonology in spite of its promising title, *An Introduction to Biblical Hebrew Syntax*.[62] A quick perusal of the main historical grammars and histories of the Hebrew language will not turn up anything like a prolegomenon to the study of language. One exception to this might be the somewhat-neglected study of Zelig Harris, *The Development of the Canaanite Dialects*.[63] The study of Hebrew, especially classical Hebrew, has been quite conventional. And "conventional" means that the traditional grammars and histories of Hebrew have been neogrammarian and descriptive.

As early as the 1950s, Chaim Rabin wrote an article on the social background of Qumran Hebrew.[64] In the 1970s he published a very short book entitled *A Short History of the Hebrew Language*, which was expressly concerned with the relationship between language and Jewish social life.[65] And his now-standard article on the emergence of classical Hebrew gives a decidedly sociohistorical interpretation.[66] Rabin's work reflected his broad training in linguistics and his interest in practical fields like translation theory. Although Rabin's articles on the emergence of classical Hebrew and on Qumran Hebrew have been well received, his sociolinguistic history of Hebrew is relatively unknown. Several other authors have addressed quite-limited issues that would fall into the purview of sociolinguistics. The classic work of Harris was concerned with the linguistic conditions in Syria-Palestine as these shaped the structure of the Canaanite language(s). The important recent work of Randall Garr employs a thoroughgoing descriptive approach in mapping a dialect geography of Syria-Palestine.[67] This forms a foundation for any sociolinguistic analysis. Gary Rendsburg's revised dissertation, published in 1990 under the title *Diglossia in Ancient Hebrew*, points to twelve grammatical features that he considers colloquial. He points out that these features become especially prominent in LBH but that they also appear in SBH. He reasons that "the dialect that later emerged as MH was already in use in the early Biblical period too."[68] Relying on Rabin's analysis of the emergence of biblical Hebrew, Rendsburg notes recent trends in linguistics that emphasize "the effect that political and social change may have on a language."[69] The subject, unfortunately, is dropped there. Rendsburg's more-recent work focusing on dialect geography and the history of Hebrew is not explicitly sociolinguistic, yet his work nevertheless touches on sociolinguistic issues time and again.

Perhaps the most extensive foray into the social groups behind the Hebrew language is Ian Young's *Diversity in Pre-Exilic Hebrew*.[70] Young eschews the traditional approach that tends to minimize linguistic diversity in order to create a standard biblical grammar. He argues that "orthodox scholarship" (as he calls it) relies too heavily on chronological explanations to account for the linguistic diversity in biblical Hebrew. According to Young, the diversity of preexilic Hebrew begins with the social diversity of the Israelite tribes themselves. He points to the impact of social forces on the linguistic evolution of preexilic Hebrew. The united monarchy, for example, becomes the catalyst for a standardization of Hebrew. Young's work is an important first step. He collects and analyzes many of the possible types of preexilic Hebrew and ascribes a variety of social settings to account for diversity. As I hope this work shall make clear, his work can be developed further in three important respects. First, there is little use of sociolinguistics or anthropological linguistics to inform his social analyses. As Labov pointed out, "The forces operating to produce linguistic change today are the same kind and order of magnitude as those which operated in the past five or ten thousand years."[71] This observation certainly invites broader interdisciplinary reflection on language diversity and change. Second, contributions from archaeology create a more nuanced understanding of the historical forces that shaped the evolution of classical Hebrew. Without a clear idea of the social forces at work, it is impossible to draw proper conclusions about the evolution of the Hebrew language. Finally, Young relies too heavily on assumptions about linguistic diversity generated by spoken languages, whereas biblical Hebrew is a literary language, and its written linguistic forms were formulated in scribal schools. For these reasons, Young's emphasis on synchronic linguistic diversity seems overstated.

One way to describe the field of classical Hebrew would be "formalist." By this we mean that classical Hebrew has often been treated as though the essential nature of Hebrew is intrinsic. The Hebrew language has been studied in isolation from other external forces, most notably sociological forces. We may further illustrate the problem by analogy to the related field of literature. I. R. Titunik explains the formalist position in literary theory: "Literature was an extrasocial phenomenon, or rather, that which constituted the 'literariness' of literature—its specificity—was something self-valuable, self-contained, and self-perpetuating that should and must be isolated from the social surrounding in which it existed in order to be made an object of knowledge; that while social forces and events could, and did sometimes even drastically, affect literature *from the outside*, the real, intrinsic nature of literature remained immune, exclusively and forever true to itself alone; that, therefore proper and productive study of literature is possible only in 'immanent' terms."[72] By substituting *language* for *literature*, we encapsulate a formalist approach to Hebrew that steers clear of social explanations. Indeed, one finds only occasional mention of social forces in traditional grammars. It is recognized, for instance, that the enormous influence that Aramaic exerted on Hebrew began with sociohistorical factors. The present work, in contrast, is predominantly concerned with such issues.

Sociolinguistics has by no means been a completely unexplored territory in the study of ancient Hebrew, and recently there has been increased interest. My own articles, "Prolegomena for the Sociolinguistics of Classical Hebrew," published in 2004, and "Sociolinguistic Reflections on the Letter of a Literate Soldier (Lachish 3)," published in 2000, are by no means the only examples of this recent interest. Several important contributions have also been made by Frank Polak, including his broad-ranging article entitled "Sociolinguistics: A Key to the Typology and the Social Background of Biblical Hebrew," published in 2006.[73] Attention to the field of sociolinguistics was also marked by a conference organized in 2003 by Seth Sanders, whose papers (including my own) were published in a volume entitled *Margins of Writing, Origins of Culture*.[74] These examples hopefully are the beginning of a more robust sociolinguistic approach to classical Hebrew.

Methodological Problems

Several significant methodological problems for studying the history of classical Hebrew must be acknowledged. An obvious obstacle to a sociolinguistic approach lies in the limited nature of the data. This pertains both to language and to social history. Moreover, the evidence of classical Hebrew comes only from sporadic written sources. Not surprisingly, there is scant evidence for spoken Hebrew—that is, for the real *language*. Moreover, the main written sources themselves are generations removed from their purported historical periods. A main literary source, the Hebrew Bible, was largely known from medieval manuscripts, until the discovery of the Dead Sea Scrolls provided witnesses as early as the third century B.C.E.[75] Even the Dead Sea Scrolls come to us quite removed from the autographs and incorporate some changes in their transmission.[76] Epigraphic sources, as well as the Dead Sea Scrolls, are primarily consonantal, although a restricted use of vowel letters does develop. Likewise, the Mishnah is known only from much-later manuscript evidence.

Another problem stems from the representation of the phonemic inventory (that is, sounds) of the Hebrew language by only twenty-two graphemes (that is, letters). The choice of a twenty-two-letter alphabet to represent the Hebrew language reflected the influence of the Phoenician scribal schools in the early Iron Age (ca. 1100 B.C.E.). Although transcriptions of Hebrew into other languages such as Greek made it clear that the Hebrew graphemic inventory simplified the richer phonemic inventory, the constraints of the scribal traditions preserved this alphabet.

Still, the study of linguistic change in classical Hebrew must be limited to the study of *written* language. This problem has not been sufficiently absorbed by most scholars. One exception is Agustinus Gianto, who recognizes that the study of language is predicated upon its oral form. He contends, nevertheless, that the primacy of orality should not apply to a classical language like Hebrew. Amazingly, he argues, "What one may believe to be oral is only a derivation from the written language. In other words, elements from the spoken language derive their forms from the written language."[77] His arguments for this, however, essentially amount to special pleading. Recognizing the problem of studying classical languages using the conventional linguistic methods, he claims that the situation with classical languages is different. Indeed, it must be so if we want to simply follow a traditional historical linguistic approach. The problem is, the situation is not different. Though there may be an oral background to classical languages, the written languages themselves are embedded in a school system. Writing is not simply intended as a transcription of oral speech. It is traditional; it has its own conventions. Just because written language employs oral conventions, that does not make it language in the formal linguistic sense.

The use of neogrammarian linguistic rules (that is, rules predicated on speech) for written texts is problematic. One example can illustrate the difficulty: the Hebrew word hêkal (היכל), "palace, temple." It is universally acknowledged that this term derives from the Sumerian logogram É.GAL, literally "big house," and comes into Hebrew through the related Akkadian word *ekallu*, "palace." Neither Akkadian nor Sumerian has a grapheme to represent the phoneme *h*. So why does this grapheme *h* appear in the Hebrew loanword? The simple answer is that it got its spelling from Aramaic. Of course, this does not explain why Aramaic used the *h*. This example highlights the problem of the simplified inventory of graphemes used to represent phonemes.

Language is a code of arbitrary linguistic signs, as Ferdinand de Saussure classically pointed out,[78] and writing is all the more so. With this in mind, another messy problem may further illustrate the situation: the Akkadian term *ḫābiru*, "social outcast" (alternatively transcribed as *ḫāpiru* or *ʿapiru)*, mentioned in the Amarna letters (see discusion in chapter 2), and the Hebrew term *Hebrew*, written consonantally as *ʿbry* (עברי), with the late (or ideologically contrived) etymological meaning "those who came from across (the river)," or the ethnic designation "the descendants of Eber" (see

Gen. 10:21–25; 11:15–17). Scholars for generations have been tempted to identify *ḫābiru* with *Hebrew*, since it would give some insight into the early origins of the Israelite tribes.[79] The enterprise, however, is fraught with uncertainty. The spelling of the Akkadian word varies, though peripheral Akkadian dialects as well as Hittite and Luwian use the *b* rather than the *p*.[80] It may be objected, for example, that the Akkadian (*ḫābiru*) and Hebrew (*ʿiber*) are not *written* as precise orthographic equivalents; this objection, however, assumes a strict correspondence between graphemes and phonemes. Such an assumption is quite unfounded, given the inherent flexibility of the syllabic cuneiform writing system, on the one hand, and the terse simplicity of the consonantal alphabetic Hebrew writing system, on the other hand. The different writing systems also create difficulties; for instance, Akkadian does not have a grapheme for the phonemic guttural *ʿayin*, and Hebrew does not have a grapheme for phonemic *ḫ* (a velar fricative). The ideological component of language change also needs to be considered when assessing the term, especially here where Hebrew could be reetymologizing the negative social label into a geographically descriptive or ethnic label.[81] Since the Hebrew writing system originally did not use vowels, it was easy for later editors to manipulate the system for ideological or theological reasons.

Pseudoetymology is certainly an important form of commentary in the Hebrew Bible. A well-known example is the name of Moses, which seems to derive from the Egyptian word *ms*, "born, child," that appears in many Egyptian names, as for example in the pharaonic names Thutmose or Ramesses, meaning "born of the god Thut/Ra"; however, the biblical narrative explains the name Moses as meaning "drawn out of the water" (Exod. 2:10). This is just one anecdote illustrating the social aspect of language transmission. This example also highlights the chronological disjunction between the Late Bronze traditions and later Hebrew oral and then written tradition. For these reasons, it is difficult to make phonetic linguistic judgments with certainty, and such discussions cannot proceed based on graphemic transcriptions alone. The social context and content of language transmission play a critical role.

Mechanisms of Language Change

As a rule, Peter Trudgill suggests, "we must be able to *measure* both linguistic and social phenomena so that we can correlate the two accurately."[82] It may be argued that we cannot sufficiently measure either. This is certainly true for the earliest stages in the development of Hebrew. Many of the social changes described herein, and especially those concerning early Israel, are the subject of some discussion by scholars in the field. Obviously, there are no native informants for classical Hebrew. There is a relatively limited corpus of biblical and nonbiblical literature. These problems certainly should give some pause, but they are not sufficient reason for paralysis. Rather, they only mean that the present study begins what should be an ongoing discussion about the relationship between language and society in ancient Canaan.

In spite of the methodological difficulties, the way forward is not hopelessly overgrown. William Labov took note of the grave difficulties: "We have too little information on the state of society in which most linguistic changes took place. The accidents which govern historical records are not likely to yield the systematic explanations we need."[83] The problem of studying the sociolinguistics of Hebrew could not be more aptly put. Labov found a way through by positing his uniformitarian principle: "The forces operating to produce linguistic change today are the same kind and order of magnitude as those which operated in the past five or ten thousand years."[84] To be specific, the forces of social change, economic and political history, and physical environment tend to produce rather predictable linguistic changes. If we can adequately identify and assess the social forces that contributed to linguistic change in ancient Canaan, we should also be able to identify the impression these forces left on the Hebrew language.

There are mechanisms of language change as well as quantitative ways of measuring language and language change, which this study will employ. We may begin with some general sociolinguistic principles that William Labov outlines in his monumental work *Principles of Linguistic Change*. Labov offers three particular sociolinguistic principles that can be modified and applied to the study of classical Hebrew:

First, there is the Golden Age Principle. Namely, there is a widespread perception that "at some time in the past, language was in a state of perfection."[85] This belief informs people's attitudes about language and language change. This principle certainly reflects a nostalgia for the past. In the case of classical Hebrew, it is not surprising that the ancients asserted that God himself spoke Hebrew. On the one hand, there are critiques of vernacular Hebrew in texts such as the Dead Sea Scrolls suggesting that Rabbinic Hebrew is a corruption of the original speech of God. On the other hand, the quintessential summary of the rabbinic tradition will trace that tradition back to a direct revelation first given to Moses and then handed down orally to the rabbis (*m. Avot* 1:1).

Second, language change is governed by the Nonconformity Principle. As Labov notes, "Ongoing linguistic changes are emblematic of nonconformity to established social norms of appropriate behavior, and are generated in the social milieu that most consistently defies those norms."[86] Labov is, of course, referring to spoken language, but the principle will be all the more true for written language. Labov notes that the leaders of linguistic change are people "with a particular ability to confront established norms and the motivation to defy them." He couples this conclusion with the observation that "the leaders of change are in the central, upwardly mobile groups."[87] The scribal classes of ancient Israel, which were supported by the state, *usually* had little reason to confront or defy the established norms—that is, to generate language change. Changes in leadership, as a result, were likely to be accompanied by linguistic change. Such changes brought in new, upwardly mobile leadership groups.

Changes in social life, and thereby the speech community and institutions of writing, are important leading indicators of linguistic change. This observation also draws our attention to another contention of Labov, namely, that the speech community and not the idiolect should be the primary object of linguistic investigation.[88] This is true not only because idiolects can be idiosyncratic but also because we are interested in the broader social phenomenon of linguistic change that is represented by a speech community, or in our particular case, the writing community. Following this principle will also give a reliable guide to linguistic change. As the sociolinguist Peter Trudgill points out, "Linguistic changes follow social changes very readily, but it is not always a simple matter to make them *precede* them."[89] For practical as well as methodological reasons then, this study begins with social changes in ancient Canaan.

There is a symbiotic relationship between language and social history. On the one hand, social history provides clues for identifying periods when we might expect seminal changes in the Hebrew language. On the other hand, language change points to changes in the social life of ancient Israel and early Judaism. As Bakhtin observed, "What is important about the word in this regard is not so much its sign purity as its *social ubiquity*. The word is implicated in literally each and every act or contact between people—in collaboration on the job, in ideological exchanges, in the chance contacts of ordinary life, in political relationships, and so on. Countless ideological threads running through all areas of social intercourse register effect in the word. It stands to reason, then, that the word is the most sensitive *index of social changes*, and what is more, of changes still in the process of growth, still without definitive shape and not as yet accommodated into already regularized and fully defined ideological systems."[90] Following Bakhtin's supposition that the historical explanation of language change must directly follow changes in social life, the present study is organized by the fundamental social changes in the history of the Jewish people over the course of nearly two millennia. The way we see the world religiously, culturally, socially, and politically determines how we learn language. Thus, seminal religious, cultural, social, and political changes are antecedents for language change.

The question remains, then, how we can apply these observations to a study of the history of classical Hebrew. This book will give an overview of changes in writing technology, changes in demographics, and changes in the social and political institutions that supported and sponsored writing in ancient Canaan.

Several major social contexts shaped changes in classical Hebrew over two millennia. First, the influence of the administrative structures of the Late Bronze city-states framed the learning of writing systems in the early Iron Age. Second, the rise of nationalism in Syria-Palestine would shape an individualization of the Northwest Semitic languages. Later, urbanization and the democratization of writing would cast Hebrew with a more popular hue. In the aftermath of the Babylonian exile, the colonialism of the Persian Empire would add an Aramaic tint to the Hebrew language. Resurgent nationalism in the Hasmonean and Roman periods would be accompanied by the ideological use of Hebrew as a symbol of the Jewish nation. Religious sectarianism and social-class distinctions would work themselves out in Qumran Hebrew and the emergence of Rabbinic Hebrew.

Many of the questions raised by sociolinguistics are beyond our reach. We are limited by both historical and linguistic data. Our knowledge of ancient Jewish society is also limited. The historical sources include archaeological evidence, ancient inscriptions, and biblical narratives. Each offers something, but all have their limitations. Archaeological data is perhaps the most significant, offering insight into the social and historical processes at work in ancient Israel. The limitations of the data mean that the sociolinguistic study of classical Hebrew must remain an ongoing discourse refined both by new data and by new perspectives.

2

The Origins of Hebrew: In Search of the Holy Tongue

All the inhabitants of the earth had one language and one speech, and they used to speak in the language of the sanctuary in which the world was created from the beginning.

—*Genesis 11:1, Targum Neofiti*

The search for the origins of Hebrew should begin with the question, What is Hebrew? Put another way, should we focus on understanding the origins of Hebrew as a writing system or as a vernacular? The preference throughout this book is on the tangible writing system as opposed to the difficult-to-apprehend vernacular. Nevertheless, most studies of the origins of Hebrew conceptualize it as a vernacular. Hebrew as a spoken vernacular has been neatly fitted into a family tree of languages. Ultimately, languages should not be reduced to their writing systems, but this is the only way we are able to access the ancient Hebrew language. The focus on vernacular as opposed to writing systems would lead us in quite different directions for the origins of Hebrew.

In Jewish tradition, the origins of Hebrew were decidedly sacred. Already by the late Second Temple period, Hebrew was understood to be the language of creation. It was the holy tongue. Although it is not explicitly stated in biblical texts, it was considered implicit that when God "brought the animals to the man, to see what he would call them" (Gen. 2:19), the language the man used to name the animals was Hebrew. Or, when God said, "Let there be light" (Gen. 1:3), the words of Genesis, which were in Hebrew, reflected the language of God. Likewise, the story of the Tower of Babel, which takes place when "everyone on earth had the same language and the same words" (Gen. 11:1), reflects a more perfect time when the whole world spoke Hebrew. God came down and confused human language, creating the "Babel" of the multiplicity of human languages. It was regarded as implicit in the story that this original language that was confused was Hebrew. This may be contrasted with the story of creation when it is retold in the Hellenistic period. For example, in the book of Jubilees (ca. 200 B.C.E.), linguistic consciousness is quite explicit. Thus, when God gives Abraham his blessing, he does so in Hebrew:

> And the Lord God said: "Open his mouth and his ears, that he may hear and speak with his mouth, with the language which has been revealed"; for it had ceased from the mouths of all the children of men from the day of the overthrow (of Babel). And I opened his mouth, and his ears and his lips, and I began to speak with him *in Hebrew in the tongue of the creation.* And he took the books of his fathers, and these were written in Hebrew, and he transcribed them, and he began from henceforth to study them, and I made known to him that which he could not (understand), and he studied them during the six rainy months. (Jub. 12:25–27)

This idea became increasingly explicit in Jewish tradition. For example, in the ancient Aramaic translation known as Targum Neofiti, which probably dates to the second century C.E., we read that mankind spoke in "the language of the sanctuary in which the world was created from the beginning." The Bible never makes the issue of linguistic consciousness part of the story of creation. Indeed, the people of preexilic Judah lived a largely monolingual context that made it unnecessary to specify that the language of creation was Hebrew. In contrast, elevated linguistic consciousness becomes especially acute in multilingual settings.

In the rabbinic tradition, the Hebrew script itself would trace its origins to creation. According to the Mishnah, the letters of the Hebrew alphabet as well as the art of writing were created on the sixth day (*m. Avot* 5:6). The idea that writing was given to mankind as part of the very creation of the world was known also in ancient Egypt and Mesopotamia. Writing was not mundane but rather was used to communicate with the divine realm by ritual actions or formulaic recitations in order to affect the course of present or future events. According to Jewish tradition, the stone tablets given on Mount Sinai were also created on the sixth day. God himself writes on these two tablets with his very finger. Ancient Mesopotamians also described heavenly tablets (known as the Tablets of Destiny) in their creation myth, *Enuma Elish*. According to biblical literature, God himself actually keeps a heavenly book, inscribed with people's names, which he adds or erases, thereby inscribing each person's eternal fate. Such mysterious and numinous understandings of writing are typical of largely oral societies like early Israel.[1]

The search for Hebrew predates the storied arrival of the ancient Israelites into the land, purportedly at the end of the Late Bronze Age (thirteenth century B.C.E.). The historical search for Hebrew can begin with its writing system—the early alphabet. The spread of alphabetic writing began in the context of the rise and fall of Egyptian hegemony in the Levant—that is, the eastern Mediterranean world. Archaeologically speaking, this is the Late Bronze Age (1530–1200 B.C.E.) through the Iron I period (1200–980 B.C.E.). The first purported Hebrew inscriptions date to the tenth century B.C.E., perhaps later. Although we have written texts preserved from this early period, they do not fully reflect the nuances of Canaanite dialects that must have existed among the cities, towns, and villages of the Levant during the late second millennium B.C.E. The inhabitants were undoubtedly aware of dialectal differences separating the region into small enclaves. For example, scholars have long debated the nature of the dialectal difference between the Gileadites and the Ephraimites that underlies the shibboleth-sibboleth story (Judg. 12:5–6). More important, the story underscores the regional dialects that separated kin groups and chiefdoms in antiquity. The biblical writers well understood the role that language played in distinguishing peoples, as we see in the "Table of Nations" in Genesis 10, where the Canaanites are divided "by their families, by their languages, in their lands, and in their nations" (vv. 1, 5, 20).

Linguists generally have classified Hebrew as a *Semitic* language, and more specifically a *Northwest Semitic* language. This terminology actually comes from the Bible, being derived from the name Shem, one of the three sons of Noah (see Gen. 5:32; 6:10; 10:31). Although Semitic is the standard terminology, it should be acknowledged as a provincial term reflecting an ethnolinguistic classification based on the Bible. Hebrew belongs within a larger family of Near Eastern languages that includes Arabic, Akkadian, and Ethiopic languages (for example, Ge'ez). Hebrew is even more distantly related to languages like Egyptian as part of the *Afro-Asiatic* family tree.

The Rise and Fall of Egyptian Hegemony

Scholars have drawn up basic outlines of the branches of the Semitic languages. Usually, a hypothetical ancestor, *Proto-Semitic*, is posited as lying behind the Hebrew language. This hypothetical ancestor also allows scholars to explain the similarities and differences between the various languages of the ancient Near East. Hebrew belongs to the *West Semitic* branch that emerged by the end of the second millennium B.C.E. Within the West Semitic branch, scholars have grouped several languages, including Hebrew, Phoenician, Ugaritic, Amorite, and Aramaic. A precursor to Hebrew was already spoken by the inhabitants of Canaan in the second millennium B.C.E., long before the biblical account of the Israelite settlement in Canaan. This is made evident, for example, by the Canaanite Amarna letters written in the fourteenth century B.C.E. The Amarna letters are a cache of letters written by the rulers of Canaanite cities and towns to their Egyptian overlords and depict a fractured political landscape in the region that was undoubtedly reflected in local dialects.[2] Although these letters are written in a type of Akkadian language using cuneiform script, scribal glosses (that is, the insertion of Canaanite words with syllabic spelling) indicate that the vernacular of the scribes was related to Hebrew.

One important early ancestor of Hebrew was *Amorite*, a language spoken by seminomadic peoples, known in cuneiform texts as the *Amurru*.[3] Unfortunately, there are no texts written in the Amorite language. Amorite had no writing system, but rather is only known in a derivative manner through proper names in Akkadian cuneiform texts. The Amorite personal names are identified by linguistic and contextual features that distinguish them from typical Akkadian names. Gelb identified more than six thousand Amorite and non-Akkadian names, and some Amorite words also appear in various cuneiform sources. From what may be gleaned from the study of personal names, Amorite is an early and independent branch of Northwest Semitic.[4] The lexicon of Amorite has striking similarities to West Semitic, which was the first clue to its affiliation with the Northwest Semitic languages. More tellingly, the Amorite verbal system uses prefixes and suffixes in a manner that parallels West Semitic; in particular, the use of the verbal prefix *ya-* (as opposed to *i-* in Akkadian) indicates its affiliation with Northwest Semitic. Indeed, it has often been pointed out that patriarchal names such as Jacob (Hebrew, *ya*^{ca}*qōb̲*) may be analyzed grammatically as Amorite prefixed verbs, a formation that is atypical of Hebrew in later periods. In this regard, perhaps it should not be surprising that the prophet Ezekiel would later describe the Israelite heritage as drawing from Amorite. There is an interesting geographical tension in this text because the Amorites and the Hittites came from outside Canaan—namely, Asia Minor and Mesopotamia. This is a cultural memory of Israel's complex ethnogenesis; ethnicity often has some bearing on linguistic self-classification.[5] The ancient Israelites perceived their origins as coming from outside of Canaan, even though the land and nation were birthed in Canaan.

The Emergence of Writing in Canaan

The ancient Israelites had cultural memories that identified them with foreigners (like the Amorites), and they subdivided themselves by dialects (like Gileadite and Ephraimite). Likewise, the Hebrew language and its writing system were not completely original. They had their predecessors and precursors. For this reason, the search for the origins of Hebrew in this book will begin with its written precursors in the ancient Near East.

Early writing systems were already known in the ancient Near East, in both Mesopotamia and Egypt, by the end of the fourth millennium B.C.E. The cuneiform writing system originated in southern Mesopotamia and appears to have the pride of priority. More important, cuneiform seems to have been the primary writing system used when writing began to spread throughout the Levant during the second millennium B.C.E. To be sure, the Egyptian hieroglyphic writing system was also used in the Levant during the second millennium B.C.E.—mostly by Egyptians and for local Egyptian affairs.

The scribal infrastructure for the cuneiform and hieroglyphic writing systems became highly developed in their respective centers, Mesopotamia and Egypt. Akkadian, however, spread more widely than Egyptian and was widely used outside of the Mesopotamian heartland. Yet the scribal infrastructure in the Levant, particularly southern Canaan, was relatively limited in the second millennium B.C.E. This is important because, as Stephen Houston points out, "Complex societies do not ensure the invention of writing, but they do enable its large-scale use and maintenance."[6] Cuneiform and hieroglyphic writing were enabled by the complex societies that invented them, whereas the Levant during the second millennium used writing in the service of these complex societies.

The use of writing in Canaan during the second millennium B.C.E. was tied to the political ebbs and flows of the era. In the early second millennium, that is, the period that archaeologists call the Middle Bronze Age II (ca. 1900–1530 B.C.E.),[7] Mesopotamia cast a long shadow over Canaan. It is not surprising, then, that cuneiform writing was found at a variety of sites throughout Canaan beginning in the Middle Bronze Age. Most of these discoveries are cataloged in *Cuneiform in Canaan: Cuneiform Sources from the Land of Israel in Ancient Times.*[8] The catalog includes a total of ninety-one cuneiform texts from twenty-eight separate sites. Scholars are still looking for a large cache of cuneiform texts that would represent a library or archive, but the quantity and distribution of the discoveries is enough to demonstrate the widespread use of cuneiform among the various polities of Canaan. In contrast, major archives of cuneiform texts have been discovered in many cities in Mesopotamia and northern Syria.[9] Indeed, the lack of large archives like those found at other major Middle Bronze Age cities along the Fertile Crescent likely reflects the relatively limited scribal infrastructure of Canaan during this period—an infrastructure that was heavily dependent on the economically more prosperous, as well as politically more dominant, polities in Mesopotamia, northern Syria, and Egypt.

A conduit for cuneiform culture arriving into Canaan was the great Middle Bronze Age city of Hazor, the largest city of ancient Canaan. Although settlement in Hazor had already begun in the third millennium B.C.E. (Early Bronze Age), it was confined to a small acropolis during that period. In the Middle Bronze Age, sometime around 1800 B.C.E., the city mushroomed. The city covered the entire tell until the thirteenth century B.C.E., when both the upper and lower tell were violently destroyed. The city is mentioned in several texts dating to the Middle Bronze Age, beginning with the Egyptian Execration texts (nineteenth century B.C.E.). Hazor is also mentioned fifteen times in important archives from Mari, a large northern Syrian city of the seventeenth century B.C.E., and served as one of its major trading partners.[10] The Mari archive highlights Hazor's far-reaching economic and political ties with Mesopotamia during the Middle Bronze Age. It is the only Canaanite city mentioned in these archives and served as the western frontier for the spread of Mesopotamian culture. Hazor also appears in the Amarna archive, and there are several references to Hazor in the military accounts of the New Kingdom pharaohs (fifteenth to fourteenth centuries B.C.E.) as well. The small corpus of texts from Hazor "display scribal features best known to us from the Mari archives."[11] In addition, there are at least three school texts that suggest that Hazor may have served as a regional center for training scribes. These school texts include a mathematical text with multiplication tables, a lexical text with lists of terms for economic exchange, and liver models used for educational purposes in either the general training of scribes or the specific training of diviners.[12] Archaeologists are still hoping to find a major archive of cuneiform texts from Hazor, but the smaller finds point to Hazor's role in disseminating cuneiform writing throughout Canaan.

Writing was thus well entrenched in the Levant long before we have any written Hebrew texts. Whereas early cuneiform and hieroglyphic writing systems were logographic and developed into logographic and syllabic systems (meaning that each written symbol represented a morpheme or a syllable),[13] Hebrew writing would use an alphabetic writing system.

Alphabetic Writing

There is some debate over what may properly be labeled an "alphabetic" writing system and, therefore, whether the early West Semitic "alphabets" should strictly qualify. The earliest alphabetic writing systems were consonantal (without vowels), a type of alphabetic writing that has been termed *abjad*, to distinguish it from alphabetic writing systems that have both consonants and vowels. However, as the linguist Florian Coulmas points out, the description of the Semitic alphabet as either uninterested in vowels or deficient because of its focus on consonants overlooks the problems of all writing systems.[14] *Writing systems* should not be confused with *transcription systems*, which attempt to record all phonetic details. All writing systems—including the lauded Greek alphabet—omit some phonetic distinctions. For example, it may be observed that vowel letters, even in the Greek and Latin alphabets, are quite polyvalent, much more so than consonants. Consonants tend to adhere to the alphabetic principle of one grapheme for each phoneme much more closely than vowels do. Thus, although there are five vowel letters in the Latin alphabet (*a, e, i, o, u*), there are as many as twenty-three vowel sounds in English and at least eighteen in German. In short, all alphabetic writing systems have deficiencies as transcription systems, but they share the common principle of segmentation, that is, the breaking of the natural syllables of speech into the smaller units of vowels and consonants.[15]

It is noteworthy that the alphabet (unlike other writing systems) was invented only once, and that all alphabets—including Hebrew—are adaptations from this original innovation. Greek and Latin sources almost universally attribute the invention of the alphabet to the Phoenicians. For example, the fifth-century B.C.E. Greek historian Herodotus writes that "the Phoenicians . . . taught them [that is, the Greeks] the alphabet" (*Hist.* V, 58:332), and later writers largely follow the account of Herodotus. In fact, however, alphabetic writing precedes the Phoenicians, already appearing in the early second millennium B.C.E. Although most Greek and Latin sources associate the alphabet's origin with the Phoenicians, who disseminated it, the Latin historian Tacitus recalls that the Egyptians "claim to have discovered the alphabet and taught it to the Phoenicians who, controlling the seas, introduced it to Greece and were credited with inventing what they had really borrowed" (*Annals* xi, 14).[16] This account received credibility because of the antiquity of the first alphabetic inscriptions as well as the location of their discovery.

The earliest example of alphabetic writing is from Wadi el-Hôl in Egypt. The site is on a caravan trail, not far from the ancient city of Luxor. Egyptologists J. C. Darnell and D. Darnell discovered alphabetic inscriptions while surveying the desert roads around Thebes. Although the preponderance of inscriptions in the area were written in formal Egyptian hieroglyphic or cursive hieratic writing, a few strange inscriptions caught the Darnells' attention. These inscriptions turned out to be two of the earliest known alphabetic texts.[17] Evidence from the material culture surrounding the finds suggests that this alphabet was being used by common people—that is, soldiers, merchants, and traders—and not scribal elites. In particular, the name of a certain Bebi, "General of the Asiatics," linked these alphabetic inscriptions with Semitic laborers and mercenary soldiers working in Egypt. The second inscription mentions "the scribe of the storehouse of the mayor, Sawepwaut." These inscriptions suggest that the texts might be related to the "Asiatics" and also point to the role of Egyptian scribes in administrative positions outside of Egypt. The innovation of these alphabetic inscriptions must be related to the spread of Egyptian hegemony outside of Egypt.

New cultural settings allow for the expression of nontraditional forms, and new scripts tend to emerge at moments of societal change. Anthropologists have observed that "the more dramatic leaps from logographic to phonic scripts appear on the margins of areas where logosyllabic scripts reign."[18] The earliest alphabetic inscriptions, to be sure, are found at the margins of Egyptian civilization. The invention of the alphabet also began the process of democratizing language, that is, giving access to writing to people outside the scribal elites. The letters of these alphabetic texts are clearly the early ancestors of the later Paleo-Hebrew alphabet, but this alphabet dates back to at least 1900 B.C.E. (that is, to the Wadi el-Hôl inscriptions)—many centuries before a distinctive Hebrew alphabet would emerge.

More than democratizing writing, the invention of the alphabet might have been an abandoned attempt by the Egyptians to create an administrative language. The invention of the alphabet should be tied to the deeply held language ideology of the Egyptians. They considered their own writing system, hieroglyphics, to be sacred and not for foreigners. Indeed, the Egyptians used a special type of hieroglyphs called "group writing" especially for writing foreign words and names;[19] that is, there was a certain linguistic ideology that reserved regular hieroglyphic writing for pure Egyptian language. This type of language ideology is certainly not uncommon. The alphabetic writing system could thus have developed as a mundane alternative to the sacred hieroglyphic writing. Moreover, all the earliest known alphabetic writing came from peripheral regions directly and indirectly controlled by the Egyptians. For example, the other famous early alphabetic inscriptions were found more than a century ago by Sir Flinders Petrie in the middle of the Sinai Desert at an Egyptian mining settlement (1991–1785 B.C.E.), known today as Serabit el-Khadem. Viewed together with the Wadi el-Hôl inscriptions, it becomes clear that the origins of the alphabet must be linked with Egyptian writing. This is also evident in the form of the letters in the early alphabetic inscriptions. The letter forms are pictographic, by which we mean that the pictorial character of a letter (that is, a grapheme) can be recognized. Thus, in the Proto-Sinaitic inscriptions, the Hebrew letter *ʾaleph* corresponds to the picture  (representing an ox's head), the letter *mem* to  (representing water), the letter *nun* to  (representing a snake), and the letter *resh* to  (representing a head). Moreover, pictographs such as the letters *mem* and *resh* bear striking resemblances to Egyptian hieroglyphic and hieratic forms.[20] It is again noteworthy that Serabit el-Khadem is a remote mining settlement with a prominent Egyptian temple. The Proto-Sinaitic inscriptions at Serabit el-Khadem are often attributed to Semitic workmen, but it is difficult to know for certain. The purveyors of the alphabet borrowed the icons from Egyptian forms. The writing was at a very low level—mostly personal names and names of gods or epithets like "Beloved of the Lady."[21]

Apart from these early examples of alphabetic writing in Egyptian contexts, there are a few other examples of alphabetic writing from the southern Levant.[22] The exemplars come from a variety of locations, including Lachish, Shechem, Gezer, Tell en-Nagila, and Tell el-Hesi. None of these exemplars come from contexts that would indicate that this early alphabet was being used widely by scribes in the Levant. Indeed, there was no indigenous political or social infrastructure in the Levant that would have supported the widespread use of this early alphabet. The only political and administrative infrastructures to support and develop writing would have been external—that is, coming from Egypt or Mesopotamia. Scribes in the region generally used the Akkadian cuneiform writing system, as can be illustrated, for example, by the Amarna letters. Given the lack of a formal social infrastructure and support for early alphabetic writing, it is quite remarkable that the early alphabetic writing system persisted until it finally developed into the writing system known from Ugarit and later from the Phoenicians.

The nature of early alphabetic writing points to its importance as a technological innovation that made writing accessible outside of scribal schools. Although the invention of the alphabet did not result immediately in widespread literacy, the persistence of linear alphabetic writing in the second millennium was not sponsored by the state. This is in marked contrast to the cuneiform and hieroglyphic writing systems. Alphabetic writing definitely made it easier for nonspecialists to acquire rudimentary skills in writing, as evidenced by Wadi el-Hôl and Serabit el-Khadem. Though it would require either state sponsorship or economic complexity for the alphabet to spread, it persisted in the second millennium even without these. To be sure, learning to read—even with an alphabet—is not something that happens "in a matter of days or weeks,"[23] but the ability to acquire rudimentary facility in reading is different with alphabetic scripts than with cuneiform or hieroglyphics, hence its democratizing potential.

Although cuneiform was widely used in Canaan during the second millennium B.C.E., the invention of the alphabet and the eventual adoption of the alphabet by ancient Israelite scribes reflected Egyptian influence. The invention of the alphabet began with the innovative use of Egyptian unilateral hieroglyphs, which were used as phonetic complements specifically to indicate vocalization of Egyptian logograms, as well as to aid in the writing of foreign words and names.[24] Although the unilateral hieroglyphs in Egyptian were not used as an alphabet, one may infer from them the correspondence between single graphemes and phonemes that is the basis for the invention of the alphabet. It is not surprising, therefore, that the earliest alphabetic writing borrowed the pictographic shapes from hieroglyphic writing for the shapes of the letters of a West Semitic alphabet. Egyptian influence, however, continued and extended beyond the building blocks for the invention of an alphabet.

Critical Hebrew loanwords pertaining to the work of scribes were borrowed from Egyptian. They include *ḏᵉyô*, "ink"; *gōmeʾ*, "papyrus"; *ʾêpâ*, "dry measure"; *hîn*, "unit of liquid measure"; *zeret*, "span of hand (as unit of measure)"; *ḥôṯām*, "seal"; and *qeset*, "a scribe's palette."[25] Although there are relatively few Egyptian loanwords in Hebrew, it is striking that the critical terms of the scribes' profession—terms for accounting and measuring as well as for ink, papyrus, and palette—were borrowed into Hebrew from Egyptian.[26] In addition to the Egyptian loanwords, Hebrew also borrowed the Egyptian hieratic numerals for use in its accounting, as is preserved in many Hebrew ostraca. These Egyptian hieratic numerals can be dated no later than the tenth century B.C.E.[27] Taken as a whole, Egyptian scribal influence on Hebrew suggests continuity in the scribal profession during the late second millennium B.C.E. The major period of Egyptian activity in the Levant was the late second millennium, and several Egyptian hieratic ostraca from this period have been discovered at various locations in the southern Levant, indicating the presence of Egyptian scribes working in the region.[28] The famous Papyrus Anastasi, which details "The Craft of the Scribe," in fact makes knowledge of Levantine geography one of the requisites of the competent Egyptian scribe during the late second millennium B.C.E.[29] Thus, Egyptian scribes were clearly working in the Levant in the late second millennium B.C.E. and undoubtedly continued to ply their profession even as Egyptian influence in the region began to wane in the twelfth century B.C.E. One of the striking examples of Egyptian legacy in early Judean scribal practice is the influence of the scribal text "The Wisdom of Amenemope" in Proverbs 22:17–23:10.[30] Judging from this evidence, Late Bronze Age Egyptian scribes apparently contributed to the early Israelite scribal culture.

THE UGARITIC ALPHABET

The first known systematic use of alphabetic writing by scribes came from the ancient city of Ugarit, where a cuneiform alphabetic script appeared. The cuneiform alphabet from Ugarit dates back to at least the fifteenth century B.C.E., although most of the Ugaritic texts date to about 1200 B.C.E. It is important to note that alphabetic cuneiform is also known from fragmentary inscriptions throughout the Levant; thus, it is not merely a "Ugaritic" writing system but is more generally in use in the Levant. The cuneiform alphabetic writing system was one of three writing systems used in the Levant in the late second millennium to write West Semitic dialects. These include (1) the traditional cuneiform writing system, (2) a linear alphabet (which dates as early as 1900 B.C.E., based on the Wadi el-Hôl inscriptions), most commonly associated with the later Phoenician alphabet, and (3) an alphabetic cuneiform writing system. Each of these writing systems was used for a variety of West Semitic dialects, and the writing systems crossed political boundaries. In other words, these writing systems were not narrowly tied to particular dialects or polities. Nevertheless, the choice of writing system still informs us about aspects of language ideology during the late second millennium B.C.E.

During the heyday of the Ugaritic kingdom in the fourteenth and thirteenth centuries B.C.E., the city of Ugarit served as one of the great mercantile ports on the Mediterranean and as a gateway to Mesopotamia and Asia Minor. Numerous archives suggest that several scribal schools developed both the utilitarian and intellectual uses of alphabetic writing at Ugarit. Though a large number of Akkadian texts were excavated at Ugarit, the native language was written in alphabetic cuneiform script. This writing system was an innovative blending of an alphabetic script (like Hebrew) and cuneiform or "wedge-writing" (like Akkadian). The development of alphabetic cuneiform seems to reflect the declining use of Akkadian as a lingua franca toward the end of the second millennium B.C.E.—no doubt a reflection of the waning role of Mesopotamia in the Levant. Ugaritic, as both a cuneiform and an alphabetic script, bridges the cuneiform and alphabetic cultures of the ancient Near East. Ugarit apparently adapted the pictographic alphabet into the alphabetic cuneiform used for the Ugaritic language. Many of the alphabetic cuneiform letters bear some resemblance to the early Canaanite letters (compare, for example, the letters *beth,* , and , or the letters *'ayin,* , and ).[31]

The city of Ugarit itself was located outside the borders of Canaan, but the alphabetic cuneiform script that has given Ugarit notoriety was known throughout the Levant. Although the preponderance of alphabetic cuneiform texts were excavated in Ugarit or its immediate vicinity, alphabetic cuneiform writing spread well beyond the borders of the kingdom of Ugarit. Alphabetic cuneiform texts have been found in Cyprus (Hala Sultan Tekke, near Kition), in Syria (Tell Sukas, Kadesh, Kumidi [near Damascus]), in Lebanon (Sarepta), and in Israel (Mount Tabor, Taanach, Beth-Shemesh). Indeed, one of the letters found at Ugarit and written in alphabetic cuneiform script came from Tyre. Thus, although the alphabetic cuneiform script has been closely associated with the city of Ugarit, the script itself was in much wider circulation. Ugarit, however, was in a unique situation in the Levant during this period, as it combined a highly developed and complex economy with a measure of autonomy. Thus, Ugarit developed and refined its own script and language for its local literary traditions as well as its domestic affairs.

The development of the alphabetic cuneiform script marks a certain independence from Mesopotamian polities. During the Middle Bronze Age, the Akkadian language and the cuneiform writing system were used exclusively. This reflects the political and cultural influence in the region of Mesopotamian powers. During the Late Bronze Age (that is, beginning in the sixteenth century B.C.E.), Mesopotamian influence waned. The development of new languages and different writing systems is one aspect of the political and cultural changes in the Levant. Ugarit, at the northern edge of the Levant, continued to use Akkadian and the cuneiform writing system, even while they were developing their own local writing system.

The extensive archives at Ugarit have yielded more than fifteen hundred texts written in the Ugaritic language using alphabetic cuneiform, and a significant number of the texts are cultural texts that were copied and preserved through royal sponsorship. Thus, we find one colophon to an Ugaritic epic text that identifies the scribe and his patron:

> *spr.ilmlk šbny/lmd.atn.prln.rb/khnm rb.nqdm/tʿy.nqmd.mlk ugrt/adn .yrgb.bʿl.trmn.* (The scribe is Ilimalku the Shubanite, student of Attenu the diviner, chief of the priests, chief of the shepherds, from the patronage of Niqmaddu, king of Ugarit, lord of *YRGB*, master of *THRMN.)* (*KTU* 1.6:54–58)

The major archives from Ugarit include these epic texts copied with royal sponsorship, a large number of economic and administrative texts, and letters pertaining to the royal family and the Ugaritian court. The emergence, then, of extensive writing in an alphabetic script would seem to be the direct result of royal sponsorship.

There has been some debate about the role of the alphabet in encouraging the spread of writing. The American philologist William F. Albright, for example, famously opined that "since the forms of the [Hebrew] letters are very simple, the 22-letter alphabet could be learned in a day or two by a bright student and in a week or two by the dullest."[32] Hebrew does have a *shallow orthography*, whereas English has a *deep orthography*;[33] in other words, Hebrew has a simple correspondence between letters and sounds, unlike English. This makes the acquisition of literacy in Hebrew easier than in languages with a more complex relationship between reading and speaking. Thus, Albright's observation is not completely off the mark. The invention of the alphabet could play a role in the ease of writing and reading acquisition and ultimately in the spread of writing. Still, the spread of writing beyond the scribal classes did not take place until at least the seventh century B.C.E.

The invention of the alphabet, though it lowered the difficulty of attaining proficiency in reading and writing, did not result in an immediate spread of writing beyond the traditional classes. This may be explained by several factors. First, learning to read and write is not as easy as it might seem, especially in a culture where learners do not have prior literacy. Learning the shapes of the alphabet may be a simple matter, but acquiring functional literacy is a much more difficult one. It is true that emergent literacy is possible with a few weeks of instruction, but proficiency still must be acquired over a long period.[34] Second, literacy is a cultural value that must be taught, and the invention of the alphabet itself does little to foster the cultural value of literacy. Without a cultural value of literacy, there is little motivation for its acquisition and spread. Third, the emergence and spread of writing required the establishment of social institutions and sponsorship. Thus, the conditions for the spread of writing—especially the spread of writing beyond scribal classes—did not exist in the southern Levant during the second millennium B.C.E. The invention of the alphabet needed to be accompanied by other social and political developments (which would ultimately happen only in the seventh century B.C.E. in Judah; see more on this in chapter 5).

The Precursors to the Hebrew Language

As we have seen, there were four writing systems in use in the southern Levant during the late second millennium—hieroglyphic, an early West Semitic pictographic alphabet, alphabetic cuneiform, and cuneiform. Hieroglyphic was used strictly for the Egyptian language. Beyond the headline-making discoveries of an early pictographic alphabet at Wadi el-Hôl and Serabit el-Khadem, there are only a handful of short inscriptions in the pictographic alphabet, and the limited evidence does not indicate widespread use by scribes for preserving local literary traditions or recording domestic affairs. Alphabetic cuneiform (that is, Ugaritic) provides a more extensive corpus, but there is very little evidence for the development of the alphabetic cuneiform script in the southern Levant at this point. Still, the archives of Ugarit do give us a glimpse into the language and literary traditions of the Levantine region more generally. The cuneiform texts from Canaan are also quite limited, although the Amarna corpus does provide a window into the early Canaanite language. It is worth surveying more carefully the two main precursors to Hebrew in the second millennium, namely, Ugaritic and Amarna Canaanite, to see what light they may shed on the early history of Hebrew.

UGARITIC: A COUSIN TO HEBREW

Hebrew has long been associated with Ugaritic, a language named for the ancient city of Ugarit, which lies on the northern coast of the eastern Mediterranean about half a mile (one kilometer) from the Mediterranean Sea, six miles north of the modern city of Latakia (ancient Greek, Laodikeia), and about two hundred and fifty miles north of Jerusalem. The city was located on the trade route from Mesopotamia up the Euphrates River from Mari, Emar, and Ebla—three well-known Late Bronze Age cities. Natural boundaries defined the city of Ugarit. To the west, the Mediterranean Sea shaped its history as a commercial port. To the north, east, and south, Ugarit was bounded by mountains. A valley to the northeast of Ugarit (toward Alalakh and Ebla) was a gateway for commerce with northern Syria and Mesopotamia. Nevertheless, the kingdom of Ugarit remained geographically and politically distinct from Canaan.

Ugarit was linguistically diverse. As a trade hub, Ugarit attracted merchants and foreigners from nearby maritime towns as well as more distant locations, like Egypt, Cyprus, Syria, and Mesopotamia. Phoenicians, Hittites,

Egyptians, Assyrians, Canaanites, Cypriots, and other Aegeans came as merchants and mercenaries to Ugarit. As much as 16 percent of the population came from outside of Ugarit, and the population of the kingdom probably numbered about fifty thousand, with between five thousand and ten thousand living in the city of Ugarit itself. The native language seems to have been some type of precursor to Hebrew, but Ugarit's distance from Canaan and its multiethnic population certainly suggest that Ugaritic was quite distinct from the dialects of the central highlands in the southern Levant, where Hebrew was to emerge as a distinct language centuries later.

The Ugaritic language was written in an alphabetic cuneiform script consisting of thirty letters, a reduction from the more than forty graphemes known from the early alphabetic inscriptions, but more than the twenty-two graphemes that were employed in Phoenician as well as Hebrew, which borrowed the Phoenician script. Three of the Ugaritic graphemes are used for the *ʾaleph* to represent three basic vowels: *a*, *i*, and *u*. The placement of the latter two letters at the end of the alphabet suggests that they were a secondary adaptation for the Ugaritic language, probably reflecting an innovation inspired by Akkadian. The general order of the letters in abecedary texts shows a distinct affinity with the later Hebrew alphabet.[35] The order of the twenty-two letters is the same basic order that we see in Paleo-Hebrew, including the earliest Paleo-Hebrew abecedaries from Tell Izbet Sarta and Tell Zayit. The fact that the order of the letters is similar indicates some relationship between the scribal training at Ugarit and the early Hebrew scribes.

Ugaritic preserves some characteristics that distinguish it from Hebrew. Most notably, the *Canaanite shift*—that is, the phonetic shift from /ā́/ to /ṓ/—does not occur in Ugaritic writing. Moreover, Ugaritic employs the prefix *š*- for the causative verbal conjugation (like Akkadian), as opposed to the prefix *h*- that is found in Hebrew and other Canaanite languages.[36]

Given the geographic and temporal distance between Ugaritic and Hebrew, it is actually quite remarkable that the languages show so many similarities. Indeed, Ugaritic literature is one of the sources that scholars mine in search of the supposed Canaanite heritage of ancient Hebrew literature. It has been argued that "biblical literature was but the continuation of the antecedent Canaanite literature."[37] The source of these antecedent Canaanite traditions has been seen in the Ugaritic literature. Indeed, early on, the similarities between Ugaritic and Hebrew encouraged Ugaritic's classification among the Canaanite languages (Phoenician, Ammonite, Moabite, Hebrew).[38] This classification, however, has been challenged on several fronts. Anson Rainey, for example, has pointed out that Ugarit was beyond the borders of Canaan—as the ancient Canaanites understood it—and therefore argued that Ugaritic should not be described as a Canaanite language.[39] Although Rainey's argument itself begins with descriptive linguistic observations, it also recognizes that definitions of language and dialect are equally defined by social and political boundaries, not purely linguistic ones.[40] Moreover, the social and political boundaries must ultimately have shaped the development of languages and dialects in the Levant. The difficulty of the classification of Ugaritic, however, is also a problem of chronology. On the one hand, evidence for the Canaanite languages dates largely from the tenth to the fifth centuries B.C.E., with the notable exception of the Amarna letters. Ugaritic, on the other hand, is known from texts dating from the fifteenth through thirteenth centuries B.C.E. Moreover, language classification itself usually depends more on politics (both ancient and modern) than on descriptive linguistics. For these reasons, discussions about the classification of Ugaritic have been somewhat misguided. Still, it remains undeniable that ancient Israelite culture had strong connections to the world of the ancient Near East. Furthermore, the biblical authors were quite aware of these close cultural connections; in the words of the book of Ezekiel: "Your origin and native land are from the land of the Canaanites; your father was an Amorite and your mother a Hittite" (Ezek. 16:3). Though such statements must be understood as reflections of cultural ideology and memory, they do invite us to explore the connections between Ugaritic and Hebrew language and literature.

The evidence of a shared heritage for Ugaritic and biblical scribes is far-reaching. The focal point for a projected literary tradition shared by Ugaritic and Hebrew has been the study of Hebrew poetry. Among the early scholars who recognized the affinities of Ugaritic and Hebrew psalmody was H. L. Ginsberg. Ginsberg compared linguistic patterns, geographical concepts, and mythical motifs in Psalm 29 with Ugaritic epic literature and, on this basis, argued that Psalm 29 was originally a Canaanite hymn.[41] Ginsberg's analysis was convincing, and scholars today recognize a common background shared by Psalm 29 and Ugaritic psalmody, though many would not be so bold as to label Psalm 29 a Canaanite psalm. Nevertheless, Ginsberg's study serves as a convenient point of departure for the seminal shift in the study of biblical psalmody. The importance of Ugaritic literature for biblical psalmody was pushed particularly by William F. Albright and his many students. Albright believed, "It is not too much to say that all future investigations of the book of Psalms must deal intensively with the Ugaritic texts."[42] The use of Ugaritic literature in the study of biblical psalmody reached its apex in the massive commentary on the Psalms by Mitchell Dahood,[43] which, though hailed by Albright as the most important contribution to Psalms study in two millennia, was criticized sharply by most scholars for its fanciful emendations.[44] Dahood almost completely disregarded the traditional meaning of the Psalter, using the consonantal skeleton as a framework to build his new creation—a creation that bore only faint resemblance to the Masoretic Psalter. Now Dahood's commentary is a monument to the excesses of the comparative approach. In spite of his highly speculative approach, Dahood's ruminations still highlight some remarkable similarities between Ugaritic and Hebrew psalmody. In point of fact, however, these similarities reflect the broader Canaanite and Near Eastern scribal tradition rather than a specific relationship between Ugaritic and biblical literature.

Illustrations of a general West Semitic literary tradition may be culled from Ugaritic literature. Parallelism is a common feature of Ugaritic and Hebrew poetry. It is perhaps the most often cited example of a common literary tradition. This parallelism is expressed in several distinct rhetorical forms. Typical examples from Psalms and the Ugaritic poem of El's feast can illustrate. In Psalm 93:3 we read, "The ocean sounds, O LORD, The ocean sounds its thunder, The ocean sounds its pounding"; in Ugaritic poetry we find, "The gods eat and drink, They drink wine until sated, Vintage until inebriated" (*KTU* 1.114:4–6). In these examples, a threefold parallelism is employed. Such rhetorical forms also have parallels in Akkadian, suggesting that they are of generic Semitic origin rather than specifically Canaanite. For example, this type of parallelism is also found in the Amarna letters, as in the letter of Abdi-milku:

> *Amur amêli* ^{URU}*beruti ina* ^{GIŠ}*elippi alik u amêli ṣidu*[*n*]*a ina* 2 ^{GIŠ}*e*[*lippi*] [*i*]*lak u anaku ilak qadu gab*[*b*]*i* ^{GIŠ}*elippik*[*a*]. (Behold, the men of Beirut went in one ship, and the man of Sidon goes in two ships; I will serve with all your ships.) (EA 155:67–69)

Also apparent in this last example is a similar use of numbers that is quite common in both Ugaritic and classical Hebrew but that also occurs more generally in Akkadian and Sumerian. It is widely discussed by scholars, and a few choice examples will illustrate:[45]

Hebrew: How could one have routed a thousand,
Or two put ten thousand to flight? (Deut. 32:30)
The span of our life is seventy years,
Or, given the strength, eighty years. (Ps. 90:10)

Ugaritic: Seven years may Baal fail,
Eight the Rider of the Clouds. (*KTU* 1:19:I:42–44)
Sixty-six towns he seized,
Seventy-seven villages. (*KTU* 1:4:VII:9–10)

Akkadian: I provided her with six decks,
dividing her into seven parts. (Gilgamesh XI, 60–61)
At twenty leagues, they broke off a morsel,
at thirty leagues they settled for the night. (Gilgamesh XI, 300–301)

The parallelism may be summarized by the following formulae: x // x+1, 10x // 10(x +1), and 11x // 11(x+1). Such rhetorical forms point to a continuity in oral literature that appears in the scribal tradition.

There is also shared heritage between Ugaritic and biblical literature that is specific to these two corpuses. These include formulas of transition, similes and metaphors, epithets, parallelism between words, and parallelism between phrases. So, for example, a common Hebrew expression like "he lifted his eyes and saw" finds a counterpart in Ugaritic epic literature: "Baal Most High lifted his eyes and saw; he lifted up his eyes and answered" (*wyšʾu ʿnh ʾalʾiyn bʿl wyšʾu ʿnh wtʿn*; *KTU* 1.10:13–14). Likewise, the Hebrew expression "he lifted up his voice and called" has an equivalent in Ugaritic, "he lifted up his voice and cried" (*wyšʾu gh wyṣh*; e.g., *KTU* 1.1.II:17; 1.3.III:36–37).[46] These and other examples suggest a shared West Semitic (or "Levantine") scribal training.

CANAANO-AKKADIAN: A STEPFATHER OF HEBREW

The Amarna letters are an archive of about four hundred letters written with Akkadian cuneiform script on clay tablets. The letters are diplomatic correspondence between the Egyptian administration and rulers in Canaan and Syria during the New Kingdom (fifteenth to fourteenth centuries B.C.E.). Most of the letters came from Egyptian subordinates (in the southern Levant) and some came from independent kingdoms (such as the Hittites). The letters were discovered in the ancient Egyptian capital founded by the pharaoh Akhenaten (ca. 1350–1330 B.C.E.) during the Eighteenth Dynasty of Egypt and known today as Amarna. The letters from Canaanite cities are of interest to scholars of ancient Hebrew because they are written in a peculiar dialect that probably reflects the vernacular of ancient Canaan. This Amarna Canaanite dialect (or Canaano-Akkadian) is a predecessor to the Hebrew language. I have coined the odd description of Amarna Canaanite as a "stepfather" to Hebrew in order to express two aspects of the relationship. First, being written in the Akkadian cuneiform script and retaining aspects of that language in their writing, the Amarna letters are not a direct relative of the Hebrew language. At the same time, they do reflect the local Canaanite dialect in the region that directly preceded Hebrew. The Egyptian scribes, however, were familiar with both Canaano-Akkadian and the standard Middle Babylonian dialect used in northern Syria and Mesopotamia. Only letters coming from the general limits of Egyptian hegemony in the Late Bronze Age are written in the Canaano-Akkadian dialect.

The Amarna letters reflect aspects of the complex political and linguistic situation of Canaan in the late second millennium B.C.E. The region was dominated by the Egyptians during the Late Bronze Age (ca. 1530–1200 B.C.E.), and the Canaano-Akkadian Amarna letters seem to represent the language of the Egyptian administration. For example, the linguistic dialect of the letters from the southern Levant differs from the dialect in the letters that came from the north of Canaan (that is, beyond Egyptian control). The northern letters are written in the typical peripheral Akkadian of northern Syrian city-states, whereas the southern letters are written in a peculiar dialect that adapts the cuneiform writing system and Akkadian grammar to the local Canaanite dialects.[47] The fact that this language is being used in correspondence with Egypt suggests that the Egyptian administration may have sanctioned and even encouraged the development of this idiosyncratic writing system. In this case, the Egyptians would have been encouraging the development of an administrative lingua franca for the administration of their conquered territories, while restricting the use of Egyptian hieroglyphic writing to their own people and indigenous culture. At the same time, the Egyptian scribes had knowledge of the standard Akkadian dialect for diplomatic use with northern Syrian polities like that of the Hittites. The choice of written codes—Egyptian, Canaano-Akkadian, and Middle Babylonian languages—had political and ideological implications.

The best proof of the Canaanite scribes' knowledge of standard Akkadian is the use of *code-switching*. Code-switching is a linguistic term that refers to the use of more than one language or dialect. Although the term normally describes speech, it is certainly applicable here to written language. Code-switching requires that the speaker (or writer) have the ability to use elements of multiple languages. In the Amarna letters, Canaanite scribes would switch to standard Akkadian forms when referring to the pharaoh. This includes not only direct quotes of the pharaoh (or his officials) but also references to and paraphrases of the pharaoh.[48] Examples of code-switching can be illustrated especially in the verbal system, which is perhaps the most distinctive feature of the Canaano-Akkadian dialect of the letters. For example, in a letter from the ruler of Byblos to the pharaoh (EA 106), the writer uses standard Canaano-Akkadian forms when speaking about the Canaanite ruler Ribhaddi:

> (13) *šá-ni-tam a-na mi-nim* (14) *yi-iš-tap-ru* ^{m}*ri-ib-*^{d}*IŠKUR ki-na-an-na-ma* (15) DÚB-*pa a-na* É.GAL. (Furthermore, why does Ribhaddi *keep sending* a tablet this way to the palace?)

Here, the writer uses the typical Canaano-Akkadian verbal form with a prefix *yi-*. In contrast, the writer will employ code-switching, using standard Akkadian forms, when he refers to what Pharaoh has told Ribhaddi:

> (30) *ú ki-i i-qa-bu* LUGAL *a-na mi-nim iš-tap-r*[*u*] (31) ^{m}*ri-ib-*^{d}*IŠKUR* DÚB-*pa a-na ma-ḫar be-li-š*[*u*]. (And how can the king *say*, "Why does Ribhaddi *keep sending* a tablet to his lord?)

The writer uses the standard Akkadian forms with the *i-* prefix instead of the more typical Canaano-Akkadian forms with the *yi-* prefix. Shlomo Izre'el gives several other examples of this phenomenon,[49] but this example suffices to illustrate the point. The Canaanite scribes of the Amarna letters were aware of the "standard" Akkadian forms, but such forms were not their standard. The writers associated the standard forms with their Egyptian liege, even though Akkadian was not the language or writing system of the Egyptians. However, Canaanite scribes could also reasonably expect their Egyptian counterparts to be versed in both Canaano-Akkadian and the standard Akkadian dialect.

The most striking contribution of the Canaano-Akkadian Amarna letters has been to our understanding of the Hebrew verbal system.[50] Most important has been the outlining of the early Northwest Semitic prefix conjugation:

INDICATIVE		INJUNCTIVE	
Preterite	*yaqtul, -û*	Jussive	*yaqtul, -û*
Imperfect	*yaqtulu, -ûna*	Volitive	*yaqtula, -û*
Energic	*yaqtulun(n)a*	Energic	*yaqtulan(n)a*

The recognition of the preterite (short) and imperfect (long) indicative prefix conjugations shed new light on the Hebrew verbal patterns, particularly the so-called *waw* consecutive, which derives from the short prefix form of the verb and is preserved in narrative as a preterite verb. Forms such as the *waw* consecutive are purely scribal forms, hence the description of it sometimes as a "narrative tense." The so-called enigma of the Hebrew verbal system lies in its transition from the older aspect-oriented West Semitic system with two prefix conjugations to a more tense-oriented system that only fully emerges in Rabbinic Hebrew.[51]

The Canaanite Amarna letters show a number of marked similarities with the later classical Hebrew dialect. Most notably, the *Canaanite shift*—that is, the phonetic shift from /ā́/ to /ṓ/—becomes standard in the Amarna letters (as opposed to Ugaritic). For example, the pronoun in Akkadian, *anāku* "I," also appears in Ugaritic as *ʾanāku*, whereas the Amarna letters show the Canaanite shift, *a-nu-ki* (compare Hebrew, *ʾanōki*). Another interesting feature is the use of the typical Canaanite *h*- prefix for the causative verbal conjugation (alongside the *š*- prefix that was used in Akkadian).[52] Although the Amarna letters were not written in a standard Akkadian dialect, the scribes were not merely writing deficient Akkadian. Rather, the scribes were aware of the standard Akkadian forms but chose to write in their own special dialect, which we may call Canaano-Akkadian.

Whose "standard" was it then? *Standard* Akkadian is defined by scholars as the language that emanates from the Mesopotamian heartland. Quite typically, the standard language is the language of those in political power who support the schools and the scribes. As Eva Von Dassow has pointed out, "It has become a truism that Akkadian, the principle Semitic language of ancient Mesopotamia, was the lingua franca of the Near East during the second millennium B.C.E."[53] It is quite typical then for modern scholars to denigrate Canaano-Akkadian as if it were inferior. Even an Amarna expert such as Izre'el can write, "From a sociolinguistic point of view, the language of the Egyptian scribes [who wrote in "standard" Akkadian] was superior to that of the Canaanite scribes."[54] This is, however, certainly not a *sociolinguistic* perspective. The dialect used by the Egyptian scribes may have had a broader usage in the Near East, and Akkadian was certainly used by the dominant political polities of the late second millennium, but this does not make it *superior* from a linguistic point of view. The word *superior* implies a value judgment—a colonialist perspective—that is simply not appropriate for comparing languages or dialects. Moreover, the ascendancy of the Akkadian language itself was in decline during the late second millennium B.C.E. As the political fortunes of Mesopotamia waned, so also did the fate of "standard" Akkadian.

The ancestors of the Hebrew language can be glimpsed in the languages of the second millennium B.C.E.—Ugaritic, Canaano-Akkadian, and even Amorite. However, there is no direct or simple lineage. In addition, the linear alphabetic writing system (that is, what is commonly known as the "Phoenician" alphabet) that came to be used for Hebrew was invented in the early second millennium, but it apparently saw little use before its development by the coastal Canaanite city-states in the early Iron Age. In sum, the building blocks for the Hebrew language were already present in the Late Bronze Age, but the development of classical Hebrew as a language and a writing system would await the social and political events surrounding the emergence of the Israelite and Judean kingdoms in the early first millennium B.C.E.

Whence Came the Israelites and Their Language?

Although it is clear that the Israelites borrowed the Canaanite/Phoenician writing system (that is, the alphabet), it does not necessarily follow that Hebrew is a Canaanite language. In a series of articles, Anson Rainey has argued that Hebrew is a Transjordanian language (that is, modern-day Jordan or ancient Moab, Ammon, and Edom).[55] This conclusion directly contradicts the conventional wisdom that Hebrew is a Canaanite language, which is based first of all upon the shared alphabetic writing system. Certainly, ancient Hebrew borrowed its writing system from the Phoenician city-states. At the same time, the problems with this are evident in the fact that Hebrew has at least twenty-five consonantal phonemes, whereas the Phoenician writing system had only twenty-two letters. The alphabet was a writing system but not a language; and the differences between Hebrew and Canaanite are underscored by the limitations of this writing technology for Hebrew. But does it follow that Hebrew is not a Canaanite language? A language is not its writing system, yet the writing system is our key to understanding the origins of Hebrew—which we essentially know as a written language.

The argument that Hebrew is fundamentally a Transjordanian language dovetails nicely with the biblical accounts of the origins of Israel as wandering in the southern desert (or Negev) and entering the Promised Land from the east (that is, from Transjordan). Rainey utilized a combination of archaeological and linguistic evidence to make his case. The archaeological evidence is equivocal; that is, it shows evidence of connections among early Israelite settlements and the coastal plain, the early Late Bronze Age hill-country settlements, and settlements from Transjordan. Archaeology will not categorically answer the question of how to categorize the origins of the Hebrew language.

The linguistic evidence is more enticing. There are a number of important distinctions between the Phoenician dialects and Hebrew. One such major distinction is the verb *to be*; Hebrew and Moabite use the root **hyy* (which becomes *hyh* [היה] in Hebrew), whereas Phoenician uses *kwn*. This distinction in verbs is reinforced by fundamental differences in the verbal systems of Hebrew and Moabite as opposed to Phoenician. Hebrew and Moabite (as well as southern Aramaic dialects) use a narrative tense (usually termed the *waw* consecutive) in prose (for example, *wyhy*, "and it came to pass"),[56] whereas Phoenician uses a form of the old West Semitic infinitive absolute as its narrative tense. Another important isogloss between Hebrew and its Transjordanian cousin, Moabite, was the word *ʿśh* (עשה), "to do," which stands in contrast with the Phoenician *pʿl*. The different relative particles are also noteworthy in this regard. Phoenician (and Northern Hebrew) use a relative particle, "which, that" derived from *š* (being spelled with a prosthetic *ʾaleph* in Phoenician, *ʾš*), whereas Judean Hebrew and Moabite have the relative *ʾšr* (אשר) that can be derived from the West Semitic word for "place," **ašru*. Finally, there is a significant administrative isogloss between Phoenician and Amarna Canaano-Akkadian, namely, the use of *skn* or *saknu* for a "governor, chief administrator"; this stands in contrast to Hebrew, which employs the expression *ʾšr ʿl hbyt* (אשר על הבית), literally, "the one who is over the house." This also highlights that Amarna Canaano-Akkadian shares significant isoglosses with Phoenician dialects. In sum, there are significant distinctions between Hebrew and Canaanite/Phoenician, but does this make it a different language?

Hebrew also shares striking similarities with Phoenician dialects. The most important of these is the Canaanite shift, namely, the vocalic shift from long *a* to long *o*, which did not take place in Aramaic. Hebrew and Phoenician also share the prefixed *heh* as a definite article, in contrast with the suffixed *ʾaleph* used in Aramaic; yet, the Transjordanian dialects of Moabite, Edomite, and Ammonite also used a prefixed *heh* for the definite article. In the end, linguistic classification—as we have argued—is more about politics than identity and origins. The borrowing of the alphabet was the borrowing of a technology. It does not tell us too much about linguistic classification. Distinction in the basic linguistic terminology—that is, words for "to be," "to do," definite articles—lend themselves to creating distinctions in identity, and it is in these respects that Hebrew is not a coastal or Canaanite language. Indeed, geographically and politically speaking, it is likely that the ancient Judeans would have created a separate linguistic identity from the coastal plain. Culturally and geographically, the hill country of Judah and the Transjordanian highlands had much in common. Eventually, however, the Judean state would push down into the coastal plain. The coastal plain by the twelfth century B.C.E. was already inhabited by the Philistines, who would eventually also adopt the Phoenician writing system and language. In sum, the late second millennium witnessed the exchange of one transnational writing system, syllabic cuneiform, for a new transnational writing system, the alphabet.

So, returning to the question that began this chapter, What is Hebrew? In this early period at the end of the second millennium, Hebrew is encoded in a new transnational writing system. This is a reflection of the fact that writing is not to be equated with language in this period. Vernacular languages are closely associated with local speech communities and identity. Using a writing system that transcends the boundaries of local dialects and languages underscores the role of writing as a communication technology. There have been interesting debates among archaeologists about the use of pottery or architecture for isolating ethnic identity that have highlighted the complicated nature of identifying such technologies with ethnic identity.[57] There is a variety of archaeological evidence pointing to the emergence of an early Israelite culture in the hill country, and vernacular dialects would have been part of the emerging Israelite culture; however, writing was not uniquely part of emergent Israelite cultural identity. Rather, writing was still a transnational technology. Social and political changes in subsequent centuries would result in a distinct Hebrew language that can be identified through its writing system; however, that time had not yet come. In the late second millennium B.C.E., Hebrew was only known from common West Semitic systems of syllabic cuneiform, alphabetic cuneiform, and linear alphabetic writing.

Commonly Proposed West Semitic Features

1. Canaanite shift. The phonetic shift from /ā́/ to /ṓ/ occurs in "Canaanite" languages (e.g., Phoenician, Hebrew, the Amarna texts) but not in Aramaic or Ugaritic.
2. Two prefix conjugations. The Amarna letters provide evidence for a long-prefix *yaqtulu* conjugation (the imperfect) as well as short-prefix *yaqtul* conjugation (the preterite). The short form survives in BH as a narrative tense with the *waw* consecutive as well as the frozen formula *ʾz* + *yaqtul* (e.g., *ʾz yšyr mšh*, "then Moses sang," Exod. 15:1).
3. No definite article.

3

Early Hebrew Writing

A language is simply a dialect that has an army and a navy.

—*Max Weinreich*

The rise of Hebrew is conventionally connected with the emergence of monarchy in ancient Israel and particularly with the reigns of David and Solomon. In this event, the tongue-in-cheek cliché in linguistics that "a language is simply a dialect that has an army and a navy" might apply. Not only are David and Solomon credited with standing armies, Solomon is even credited with building a navy at the Red Sea port of Eilat (1 Kings 9:26–28). This cliché also speaks to the role of language in creating group identity in nations. Unfortunately, there is no evidence that ancient Israel had any special language ideology concerning writing in the early Iron Age. Rather, the transnational role of scribes and writing that characterized the Middle and Late Bronze Ages (2000–1200 B.C.E.) continued into the early Iron Age (1200–840 B.C.E.). Scribes and writing were not nationalized but were part of transnational Canaanite culture. What we call "early Hebrew writing" was nearly indistinguishable from the other early Canaanite inscriptions.

Even though Israel emerged as a people in Canaan by the end of the second millennium B.C.E., a unique Hebrew writing system did not emerge. It could not. Hebrew was still searching for its voice—that is, for its own unique writing system and nationalized scribal schools to put the vernacular of the ancient Israelites into writing. There were two polities that helped shape the emergence of Hebrew. First, the Egyptians during the late second millennium B.C.E. instituted an administrative system that included writing and scribes, which was the scribal foundation for the early Canaanite kingdoms. Second, the Phoenicians developed and refined the alphabet, and through their commerce spread the alphabetic writing system throughout the eastern Mediterranean.

The sharp decline of the Egyptian New Kingdom and its pharaohs from Thutmose III to Ramesses III also marked a political, social, and demographic transition in the Levant. The Levant was dominated in the fifteenth through thirteenth centuries B.C.E. by Egypt. The decline of Egypt is usually associated with the arrival of the Sea Peoples and their battle with Ramesses III in 1185 B.C.E. Egypt retreated from the international stage in the twelfth century, and the Levant transitioned to new independent polities including the Philistines, the Phoenicians, the Israelites, and the Aramaeans. The more urban culture of the second millennium—specifically, the Middle Bronze Age (2000–1550 B.C.E.) and the Late Bronze Age (1550–1200 B.C.E.)—devolved into the more pastoral and agrarian society that characterized the early Iron Age (1200–840 B.C.E.).

The period of the early Israelite monarchy associated in biblical history with the kings David and Solomon now appears as more of a foundational period rather than a period of great affluence and complex state development. Nevertheless, the rise of the classical Hebrew language was associated with the emergence of monarchy in ancient Israel, particularly in a classic article by Chaim Rabin: "The great turning point in the history of the Hebrew language, as in so many other cultural and religious aspects, was the brief spell (about seventy years) during which North and South were united under David and Solomon, and in particular the establishment of the administrative and religious capital in Jerusalem, a city not previously connected with any tribe. After its conquest the city was populated by David with people from different tribes. The cult, which existed in David's time, was carried on by priests from all parts of the country (I Chron. 13:2), and of course even more so once the Temple had been established."[1] Rabin's conclusion was based, on the one hand, on a theoretical cornerstone of sociolinguistics, namely, that language change and social history are mutually dependent, and, on the other hand, on the consensus that the period of David and Solomon was a period of political consolidation and great economic prosperity and expansion. The former cornerstone still holds, but the latter consensus has crumbled in the face of archaeological evidence. Indeed, an entire school of biblical history has risen around the critique of the golden age of David and Solomon—a "united monarchy," as it were.[2] The idea of the united monarchy, that is, of political and social centralization under Saul, David, and Solomon, also has its defenders, and recent archaeological discoveries undermine the more radical denials of the united monarchy.[3] The critiques of history aside, the archaeological evidence indicates that the high points of political consolidation and economic prosperity in the southern Levant came in the late eighth and seventh centuries rather than in the tenth and ninth centuries B.C.E.[4] In this chapter, we will focus on the early Iron Age. In archaeological terms, we are interested in language, writing, and society during the Iron I through the Iron IIA periods, or between 1200 and 840 B.C.E.[5]

For the study of early Hebrew, however, we face an even more fundamental issue: In antiquity, writing gave language its voice, thus scribes and their employers shaped the contours of early Hebrew. There was no specifically Hebrew writing system. The scribes were deeply entrenched and inseparable from the larger world of ancient Canaan.[6] Before discussing the nature of early Israelite scribal schools, we begin with a delineation of the chronological and geographical boundaries of *early Hebrew*, which must be distinguished from *Archaic Biblical Hebrew* (ABH). By early Hebrew, I refer generally to the inscriptions from the territory of the kingdoms of Israel and Judah, but there is no distinction between Old Canaanite writing and specifically Hebrew writing during this early period. Early Hebrew is described by *geography* rather than linguistics. The presumed vernacular behind inscriptions such as the Gezer Calendar or the Qeiyafa inscription found within the borders of Israel and Judah is presumably Hebrew, but the linguistic description of early Hebrew presumes a relationship with Old Canaanite writing and a local vernacular. In contrast, ABH is specifically the poetry of a few apparently archaic poems in the Bible; the texts conventionally labeled as ABH include the Blessing of Jacob (Gen. 49), the Song of Moses (Exod. 15), the Oracles of Balaam (Num. 23–24), the Poem of Moses (Deut. 32), the Blessing of Moses (Deut. 33), the Song of Deborah (Judg. 5), and early Psalms (for example, Pss. 18, 68). And, by ABH, I refer to the Hebrew language used *before* the rise of an official standardized Hebrew that would be defined by the kingdom of Judah and the scribal tradition centered in the city of Jerusalem in the eighth and seventh centuries B.C.E. (see chapter 4).

The Rise of Alphabetic Writing

At the close of the second millennium and into the first centuries of the first millennium, there was significant cultural continuity in the southern Levant. This cultural continuity included language and writing. The first indicator for linguistic continuity, especially with regard to writing, was the alphabet. The alphabet, which had been invented at the beginning of the second millennium, finally began to spread widely at the close of the second millennium B.C.E.

The first "Hebrew" inscriptions did not use a uniquely Israelite alphabet. Rather, early Hebrew writing employed an alphabet attributed to the Phoenicians in spite of its deficiencies for accurately reflecting the phonology of Hebrew. The Phoenician alphabet had twenty-two letters, which is much reduced from the thirty letters known from the Ugaritic alphabet and the even larger number of letters known from the early alphabetic texts from Serabit el-Khadem and Wadi el-Hôl.

Two processes were used in compressing the Proto-Semitic inventory of consonantal phonemes (sounds) into a reduced Phoenician inventory of graphemes (letters): *assimilation* and *polyvalence*.[7] Once the assimilation of consonantal phonemes has been accounted for, Hebrew still had at least twenty-five consonantal phonemes that had to be represented by the twenty-two graphemes of the Phoenician alphabet. Thus, there are three polyvalent graphemes: ש representing /š/ and /ś/, ח representing /ḥ/ and /ḫ/, and ע representing /ʿ/ and /ǵ/. As a result, there are many homographs, that is, words that are spelled in the same way but have different etymologies resulting from the more limited graphemic inventory of the Phoenician alphabet.[8] The most obvious examples are the consonantal phonemes /š/ and /ś/, which were both written with the Hebrew letter ש until the Masoretes added a diacritical mark to distinguish שׂ /ś/ from שׁ /š/. In addition, there is evidence from Hellenistic sources to suggest that one Hebrew grapheme was used to represent two distinct phonemes; respectively, ח was used for the phonemes /ḫ/ and /ḥ/, and ע for /ʿ/ and /ǵ/, which were pronounced distinctly in certain Hebrew dialects at least until the end of the first millennium B.C.E. Thus, the consonantal spelling *ʿnh* could reflect two pronunciations, /*ʿānâ/, "he answered," and /*ǵānâ/, "he sang," a result of the use of this one grapheme ע for two phonemes, /ʿ/ and /ǵ/. Similarly, the word *ḥrym* (חרים) was a homograph for *ḫrym*, "holes, Hurrians," and *ḥrym*, "nobles, freemen." Cognate languages such as Old South Arabic, Arabic, Aramaic, and Akkadian give insight into the phonetic mergers that took place by the end of the second millennium B.C.E., giving us the more limited phonetic inventories (as well as graphemes) that we see in the Canaanite dialects of the first millennium.

The spread of the old West Semitic linear alphabet has been tied to the Phoenicians. However, it is not precisely correct to label this a "Phoenician" alphabet, inasmuch as *Phoenicians* is an anachronistic term. Phoenicia was actually several independent coastal city-states, including Tyre, Sidon, Arwad, and Byblos, which maintained their own autonomy. Those who lived in loosely connected city-states only came to be called "Phoenicians" by later Greek writers. In antiquity, the Levantine coast was called "Canaan," which later became a term for the entire Levant. These coastal city-states flourished at the end of the second millennium and into the early first millennium and seem to have been responsible for the spread of alphabetic writing, yet the alphabet was not a specifically Phoenician invention. The alphabet was not invented as a national script and was used throughout the Levant in the second millennium with little sense of identification with one ethnic group.[9] Although all labels have their limitations, the generic term *Canaanite* best describes the reduced twenty-two-character alphabet that spread throughout the Levant at the end of the second millennium into the early first millennium (about 1200–900 B.C.E.). The term *Phoenician* most aptly refers to the later development, by the eighth century B.C.E., of a local script that was distinct from the contemporary local Hebrew and Aramaic scripts.

Another caution must be noted regarding the tendency to oversimplify the relationship between sounds and writing. Even among the coastal city-states there were differences in writing conventions and dialects. So, for example, Byblian has been described as a "dialect island" in Phoenician.[10] These differences were naturally more significant in other Levantine kingdoms that utilized the alphabet. Because of the limited inventory of letters in the Canaanite alphabet, there are special considerations regarding how phonemes would be expressed by graphemes in the various Northwest Semitic languages that borrowed the Canaanite alphabet. A prominent example of this problem is the word for "land," usually reconstructed as coming from /*ʾarḍ/ in Northwest Semitic; this word was written as *ʾrṣ* in Phoenician and Hebrew, but written in two different ways in Aramaic. In the Old Aramaic dialects "land" is usually written as *ʾrq*, but later in Imperial (and later) Aramaic dialects it is usually written *ʾrʿ*. Is the writing of the hypothetical Proto-Semitic sound /ḍ/ with the letter *q* and then *ʿ* in Aramaic as opposed to *ṣ* in Hebrew and Phoenician really simply the result of different phonological mergers or shifts? Likely not. Sociolinguistic research has shown that spelling practices are quite often dictated by social, political, and ideological factors,[11] and we can hardly rule out such issues in a highly loaded word like *land*. This variance should alert us to the problematic relationship between graphemes (that is, writing) and phonemes (that is, speech), and it should remind us that choices about spelling can reflect much more than an attempt to correlate sounds with letters.

The coastal city-states developed an alphabet, and it spread throughout the Levant at the end of the second and beginning of the first millennium B.C.E. For example, the various Aramaean and Hittite kingdoms used the Phoenician alphabet, even though the limited number of graphemes in Phoenician did not fully represent the phonemes of the local dialects. Likewise, the ancient Israelites also employed the Phoenician alphabet. This raises the question, Why was the Phoenician alphabet used, in spite of its limited inventory of letters, for writing throughout the Levant at the end of the second millennium and into the early first millennium B.C.E.?

Egypt's Role in Early Levantine Scribalism

As previously mentioned, one of the remarkable achievements of the late second millennium B.C.E. was the development of a coherent writing system known from the Amarna letters. The correspondence comes from an archive excavated at the Egyptian capital of Akhetaten (1350s–1330s B.C.E.). Amarna is the modern name for this Egyptian capital dating to the Eighteenth Dynasty and located in Upper Egypt. The letters are addressed to the pharaoh from his representatives in Canaan and Amurru during the New Kingdom. The known tablets number about four hundred in total, with a majority deriving from the Canaanite towns.

The problem of the Canaanite Amarna letters begins with the fact that they were written in a consistent but distinct dialect. This dialect has been described in a number of studies, including Anson Rainey's monumental four-volume work, *Canaanite in the Amarna Tablets*. The writing system of the Canaanite Amarna letters, surprisingly, exhibits the waning of Mesopotamian scribal influence in Canaanite. The letters were not written in the standard Akkadian dialect of the Late Bronze Age, but they already exhibit a decisive break with the contemporary cuneiform culture to the north (see further discussion of the Amarna letters in chapter 2). They employ as their base language Old Babylonian (that is, of the early second millennium B.C.E.) rather than the contemporary Middle Babylonian dialect that underlies the cuneiform culture of the northern Levant and Syria. That is, the Canaano-Akkadian of the Amarna letters is a vestige of Middle Bronze Age scribal culture mixed with innovative linguistic characteristics of Canaanite. However, *there is no political polity within Canaan itself that can account for the creation of this independent writing system*. The Canaanite city-states of the region were too weak, independent, and dominated by Egypt to have created a new writing system and enforced a standardization throughout the southern Levant. So who then created the Canaano-Akkadian writing system of the Amarna letters?

The answer will not be found by looking to the north. The language of the Amarna letters, with its use of the Old Babylonian base language (instead of the contemporary Middle Babylonian used in northern Syria), demonstrates that it was not a creation of northern Syrian scribes. Other cuneiform texts can serve as further signposts pointing to independence from Mesopotamia and also the decline in cuneiform culture during the Late Bronze Age.[12] Most of the cuneiform evidence from Canaan dates to the early part of the Late Bronze Age (that is, fifteenth and fourteenth centuries), and by the end of the Late Bronze Age, cuneiform culture had completely disappeared from the southern Levant and would not reemerge until the resurgence of Assyria in the eighth century B.C.E.[13] Cuneiform had been the local writing tradition through most of the second millennium B.C.E., until the thirteenth century B.C.E., but it began to be replaced during the thirteenth and twelfth centuries, in favor of a local alphabetic tradition influenced by Egyptian scribal traditions.

Who then was responsible for creating the writing system used in the Canaano-Akkadian Amarna letters? The only alternative is to look to the south. Indeed, *Canaano-Akkadian was the language employed by areas under Egyptian hegemony in addressing the pharaoh*. Egypt was the only polity capable of creating this new writing system and spreading a standardization throughout the southern Levant. Canaano-Akkadian was an administrative tool of the Egyptians in the southern Levant. Moreover, the content of the Amarna letters underscores the increased Egyptian presence in the southern Levant that so characterizes the Late Bronze Age. And, the appearance of this new writing system happened to coincide with the expansion of systematic Egyptian hegemony into the Levant, for the first time in its history, during the New Kingdom. By the time of the Nineteenth Dynasty (ca. 1292–1190 B.C.E.), the Egyptians had set up administrative centers along the coast (in towns like Gaza, Jaffa, and Sumur) and along the major trade routes (in cities like Aphek, Beth-Shean, and Kumidi) in the southern Levant.[14] The Canaanite Amarna letters also refer to various Egyptian administrative officials working in various capacities in Canaan. In addition, the well-known Egyptian text "The Craft of the Scribe" (Papyrus Anastasi I), which was written during the reign of Ramesses II (ca. 1279–1213 B.C.E.), highlights the importance of the Levantine topography for Egyptian scribes.[15] According to this text, the Egyptian scribe had to serve as a *mahir*, which is a Semitic term for an officer with knowledge of logistics and reconnaissance, for the Egyptian military and administrative operations in the Levant. The text is replete with loanwords from West Semitic and highlights the scribes' education in foreign topography and accounting. As this text makes clear, Egyptian scribes played important roles in the administration of the southern Levant.

Further evidence of Egyptian scribes working in Canaan comes from several other literary and archaeological sources. First of all, several hieratic inscriptions reflecting mundane administrative work of Egyptian scribes have been excavated in Israel.[16] The hieratic inscriptions testify to a robust Ramesside administration in the southern Levant, a main function of which was the taxation and administration of grain deliveries. These inscriptions are in typical Egyptian hieratic, written in ink on potsherds, and are ephemeral records of day-to-day transactions; papyrus and ink were undoubtedly also used for more-permanent records, but the environment in the southern Levant makes it unlikely that any papyrus documents would be recovered in excavations.

The activities of these Late Bronze Age Egyptian scribes left a lasting mark, continuing to influence the scribal culture in the Iron I period and later.[17] Already in the previous chapter, I detailed the legacy of Egyptian scribal schools from the Late Bronze Age, and it may be useful to develop further some of the evidence in this context. To begin with, the use of ink on papyrus as a medium of writing (as opposed to a stylus on wet clay) became a normative practice in the Levant. Not surprisingly, the Hebrew words for "ink" (*ḏᵉyô*) and "papyrus" (*gmʾ*) are borrowed from Egyptian.[18] The use of ink for writing begins in the Late Bronze Age and continues into the Iron Age. Along with ink, the use of papyrus comes directly from Egyptian scribal practice and technology. The use of papyrus, of course, went hand in hand with the introduction of ink as a writing technology.

In addition to the changing technology for scribes, there were new accounting methods borrowed from the Egyptians. Most important, the hieratic numerals that Egyptian scribes were using in their local administration of taxation became standard for ancient Israelite scribes (but not for Phoenician or Aramaean scribes to the north).[19] This use of Egyptian hieratic numerals for accounting must date back to at least the tenth century B.C.E. but more likely can be traced back to vestiges of the Ramesside administration in the Levant. Indeed, there was little or no difference in the hieratic numerals between the thirteenth and tenth centuries B.C.E., but a major transition in Egyptian writing occurs between the tenth and eighth centuries B.C.E., when demotic numerals appear instead of hieratic.[20] As a result, the hieratic numerals that would be used in Hebrew inscriptions throughout the Iron Age must be regarded as the residue of the Egyptian administration during the Nineteenth and Twentieth Dynasties in the southern Levant. Even as the Egyptian presence diminished during the Twenty-First Dynasty (1069–945 B.C.E., or the beginning of the Third Intermediate Period), the tokens of their presence remained.

The influence of Egyptian scribal culture would become quite widespread in early Israel. In addition to learning the practices of accounting (that is, using hieratic numerals) and of writing with ink, the early Israelites borrowed several linguistic terms relating to the scribal profession from Egyptian. To begin with, it is worth noting that the Hebrew word for "scribe" (*sōp̄ēr*) derives from the root *spr*, which originally meant not "to write" but rather "to count," reflecting the administrative roots of the scribal profession. We have already mentioned the terms for "ink" and "papyrus," but other Egyptian (Eg.) loanwords include those for "a scribe's palette" (Eg. *gśty*; Heb. *qeseṯ*), "seal" (Eg. *ḫtm*; Heb. *ḥôṯām*), "signet ring" (Eg. *ḏbʿt*; Heb. *ṭab̄aʿaṯ*), "ephah" (a certain measurement for grain; Eg. *ypt*; Heb. *ʾêp̄â*), "hin" (a certain liquid measure; Eg. *hnw*; Heb. *hîn*), and "zeret" (a span of measurement; Eg. *ḏrt*; Heb. *zereṯ*).[21] There are very few Egyptian loanwords in Hebrew, but most are related to the scribal technology and profession, most likely reflecting the continuing work of Egyptian natives or Egyptian-trained locals after the retrenchment following the Twentieth Dynasty.[22]

The biblical records concerning the first scribes of the Israelite kingdoms also point to a lingering Egyptian scribal presence. For example, a list purported to be David's officials includes the figure of "Sheva, the scribe" (2 Sam. 20:25), and a list of officials for King Solomon also includes two court scribes: "Elihoreph and Ahijah, the sons of Shisha" (1 Kings 4:3). The name Elihoreph is Egyptian, deriving from *ʾr-ḥp*, "Apis is my God."[23] The name Shisha seems to be a straightforward Hebraizing of the Egyptian word *sš*, "scribe."[24] The name Sheva seems to be an appellative derived from the Egyptian title *sš šʿt*, "the writer of letters," rather than a proper noun.[25] Given the context, the name Shisha seems to be a simple misinterpretation by a later Hebrew scribe of the Egyptian word *sš*, "scribe," as a personal name; thus, it is possible that the original meaning of the Hebrew expression *bny šyšʾ*, which is usually translated as "sons of Shisha," may have been "members of a scribal guild"—since the Hebrew term *bn*, "son," often means "guild member" when combined with a profession. These members of the scribal guild would have had their roots in the Ramesside administration. In any event, the Egyptian scribal legacy in Canaan is abundantly clear.

The Egyptian influence also extends to the alphabet itself. There is some debate among scholars about who invented the alphabet. Some scholars think that Canaanites (that is, the Egyptian "Asiatics") knew the Egyptian writing system and used this knowledge in inventing a writing system suited to their own language; other scholars believe that the differences between Egyptian and the alphabet suggest that the inventors of the alphabet were Canaanites who could not have known how to write the Egyptian writing system.[26] There is a debate about the exact identity of the inventors of the alphabet, but the graphic similarities between the early alphabet and hieroglyphic writing point to familiarity with Egyptian writing.[27]

The two main writing technologies for mundane writing in the second millennium were stylus on wet clay and ink on papyrus or potsherds. Cuneiform writing was not suited for papyrus or ephemeral materials like ostraca; likewise, ink was not suited for cuneiform writing. Cuneiform writing on wet clay was the provenance of Mesopotamian scribal culture, whereas Egyptian scribal culture used ink and papyrus for its hieratic writing (and hieroglyphics for monumental writing). The alphabet had representatives that drew their origins from both Mesopotamian and Egyptian scribal culture. The cuneiform alphabet used in Ugarit (and known even in the southern Levant) clearly drew on Mesopotamian scribal culture and technology, whereas the early alphabetic texts beginning with Wadi el-Hôl and Serabit el-Khadem drew upon Egyptian scribal culture and technology. The Late Bronze Age would begin a transition from Mesopotamian to Egyptian scribal culture in the southern Levant.

A Decisive Break?

What we have described here is the continuity between Late Bronze and Iron Age scribal institutions, particularly those related to the Egyptian administration that dominated the southern Levant in the Nineteenth and Twentieth Dynasties (that is, the thirteenth and early twelfth centuries B.C.E.). The arrival of the Sea Peoples in the early twelfth century B.C.E., however, is thought to mark a decisive cultural break throughout the Levant.

The theory of a decisive linguistic break was popularized by the work of George Mendenhall. Mendenhall argued that a break between the second- and first-millennium literary dialects reflected the discontinuity of the educated elite during the upheavals around 1200 B.C.E.[28] This theory, however, relies on weak evidence.[29] Mendenhall points, for example, to the breakdown of case vowels in the first millennium; however, he overstates the literary and linguistic break. A breakdown in case vowels is not simply a first-millennium phenomenon; it is already evident in Ugaritic.[30] At the same time, ABH preserves vestiges of case endings.[31] Given the conservative nature of written tradition, one must suspect that case endings had already largely disappeared from the spoken West Semitic dialects by the end of the second millennium B.C.E., yet the limited use of case endings in ABH shows the strong power of the conservative scribal tradition. Likewise, Hebrew literary traditions show striking similarities with Late Bronze Age traditions at Ugarit. Though the "educated elite" that Mendenhall speaks of may have lost their patrons under the Egyptian hegemony of the Late Bronze Age, the scribal profession was not merely or even primarily a palace institution during the Late Bronze Age. The study of the scribes of the Late Bronze city of Emar, for example, points to a striking independence of the scribal profession, even though scribes may have been primarily employed by the state. Shifting political sands certainly would have changed their allegiances and may have shrunk their numbers, but their craft did not disappear. Indeed, the persistence of Egyptian technical terms and technology into the Iron Age demonstrates that there was no clean and decisive break in the scribal profession but rather a transition.

In his recent study of Iron Age scribal schools, David Jamieson-Drake argues, "There is no evidence of strong pressure to modify or enhance existing administrative controls during the period [twelfth–tenth centuries B.C.E.]. The level of growth and lack of concentration of population at this time calls not so much for increasing administrative control as for the stability in pre-existing administrative systems, whatever those were." However, Jamieson-Drake assumes weak and dispersed administrative controls and thus concludes, "There is no reason to posit scribal institutions of any kind for Israel during this period."[32] Jamieson-Drake's assumption, unfortunately, relies heavily on the model of peasant revolt posited by Mendenhall and Gottwald.[33] This model envisions a social upheaval at the end of the Late Bronze Age that resulted in a complete disintegration of the Late Bronze administrative structures. More recent archaeological studies of the Late Bronze–Iron Age transition have found little evidence that would support such a model.[34] Rather, there were elements of both continuity and change in the Late Bronze–Iron Age transition. Moreover, change did not take place everywhere at the same time. Some settlements even show relative continuity from the Late Bronze Age into the Iron Age.

Jamieson-Drake's reliance on the Mendenhall and Gottwald settlement theory underscores that theory's importance for the formulation of early Judean scribal schools. As Jamieson-Drake points out, Mendenhall had to hypothesize a scenario wherein an entirely new cadre of professional scribes would have arisen in the tenth century.[35] Mendenhall suggested that the Israelite disdain for the Canaanite urban administration systems disappeared when David needed Canaanite expertise to establish his empire. Such descriptions, however, reflect the attitudes of the late- (that is, seventh-century B.C.E.) Deuteronomistic editors toward foreign influence rather than the archaeological and linguistic evidence from the Late Bronze–Iron Age transition. More plausible is that skilled craftspeople of all types (including those working with scribal and administrative technologies) looked for and found employment among local polities in the wake of the demise of Egyptian control at the beginning of the twelfth century B.C.E.

Early Alphabetic Inscriptions in Israel

Although we have evidence of alphabetic writing from the beginning of the second millennium, the evidence is quite meager and sporadic.[36] Chronologically, we can separate the evidence into three periods. We have already addressed the earliest inscriptions from the Middle Bronze Age (2000–1550 B.C.E.) and Late Bronze Age (1550–1200 B.C.E.). We now turn our attention to the early Iron Age (1200–840 B.C.E.), which I will divide into two periods: Iron I (1200–980 B.C.E.) and Iron IIA (980–840 B.C.E.). The evidence is meager enough that it is possible to survey the corpus, although it is not necessary to examine every fragmentary exemplar of writing from the early Iron Age.

During the early Iron Age, the term *Hebrew writing* is problematic. It is better to employ a local geographical term like *Israelite writing* or a more-general term like *Levantine* or *Canaanite writing*. Though the ancient Israelites undoubtedly had their own local dialects and speech communities, there is little evidence to suggest that they had developed an independent writing system or scribal community. The term *Israelite*, which I have suggested here, is an ethnic and geographic (rather than linguistic) term that is borrowed from its use in the Merneptah Stele (ca. 1207 B.C.E.), which mentions a foreign people called Israel:

> Canaan is plundered, Ashkelon [city-state] is carried off, and Gezer [city-state] is captured. Yenoam [city-state] is made into nonexistence. Israel [foreign people] is wasted, its seed is not; and Hurru is become a widow because of Egypt. (See *COS* §2.6.)

Egyptian uses determinatives, which are translated in the brackets, to mark the categories of nouns. In this case, the Egyptian enemies are given the determinative for a "city-state," whereas Israel is categorized as a "foreign people."[37] Alternatively, we could borrow another term from the stele, *Canaanite*, though this is a much broader geographical term and seems especially to refer to the Levantine coast (as opposed to the hill country). Hence, the term *Levantine* would be preferable to *Canaanite*. The choice of terminology also raises important linguistic questions, particularly the question of when Hebrew became a separate writing system from Canaanite. Our written artifacts from this early period have very little that is distinctively *Hebrew*, but they do come from the geographic territory that was inhabited by the early *Israelites*. Hence, we use the category *Israelite* here as a geographical term describing the central hill country (as opposed to the coastal plain) that runs from north to south between Shechem and Hebron. At present, all of our early inscriptions from Israel are too short to be useful for a substantive description of archaic Hebrew writing or language.

IRON I (1200–980 B.C.E.) ISRAELITE WRITING

A selected survey of some of the early inscriptions in the region gives further indication of the continuity in writing technologies and scribal culture after the demise of the Egyptian administration in the early twelfth century B.C.E. Technologically, we may separate early alphabetic writing into two categories: inscribed and ink. In general, inscribed writing is preserved better and is more easily recognizable when excavated, whereas ink writing can often only be seen after an artifact has been dipped in water. Ink inscriptions are poorly preserved and thus more difficult to interpret. A brief survey of the inscribed and ink-based textual artifacts will underscore how meager the evidence is for early Israelite writing.[38] Only a handful of inscriptions have been found, and most are very short and/or fragmentary. The paucity of evidence is not just a matter of luck—or the lack thereof. Rather, the meager epigraphic evidence indicates that this was a formative period in the development and spread of the alphabet. The scribal infrastructure of Canaan was in turmoil, transitioning from the cuneiform-based writing that we know from the Amarna letters to the more native West Semitic alphabetic writing system that had been invented centuries before but had never been able to flourish without some kind of indigenous institutional support. Thus, in this period begins the ascendancy of the alphabet as a writing system. Eventually, alphabetic writing systems would come to dominate, but in this period the multiplicity of emerging polities meant that the alphabet did not benefit from an infrastructure that could support standardization.[39]

Lachish Ewer Bowl. Broken potsherds discovered in the debris outside the Fosse Temple at Lachish (ca. 1350–1200 B.C.E.) were pieced together to reveal an important ink inscription and iconography that may be dated to about 1200 B.C.E. The inscription reads *mtn šy* [°°]*ty* ʾ*lt*, which may be translated, "Mattan. An offering to my [Lady] ʾElat." Alternatively, the first word could also stand for "gift" rather than a personal name, which might yield a translation something like, "A gift that is [offered to] ʾElat." The Lachish Ewer is unique because it is an *ink*-on-clay inscription, whereas most other early inscriptions are inscribed on clay, stone, or metal. A second, more-fragmentary ink bowl inscription, consisting of five letters, *lšlšt*, "belonging to šlšt" or "at the third," was also found in the Lachish Fosse Temple. Although it only has a few legible letters, it provides additional evidence of scribal activity. The use of ink points to a technology borrowed from the Egyptians, and indeed other ink hieratic inscriptions dating to the same general period have been excavated at Lachish. Thus, Lachish provides direct evidence of a conduit for Egyptian scribal influence on early alphabetic writing in the southern Levant.

Izbet Sarta Ostracon. A five-line incised potsherd was discovered at Tell Izbet Sarta, which was occupied between 1200 and 1050 B.C.E. It includes four lines of seemingly meaningless letters and a fifth (that is, bottom) line with an apparent abecedary.[40] The abecedary, however, is written from left to right rather than the typical right-to-left writing of later Hebrew inscriptions, and the letters *zayin* and *ḥet* are reversed from the order known from other abecedaries. The reversed order of *zayin-ḥet* may be a mistake, or perhaps the order of the alphabet was not yet firmly established. Calling this a mistake implies the standardization of the alphabet that requires well-established political and social institutions during a period—Iron I—when Canaan was politically and socially in transition. The inscription thus may reflect aspects of this political and social transition. The use of left-to-right writing recalls cuneiform culture, which was written left to right, or Egyptian tradition, which used writing in either direction. Most scholars believe that the text is a student exercise, especially because of the crude nature of the alphabetic handwriting.

Beth-Shemesh Ostracon. The early excavations by Elihu Grant uncovered a poorly preserved ostracon written with ink.[41] Although it is difficult to date precisely, the script places it somewhere about 1200 B.C.E., that is, during the last days of the Egyptian administration in the southern Levant. The inscription appears to be scribbles of a variety of letters with no particular orientation; this suggests perhaps a school exercise or some sort of magic or ritual use.

Tell es-Safi Inscription. An incised inscription with one line in early Canaanite alphabetic writing was discovered in excavations at Tell es-Safi.[42] The inscription dates to the late eleventh or early tenth century B.C.E., and it is written from right to left. The inscription appears to have two names, perhaps Philistine names of Aegean or Anatolian origin. The material culture at Tell es-Safi during this period was Philistine, and the names on the inscription were likely also typical Philistine names, but the writing system is borrowed from contemporary Canaanite culture.

Manaḥat Ostracon. A potsherd with alphabetic writing, usually dated to about 1100 B.C.E., was recovered from an Iron I burial cave just west of Jerusalem.[43] The pot was likely part of the burial goods of the tomb and includes four letters scratched on the surface dedicating the contents to its owner: *lšdḥ*, "belonging to *šdḥ*." This type of dedicatory inscription beginning with the Hebrew preposition *l*-, "belonging to," would become quite common in the late Judean monarchy (ca. 725–586 B.C.E.).

Khirbet Qeiyafa Inscription. This is a late eleventh- or early tenth-century B.C.E. inscription written in ink, five lines long. The script is difficult to date more precisely. It is more archaic than the Tell Zayit abecedary; however, it is problematic to compare an ink inscription like the one from Qeiyafa with the inscribed artifacts (like the Gezer Calendar or the Tell Zayit abecedary) that make up most of our corpus. The material context generally accords with the paleographic dating, namely, the late Iron I period.[44] The script is still not distinguishable as Hebrew but rather must be classified as an early Canaanite alphabetic script.[45] The use of ink continues a writing technology borrowed from the Egyptians. This is one of the earliest alphabetic inscriptions in ink and certainly the longest. More interestingly, the inscription is also "ruled"; that is, each of the five lines on the inscription is separated by a line drawn in ink.

The inscription is difficult to read, which has given rise to a number of transcriptions and translations. Although it is clear that Canaanite writing had not yet evolved into a distinguishable national script—that is, it is not a "Hebrew" script—there is more debate about whether there may be dialectal features that point to a Hebrew vernacular. Of course, the first problem of identifying the dialect of the inscription is establishing an agreed-upon transcription. The original publication actually offers two different transcriptions, and subsequently there have been several different transcriptions offered for the text. The original publication by Haggai Misgav[46] is perhaps the most conservative attempt at reading the inscription:

1) אל תעש[ק/ה] ועבד א[ל]
2) שפט ובואלם [ ]אלט
3) א?ל? ובעלל
4) א[ ]מ ונקם יח/סד מלכ ג[ת]?
5) סרנ ע[זה] מג/דרת

1) Do not make/do [ ], and serve th[e]
2) ruler/judge ?
3) ?
4) [ ] and take vengeance ? king of Ga[th]
5) ruler of G[aza ?]

Other, more creative readings have also been attempted, which in the end only serve to underscore the fragmentary and difficult nature of the inscription.

Some scholars have suggested that the language is Hebrew on the basis of words like *ʿśh* (עשה), "to do"; *ʾl* (אל), "to, for"; *ʿbd* (עבד), "to serve"; and *špṭ* (שפט), "judge"; however, these lexemes (assuming that Misgav's decipherment is correct) are known outside of Hebrew and do not definitively identify the vernacular dialect. So, for example, the language could just as easily be classified as Moabite, except for the geographical location of the discovery. The writing system is, however, most definitely Proto-Canaanite alphabetic writing. It reflects an early stage of the crystallization of the Canaanite writing system and may be compared with texts like the Gezer Calendar, the Tel Zayit inscription, the Izbet Sarta inscription, and the Tell es-Safi inscription. The debate about the identification of the language of the Qeiyafa inscription only illustrates how easy it is to confuse the difference between a writing system and a vernacular.

One of the most curious aspects of this inscription is the lack of standardization in the script. For example, the Canaanite letter *ʾaleph* (𐤀) appears with three different orientations—(compare lines 1, 2, and 4, where it faces right, down, or up). It is difficult to explain this variability; even if this were a school text, one would expect a student to have mastered the orientation of the letter. In addition, the inscription is oriented for reading left to right (instead of right to left, as is typical of the later Phoenician, Hebrew, and Aramaic inscriptions). The orientation of the letters may reflect variability in the direction of writing. Indeed, the possibility of writing in different directions (left-right, right-left, and up-down) is a characteristic of Egyptian writing and is also reflected in the orientation of hieroglyphic signs. The use of dividing lines to separate each line of text is also a typical Egyptian scribal practice. Is it possible that Egyptian exerts an influence here? The difference is that the orientation of the Egyptian signs follows rigidly the direction of the writing, even where the writing is boustrophedon (that is, alternating between left to right and right to left). In other words, this text does not give evidence for a refined scribal hand reflecting a highly developed scribal institution. Rather, it seems to suggest just the opposite, but we need to be careful about drawing conclusions from such a limited data set.

IRON IIA (980–840 B.C.E.) ISRAELITE WRITING

Moving into the Iron IIA, which corresponds generally with the emergence of the Israelite and Judean kingdoms, according to biblical accounts, the sample of excavated inscriptions in the central hill country does not increase to any remarkable degree. By the late tenth to early ninth century, there is some evidence indicating a standardization of the Canaanite alphabet, even though there is little evidence for differentiation between the national scripts (that is, Phoenician, Hebrew, Aramaic, Moabite, Ammonite).

Gezer Calendar. A small, soft limestone tablet with seven lines of text was a surface find at the site of Tell Gezer. Consequently, it can only be dated on the basis of paleography. Although precise dating is difficult, it is usually dated to the tenth or early ninth century B.C.E. The content is poetic, describing the agricultural calendar. It is usually understood as a school-exercise tablet because of the soft limestone material, which could be erased (or, more properly, effaced) and used again. This characteristic of the tablet, however, makes it just as likely to be a ritual tablet used in some sort of blessing on the agricultural new year. That is, rituals and magic often used the washing or effacing of writing as part of the magical ritual (see, for example, Num. 5). In this case, the writing might be rubbed off into the field and the text recited as a ritual blessing for the agricultural cycle.

The most striking feature of the inscription is the use of *-w* as a third masculine singular pronominal suffix, though scholars have debated the exact linguistic value of this letter.[47] As it is one of the longest decipherable early Hebrew or Canaanite inscriptions, it is worth examining it more carefully. The suffix is the main problem of interpretation and can illustrate some of the issues concerning the linguistics of writing.

ירחו אספ̊ ירחו ז̊	1	*yrḥw ʾsp* ǀ *yrḥw z*	Two months of gathering; two months of
ר̊ע ירחו ǀ לקש רע̊	2	*rʿ yrḥw* ǀ *lqš rʿ*	sowing; two months of late vegetation;
ירח עצד פשת	3	*yrḥ ʿṣd pšt*	month of cutting the spring growth;
ירח קצר שערמ	4	*yrḥ qṣr šʿrm*	month of barley harvest;
ירח קצר וכ̊ל	5	*yrḥ qṣr wkl*	month of wheat harvest and measuring;
ירחו זמ̊ר	6	*yrḥw zmr*	two months of vine-tending;
ירח קצ ǀ	7	*yrḥ qṣ* ǀ	month of summer fruit.
אבי	[Margin]	*ʾby*	Abija(h)

The calendar is a list of eight agricultural activities, and by assuming that the marker *-w* suffixed to the word *month* four times is dual, indicating two months, we get an agricultural cycle of twelve months. This is an obvious interpretation, yet the suffix *-w* is not generally used as a plural marker in other texts from this period. Thus, scholars have usually assumed that the *-w* is an attempt to represent the *phonetic* realization of a pronominal suffix of some type. But why do we assume that its primary purpose is phonetic transcription? Isn't writing fundamentally an arbitrary linguistic code? In this case, the *-w* is an arbitrary sign marking a dual or plural,[48] and its phonetic value is also arbitrarily assigned by modern scholars. Other Near Eastern writing systems, for example, typically mark the plural with a linguistic marker that has no phonetic value. Akkadian, for instance, might write "gods" with the cuneiform signs AN.MEŠ = the logogram for "god" (AN) followed by a plural determinative (MEŠ), whose phonetic realization would be /ilū/. In English, should the grapheme *-s* (and *-es*) be understood as simply phonetic or as a marker of the plural? The *sound* of the English plural marker can be /-s/ (as in books), /-z/ (as in dogs), and /-əz/ (as in buses), as well as a variety of other special irregular cases. The graphemic representation of the plural marker is a simplified form of the phonetic realization of the plural. Of course, it is not possible to study such intricacies in phonology and morphology for ancient texts like the Gezer Calendar.

Tell ʿAmal Storage Jar. A large Iron IIA storage jar bears the incised inscription *lnmš*, "belonging to Nimshi," on the rim. This is the earliest example of the use of "Hebrew" alphabetic writing as a label on a storage jar, although the characterization as "Hebrew" results from the typology of the storage jar, not from linguistic or paleographic analysis.

Tell Zayit Abecedary. This is an unusual abecedary carved into a large limestone grinding bowl embedded in the wall of a building. The excavators date the building to the Iron IIA period (ca. 980–840 B.C.E.), and paleographers date the inscription to the tenth century B.C.E.[49] The purpose of an abecedary would seem to be a school text, though it is difficult to understand how this particular inscription could have served in such a manner since it was embedded in a wall inside a building, where it would have been quite difficult to read or use for instructional purposes. This leads us to look for alternative explanations, such as the possibility that the written alphabet served some numinous function.

Tell Rehov Inscriptions. Three incised inscriptions were excavated at Tell Rehov. Two of these inscriptions come from archaeological contexts dated to the ninth century, and the third from the tenth century—that is, to the Iron IIA period.[50] Each of the inscriptions preserves only a few letters, presumably all personal names; the writing seems to have been on storage jars that were used for administrative purposes. The shapes of the letters in these short inscriptions have several anomalies that have made their decipherment and dating not altogether clear.[51]

Early Arad Letters. Five ostraca (numbers 76–80) from Arad are dated by the excavators to the tenth century B.C.E. Although there is some debate about the date of stratum XI from Arad—namely, either tenth or ninth century—the inscriptions correlate with the Iron IIA period. An additional ostracon is associated with stratum XII, but it contains only one letter and four hieratic numerals. The hieratic numerals provide the earliest evidence of the Judean use of Egyptian hieratic numerals and can only be understood as a vestige from the Late Bronze Age Egyptian administration in Canaan.

The early inscriptions from Israel are quite limited. Many of the inscriptions are short inscribed personal names that would seem related to administration. The early Arad ostraca use hieratic numerals, which is hardly unexpected, and further the impression that early Israelite writing was connected with administration. There are some curious examples that have not been fully explained. These include the abecedaries from Izbet Sarta and Tell Zayit, and the literary/poetic texts from Qeiyafa and Gezer. Seth Sanders commented about the early history of the alphabet (namely, Wadi el-Hôl and Serabit el-Khadem): "There is no high culture here. . . . The decisive political feature of the oldest alphabetic inscriptions is that, unlike Babylonian, they are not standardized."[52] This is all the more true of the alphabet in the early Iron Age. Many of the inscriptions seem more like scrawling. They also show striking failures in consistency. The Tell Zayit abecedary seems to have the order of the alphabet wrong. The Qeiyafa inscription cannot get the orientation of the *ʾaleph* figured out. The Izbet Sarta abecedary begins with incomprehensible doodles followed by a poorly executed alphabet. Often these problems are explained as "school texts," but the number of inconsistencies or unorthodoxies in the corpus of early inscriptions suggests that the school-text explanation may be just an easy way to dismiss features (rather than "mistakes") in these artifacts. Clearly, an active writing tradition must be posited to account for the variety of places and types of early alphabetic inscriptions that have been found. Indeed, writing is found at rather insignificant sites, such as Izbet Sarta and Tell Zayit. At the same time, there is no indication of a standardization of alphabetic writing during the early Iron Age. Rather, this was a period of decentralized political leadership when a variety of small polities adopted a "Canaanite" writing system to replace the cuneiform and hieroglyphic writing systems that dominated the Levant in the Middle and Late Bronze Ages.

The Social Location of Scribal "Schools"

It is worth reflecting briefly on the idea of scribal schools in ancient Judah. Unfortunately, the only evidence for "schools" is implied from epigraphic and literary evidence. There is, for example, no archaeological evidence in Judah for a building that was dedicated to the training of scribes. There is also no extensive discussion in the Hebrew Bible dealing with the training of scribes. The comparative evidence from the Near East would suggest that scribes were trained in family houses and that scribal training worked on an apprenticeship-type system.[53] However, it is dangerous to rely too heavily on comparative evidence. From Mesopotamia, for example, there is extensive literary evidence about the *edubba*, the cuneiform scribal school, as well as the nature of the scribal training and curriculum.[54] Egypt also had excellent evidence about scribes, their curriculum, and their training. Nothing like this exists in the archaeological, epigraphic, or literary record for ancient Israel.

A comparison with ancient Ugarit might suggest that the limited evidence for scribal schools in ancient Israel might not be just the misfortune of discovery. At Ugarit, there is evidence for extensive training in Akkadian cuneiform, but not in alphabetic writing. Akkadian school texts at Ugarit include syllabaries, lexicons, practice texts, literary texts—that is, most of the evidence of the full-fledged Mesopotamian scribal schools.[55] In contrast, the evidence for training in alphabetic cuneiform is quite circumscribed; it includes only a few abecedaries and practice texts for writing letters. There is no evidence for extensive training for scribes in alphabetic writing. The main patron for the scribes was the palace and secondarily the temple. Most texts are administrative texts related to the royal economy, and the temple economy was a derivative of the royal economy.

The epigraphic and literary evidence from early Israel is so meager that we can only hypothesize about the social location of scribes. From what we may gather from the Late Bronze Age, there were very few scribes, and their main employer was government—whether that be a governor, a mayor, or a king. The scribal craft was learned through apprenticeship, probably in the homes of extended families. A main part of the scribal profession was to be a courier that delivered messages to other rulers. As a result, it was not desirable for the scribal art to be too localized. Writing had to be able to transcend boundaries, and scribes utilized one script—the Phoenician alphabet—to write a variety of local dialects. Indeed, the lack of vowels in the Phoenician script actually benefited the transnational profession of the scribe since much of the difference between local dialects would be phonological and especially vocalic. The traces of a common Levantine poetic literature, as especially evidenced by comparisons between ABH and Ugaritic poetry, are also likely to be a legacy of the transnational nature of the scribal profession in the Late Bronze Age that continued into the early Iron Age.

Commonly Proposed Features of Archaic Biblical Hebrew

The earliest stage of the Hebrew language in the Bible is preserved by a few biblical poems. The usual examples of Archaic Biblical Hebrew (ABH) are Genesis 49, Exodus 15, Numbers 23–24, Deuteronomy 32, Judges 5,

2 Samuel 22 (which parallels Psalm 18), Psalm 68, and Habakkuk 3. Some scholars have tried to date these texts, but the evidence is only a relative chronology (not an absolute chronology).[56] In other words, there are few objective criteria by which we could date the Song of the Sea from Exodus 15 to the thirteenth century B.C.E. as distinguished from the tenth century B.C.E. On a relative basis, these texts do have linguistic features that precede Standard Biblical Hebrew (SBH)—that is, the Hebrew reflected in most of the Hebrew Bible from the Iron IIB–IIC periods (840–500 B.C.E.).

There is a decided tendency for later scribes to normalize archaic language. For example, in Genesis 49:11 the Masoretic Qere (that is, the pronunciation tradition) normalizes the archaic pronominal suffix *-h* to *-w*. Or, in the case of *ḥytw ʾrṣ*, "wild beasts" (Gen. 49:1, 24), the Samaritan Pentateuch omits the *w*, which presumably marked the case. Furthermore, the enclitic *mem* in Psalm 18:16, *ʾpyqy mym*, "sea beds," is omitted in the parallel version in 2 Samuel 22:16, *ʾpyqy ym*. Thus, we may ask how such archaic features are preserved at all in the face of later scribal standardization. Some of this may reflect the register; namely, the use of poetry invites the retention of quaint or archaic forms. Thus, archaic forms are preserved in the Psalms, whereas they tend to be eliminated when the poetry becomes part of narrative (as in Samuel). In addition, for a variety of different reasons, forms may sometimes appear as though they are normal in the later dialect of the scribes. For example, the archaic verbal suffix *-ty* (2fs) is also found in Aramaic from a much later period; thus, an example like Judges 5:7 could be interpreted as Aramaic influence, if it were not ABH.

Commonly proposed features of ABH include the following:

1. Archaic pronominal and verbal suffixes. The 3ms pronominal suffix *-h* instead of the SBH *-w*, as in *ʿyrh*, "his ass," and *swth*, "his garment" (Gen. 49:11). The 3mp suffix *-mw* instead of SBH *-m*, as in *ksmw*, "(sea) covered them" (Exod. 15:10).
2. Archaic verbal forms of the suffix tense with the morphology /-ti/, /-at/, and /-a/.[57] A classic example would be Judges 5:7, *ʿd šqmty dbwrh šqmty ʾm byśrʾl*, "until you arose, Deborah, you arose as a mother in Israel."
3. Retention of case endings. This is usually preserved in the construct state, as in *ḥytw ʾrṣ*, "wild beasts" (Gen. 49:1, 24).
4. Verbal suffixes using the so-called energic forms—that is, the energic or paragogic *nun*. Energic forms are known from West Semitic; classic examples can be seen in *wʾrmmnhw*, "and I shall exalt him" (Exod. 15:2), and *tšlḥnh*, "she extends" (Judg. 5:26).

5. The enclitic *mem*. One well-known example appears in *mtnym qmyw*, “loins of his enemies” (Deut. 33:11);[58] this is sometimes thought to be the remnant of a genitive particle.
6. A prefix conjugation (later called “imperfect conjugation” in SBH by most Hebrew grammars), used for all “tenses.” This feature of the verb is usually considered to result from the merger of two different prefix conjugations in West Semitic: a short prefix conjugation, *yaqtul* (usually identified with a West Semitic preterite), and a long prefix conjugation, *yaqtulu* (usually identified with a West Semitic imperfect).
7. The *qal* passive verbal conjugation. This form seems likely in ABH but disappears in later Hebrew and was consequently vocalized by the Masoretes as a *puʿal* conjugation (even though there is no corresponding *piʿel*), as in *ywld* (יוּלַּד), “to be born.”[59]
8. Relative pronouns. *š*, *zw*, and *zh* are used for the SBH term *ʾšr*, “which, that” (see Exod. 15:13; Judg. 5:5, 7).
9. Vocative use of the *lamed*. For example, in *lrkb*, “O, Rider” (Ps. 68:34), which finds parallels in Ugaritic poetry but disappears in later Hebrew.[60]
10. Lexicon.[61] Hapax legomena (that is, words used only once in the biblical corpus) or rare words are typical of archaic texts. The problem of identifying archaic vocabulary is complicated by the limited nature of our sources. For example, Jonas Greenfield speaks of vocabulary that has “leaped over a level of language”; that is, sometimes words known in Ugaritic but not in biblical Hebrew or Phoenician reappear in RH.[62]
11. Defective orthography. Purely vowel letters are not used in early Hebrew inscriptions.
12. Retention of the final *yod* or *waw* in verbs originally III-weak. E.g., *yk̲symw*, “they cover them” (Exod. 15:5, יכסימו).
13. Extra vocalic endings on nouns and certain verbal forms. Final *-i* (*ḥireq campaginis*) and *-o*, spelled with *y* or *w*, are unexplained but parallel examples from the Canaanite Amarna letters,[63] e.g., final *-i*: e.g., *nʾdry*, “is glorious” (MT נֶאְדָּרִי, Exod. 15:6), and *bny ʾtnw*, “the offspring of his donkey” (MT בְּנִי אֲתֹנוֹ, Gen. 49:11); final *-o*: e.g., *bnw ṣpr*, “his ass’s foal” (MT בְּנוֹ צִפֹּר, Num. 23:18), or *wḥytw-ʾrṣ*, “beasts of the earth” (MT וְחַיְתוֹ־אֶרֶץ, Gen. 1:24).

4

Linguistic Nationalism and the Emergence of Hebrew

The degree of centralization in society and concentration of economic power is mirrored by the relative strength of the standard (or official) language.

—*A. Malmberg and B. Nordberg*

The eighth century B.C.E. stands as a watershed in the linguistic history of Western civilization. Those tumultuous times witnessed the emergence of a linguistic imperialism in the Near East. Language ideology began to drive the creation of national literatures in Assyria and Egypt as well as in the kingdom of Judah. Indeed, the emergence of a distinct written Hebrew language should be understood as a political as much as a linguistic event.[1] Comparative examples abound. For instance, the distinction between Norwegian, Danish, and Scandinavian as three "languages" was more a reflex of nationalism and borders in the early twentieth century than it was the result of descriptive linguistics; likewise, the distinction between Serbian and Croatian is a reflex of political events, not linguistic events.[2] Such linguistic nationalism is not just a recent phenomenon; as Joshua Fishman points out, the notion that "a people's individuality resides in its language is very old."[3]

Indeed, it is perhaps as old as humanity itself. What was momentous in this period was the attachment of cultural identity to a national writing system.

In this chapter, we will see how the emergence of competing petty nations in Syria-Palestine, which characterized the early first millennium B.C.E., would mark a turning point in the history of the West Semitic languages. And, in particular, the rise of the Assyrian Empire would—for the first time—serve as a catalyst for the creation of the language of the Judean state—that is, Standard Biblical Hebrew (SBH), which would develop as the literary language of Judean scribes from the late eighth century until the disappearance of these scribes by the end of the sixth century B.C.E.

Though the sources for Judean Hebrew are straightforward, the language of the northern kingdom of Israel, *Israelian Hebrew* (IH), is more difficult to isolate. There is little doubt that there were different dialects of Hebrew in Israel and Judah during the Iron Age. This is indicated, for example, by the intentional use of nonstandard forms and words in texts dealing with the northern kingdom or in speech put into the mouths of northern figures. Thus, for example, when the northern prophet Elijah speaks, he uses forms like the imperative *liqḥî*, "take" (reflecting northern dialects that preserve the initial *lamed*), when the Standard Biblical form is *qᵉḥî*. Many more examples have been gathered by scholars,[4] but this serves to illustrate that the authors of the Bible were aware of different dialects and used these differences to distinguish group identity—north from south—in biblical literature; and it is hardly surprising that there would be different dialects of Hebrew in the various areas of Israel and Judah. Indeed, general studies in dialect geography lead us to expect a variety of dialects in the regions of Galilee, Samaria, and Judah. More problematic, however, is the question of whether there was a distinctive Israelian *written* standard. This seems unlikely. Whereas vernacular language is critical to group identity, there is no evidence that written language was associated with smaller groups before the rise of the Neo-Assyrian Empire. In fact, the only fragment that we have of an Israelian monumental inscription—that is, an inscription in which a standard Israelian written register might be expected—apparently uses the typical Judean word *ʾšr*, "which, that," instead of the word *š*, which is typically associated with IH.[5] To be sure, this is meager evidence indeed, but this only underscores the minimal evidence for a standardized written IH. Ironically, most of what we know about IH was preserved by Judeans in the biblical corpus.

Even the name for the northern dialect(s) of Hebrew is unknown. Herein, we use the term *Israelian*, which utilizes a term known already for the people and the region on the Merneptah Stele in the thirteenth century.[6] Moreover, the term *Israel* in Standard Biblical Hebrew is used to refer to the northern kingdom as distinct from the southern kingdom of Judah. Since *Israel* is a term for both the territory and the people, it is natural to use the related term *Israelian* for the language. It is clear, however, that there were also regional dialects that were closely associated with groups like the Gileadites or the Ephraimites (as in Judg. 12:4–6). Groups naturally associate dialect with territory, and it usually follows that the regional dialects or languages have their own names associated with the territories and ethnic groups. Indeed, the catalog of nations in Genesis 10 repeatedly used the classification "These are the descendants *by their language, their land, and their people*." Thus, it seems likely that Gileadite, Ephraimite, Benjaminite, Samarian, and Galilean would have been used to refer to the ancient regional dialects. There is no direct evidence of exactly what those dialects were called. The example in Judges 12 does suggest that Gileadite and Ephraimite were separate speech communities and thus are legitimate linguistic terms.

Although there is little doubt that there were "Israelian" dialects of Hebrew in antiquity, our sources are limited, sometimes disputed, and poorly encode dialect.[7] First, there are very few Israelian inscriptions; the only significant corpus is the Samaria ostraca. A major feature that distinguishes dialects is pronunciation, which is poorly encoded by writing systems. Indeed, an often-paraded example between British and American English would be the spelling of words like *colour/color*, yet ironically this difference in spelling actually does *not* describe a significant phonological difference between British and American English. Usually, differences in dialect are not encoded in the writing system, and consequently writing systems have a difficult time expressing the precise differences in dialect. The Canaanite shift, which describes a linguistic shift from /ā/ to /ō/ that occurred in the West Semitic languages, serves as a good illustration of this problem in Northwest Semitic dialects. We also know that the extent of this shift became more pronounced in Phoenician than in Judean. From the perspective of dialect geography, the Israelian dialect lies between Judah and Phoenicia; however, we have almost no tools to describe the extent to which this /ā/ to /ō/ shift might have affected IH. The Hebrew writing system is a poor transcription system, and the vocalic differences that make up dialects are not well represented. Nevertheless, there are more than a few indications of an IH dialect.

The classic corpus for Israelian Hebrew is the Elijah-Elisha narratives (1 Kings 17–2 Kings 8).[8] Other texts that are commonly proposed as Israelian Hebrew include Genesis 49, Deuteronomy 32–33, Judges 5, Ecclesiastes, Song of Songs, Hosea, Amos, selected Psalms, and Proverbs.[9] In addition, any narratives or poetry that deal with northern Israel, such as the Judges stories about Gideon, are often utilized in the search for IH. Although the extent of the IH corpus is a matter of discussion, it is quite clear that biblical literature employs style-switching and addressee-switching when speaking of foreigners. Thus, for example, the stories about Balaam or the prophetic oracles against foreign nations utilize a number of nonstandard Hebrew features that are best understood as resulting from literary style but are also meant to indicate dialect.[10] The epigraphic sources for IH are still rather limited. The largest epigraphic corpus, the Samaria ostraca, includes sixty-three legible texts written on potsherds; however, they are short administrative texts that provide limited linguistic information. Also important are the ostraca from Kuntillet ʿAjrud, a remote outpost in the Negev south of Judah, where twenty-one separate texts were discovered that have been identified as IH. It will be interesting to speculate about how and where the Israelian dialects might have survived the conquests of Galilee and Samaria by the Assyrians in 732 and 721 B.C.E.

Demography is one of the important indicators for linguistic change, and the Iron IIB period (840–700 B.C.E.) was characterized by wholesale shifts in the demography of the ancient Near East, including Israel and Judah. Assyrian incursions into the Levant began in 745 B.C.E. under Tiglath-pileser III and continued with the conquest of Galilee in 732 B.C.E. and Samaria in 721 B.C.E. The Philistine coastal cities were overtaken by Assyria by 712 B.C.E., and Sennacherib's campaign against Judah and Jerusalem in 701 B.C.E. devastated the Judean state. The rise of Assyria in the mid-eighth century devastated smaller states and urbanized the landscape of the entire Near East.[11] The Assyrian invasions had a particular impact on Jerusalem, which saw an influx of refugees from the north.

Refugees probably began arriving in Jerusalem after the Assyrian conquest of Samaria in 721 B.C.E. A few years later an influx of dispossessed Judeans came into the Jerusalem region from the foothills of Judah following the campaign of Sennacherib against Judah in 701 B.C.E.[12] The total built-up area decreased by about 70 percent, suggesting that the depopulation especially affected smaller agricultural towns and villages, more than larger cities.[13] These events can be placed within a larger context that shaped the city of Jerusalem, where SBH as a written language was forged. Rather than trying to barricade his borders, Hezekiah tried to integrate these refugees into his realm, with the hopes of restoring an idealized golden age of Israel, the kingdom of David and Solomon.[14] These events raise the question of how the language of the refugees from northern Israel might have influenced Judean

Hebrew. Gary Rendsburg, for example, has estimated that at least 16 percent, and perhaps as much as 30 percent, of the Hebrew Bible may directly reflect IH.[15] The influx of northern refugees certainly helps to account for the substantial quantity of northern texts and IH in the Hebrew Bible.

The exile of the northern kingdom by Assyria and the subsequent urbanization of the rural south were catalysts for literary activity that resulted in the composition of extended portions of the Hebrew Bible.[16] It gave rise to the prophetic works of Amos, Hosea, Micah, and Isaiah of Jerusalem, to priestly liturgies and ritual texts, as well as to a pre-Deuteronomic historical work. The northern kingdom takes a prominent place in the Hebrew Bible, with accounts of its history (in the book of Kings), its prophets (for example, Amos and Hosea), and its tribal ancestors (in the Pentateuch and the book of Judges). The literary idealization of a golden age that united north and south, Israel and Judah, under the aegis of David and Solomon also presumes the standardization of a literary language. On the one hand, the use of writing as a transnational communication technology would *not* have encouraged the localization of a national script; on the other hand, the development and preservation of cultural traditions and history would have encouraged the nationalization of writing technology. The social and political events of the eighth century apparently encouraged both the preservation of literary and cultural traditions in writing and the nationalization or localization of writing technology—that is, the full development of Hebrew writing alongside the local vernacular.

Even though many Israelian traditions found their way into the Hebrew Bible, they were collected and transmitted in Judah and Jerusalem. This fact is an important caveat in the search for IH. The natural place to begin a search for an IH dialect in the Bible might be the supposedly northern prophets Amos and Hosea. This search, unfortunately, is not entirely satisfying. With regard to the book of Hosea, early scholars generally did not find strong indications of a northern dialect. For example, William Rainey Harper concluded, "It cannot be maintained that the peculiarities of Hosea furnish any considerable data toward the hypothesis of a Northern dialect as distinguished from the Southern."[17] Actually, these examples only remind us that the Hebrew Bible was collected, edited, and written in Jerusalem and Judah. The well-known wordplay in Amos 8:2 between *qāyiṣ*, "summer," and *qēṣ*, "end," derives in part from the dialect difference between the south and the north, namely the well-known contraction of diphthongs in IH, so the scribe is aware of the dialect differences and even utilizes them.[18] Yet the book as a whole is transmitted in the standard biblical dialect. Thus, even though there are northern texts and traditions that are compiled into the Bible, this was done in the south. The evidence for the standardization of Hebrew is Judean.

The emergence of a standardized Hebrew *language* again raises the question, What do we mean by "language"? For practical reasons, when discussing ancient languages we must speak of *written codes* rather than *vernaculars*. Through the lenses of our written artifacts, at best we only see glimpses of vernacular dialects. These glimpses suggest that dialects were differentiated in the southern Levant in all periods and that the early Israelites had their own vernacular language that they could use to differentiate both internally between tribes and clans and externally from the *gēr* (that is, "resident alien") and *nok̲rî* ("foreigner") in their midst. The famous shibboleth-sibboleth incident in Judges 12 illustrates both a linguistic consciousness and the use of dialect for differentiating identity. Writing, however, was not a vehicle for ethnic or tribal identity in the ancient Near East during the second millennium. For example, the Amarna letters employ a Canaano-Akkadian language unique in the cuneiform world of the second millennium B.C.E., but this language levels the differences between individual dialects. Although we may glimpse some indications of individual dialects in the letters, the writing system was primarily a means of leveling the differences between the vernaculars of the Levant rather than a means of differentiating the various speech communities (to use the linguistic jargon)—or tribes (to use the biblical or anthropological category).

The widespread adoption of the linear alphabet made writing largely autonomous from Levantine dialects at the beginning of the first millennium B.C.E. More generally, written language in Mesopotamia and the Levant was a transnational phenomenon, and the profession of scribes in the Near East was transnational. The exception was ancient Egypt. There, hieroglyphic writing was always strictly part of the Egyptian cultural system, and the Egyptian writing system was not borrowed by foreign cultures for the writing of a wide variety of languages and dialects in the manner of Mesopotamian cuneiform or the West Semitic alphabet. Egyptian writing was always a local phenomenon. Not so with writing in the Levant. Through the second millennium and into the early first millennium, writing was a transnational cultural phenomenon. This began to change by the ninth century and especially in the eighth century B.C.E. Eventually, a local writing tradition became incorporated into Judean ethnic and national identity. That is to say, writing was nationalized in ancient Judah. The only questions are, When exactly did *written* language emerge as a unique part of Judean culture? And why did writing change from being an autonomous to a nationalized technology?

In the ninth and eighth centuries B.C.E., a sense of ethnicity and national identity began to consolidate in Syria-Palestine, even while (and perhaps because) the Assyrian Empire emerged and began to grow beyond "the two rivers."[19] The growing sense of ethnic identity in the Near East included a sense of Judean identity. Implicit in this sense of identity was linguistic distinctiveness that spread beyond vernacular to local written language. Out of the political turmoil that marked the end of the Late Bronze Age throughout the eastern Mediterranean world arose petty kingdoms—Israel, Judah, Ammon, Moab, Philistia, Tyre, Sidon, Damascus—competing for supremacy in the Levant. These kingdoms would develop a sense of ethnic identity characterized by national gods, border conflicts, and a growing linguistic differentiation. Classical Hebrew (and by "classical Hebrew" we mean specifically the written language) emerged from the developing sense of a national identity in Judah. In contrast, the northern Syrian states that had used Phoenician to write their local inscriptions began using Aramaic—using both local Aramaic dialects and developing a distinctive Aramaic ductus.

The period needs to be broken down into at least three distinct historical eras: 1200–840 B.C.E., 840–500 B.C.E., and 500–250 B.C.E., which correspond with some seminal political periods and reflect aspects of continuity and distinction in material culture.[20] The first period (1200–840 B.C.E.) is the period of *Phoenicianizing* language, that is, when Levantine kingdoms all used a similar script. The second period (840–500 B.C.E.) witnessed the emergence of a distinct Paleo-Hebrew national script, whereas the third period (500–250 B.C.E.) reflected the pervasive use of Aramaic script for writing in the Levant (including Judah/Yehud). The use of the Aramaic script had already begun with the Neo-Assyrian administration, but it became normative in Yehud during the Babylonian period (post-586 B.C.E.) as a result of Babylonian administration in the Levant. Eventually, the Jews embraced the Aramaic script during the Persian and early Hellenistic periods (500–250 B.C.E.), so much so that it came to be known as "Jewish script," and the Hebrew script that we use today is really a development of this branch of the Aramaic script.

Aramaic and Hebrew inherited a common Northwest Semitic linguistic tradition. Already in the Late Bronze Age and early Iron Age (that is, up until the ninth century B.C.E.), Aramaic and Hebrew scribes shared a common scribal tradition. However, it was the use of Aramaic as a diplomatic language in the Neo-Assyrian Empire beginning in the eighth century B.C.E. that especially elevated its role in the history of the Hebrew language. Indeed, it is in this context that we may recall the scribes of Hezekiah asking the Assyrians to speak Aramaic (2 Kings 18:26). The Assyrians apparently sent administrators with training in Aramaic, called the LÚA.BA scribes in Akkadian (with A and BA being a code for the first two letters of the alphabet), who spread Assyrian administration and ideology into the new provinces of the empire.[21] Judean scribes—those responsible for the composition and editing of the Hebrew Bible—would likely have learned Aramaic from Assyrian administrators (that is, the LÚA.BA, or *sepīru*), so it is hardly surprising that Aramaic influence creeps into biblical texts as well as Epigraphic Hebrew of the late Iron II period. As a result, the chronological significance of Aramaisms in Hebrew is quite complex.[22] It is often difficult to be certain whether Aramaic loanwords in biblical literature derive from the late Judean monarchy (eighth to seventh century B.C.E.), the period of Babylonian and Persian rule (sixth to fourth century B.C.E.), or the later Hellenistic period (third to second century B.C.E.).[23] To be sure, the most pervasive influence of Aramaic on Hebrew came in the Persian, Hellenistic, and Roman periods, when Aramaic became the first language for many people in Syria-Palestine (especially outside of the immediate environs of Jerusalem). Still, the beginnings of Aramaic influence on Judean scribes must be traced back to the Neo-Assyrian period (as will be discussed further in chapter 5).

Hebrew vernacular was part of a cultural system. If the cultural system asserts some distinctiveness, then this distinctiveness will be reflected in language. As much as the Hebrew language is part of the cultural system, so the assertion of cultural distinctiveness in Israel would have had linguistic implications. This chapter takes issue with Seth Schwartz, who argued that Hebrew was not central to the self-understanding of the Israelites before Alexander the Great.[24] Schwartz offers two arguments for his conclusion. First, in contrast with Greek, there is no "elaborate metalanguage to describe different types of written (and spoken?) discourse."[25] Second, the books of Ezra and Daniel switch between Hebrew and Aramaic, demonstrating that each book was "unselfconscious about what language it happens to be using."[26] Actually, the use of Aramaic in Ezra begins quite intentionally with diplomatic correspondence, namely, they "wrote to King Artaxerxes of Persia; the letter was written in Aramaic and translated" (Ezra 4:7). When discussion of the official business detailed in Persian documents concludes in Ezra 6:18, the narrative switches back to Hebrew. The linguistic code thus corresponds to the content. The sociolinguistic practice of code-switching, that is, the moving between languages or registers, is always loaded with social and ideological importance.[27] Typically, code-switching reflects group membership or social prestige. Although the code-switching in Daniel may be more complex, the switch from Hebrew to Aramaic occurs at a point where the Aramaic linguistic code was expected, in a public address to a foreign king: "The Chaldeans spoke to the [Persian] king in Aramaic" (Dan. 2:4). Rather than suggesting that these texts were "unselfconscious" or random in their interchange between languages, the changes occur at points where code-switching is an expected, self-conscious sociolinguistic strategy. To be fair, code-switching is usually discussed in social situations where people are speaking, and the movement between languages can be rather fluid. In a literary text, code-switching is much more intrusive and intentional. Yet one must conclude that the use of both Aramaic and Hebrew and the intentional code-switching between the two underscores the roles of these two languages for group identity and social prestige that are so typical of this phenomenon in sociolinguistic studies.

The period following the Babylonian invasions and exiles ushered in profound changes in the social life of the people, and languages played specific roles in this new historical context. Jews in the Second Temple period were well aware of the encroachment of Aramaic upon Hebrew, and they were conscious about the role of language for their culture and identity (see chapter 7). Indeed, the book of Nehemiah will pointedly make the connection between language and identity:

> In those days also I saw Jews who had married women of Ashdod, Ammon, and Moab; and half of their children spoke the language of Ashdod, and they could not speak the language of Judah, but spoke the language of various peoples. (Neh. 13:23–24)

In Qumran Hebrew there would be a marked avoidance of Aramaic (see chapter 8). As for the former argument, it is essentially an argument from silence. We do not have enough sources to know much about metalanguage in the eighth century B.C.E. Moreover, it does not require an elaborate metalanguage for people to recognize the centrality of language in cultural and ethnic identity. It should not be surprising that a short-lived uprising during the Persian period tried to reclaim linguistic identity by using Paleo-Hebrew script on coins, just as the Hasmoneans would a couple of centuries later.[28] At the same time, the coining of the term *Judean*, known from the book of Isaiah as well as the book of Kings (Isa. 36:11; 2 Kings 18:26), already indicates some development of a metalanguage to distinguish Hebrew from other Levantine dialects. Indeed, the term *Judean* even shows a conscious distinction from IH.

What about the Hebrew script? Vernacular dialects are always part of social identity, but not necessarily writing systems. Christopher Rollston has cogently pointed out that "the fact that the Phoenician script persisted during the tenth and early-ninth centuries in Israelite territories is a demonstration that the Old Hebrew script had not yet developed."[29] Indeed, the Phoenician script persisted throughout the Near East into the ninth century. Perhaps the most interesting example of this is the Tell Fakhariyeh inscription, which was discovered in north Syria. The inscription dates to the ninth century B.C.E. and was written using an "archaic" Phoenician script but in the Aramaic language.[30] Even into the late eighth century, the Phoenician script continued to be used in Anatolia and north Syria.[31] The situation changed after the ninth century B.C.E. Phoenician script was no longer used throughout the Near East, and local varieties began to develop.

By the late eighth century, the Hebrew script was differentiated from Phoenician. Exactly when the transition took place is more difficult to pinpoint. Rollston understands the creation of a Hebrew national script as a "conscious decision" intended as a nationalistic statement and not merely an evolutionary development.[32] Although he does not explain his reasoning, his conclusion is certainly sound. Localizing a script is a way of culturally appropriating writing. Hebrew writing was no longer simply a communication technology; it became part of Judean culture. Moreover, the function of the scribe became increasingly part of local administration and economy as opposed to international correspondence and relations. Rollston's dating, however, is more problematic. He locates the nationalization of the Hebrew writing system in the ninth century primarily on the basis of the Moabite Stele, a Moabite monumental inscription from the mid-ninth century B.C.E. There is very little evidence of Hebrew writing from the ninth century, and the evidence from Moab is not altogether convincing for a *Hebrew* national script. The other (more meager) evidence cited is also not Judean, namely, the short Moabite el-Kerak inscription and the (Israelian) Kuntillet ʿAjrud inscriptions. The elongation of tails on letters that Rollston identifies as the beginnings of a distinctive Hebrew script seems just as likely to be simply a cursive form of the Phoenician script, which can be seen in the Kition Bowl that dates to the eighth century from Cyprus.[33] Unfortunately, the early Phoenician script is known mostly through monumental inscriptions, so there is only later evidence from ostraca (like the Kition Bowl) or papyri where a cursive might have been employed. The evidence is still sketchy for the exact timing of the development of the Hebrew national script, although it is clearly in full bloom when we begin to see the large numbers of Hebrew inscriptions in the late eighth century B.C.E. By contrast, there is much more evidence for the development of a distinctive Aramaic script, which Rollston places in the eighth century B.C.E. For Hebrew, the inscriptional evidence from the ninth century is too limited to place the development of a distinctive Hebrew national script that early; rather, based on the present evidence—namely, the appearance of large numbers of Hebrew inscriptions (and particularly seals and seal impressions) in the late eighth century—we must place the distinctive Hebrew (or, more specifically, Judean) national script in the eighth century.

The distinctive feature of the Old Hebrew script is its cursive style, in contrast with both Phoenician and the developing Aramaic script. A critical part of paleographic evolution is the writing technology used—that is, writing with ink versus inscribing on wet clay. The writing technologies affect the ways letters or signs develop. Clay, for example, was used in northern Syria as the material for accounting texts well into the seventh century for Aramaic texts. The use of clay as a writing technology is a legacy of Mesopotamian cuneiform culture. In contrast, ink and papyrus were inventions of the Egyptians and mostly influenced writing in the southern Levant. The use of ink encouraged the development of more cursive letters, whereas impressing or carving letters into wet clay encouraged more angular shapes, and this is exactly what we see in comparing Old Aramaic with Old Hebrew. In this respect, it is actually surprising that the more formal monumental style of the Phoenician script lingered in the southern Levant into the ninth century B.C.E.

Linguistic Imperialism

In contrast to the conceptually fixed boundaries of nations, the boundaries of *empires* are continually in flux. The size of the empire is not determined but rather is contingent on territorial expansion (and sometimes contraction). The absence of fixed boundaries in empires means that territories and their inhabitants are sociologically heterogeneous. Empires consist of many different peoples and distinct territories. Likewise, empires can accommodate, to some extent, a diversity of religion, as the Assyrian Empire did.[34] The Persian Empire even encouraged the diversity of religion. The Assyrian Empire does present some interesting problems. The empire began as a nation with fixed boundaries and a national god, Ashur. This national ideology remained even as boundaries and ethnicity were reinvented. Assyrian rulers had known a defined national border, even as they conquered diverse territories and incorporated them within the borders of Assyria. Language divided the diverse peoples of the emerging Assyrian Empire. As Peter Trudgill observed, linguistic subjugation or unification (depending on one's viewpoint) is a strategy in implementing political subjugation (or unification).[35] Linguistic imperialism was part of the Assyrian imperial strategy and would have a lasting impact on the linguistic landscape of the Near East.

The Assyrian Empire and its administration had paved the way for the more mundane use of writing by introducing a special type of scribe (^{LÚ}A.BA). The A.BA scribal training was restricted to Aramaic for administrative purposes, and Aramaic writing thus became a technological tool utilized for administration and commerce. Scribes no longer needed the complete training in the Mesopotamian *edubba* (from the Sumerian, É.DUB.BA, "house of tablets"), which was the traditional Mesopotamian place of learning that included a repository of school curricula for the training of scribes. The *edubba*, however, was a tradition for the training of scribes in the prestige language of the empire, that is, Akkadian cuneiform. The Assyrian linguistic ideology associated elite scribal training specifically with cuneiform writing as opposed to the more mundane alphabetic (Aramaic) writing system. In fact, Aramaic was held in a certain level of contempt, as we see, for example, in a letter from King Sargon II:

> [As to what you wrote]: "There are informers [. . . to the king] and coming to his presence; *if it is acceptable to the king, let me write and send my messages to the king on Aram[aic] parchments*"—why would you not write and send me messages in Akkadian? Really, the message which you write in it must be drawn up in this very manner—this is a fixed regulation! (*SAA* 17, 2:13–18; emphasis added)

There is a measurable sense of hostility at the thought that correspondence within the eastern part of the Assyrian realm might be written in Aramaic. As Barbara Porter points out, the Assyrians continued to erect royal monuments in the west using Akkadian because "the cuneiform signs by their very presence and quantity demonstrated the wealth and power of . . . the foreign overlord."[36] This may be contrasted with Fales's characterization of Aramaic as a "second recognized official idiom *of social and economic interest* within the empire itself."[37] The Aramaic writing system was a technological tool used by Assyrian administrators in the Levant, but it was limited to social and economic interests in the west and did not carry the same prestige of cuneiform with its literature and history that were bound up in the *edubba*. The Assyrians sent these administrative scribes to the far reaches of their kingdom in order to teach fealty to Assyria and to oversee the administration of the empire. It was through such Assyrian linguistic imperialism that Aramaic came to play a role in administration and commerce (for example, 2 Kings 18:26) and to be known as a lingua franca by the officials in Jerusalem.

The Assyrians began using Aramaic as a unifying administrative language in the eighth century B.C.E. The Assyrians recognized a close relationship between language and their imperial goals, and a central part of Assyrian imperial ideology was to unify peoples of "divergent speech" into a people of "one language"—at least metaphorically if not in practice. According to the Dûr-Sharrukîn Cylinder inscription, language ideology played a significant role in Sargon II's (r. 721–705 B.C.E.) conception of the empire. According to the old standard translation of Luckenbill:

> Peoples of the four regions of the world, *of foreign tongue and divergent speech*, dwellers of mountain and lowland, all that were ruled by the light of the gods, the lord of all, I carried off at Assur, my lord's command, by the might of my scepter. *I made them of one mouth* and settled them therein. Assyrians, fully competent to teach them how to fear god and the king, I dispatched as scribes and officials. The gods who dwell in heaven and earth, and in that city, listened with favor to my word, and granted me the eternal boon of building that city and growing old in its midst.[38]

The phrasing of the Dûr-Sharrukîn Cylinder inscription, especially in the old translation of Luckenbill, shows an acute linguistic ideology: "peoples of . . . foreign tongue," "divergent speech," uniting with "one mouth," and sending "scribes" "to teach." The creation of a vast empire meant dealing with language barriers and differences: "peoples of . . . foreign tongue." The Akkadian expression translated "foreign tongue and divergent speech" is pejorative. Specifically, the expression "foreign tongue," translating the Akkadian *lišānu aḫītu*, has quite negative connotations. It is more than a "foreign" language; it implies a language of "secrecy, hiding, and falsehood," that is, languages that could undermine an empire.[39] This is typical linguistic ideology regarding foreign languages. The languages of the conquered peoples are both foreign and suspicious. These peoples with their strange languages, Sargon claims, he literally gave "one mouth" by supposedly sending "scribes" to teach them.[40] There are Neo-Assyrian references to Aramaean scribes writing Aramaic: ^{LÚ}A.BA *armaja ana muḫ[ḫi . . . iš]apparuma*, "the scribe writing Aramaic."[41] This would suggest that *Aramaean scribes* were being sent to teach and make the peoples of divergent tongues "one mouth." The Akkadian noun *šāpiru* invariably bears the standard Akkadian meaning of merely an administrator, which would suggest that these administrators were scribes whose administrative training was limited to Aramaic. Sargon sent administrators who had limited and utilitarian training in Aramaic to teach the "peoples of . . . foreign tongue." This raises the question, What exactly were these "foreigners" being taught? Certainly not the written Akkadian language, and probably not even the vernacular Assyrian language. More likely, they were being trained for the Assyrian administration and loyalty to the crown. With regard to loyalty, recall the idiom in the above inscription, "I unified them," which translates the Akkadian expression *pâ ištên ašaškinma*, which Luckenbill translated literally as "I made them of one mouth." Such a translation still leaves the nature of this "unification" unclear. By one mouth, can we infer that there was one language? Not likely. More likely, "one mouth" implied swearing fealty to the Assyrians and not necessarily acquiring their language. The Aramaic language was a critical tool of Assyrian administration for incorporating and indoctrinating its vassals.

The Assyrian administrators teach the peoples of foreign tongue "to fear [the Assyrian] god" and to swear fealty to their Assyrian "king." Swearing loyalty to the king would imply knowledge of Assyrian treaty language and ideology. Indeed, intimate knowledge of Assyrian vassal treaties is evident in the Aramaic Sefire inscription as well as in the book of Deuteronomy. Such knowledge of Assyrian treaty language was likely communicated by Assyrian administrators (with training as Aramaic scribes). In the final analysis, a cylinder inscription such as Dûr-Sharrukîn certainly reflects pure ideology, and its concern for language should make us aware of how critical language issues were to the forging of the empire.

Chaim Tadmor pointed out many years ago in his classic article "The Aramaization of Assyria" that there were practical aspects to the use of Aramaic for the Assyrian administration of the west. Tadmor points to "evidence that in the Western parts of the Empire, Aramaic served as the language of diplomacy and administration alongside of, or instead of, Akkadian."[42] Tadmor cites three texts from the Assyrian royal correspondence. First, there is Nimrud letter 13 from the period of Tiglath-pileser III (r. 744–727 B.C.E.), in which Qurdi-ashur-lamur writes to the king as follows: "I have had Nabu-ushezib bring this sealed Aramaic letter [*kanîku annîtu armêtu*] from the city of Tyre." This explicitly mentions the use of Aramaic in diplomatic correspondence in the west. In the case of Nimrud letter 14, we are left to infer that Aramaic was used when the letter refers to a "sealed letter" written from Ayanuri, apparently a Moabite, which we may safely assume was not written in cuneiform. Tadmor also notes the reference to an Aramaic letter (literally, *egirtu armêtu*) in *ABL* 872, allegedly dating to the time of Shalmaneser III (r. 858–824 B.C.E.). Since the publication of Tadmor's article, more evidence has come to light. Some of this evidence has been nicely summarized by Frederick Fales in several publications, particularly his article "The Use and Function of Aramaic Tablets," in which he argues for the role of Aramaic as an official administrative language within the empire.[43]

One of the most interesting illustrations of the increasing role of the Aramaic language and scribes in the Neo-Assyrian period is the appearance of a new logogram for scribes: ^{LÚ}A.BA, "the ABC scribe." Laurie Pearce has pointed to a distinction between the new scribal title *sepīru* and the traditional term *ṭupšarru*, which relate to the scribes' competence. The *sepīru* produced only administrative documents, whereas the *ṭupšarru* produced both literary and administrative texts.[44] It is noteworthy that surviving Aramaic texts from the Neo-Assyrian period through the Persian period are predominantly administrative and legal texts. There are almost no Aramaic literary texts, with the notable exception of the Proverbs of Ahiqar, which was part of the scribal curriculum.[45] Tradition has it that Ahiqar was a scribe of the court of Sennacherib, though the story now serves as an exhortatory tale about the proper conduct and loyalties of a scribe. The logogram ^{LÚ}A.BA seems to be related to the activities of an Aramaic scribe called a *sepīru*, which is a better normalization for A.BA than *ṭupšarru*. The ^{LÚ}A.BA logogram should be understood specifically as an Aramaean or "alphabetic" scribe, as A and BA are the Akkadian equivalents of the first two letters of the Aramaic ABCs.[46] The logogram would thus be an iconic invention to indicate an "ABC scribe." This proposal is made more plausible by the fact that the logogram seems to first appear in the early Neo-Assyrian period, namely, in a colophon from Tiglath-pileser I, and then it becomes quite prevalent in the Neo-Assyrian inscriptions.[47] By the Neo-Babylonian period, some nuances of the origin of this logogram may already be disappearing. It is also noteworthy that when late-Assyrian texts refer to foreign scribes, such as Egyptian scribes, the logogram A.BA is used instead of the older term DUB.SAR. The evidence concerning the logogram A.BA, however, is not unequivocal. For example, it has been pointed out that in Ugaritic lexical texts we find ^{LÚ}DUB.SAR equated with ^{LÚ}A.BA and *ṭupšarru* for "scribe."[48] Of course, the term *sepīru*, which is an Aramaic loanword into Akkadian, was not available to the Ugaritic scribes. The appearance of the logogram ^{LÚ}A.BA for "scribe," particularly in the mixed scribal culture of Ugarit, is itself suggestive. Thus, there may have been different nuances for the logograms ^{LÚ}DUB.SAR and ^{LÚ}A.BA, but the only available Akkadian transcription was *ṭupšarru*. Moreover, it is important to note that abecedaries were pivotal for the early training of alphabetic scribes at Ugarit, whereas cuneiform scribes began by learning signs grouped by syllables, such as *ta-ti-tu* exercises. For this reason, the understanding of ^{LÚ}A.BA as "ABC scribe" seems particularly inviting.

A national reaction to linguistic imperialism is linguistic nationalism.[49] Languages act as political lightning rods for group consciousness and solidarity. A recent example of linguistic nationalism accompanied the rapid rise of independent European nation-states during the twentieth century; the increase in nation-states was paralleled by the growth in autonomous, national, and official languages. Over the past two centuries the number of official languages in Europe has grown from sixteen to more than sixty. For example, the breakup of Yugoslavia was accompanied by the establishment of independent languages. Likewise, the breakup of the Soviet Union has encouraged the development of autonomous national languages. Peter Trudgill notes, "Where language is a defining characteristic of a minority ethnic group wanting independence, particularly where other (for example physical) characteristics are not significant (as in the case of Welsh), linguistic factors are likely to play an important role in any separatist movement they might undertake."[50] The linguistic expression of such nationalist and separatist movements is typically spelling reform. Such a scenario seems likely, a priori, in the Levant in the ninth and eighth centuries. One of the characteristic features that would distinguish the emerging Canaanite and Aramaic written vernaculars from Phoenician was the introduction of vowel letters. As we have seen, the Assyrians considered linguistic diversity in the west an impediment to their imperial aspirations. Language became an instrument of imperial administration. In both Egyptian and Akkadian texts from the second millennium, the inhabitants of the Levant from the Wadi el-Arish up to the Orontes River were considered one ethnic group that we usually refer to as Canaanite. Although the Amarna letters are ample-enough evidence of competition among the various city-states, it is also clear that this competition was not grounded in ethnicity.

From Israelian Hebrew to Judean Hebrew in Jerusalem

The Assyrian Empire brought not only globalization but also massive local population shifts. This demographic change would be critical to the formation of the Hebrew language. In particular, a massive influx of refugees migrated from the vanquished kingdom of Israel into the southern hill country after the conquest of Samaria in 721 B.C.E.[51] Archaeological excavations and surveys have pointed to a burgeoning population in Jerusalem, which can be explained by refugees from the Assyrian invasions to the north and west of Jerusalem. Estimates suggest that Jerusalem's population grew at least threefold in the late eighth and early seventh centuries. Subsequent excavations in the region surrounding Jerusalem have further continued to support these conclusions, pointing to an escalating population not only in Jerusalem itself but also in its vicinity.[52] Sites like Ramat Rahel, to the south of Jerusalem, and Gibeon (el-Jib), to the north of Jerusalem, began to thrive in the late eighth century. Throughout the immediate countryside, farmsteads and small villages cropped up and helped support the urbanization and growth of Jerusalem. Recent archaeological surveys have provided more-specific evidence about the composition of these demographic changes. The demographic disruption was especially profound in the vicinity of Bethel—that is, in the regional territory at the boundary of the tribes of Ephraim and Benjamin.[53] Bethel's demise is indicative of a more general decline: "The number of sites there decreased from 238 in the eighth century to 127 in the Persian period and the total built-up area shrank even more spectacularly, from c. 170 to 45 hectares."[54] This would indicate that the influx of population into Jerusalem was dominated by refugees from southern Ephraim and Benjamin. Such demographic changes portend the influence of northern scribes in Jerusalem.

The social and demographic changes certainly left behind some literary evidence. For example, according to the second book of Kings, King Hezekiah named his son Manasseh, a name well known as one of the leading tribes of the northern kingdom. The Judean monarch also arranged a marriage between his son and a family from Jotbah, a village in Galilee (see 2 Kings 21:19). Another tradition—namely, that Manasseh followed in the sins of King Ahab of Israel—suggests that the northern émigrés also left their mark on religious practice in Jerusalem (2 Kings 21:3). The biblical prophetic literature also has indications of the social and demographic changes. For example, the prophet Isaiah enigmatically named his son Shear-Jashub, which translates literally as "a remnant shall return" (Isa. 7:3). This seems to be a thinly veiled reference to the refugees from the north who flooded into Jerusalem in the wake of the Assyrian campaigns.[55] The book of Isaiah refers to Galilee and Samaria as a "land of deep darkness" ravaged by war, and then claims that the governance of the Davidic royal family will be their salvation (Isa. 8:23–9:6 [English versions 9:1–7]). The book of Micah expresses the social tensions that such northern refugees would have introduced: "Hear this, you rulers of the house of Jacob and chiefs of the house of Israel, who abhor justice and pervert all equity, who build Zion with blood and Jerusalem with wrong!" (3:9). The poet identifies the northern kingdom—that is, "rulers of the house of Jacob and chiefs of the house of Israel"—as those who built Jerusalem. The ties between Samaria and Jerusalem had already developed under the Judean king Jehoshaphat (r. 871–847 B.C.E.), who created an alliance with Samaria through marriage. An Israelite princess, Athaliah, even became queen of Judah according to the biblical tradition (r. 841–835 B.C.E.). Such ties perhaps made it easier to absorb refugees from the north.

The linguistic evidence of these refugees is difficult to measure precisely.[56] The very fact that we can point to texts that show some indication of northern influence, for example the Elijah-Elisha narratives, arises from the fact that these texts show *deviations from biblical Hebrew*. In the case of the

Elijah-Elisha narratives,[57] these deviations are part of the literary style of the narrative. That is, the biblical author preserves the northern idiom while incorporating folktales about a couple of northern prophets. It is also possible that the author is not so much preserving the northern idiom as giving a literary flourish to the narrative. In either case, the northern elements are included precisely because they are nonstandard. Part of the difficulty in measuring the influence of IH in Jerusalem is the problem of identifying its features. One example is the use of the feminine marker *-t* (ת-) in IH, which follows Phoenician, as opposed to the classical (and Judean) use of *-h* (ה-), as in the Judean word *šnh*, "year," which is spelled *št* in the Samaria ostraca. Another frequently cited example for IH is the contraction of diphthongs such as *yên* (ין, "wine") in the Samaria ostraca instead of the classical (and Judean) *yayîn* (יין, "wine"). It seems likely that such contractions are not merely spelling conventions but also reflect vernacular. Contraction is also apparent in the theophoric additions (that is, the use of divine names as part of a personal name) to personal names, as in the Israelian *-yāw* (יו-) as opposed to the Judean *-yahû* (יהו-), which are both shortened from the full name Yahweh (יהוה).[58] Contraction of diphthongs and shortened spelling are typical of Phoenician and likely reflect the influence of Phoenician scribal practice in Samaria. It is important to recall at this point that the script itself was also borrowed from Phoenician and does not clearly distinguish itself from Phoenician until the eighth century.

The well-known linguistic peculiarities of the Siloam Tunnel inscription may stem from the influence of northern scribes and workmen.[59] The tunnel along with its inscription were apparently completed at the end of the eighth century, that is, during a time when a substantial number of northern refugees were being assimilated into Jerusalem society. Three linguistic features of the inscription may be understood as influenced by northern scribes and workmen: (1) the *-w* suffix; (2) the verbal form *hyt*, using the 3fs suffix conjugation; and (3) the term *mwzh* for "spring" instead of the standard biblical Hebrew term *mʿyn*.[60] The last term, *mwzh*, does use the long (Judean) spelling with *w* instead of the more typical contracted Israelian spelling of the diphthong (that is, **mzh*), which may underscore a mixed dialect or perhaps reflect some unofficial aspect of the inscription.

Israelian Hebrew's contraction of spelling for diphthongs has been thought to reject the practice of so-called *historical spelling*, which some have argued is the origin of vowel letters (or *matres lectionis*, "mothers of reading") in Hebrew and Aramaic. The beginnings of the practice of using vowel letters in the West Semitic dialects has been the subject of some debate among scholars. Usually this problem begins with a discussion of "historical spelling," by which scholars refer to the retention of contracted consonant letters *yod* and *waw*, which were part of original diphthongs, as vowels. To be more accurate, however, scholars are really speaking of *historical phonology*. The contraction of diphthongs (specifically, /aw/ and /ay/), for example, is a matter of phonology, not spelling. It is worth noting that the contraction of diphthongs in speech did not require a change in spelling. Quite the contrary. Spelling changes tend to be quite conservative in spite of radical developments in speech patterns. Furthermore, the very attribution of historical spelling begs the question of which spelling was "historical"—or, more precisely, standard. Is there evidence to suggest that words such as /*yayîn > yên/, "wine," and /*bayît > bêt/, "house," as well as /*yawm > yôm/, "day," and /*mawt > môt/, "death," were first spelled with longer spellings such as *yyn*, *byt*, *ywm*, or *mwt* rather than shorter spellings such as *yn*, *bt*, *ym*, or *mt?* The opposite is the case: The first attestations of these words in any Northwest Semitic alphabetic inscriptions are with the shorter "nonhistorical" spellings, in thirteenth-century Ugaritic inscriptions and in tenth-century Phoenician inscriptions. The tenth-century Hebrew/Canaanite inscription from Gezer also points to the shorter orthography. Thus, in terms of the history of spelling, the shorter spelling is standard, and the longer spelling would be a Hebrew innovation. In this respect, there is little "historical" about historical spelling.

The Moabite inscription from King Mesha (ca. 840 B.C.E.) can serve as an example of the problem of historical spelling in ancient alphabetic inscriptions. The inscription has the word for "house" spelled with the shortened form *bt* /*bêt/ (six times; lines 7, 23, 27, 30, 31) and with the longer form *byt* /*bāyit/ (once, line 25). After considering a variety of explanations for this variation, Cross and Freedman conclude that this inconsistency must ultimately be understood as an example of historical spelling.[61] Andrew Dearman notes, "Since the letter *yod* was already being used to represent *ê* in the final position, it should not be surprising to find the same sound represented by the same letter internally, whether the scribe included it inadvertently or not."[62] These explanations all assume a close correspondence between orthography and phonology—a correspondence that cannot be proved and is not axiomatic in the linguistics of writing systems. When we examine the context of the seven occurrences of *bt/byt* in the inscription, it turns out that the single occurrence of the longer spelling *byt* appears in a direct speech. In this respect, the spelling *byt* could be labeled as an example of *mater lectionis*, or "mother of reading," or in this case, a "child of speech." That is, the spelling seems to be an attempt to differentiate standard spelling from the idiosyncrasies of speech. This phenomenon is certainly known in the Hebrew

Bible, where the direct speech of foreigners is particularly colored by dialectal elements.

The population shifts and urbanization occasioned by the Assyrian era of Near Eastern history would have had profound implications for the linguistic environment of the late Judean monarchy. William Labov observes that "we often see *a rapid transformation of the more salient features of the rural dialects* as speakers enter the city."[63] A certain homogenization of language naturally occurs. Labov further notes that "the creation of low-prestige working-class dialects . . . embodies two major linguistic trends of the past several centuries: *the decline of local dialects* and the growth of vertical stratification in language."[64] In other words, there is at the same time a tendency for linguistic homogenization (that is, "decline of local dialects") and linguistic diglossia (that is, "vertical stratification"). These trends, according to Labov, operate "wherever large capital cities are developing at the expense of the hinterland." Such trends, however, would have appeared most prominently in speech, not writing. Thus, even though this nicely describes the linguistic environment in Judah during the late monarchy, in what way would linguistic homogenization as well as diglossia be seen in the textual artifacts? Such influence might only be seen if (1) scribes from other regions were migrating into and serving in Jerusalem, or (2) writing was spreading throughout society. It is possible that examples of diglossia and homogenization might be gleaned from two types of textual artifacts: graffiti and direct speech embedded in narrative. Unfortunately, direct speech in the Hebrew Bible cannot be assumed to be a precise representation of vernacular. Though there are embedded aspects of direct speech that may be gleaned for the study of vernacular, it is still part of the written narrative. Indeed, one author studying direct speech in the Bible even came to the conclusion that "the ancients discoursed in poetry, even in daily activities."[65] Others have argued that spoken and written dialects did not differ in antiquity, even though, as Gary Rendsburg points out in his critique, this "flies in the face of linguistic consensus."[66] The linguistic consensus is that no language is spoken as it is written; there is always a measure of diglossia between the vernacular and writing.[67] Rendsburg attempts to isolate the ancient Hebrew vernacular by pointing to isoglosses between biblical Hebrew and later Rabbinic Hebrew (which was based on vernacular language; see further in chapter 9).

Linguistic Nationalism

Perhaps pushing back against the emergence of empire was the notion of national identity that seems to have emerged in the Levant by the late ninth or eighth century B.C.E. Although the term *nationalism* is typically applied to the study of modern history, the categories that typify nationalism—including language—were also operative in antiquity.[68] Peoples of the ancient Near East were aware of differences in religion, territory, history, culture, and language. This awareness of difference forms the roots of ancient nationalism, even if we would not want to compare modern nationalism with nationalism in the Iron Age.[69] Most readily traceable aspects of political nationalism include temple, territory, kingship, and the army. Calendar, law, and language are also visible in the historical process.

Ethnicity is a relatively fluid concept whose boundaries can appear and disappear in the course of history. Languages are also fluid social constructs that often appear, disappear, and change as national boundaries move and shift. Linguistic characteristics, through the shifting political tides, tend to be "the most important *defining* criteria for ethnic-group membership."[70] This was true even in antiquity, as we see, for example, in the shibboleth incident in Judges 12, where the Gileadites distinguished themselves from the neighboring Ephraimites through a linguistic marker. Language is a readily available marker of group and ethnic identity.

The identification of a language with a people is a fundamental tenet of language ideology. This romantic linguistic notion is usually associated with the eighteenth-century German Enlightenment and particularly with Johan Herder's characterization of language as the genius of a people.[71] Indeed, language acts as an important symbol of group identity. In recent history, nationalistic ideology of language has structured state policy; and an important part of the claim to nationhood is the claim to a distinct language. Although language is closely tied to nationalistic movements of the early modern era, it is intrinsic to ethnic and group identity. Ethnic consciousness rose with a growing nationalism that characterized Syria-Palestine in the ninth century B.C.E. At this time, independent states arose in Syria-Palestine, including Israel, Judah, Philistia, Moab, and Ammon, as well as Aramaean states. Evidence of an incipient nationalism comes from a variety of sources.

One prominent indication of a growing sense of nationalism was the emergence of national gods.[72] For example, the royal monument erected by Mesha, king of Moab, in the mid-ninth century reads:

> I am Mesha, son of Chemosh-[yat], king of Moab, the Dibonite. My father had reigned over Moab thirty years, and I reigned after my father, and I made this high place for Chemosh in Qarhoh [. . .] because he saved me from all the kings and caused me to triumph over all my

> adversaries. Now Omri was king of Israel, and he oppressed Moab because Chemosh was angry with his land.

Strikingly, Chemosh is the particular god of the Moabites (as opposed to a general Semitic deity like Baal or El), and Moab is "his land." Chemosh arises as a national deity in Moab just as Yahweh appears in Israel and Judah. Throughout the southern Levant we see the rise of such national gods. A Josianic writer provides a list of the various national deities and has the prophet Ahijah speaking for Yahweh, decrying, "For they have forsaken Me; they have worshiped Ashtoreth the goddess of the Phoenicians, Chemosh the god of Moab, and Milcom the god of the Ammonites" (1 Kings 11:33). Personal names with theophoric elements (for example, *-iah* for Yahweh, as in Isaiah, which means "Yahweh saves") provide evidence for the exclusivity of these national deities. Jeffrey Tigay's work on the corpus of names in ancient Judah illustrates the centrality of a single national deity, Yahweh, even if there were polytheistic aspects to ancient Judean religious praxis.[73] The evidence from names in Ammon, Moab, and Edom—although it has not been analyzed as systematically as the Israelite material has—shows similar patterns.[74] Stephen Grosby, for instance, notes a similar development in Edom that begins in the eighth century B.C.E.: "The names of the kings of Edom contained the divine name 'Qaush,' for example, Qaushmalaka ('Qaush has become king,' from the reign of Tiglath-pileser III, 744–27 B.C.), Qaushgabri ('Qaush is powerful,' from the reign of Esarhaddon, 680–69 B.C.)."[75] Grosby goes on to point out that the development of monolatry that is suggested by personal names would have led to an increased degree of sociological uniformity required to speak of ethnicity.

Strong nationalistic fervor could be fostered through both territorially bounded religion and a common legal code. It is commonly acknowledged that the Deuteronomic laws are central to the religious and political program of the Josianic period (the late seventh century B.C.E.). It is hardly coincidental that this written codification of law can be located in the late-Judean monarchy. Deuteronomy also begins to employ the written text as religious and cultural authority. For example, in Deuteronomy 27:2–3 we read:

> On the day that you cross over the Jordan into the land that the Lord your God is giving you, you shall set up large stones and cover them with plaster. You shall write on them all the words of this law when you have crossed over, to enter the land that the Lord your God is giving you, a land flowing with milk and honey, as the Lord, the God of your ancestors, promised you.

As many scholars have noted, the book of Deuteronomy borrows the literary features of Near Eastern treaties as its literary template. The treaty genre is a quintessentially *written* artifact. Typically, Near Eastern treaties culminate with curses for those who break the treaty, and curses are derivative of the genre of magic. Magic texts also use writing as a fundamental element of their rituals. Deuteronomy thus justifies itself through the use of writing, particularly employing the treaty genre in order to reinforce its own authority. It might be added here that the treaty genre—a covenant sealed with a written document—was particularly significant in elevating the authority of written text. Writing had long had cultural power in magic ritual, legal texts, and royal monuments, but Deuteronomy employs these genres to give its written words more-general cultural authority.

Another indication of ethnicity is an emerging interest in national boundaries, which contrasts sharply with the city-states of the Amarna period. Grosby has examined the different notions of boundaries and nationality in antiquity and has identified three basic categories: empires, nations, and city-kingdoms.[76] An extended yet bounded and sociologically homogenous territory characterizes *nations*. The boundaries of nations are conceptually fixed, even if they are ideological and even fictional. Israel's conceptual boundaries (Num. 34),[77] for example, seem to bear little resemblance to the historical realia for most—if not all—of the monarchy.

Nations typically have a common name for the land, people, and language. The names Israel and Judah come to refer to both the territory and the people inhabiting the territory. This meaning for Israel is already clear in the Tell Dan inscription (ca. 825 B.C.E.), where a clan-based designation is used for Judah: The Aramaean inscription refers to "the king of *Israel* and the king of the house of David."[78] A similar use of the clan-based designation *house of David* for Judah, as against *Israel* for the northern kingdom, apparently can be found in the contemporary Moabite Stone (ca. 850).[79] In the Moabite Stone, Israel quite clearly refers to a people, though perhaps also to a nation. The first use of *Israel* as the name of a people goes back to the famous line in the Merneptah Stele (ca. 1207 B.C.E.): "As for (the people) Israel, their seed is not!" The text clearly uses the determinative for a people with Israel, but there is insufficient context to make any broad conclusions other than that Israel was an early term for a people. Another ninth-century text (ca. 840 B.C.E.), the Kurkh Monolith of the Assyrian king Shalmaneser III, mentions a coalition of kings that included "from the *land* of Israel" (^{KUR}*sirʾalāia*).[80] The various uses of Israel in these passages suggest that Israel had become a flexible term referring to a people but also to a land and perhaps even to a nation.

Interestingly, the references to *ʾeretz yisraʾel* (ארץ ישראל), "the land of Israel," in the Bible derive mainly from the Elijah-Elisha narratives, where they refer to the northern kingdom. A later (probably sixth-century B.C.E.) text such as Ezekiel 27:17, which reads, "Judah and the land of Israel were your merchants," separates Judah from "the land of Israel." Wherever it is clear in the Hebrew Bible, the land of Israel refers to the territory of the northern kingdom (see 2 Kings 5:2; 6:23; Ezek. 27:17; 2 Chron. 30:25). The use of the term *ʾeretz yisraʾel* to refer to the territory of both Judah and Israel is a later development of Jewish tradition. This development is already implicit in the use of *yisraʾel* in late-biblical (postexilic) literature to refer to the community in Persian Yehud.[81]

Evidence for the common use of land and people for Judah appears only in the eighth century—about a century later than in Israel. A building inscription (ca. 740 B.C.E.) from the Assyrian king Tiglath-pileser III mentions Jehoahaz of Judah (*ia-ú-ḫa-zi ia-ú-da-a-a-a*);[82] and the famous description of Sennacherib's third campaign in Judah and Jerusalem (in 701 B.C.E.) mentions "Hezekiah, the Judean" (*ha-za-qi-ia-ú* ᴸᵁ́*ia-ú-da-ai*).[83]

Concomitant with this terminological conflation between *land* and *people* is the development of a territorial kinship—that is, a social fiction that a territorially bounded people are related by blood.[84] In the present case, the fiction is that the *Israelites* are the sons of Abraham, even though it is clear even in biblical literature that nonkin groups became part of *Israel*—as, for example, the Kenites (cf. Gen. 15:18–21; Judg. 1:16). Ironically, literature is one of the means by which a territorial, extensive kinship is advanced, but close reading also demonstrates the fictive nature of this kinship. These national and ethnic linguistic identities have a tendency to correspond with a distinct geographic boundary and religious practice. Thus, city-states have no extended, bounded relation of center to the periphery, whereas nations do. Likewise, although city-states may have patron deities, they are not necessarily exclusive to the city. The recording of extensive boundary lists (for example, Josh. 15–18) is usually related to political activities of the late eighth century B.C.E. Likewise, the beginnings of religious centralization are not merely coincidentally related to the political and linguistic identity that seems to be crystallizing in the late eighth century B.C.E.

Finally, language is an important basis for kinship affiliation, and in our case, the Judean language is the common denominator for the Judean people. *Judean* (*yhwḏyṯ*; יהודית) is a derivative of the tribal and geographic name Judah (*yhwḏh*), and its use to refer to the Hebrew language first appears in the Hebrew Bible in the story of the Assyrian assault on Jerusalem, where an Assyrian emissary insists on speaking "Judean" rather than Aramaic (see

2 Kings 18:26–28; Isa. 36:11–13). It is probably not a coincidence that the Assyrians, whose own literature betrays strong linguistic consciousness and language ideology, are credited with using the term *Judean* to refer to the Hebrew language. The Assyrians made language ideology part of their imperial plan, so it is not surprising that language ideology was also elevated in local states like Judah.

Assyrian imperialism also resulted in the disappearance of northern Hebrew dialects. By this, I do not mean to infer that there is no evidence for IH. Indeed, scholars have successfully identified aspects of IH in the literary and epigraphic record. Still, the disappearance of northern Israelite towns and villages after the Assyrian invasions resulted in the disappearance of the speech communities that would have been necessary for the preservation of vernacular dialects. At the same time, the migration of northern refugees into Jerusalem and Judah did lead to the preservation of IH, if only in fragments and glimpses, in the biblical literature compiled and edited during the late eighth century B.C.E. It has been argued that later Rabbinic Hebrew was influenced by IH,[85] but this could not have been a direct lineage. Samaria and Galilee became Assyrian then Babylonian and Persian provinces after 721 B.C.E. Speech communities were disrupted and dislocated. No longer inscriptions have been found that were written in IH after 721 B.C.E. The local administrative language became Aramaic, and the local vernaculars were also Aramaic. The later Samaritan Hebrew seems to have little direct relationship with the earlier IH dialects. Rather, Samaritan Hebrew is a religious language based on the Bible and colored by local Aramaic dialects. Israelian Hebrew disappeared and is now preserved by a few inscriptions and through linguistic analysis of biblical literature.

Commonly Proposed Israelian Hebrew Features

The following are the some commonly proposed features of IH:[86]

1. Monophthongization of diphthongs, e.g., /ay/ > /ê/. See Samaria ostraca, *yn* /*yēn/ (cf. SBH *yyn* /*yayin/), "wine"; 1 Samuel 10:14, *ʾn* (cf. SBH *ʾyn*), "where"; and Gezer 1:7, *qṣ*, "summer" (cf. SBH *qyṣ*). Compare Ugaritic and Phoenician.
2. Feminine-singular nominal ending *-t*. Compare Phoenician, Moabite, Aramaic, and Rabbinic Hebrew. See Samaria ostraca *št* (cf. SBH *šnh*), "year"; Genesis 49:22, *prt*, "she-ass"; Judges 5:29, *ḥkmt*, "wise lady"; 2 Kings 6:8, *tḥnt*, "camp"; 2 Kings 9:17, *špʿt* (cf. SBH *špʿh*), "multitude"; Hosea 7:5, *ḥmt*, "poison."

3. Shortened theophoric prefix and suffix using *-yw* (cf. SBH *-yhw*). See Samaria ostraca, Kuntillet ʿAjrud inscriptions.
4. The relative pronoun *š-* (instead of SBH *ʾšr*). Compare Phoenician and Ammonite. See Judges 5:7; 6:17; 2 Kings 6:11; Psalm 133:2; Song of Songs; Ecclesiastes. This also becomes the standard form in Rabbinic Hebrew. Sometimes it is also described as ABH (e.g., Judg. 5:7), though it seems more appropriate to list it as IH.
5. Suffix form of verbs (III-*yod*) with *-t*. Compare Aramaic and RH. See 2 Kings 9:37, Qere *hyt* (cf. SBH *hyth* used in the Ketibh), "she was"; Leviticus 25:21, *ʿśt*, "it shall make"; note the Siloam Tunnel inscription, line 3, *hyt*.[87]
6. The use of *ʾḥd*, *ḥd* (חד/אחד), "a certain (indefinite)," as an indefinite pronoun. See examples in Judges 9:53; 13:2; 1 Samuel 1:1; 7:9, 12; 2 Samuel 18:10; 1 Kings 19:4, 5; 20:13, 35; 22:9; 2 Kings 4:1; 7:8, 13; 8:6; 12:1. Some external evidence is provided by the Deir ʿAlla inscription (ii.10, *kḥd*).
7. 2fs pronoun *ʾty*, "you" (contrast SBH *ʾt*), e.g., 2 Kings 4:7µ, 16, 23; 8:1; and the 2fs suffix *-ky* (contrast SBH *-k*, Judg. 17:2; 2 Kings 4:2; Jer. 4:30).
8. Lexicon. Terms such as *ʾdrt*, "coat" (1 Kings 19:13, 19; 2 Kings 2:8, 13; contrast SBH *mʿyl*); *kd*, "jar" (Judg. 7:16–20; 1 Kings 17:12, 14, 16; 18:34; Tell el-ʿOreme inscription); *nqd*, "shepherd" (2 Kings 3:4; Amos 1:1; Mesha Inscription; contrast SBH *rwʾh*); *ghr*, "to crouch, bend" (1 Kings 18:42; 2 Kings 4:34, 35; contrast BH *rbṣ* and *škb)*; *šns*, "to gird" (1 Kings 18:46; contrast SBH *ḥgr* and *ʾzr)*; *ʾrmwn*, "palace" (Hos. 8:14; contrast SBH *byt-hmlk, hykl*); *tny*, "repeat" (Judg. 5:11; 11:40; Hos. 8:10; contrast SBH *šnh*).

5

The Democratization of Hebrew

The more complex the organization of the state and the economy, the greater the pressure toward graphic representation of speech.

—*Jack Goody*

The development of government bureaucracy was a natural catalyst for the development and spread of writing beginning in the eighth century B.C.E. Writing was democratized in ancient Judah. That is, it became widely available and started to become a Judean cultural value. The catalyst for the democratization of writing was—to use a modern term—the *globalization* of society. In this chapter we examine the Hebrew language in the last hundred years before the Babylonian destruction of Jerusalem in 586 B.C.E. It is during this period that we see the flourishing of Hebrew writing as preserved in all kinds of written (or epigraphic) evidence. We find hundreds of seals and seal impressions, dozens of letters, tomb inscriptions, a variety of economic texts, and even graffiti. And not surprisingly, it is in this context that a written text, the scroll of the covenant supposedly discovered in the temple (2 Kings 23:2), became the basis for the religious reforms of the late Judean monarchy. The written word had reached its zenith in ancient Judean culture. At the same time, the democratization of writing—its spread to nonscribal classes—undermined the tight control of writing standards. Democratization of writing extended outside the boundaries of those who would strictly control its standards.

Inscriptional Evidence for the Spread of Hebrew Writing

Hundreds of Hebrew inscriptions testify to the widespread use of writing during the late Judean monarchy. As the archaeologist Ephraim Stern notes, "Taking into consideration the size of the Judean kingdom during this period, this large body [of inscriptions] is truly astonishing."[1] The marked increase in epigraphic remains begins already in the late eighth century, but it reaches its apex in the seventh and early sixth centuries. Parenthetically, such a spread of writing was also critical to the formation and religious authority of biblical literature. Indeed, it is hardly surprising that this period also is marked by the appearance of the "writing" prophets (for example, Isaiah, Micah, Amos, Hosea, and Jeremiah) and by a religious reform supposedly prompted by the discovery of a written text. Such examples from biblical literature accord well with the epigraphic picture that emerges from the late Iron Age.

What impact did this marked increase in writing have on the development of the Hebrew language? The spread of writing throughout Judean culture results in a decline in the standardization in writing. As writing is no longer tightly confined to scribal elites, the ability to standardize an "official Hebrew" actually diminishes. This is easy to understand by modern analogies, such as e-mail, texting, and other social media—all forms of writing that challenge the established standards of writing because they flourish outside the realms of those who standardize writing. Thus, this type of democratization in writing results in inconsistencies in grammar and spelling. In ancient Hebrew, the democratization of writing resulted in unevenness in spelling and script. Although the epigraphic evidence for writing during the late Judean monarchy is so vast that we cannot rehearse it all here, it will be useful to examine some examples of writing during the last century of the Judean monarchy, before the conquest of Jerusalem by the Babylonians in 586 B.C.E. This will serve to illustrate some of the types of linguistic changes that we begin to see as well as the role that Hebrew comes to play in the life of the Judean people. Examples will be drawn from seals and seal impressions, letters, economic texts, tomb inscriptions, and graffiti.

WRITING FOR ADMINISTRATION

A variety of different types of texts illustrate the importance of Hebrew writing for administration in the late monarchy. These include economic texts, seals and seal impressions, and inscribed weights. The teaching of Hebrew reading and writing skills began specifically for administration and commerce, and the commercial and administrative uses of writing would be critical to the spread of writing to a variety of social classes during the late Iron Age.

Excavations at Kadesh Barnea (Tell el-Qudeirat) have recovered some of the best examples of scribal exercises in ancient Judah. Kadesh Barnea was a remote fortress that served trading caravans in the middle of the vast Negev highlands. The excavations recovered ten ostraca dating to the late monarchy. Ostraca 1–6 and 9 date to the last phase of the Iron Age fortress (ca. 600 B.C.E.) and appear to be scribal exercises. The most elaborate example includes six columns with lists of hieratic numbers as well as hieratic abbreviations for accounting terms such as *shekel* and *homer*. It also includes the Paleo-Hebrew letter *b* (𐤁, column 1, line 2) used as an abbreviation for "bath" (as in Arad letter 2:2). The corpus of scribal exercises from this remote outpost highlights the central role that accounting played in trade and commerce.

The large corpus of inscribed jar handles from Gibeon also highlights the use of Hebrew writing in administration. The inscriptions from Gibeon also include a variety of other types of inscriptions, including eighty-four *lmlk*, "belonging to the king," jar-handle inscriptions dating to the late eighth century, which was when the town of Gibeon first became a commercial center for the production of wine. There are sixty-two inscriptions on wine-jar handles from Gibeon that date to the late seventh century or early sixth century B.C.E. They are linguistically uninteresting, mostly comprising scrawled names and references to a *gdr* (גדר), "walled plot", as well as references to the name of the town itself. The script is legible but not carefully or elegantly executed. The two types of inscriptions from Gibeon are suggestive of the changing role of writing in the late Judean monarchy, that is, from the royal jar handles of the late eighth century to the commercial jar handles of a century later. Writing begins at Gibeon as part of royal administration and develops into nonroyal and commercial use. The royal seals are carefully executed seals, whereas the later commercial inscriptions are scrawled on the storage jars.

Weights belong to the growing corpus of inscribed items relating to commerce.[2] They often have abbreviations for different measurements as well as hieratic numerals (borrowed from Egyptian). Some of the terminology inscribed on weights, like the term *škl* (that is, "shekel"), continued to be used until the Roman period. Other terms, like the term *pym*, which refers to "two-thirds of a shekel," are known only from Iron Age Hebrew inscriptions and the Hebrew Bible. Such inscribed weights testify to the spread of the commercial use of writing in the late monarchy. They provide further evidence that ties the growth of writing with developing economic activity.

A variety of seals dating to the late monarchy have been found. The most prominent examples are the royal seal impressions, the earliest of which are the so-called *lmlk*, "belonging to the king," seals. These are a group of royal seal impressions with the *lmlk* inscription and the name of one of four administrative centers (Hebron, Ziph, Socoh, and *mmšt*). These royal stamps give way to the rosette-style seals and eventually the "Mozah" seals of the Babylonian period (sixth century B.C.E.).

There were also fiscal seal impressions (or fiscal bullae). Two such fiscal seal impressions are published in *West Semitic Stamp Seals*: number 421 reads *b26/šnh/ʾltld/lmlk*, "in the twenty-sixth/year/Eltolad/for the king," and number 422 reads *b13/šnh/rʾšny/lkšl/mlk*, "in the thirteenth/year/the first crop/of Lachish. For/the king." Bulla 421 refers to the town of Eltolad, which was apparently paying taxes to the king in the twenty-sixth year of his reign (likely referring to King Josiah, which would be in the year 614 B.C.E.). Bulla 422 is very crudely or quickly carved, probably reflecting the relatively ephemeral nature of these fiscal bullae (which could only be used for one season). The spelling of the word *rʾšny*, "first," is linguistically problematic. The *nun* points to the Hebrew word *rʾšn*, "first in rank," but this is never spelled with a final *yod*. The final *yod* points to the Hebrew *rʾšyt*, which is always spelled without a *nun* and with a final *tav*. Thus, the term seems to be a misspelling. Most likely, then, it simply reflects the limited scribal education of the writer of this economic seal impression. The writing—both script and grammar—is crude, but it was nonetheless perfectly functional. Both seals use hieratic numerals, which are known in Hebrew inscriptions dating back to the tenth century B.C.E.

The most mundane yet powerful evidence for Hebrew writing during this period is the considerable mass of personal seals and seal impressions. A recently published collection by Nahman Avigad of West Semitic stamp seals includes about seven hundred Hebrew seals, mostly dating to the seventh and early sixth centuries B.C.E. With every excavation season, more seals are being added to this corpus. These clay objects point to a great number of papyrus and parchment documents that did not survive the vicissitudes of climate and military conflict. Only one papyrus letter has been discovered that predates the Babylonian conquest of Jerusalem in 586 B.C.E. This is an extremely fragmentary letter (Papyrus Muraba'at 17) dating to the seventh century B.C.E., which was preserved in the arid region near the shores of the Dead Sea. The corpus of seals and seal impressions is substantial enough to establish that a comparatively large number of papyrus and parchment documents have been lost. The large number of lost documents can be illustrated by one collection of forty-nine epigraphic seal impressions excavated in the "House of the Bullae" in 1982 in the City of David (Jerusalem).[3] The archive was discovered in 1982 during excavations. Several of the seal impressions reflect quite elegantly executed seals and represent the highest levels of wealth and power in Jerusalem during the late monarchy. Others, however, are less impressive. Although many of the seal impressions are damaged and only partially legible, the editor describes twelve of them as careless, crude, coarse, or unskilled.[4] This suggests that seals were also being executed for a wide variety of people who often did not have the means to hire a highly skilled scribe-craftsman to execute their seals. In other words, the corpus of seal impressions reflects the activity of both private citizens and skilled government artisans. Yet, all these bullae come from one archive that was burned in 586 B.C.E. in the Babylonian destruction of Jerusalem.

There are even seals from people known from biblical literature. The most prominent example is perhaps the exquisitely executed seal impressed by "Gemaryahu, son of Shaphan," a royal official in Jerusalem (see Jer. 36:10).[5] There are scholars who have doubted the identification of the Gemaryahu seal impression with the biblical figure; however, the appearance of exactly the same name, dating to precisely the same period of time, and located in the same place (that is, Jerusalem), seems sufficient for this identification. The identification, in any case, is irrelevant to the more important discovery—namely, that a plethora of seals executed in diverse ways points to the variety of people involved in the production and use of writing.

The large number of seals and seal impressions reflects the entire scope of Judean society, including the lower classes. Nahman Avigad, who published another large collection of more than two hundred seal impressions, also points to carelessly executed seal impressions and clumsy letter forms in his hoard. He suggests that many of these seals were executed by their owners, but this is difficult to know for certain. Nevertheless, it seems that seal ownership became something of a status symbol in these times. Avigad also makes the interesting observation, "In none of the neighbouring cultures, including Egypt, has so large a hoard of bullae bearing private names come to light from the period of the Judean monarchy."[6] Moreover, it seems that Hebrew writing itself was a central part of this widespread use of seals. It is important to reiterate that Hebrew seals are unique in their preference for writing rather than iconography.

Judah represents the first evidence for the widespread use of aniconic seals, that is, seals without pictures. Until at least the mid-eighth century B.C.E., seals in ancient Israel were anepigraphic—that is, without writing. Thus, a hoard of seal impressions excavated in the royal palace at Samaria dating to the mid- to late eighth century B.C.E. bear no names at all, only images.[7] This observation has recently been sharpened by new discoveries of seal impressions from the ninth century B.C.E. in Jerusalem; in excavations led by Ronny Reich, more than 170 clay bullae used for sealing documents were discovered in the City of David in Jerusalem.[8] These seal impressions are exclusively anepigraphic; that is, not a single bulla has any letters or writing. They all utilize iconography instead of written names and titles to indicate their owners. This stands in stark contrast to seals of the later eighth and seventh centuries that primarily utilize written names to indicate ownership. It marks a watershed in the role of writing in Judean society.

In the ancient Near East, seals generally used graphic images to tell something about the owner. Alan Millard notes the contrast with contemporary Phoenician seals: "Almost all published Phoenician seals bear a design of some sort, whether a simple divine emblem or an elaborate scene, and so that by itself could be sufficient to express identity. On those seals the letters of an owner's name are strictly superfluous."[9] This is especially important in a largely nonliterate society. The widespread use of aniconic seals, in contrast, presumes that seals could be readily identified by the writing. This may be rather mundane literacy, but it also implies that writing itself has become a mundane or common part of the culture. The widespread use of seals is also evidence for an increasingly complex economy that prompted the rise of literacy itself. It is representative of the spread of writing through different classes of Judean society—hence, the reason for the title of this chapter, "The *Democratization* of Hebrew."

Though there is limited linguistic information to be gleaned from seals, a few trends become clear. For example, the City of David excavations illustrate that even seals begin to use vowel letters, that is, what would technically be termed *plene* or "full" spelling. For example, seal B37 inscribes *lʾḥyʾb*, "belonging to Achiab," where the *y* is an internal vowel letter. Concerning this seal, the epigrapher Yair Shoham observes that "the script is careless."[10] Other examples of medial vocalic spelling are written in fine script (see B28, B29, B30). Shoham also notes, "At the end of the word *plene* spelling was always used. . . . There is not a single example of defective spelling at the end of the word."[11] Thus, the use of vowel letters, particularly medial *-w-* (ו) or *-y-* (י) and final *-h* (ה), becomes increasingly commonplace.

The spread of writing does not mean that everyone was literate, but rather that writing was no longer restricted to highly trained scribal elites. For example, the pervasive use of seals and weights minimally points to signature literacy or craft literacy, that is, the ability to read and write one's own name, to read and write receipts, and perhaps to read short letters. Christopher Rollston has rightly dismissed assessments that proficiency in alphabetic writing can be easily attained; however, Rollston's critique focuses on advanced proficiency and not the ability to read a seal or write a receipt.[12] It is noteworthy in this regard that there is no evidence of an elaborate school curriculum in Judah. This is not just happenstance, as we learn by comparing school texts in ancient Ugarit, which had elaborate school texts for Akkadian cuneiform but limited school texts (essentially the alphabet) for learning alphabetic cuneiform in their own Ugaritic language. The alphabet creates the potentiality for writing, which a more complicated writing system did not. One can learn an alphabet rather quickly, and it is quite flexible. Therefore, it is hardly surprising that rudimentary literacy, which I would call "craft literacy," is evident throughout the epigraphic record. It did not require years of training. This beginning level of literacy is illustrated, for example, by a recently published ostracon that contains a list of seventeen different signatures of individuals apparently signing for a receipt or payment.[13] This ostracon is one of the better-preserved and more elaborate ostraca representing the use of writing in the everyday economic activity of the late Judean kingdom. It is evident in the record of seals, weights, graffiti, and even letters. This does not mean that ancient Judah was a nation of scribes or widely literate, but merely that writing as a technology had transcended the bounds of scribal elites. This is nicely illustrated in the so-called "Letter of a Literate Soldier."

THE LETTER OF A LITERATE SOLDIER

Excavations at the site of ancient Lachish in the Judean foothills uncovered thirty-four ostraca along with other assorted seals, seal impressions, and inscribed weights. The ostraca date to the final stage of the Iron Age occupation (ca. 586 B.C.E.). One particular ostracon discovered at Lachish provides rather remarkable testimony for the cultural prestige of basic literacy in the early sixth century B.C.E. Lachish letter 3, which has been dubbed the "Letter of a Literate Soldier," captures a debate between a junior and a senior officer on the topic of the ability to read.[14] The commanding officer, Yaush, had obviously questioned his junior officer's ability to read in a previous letter. Hoshayahu, the junior officer, writes back, offended by the suggestion that he cannot read. Put differently, the whole letter is addressing the issue of literacy in a nonscribal class of society. The ostracon is written on both sides, and the text reads as follows:

ʿbdk.hwšʿyhw šlḥ.l	(1	עבדכ·הושעיהו שלח·ל
hgd lʾdny yʾwš.yšmʿ	(2	הגד לאדני יאוש·ישמע
yhwh ʾt ʾdny šmʿt.šlm	(3	יהוה את אדני שמעת·שלמ
wšmʿt ṭb [.] *wʿt.hpqḥ*	(4	ושמעת טב [·] ועת·הפקח
[*nʾ*] *ʾt ʾzn ʿbdk.lspr.ʾšr*	(5	[נא] את אזנ עבדכ·לספר·אשר
šlḥth ʾdny lʿbdk ʾmš.ky.lb	(6	שלחתה אדני לעבדכ אמש·כי·לב
ʿbd[*k*] *dwh.mʾz.šlḥk.ʾl.ʿbd*	(7	עבד[כ] דוה·מאז·שלחכ·אל·עבד
k wky ʾmr.ʾdny.lʾ.ydʿth.	(8	כ וכי אמר·אדני·לא·ידעתה·
qrʾ.spr ḥyhwh.ʾm.nsh.ʾ	(9	קרא·ספר חיהוה·אמ·נסה·א
yš.lqrʾ ly spr lnṣḥ.wgm.	(10	יש·לקרא לי ספר לנצח·וגמ·
kl spr ʾšr ybʾ.ʾly ʾm.	(11	כל ספר אשר יבא·אלי אמ·
qrʾty.ʾth wʿwd ʾtnnhw	(12	קראתי·אתה ועוד אתננהו
kl.mʾwmh wlʿbdk.hgd	(13	כל·מאומה ולעבדכ·הגד
lʾmr yrd śr hṣbʾ.	(14	לאמר ירד שר הצבא·
knyhw bn ʾlntn lbʾ.	(15	כניהו בנ אלנתנ לבא·
mṣrymh.wʾt	(16	מצרימה·ואת
hwdwyhw bn ʾḥyhw w	(17	הודויהו בנ אחיהו ו
ʾnšw šlḥ lqḥt.mzh	(18	אנשו שלח לקחת·מזה
wspr.ṭbyhw ʿbd hmlk.hbʾ	(19	וספר·טביהו עבד המלכ·הבא
ʾl.šlm.bn ydʿ mʾt hnbʾ lʾm	(20	אל·שלמ·בנ ידע מאת הנבא לאמ
r.hšmr.šlḥh.ʿb<d>k.ʾl.ʾdny	(21	ר·השמר·שלחה·עב<<ד>>כ·אל·אדני

> Your servant Hoshayahu sent to inform my lord Yaush: May YHWH cause my lord to hear a report of peace and a report of good things. And now, please explain to your servant the meaning of the letter which you sent to your servant yesterday evening because the heart of your servant has been sick since your sending to your servant and because my lord said, "You do not know how to read a letter" [*lʾ ydʿth qrʾ spr*]. As YHWH lives, never has any man had to read a letter to me. And also every letter that comes to me, surely I read it and, moreover, I can repeat it completely! And concerning your servant, it was reported saying, "The commander of the army, Konyahu ben-Elnathan, came down to enter into Egypt. And he sent to take Hodavyahu ben-Ahiyahu and his men from this place." And as for the letter of Tobyahu, servant of the king, which came to Shallum ben-Yada through the prophet, saying, "Beware!" your servant sent it to my lord.

We may infer from the passion of the junior officer's protestation—"As YHWH lives, never has any man had to read a letter to me"—that illiteracy had a social stigma. This would be the first time in history that illiteracy among nonscribal classes was actually socially stigmatized.

One Neo-Assyrian letter provides a useful comparison to the Letter of a Literate Soldier. An administrator during the reign of Sargon II (r. 721–705 B.C.E.) writes as follows:

> To the king my lord; your servant Sin-na'di. Good health to the king, my lord! I have no scribe where my lord sent me to. Let the king order either the governor of Arrapha or Aššur-belu-taqqin to send me one.[15]

This letter exhibits several "peculiarities, even blunders" that reflect the limited scribal training of the writer.[16] Yet, the writer also recognizes the need for a professional scribe and is not ashamed to ask for one to be sent to him. This contrasts with the proud boasts by the Assyrian king Assurbanipal (r. 668–627 B.C.E.) about his ability to read, which might suggest that the scribal education was a desired ability even outside of the scribal classes; however, Assurbanipal was probably not trained in the scribal arts as preparation for kingship. Rather, his brother Siniddinapli, the crown prince, died prior to 672 B.C.E. As a result, Assurbanipal had been trained in scholarly pursuits, including divination, mathematics, and scribal arts, before he became crown prince. In Assurbanipal's case, this later autobiographical boasting relates to fortuitous early scribal training. In contrast, the Judean kings are encouraged to be literate by the Deuteronomic "law of the king" (Deut. 17:18–19a): "When he is seated on the throne of his kingdom, he shall write for himself a copy of this teaching in a scroll before the levitical priests, and it shall be with him and he shall read in it all the days of his life."[17] This Deuteronomic law was particularly critical for the Josianic reforms in the late seventh century. Indeed, the "law of the king" in particular was utilized in the religious critique of kingship by the Deuteronomistic historian(s).[18] This suggests that the rising social status of literacy in Judah was partially grounded in religion.

It is sometimes suggested—incorrectly—that the Letter of the Literate Solder is part of a corpus of Lachish letters that represent "official Hebrew."[19] This assumes two things: first, that there is a standardized or "official" Hebrew, and, second, that the junior officer had a professional scribe or that his scribal skills were equivalent to a well-trained scribe. Yet the second assumption is challenged by the content of the discourse itself. After all, Lachish letter 3 is mostly devoted to protestations that the junior officer needed no professional scribe. The very content of the letter undermines assertions that it is from the pen of a trained scribe. In an earlier article, I argued that the linguistic idiosyncrasies of the letter suggest that it was penned by a junior military officer with rudimentary linguistic skills.[20] These linguistic problems include spelling errors, grammatical errors, and the use of nonstandard formulas in the letter. The first clue comes in lines 1–2: "Your servant Hoshayahu sent to inform my lord Yaush," which does not conform to standard epistolary style.[21] Dennis Pardee describes it in his *Handbook of Ancient Hebrew Letters* as "unparalleled."[22] An example of standard epistolary style can be seen in Lachish letter 2, which begins, "To my lord Yaush, may Yahweh cause my lord to hear peace." It is also worth comparing the more typical formula used in Genesis 32:4–6:

> Jacob sent messengers ahead to his brother Esau . . . and instructed them as follows, "Thus shall you say, '*To my lord Esau, thus says your servant Jacob*: I stayed with Laban and remained until now; I have acquired cattle, asses, sheep, and male and female slaves; *and I send to declare* (*lhgyd*) *to my lord* in the hope of gaining your favor.'" (emphasis added)

A formal letter should have first mentioned the superior, "To my lord Esau" or "To my lord Yaush," then followed with the inferior, "your servant Jacob" or "your servant Hoshayahu." Lachish letter 3 skips the formal introduction and proceeds immediately to the second part of the address that we see in Genesis 32:6, "I send to declare to my lord," or in Lachish 3, "Hoshayahu sent to inform my lord Yaush." The failure to employ standard epistolary protocol is the first indication that the writer's scribal training was rudimentary.

Lachish letter 3 also highlights the increasing use of vowel letters in Hebrew. The most important example of this phenomenon is the word *ʾyš* (איש), "man," in lines 9–10, which uses the medial *yod* as a vowel letter. In earlier inscriptions, such as the Siloam Tunnel inscription (from Jerusalem, ca. 710 B.C.E.) or the Mesha inscription (from Moab, ca. 840 B.C.E.), the long *i* vowel in the word for "man" /ʾīš/ is spelled without the medial vowel *yod*: *ʾš* (אש).

The increasing use of vowel letters should also influence the way that we read other parts of this inscription. In lines 6 and 7 we find the difficult verbal form *šlḥth* (שלחתה), "you sent," and on line 8 the form *ydʿth* (ידעתה), "you know." Normally, the 2ms perfect would be spelled with a final *-t* (ת-) rather than with the final vowel letter *-th* (תה-), even though it was apparently pronounced /-tā/. Although the spelling using a final *h* as a vowel letter would become quite typical in the Qumran Hebrew texts, it would not be used until Rabbinic Hebrew and does not ever seem to have been a standard spelling in Hebrew. Occasionally, the 2ms perfect is found with the longer *-th* suffix in SBH (for example, Gen. 3:12; 15:3; 21:23; Exod. 12:44; 25:12; 26:32, 33 [contrast v. 34]), but it is clearly exceptional. James Barr observes that this phenomenon in the Hebrew Bible is associated with the verb *ntn*

(נתן, "to give") and the III-*heh* class of verbs.[23] Neither of these observations, however, applies to Lachish 3. As a result, Frank Moore Cross was quite reluctant to read *šlḥth*, "you sent," and *ydʿth*, "you know," as simple verbs with the *mater lectionis* letter *heh*; instead, he suggested that the 2ms verbs here attach a 3ms suffix -*h*, thus rendering the text as "you sent *it*" and "you know *it*." Cross argued that "regularly in pre-Exilic Hebrew prose the 2.m.s. form without the suffix is written without *he*."[24] The writing with final *heh* would become frequent only in Qumran Hebrew, although it is also attested in Aramaic. Two other examples of the long spelling of the 2ms perfect verbal suffix are attested in the Arad letters (*ktbth* [כתבתה] 7:6) and the Lachish letters (*ydʿth* [ידעתה] 2:6). Cross's interpretation depends on rather rigid conceptions about the evolution of *matres lectionis* in Hebrew and does not take into consideration sociolinguistic aspects of the inscription. For example, the author of the ostracon was apparently a soldier and not a professional scribe. Surely, this must be taken into consideration just as if we were reading a letter by someone with an elementary education as opposed to a college education. Moreover, the spread of writing to nonscribal classes also results in a diminishing of the standard spelling.

In line 9 we must reckon with the contraction *ḥyhwh* (חיהוה, "as surely as Yahweh lives") from the expected *ḥy yhwh*. Several scholars have grasped this idiosyncratic writing as reflecting scribal practices in the Iron Age.[25] Dennis Pardee, however, observes, "The occurrence of the phenomenon in practically every student's paper they read should lead scholars to be wary of accepting it as a legitimate option open to ancient scribes."[26] While it is likely that this orthography reflects aspects of the spoken idiom, where the two words would be run together, this should not be regarded as normative scribal practice. More likely, this incidental influence of vernacular pronunciation on the spelling is another indication of the rudimentary level of the officer's scribal training.

Line 12, *ʾtnnhw* (אתננהו), has been interpreted in various ways. The most plausible reading takes this from the verbal root *tnh* (תנה, "to repeat"), with a 3ms verbal suffix attached, hence, "I could repeat it"; in other words, the soldier could repeat the contents of the document (/sēper/ ספר). However, the spelling *tnh* is typical of Aramaic, which regularly interchanges the grapheme *t*, where in Hebrew we find *š*. Thus, in SBH we usually find *šnh* (שנה, "to repeat, recite"), yet the lexeme *tnh* is found in Judges 5:11 and 11:40. An alternative is to read the verb as deriving from *ntn* (נתן, "to give") with a 3ms suffix, hence, the sentence in lines 12–13 might be translated: "and I would not give him anything"; in other words, the soldier would not pay a scribe (/sōpēr/ ספר) anything to read the letter for him. However, this reading is also problematic, as it cannot easily account for the extra *n*. Perhaps it is the infamous enclitic *nun*; however, in SBH this is spelled either *ʾtnnw* (אתננו) or *ʾtnhw* (אתנהו),[27] never, as we have in Lachish 3, *ʾtnnhw* (אתננהו). Rather than understanding this as Aramaic influence, it again seems prudent to consider the possibility that the variant simply arises from a writer with rudimentary training.

In short, the linguistic idiosyncrasies of the Letter of a Literate Soldier reflect a quite basic level of literacy that a junior officer might be expected to have. In this respect, the accusations of the superior officer, which prompted the junior officer's impassioned defense of his reading skills, were probably quite justified. Given the importance of clear and accurate writing in military communiqués, it made sense for the senior commander to request that the junior officer get a scribe. What is more remarkable is that he had to ask at all, and then that the junior officer is so offended at his request! This letter is powerful evidence pointing to seminal changes in the social fabric of society during the late Judean monarchy and the impact that the spread of writing could have on Hebrew itself.

A WORKER'S JUDICIAL PLEA

Another ostracon, known as the Yavneh Yam ostracon, discovered at a small military fortress on the Mediterranean coast just south of the modern city of Tel Aviv, also speaks to the spread of writing and literature in the late Judean monarchy.[28] The ostracon can be dated to about 600 B.C.E. and was found in a guardroom of the fortress that served as an agricultural administrative center at the end of the Judean monarchy. The text is a judicial plea from an agricultural worker complaining that his garment was unjustly confiscated.

yšmʿ ʾdny.hšr	ישמע אדני·השר	(1)
ʾt dbr.ʿbdk	את דבר עבדה·עבדכ	(2)
qṣr.hyh.ʿbdk.bḥ	קצר·היה·עבדכ·בח	(3)
ṣr ʾsm.wyqṣr ʿbdk	צר אסמ·ויקצר עבדכ	(4)
wykl wʾsmkymm. lpny šb	ויכל ואסמ כימכ·לפני שב	(5)
t kʾšr kl [ʿ]bdk ʾt qṣr wʾ	ת כאשר כל [ע]בדכ את קצר וא	(6)
sm kymm wybʾ.hwšʿyhw bn šb	סמ כימכ ויבא·הושעיהו בנ שב	(7)
y.wyqḥ.ʾt bgd ʿbdk kʾšr klt	י·ויקח·את בגד עבדכ כאשר כלת	(8)
ʾt qṣry zh ymm lqḥ.ʾt bgd ʿbdk	את קצרי זה ימכ לקח·את בגד עבדכ	(9)
wkl ʾḥy.yʿnw ly.hqṣrm ʾty bḥm	וכל אחי·יענו לי·הקצרמ אתי בחמ	(10)
hšmš ʾḥy.yʿnw ly.ʾmn nqty.mʾ	השמש אחי·יענו לי·אמנ נקתי·מא	(11)
[šm whʾ gzl ʾt] bgdy wʾm lʾ.lšr lhš	[שמ והא גזל את] בגדי ואמ לא·לשר להש	(12)

[b ʾt bgd] ʿb[dk wtt]n ʾlw.rḥ	[ב את בגד] עב[דכ ותת]נ אלו·רח	(13
[mm whš]bt ʾt [bgd ʿ]bdk wlʾ tdhm [. . .]	[מׄמׄ והש]בת את [בגד ע]בדכ ולא תדהמׄ [. . .]	(14

> May my lord, the official, hear the matter of his servant. Your servant was reaping, your servant was in Hatzar Asam; and, your servant reaped, and he finished. Now it was stored as usual before the Sabbath. At the time your [se]rvant completed the reaping and it was stored as usual; then, Hoshayahu son of Shobay came, and he took your servant's garment. When I had finished my reaping at that time, a few days ago, he took your servant's garment. All my companions will testify for me, all who were reaping with me in the heat of the sun; my brothers will testify for me. Truly, I am innocent from any gu[ilt. Please return] my garment. If the official does not consider it an obligation to retur[n your] ser[vant's garment, then please hav]e pi[ty] upon him [and ret-]urn your [se]rvant's [garment]. You must not remain silent [when your servant is without his garment.]

The language of the plea, besides being rather redundant and perhaps reflecting aspects of oral speech, has a couple of striking linguistic features. First is the use of the periphrastic verbal construction, that is, the use of a participle coordinated with the verb for "to be," *hyh* (היה), in line 3 *qṣr.hyh*, "was reaping."[29] This is a verbal construction that becomes increasingly common in later stages of Hebrew, probably as a result of its regular use in Aramaic.[30] However, it is also known in some BH texts, especially LBH, as well as QH. It is a regular form in RH. This verbal construction stands in contrast to the use of the *waw* consecutive (or "preterite continuative") as a narrative tense in lines 4 and 5 (*wyqṣr, wykl*) and again in lines 7 and 8 (*wybʾ, wyqḥ*). In fact, the full construction in lines 2–3, "Your servant was working at the harvest, your servant was in Hatzar Asam," is the typical use of a temporal anchor that we find in SBH to begin a sequence of *waw* consecutives; and line 6 begins with another temporal marker, "when," that is followed by *waw* consecutives. Because the verb in SBH does not primarily mark time, the time of the action must be established by a temporal marker, in this case when they were working at the harvest. The following string of *waw* consecutives encodes not past time but a continuation of the marked time, namely, when "your servant was harvesting" or "when we finished harvesting," which happens to be in the past, as is often the case with narratives that use *waw* consecutives in SBH. Thus, we see in this text aspects of the early Hebrew verbal system that emphasized aspect (temporal markers + *waw* consecutive) as well as the later development of the verbal system (for example, the periphrastic construction) that will increasingly encode tense.

It is striking that a workman's complaint from a remote agricultural center takes a written form. The issue of a garment taken in pledge was apparently a well-known legal issue (see Exod. 22:26–27; Deut. 24:10–15; Amos 2:8). Of course, the worker need not have had any direct knowledge of the written legislation in order to file his complaint. Nevertheless, the written complaint suggests the role that Hebrew writing was coming to have in this period. It is usually assumed that the worker had a scribe write out the complaint for him. Of course, the assumption that a scribe was involved is just that—an assumption, which is predicated on the implausibility of an agricultural worker being able to write. This may or may not be well founded. The real question, however, is why the complaint needed to be written at all. The use of the written word here seems to be useful in further establishing the authority and legitimacy of the complaint. This is a noteworthy development for the social role of writing in Judean society, and it can be illustrated in other examples. It is also noteworthy linguistically. Even though the complaint is rather crude in its style, it still uses classical literary forms of SBH, like the *waw* consecutive preceded by a temporal marker to indicate the time of the event (instead of encoding time within the verb itself or using the *waw* as a tense converter, that is, a *waw* conversive). This is an aspect of the Hebrew verbal system that deteriorates in LBH and disappears in QH and RH but is nicely preserved here in a worker's complaint.

GRAFFITI

Other telling evidence for the spread of Hebrew writing is graffiti. Whereas the Letter of a Literate Soldier addresses the ability to read, graffiti points to the ability to write among nonscribal classes. The two most important ancient Hebrew graffiti are the Khirbet el-Qôm inscriptions and the Khirbet Beit-Lei inscription.

The most well known corpus of graffiti was discovered in the burial caves at Khirbet el-Qôm.[31] The inscriptions are well known for their lack of religious orthodoxy. One graffito, for example, asks for a blessing "for his Asherah," *wlʾšhrth* (ולאשרתה). The workman may have known how to write, but he was apparently not well versed in monotheism! Although the inscription is clear enough, there are several problems in interpreting it.

1)	*ʾryhw.h⸢ʿ⸣šr.ktbh*	אריהו.ה[ע]שר.כתבה	Uriyahu, the ?, inscribed it.
2)	*brk.ʾryhw.lyhwh*	ברכ.אריהו.ליהוה	Blessed be Uriyahu to Yahweh;
3)	*wmṣryh.lʾšrth.hwšʿ lh*	ומצריה.לאשרתה.הושע לה	and, from his enemies, for Asherah, may save him.
4)	*ldnyhw*	לדניהו	For Daniyahu

5) *wl'šrhth* ולאשרתה And for his Asherah
6) [*wl'š*]*r*[*ht*]*h* [ולאש]ר[ת]ה [And for] his [Ashe]ra[h]

I have provided a rather wooden translation to illustrate some of the difficulties. First, the title of Uriyahu in line 1 is unclear. Some read the word as *h'šr*, "the rich one," which makes little sense but seems to be the most straightforward reading for the actual inscription. Dropping the *'ayin* gives the more intelligible reading *hšr*, "the official," which might be explained as an error or as resulting from a flaw in the rock surface. Second, the word order of line 3 is strange. The most elegant solution would be to see it as another scribal error, in this case switching the order of "and for Asherah" and "from his enemies." This yields the translation of lines 2–3 as "Blessed be Uriah to Yahweh and to Asherah. And, from his enemies, save him." Line 4 seems to be a disconnected personal name, though it may be a specification of "to him" from the end of line 3, that is, "save him, that is, Daniyahu." This, however, is an awkward solution. Finally, line 5 seems to be a disconnected repetition of "and for his Asherah." Finally, it is often observed that proper nouns—that is, Asherah—do not take suffixes in SBH, yet this is exactly what we seem to have in the construction *'šrth*, "*his* Asherah." The same grammatical construction can be seen in Kuntillet 'Ajrud ostraca 18:1 and 19:7, and therefore it cannot be considered a simple grammatical error. Yet, the Hebrew word *'šrh* can be either a common noun meaning "sacred pole" or a personal name, "Asherah," and this might account for the unusual grammatical construction. Given the nature of the inscription, namely, a graffito scrawled in a tomb, the unusual grammatical construction might simply reflect vernacular. It is also possible that it reflects the limited scribal training of the writer of these graffiti.

Another, less well-known graffito from Khirbet el-Qôm provides the identity of the writer, namely, a tomb cutter who asks for a blessing upon himself. It reads:

> *brk ḥṣrk/yškb bzh zqnm* (ברכ|חצרכ/ישכב|בזה|זקנמ). (Blessed be your stone cutter. May he rest in this place, [in] old age.)

The two lines are separated by a considerable space and should be considered separate topics (and might even be considered separate inscriptions, though they are written by the same hand). Such graffiti are not uncommon in the ancient world, but what is interesting here is the social class of the person who inscribes the graffiti. Ancient graffiti can usually be ascribed to scribes or bureaucrats doodling away under assorted circumstances. In the case of the Khirbet el-Qôm graffiti, the author identifies himself as the tomb cutter. This again suggests a type of craftsman literacy that seems to have been rather commonplace in Judah during the late monarchy.

Another group of five inscriptions was discovered scrawled in the burial caves near Khirbet Beit-Lei, about five miles east of Lachish. They date to the end of the Judean monarchy,[32] but the graffiti are difficult to decipher in the soft limestone. They are usually understood to have been written by refugees from the Babylonian invasion of Judah in the early sixth century, but it is difficult to make any linguistic comments about the Hebrew because of the uncertainty of the readings.[33] When we add to this the linguistic ambiguity inherent in graffiti as a genre, it becomes even more ambiguous. Nevertheless, there is a literary quality to the first inscription, which appears to be a psalm praising *yhwh ʾlhy kl hʾrṣ* (יהוה אלהי כל הארץ), "Yahweh, the God of all the earth," and *ʾlhy yršlm* (אלהי ירשלם), "the God of Jerusalem." As such, it reflects the use of Hebrew writing to address religious feelings in an unofficial context.

What is the purpose of such writing? In part, it seems to underscore the increasing role that writing played throughout Judean society of the late monarchy period. At the same time, graffiti do seem to draw from the use of writing in magic rituals to express power. In both the Khirbet el-Qôm and the Khirbet Beit-Lei inscriptions, the writing asks for blessing or good wishes for those who did the writing. It may be inferred that the act of writing itself actuates the blessings and the desires of those writing the graffiti. Although writing may become more mundane through its use for a variety of mundane purposes, it does not lose it sacred character.

KETEF HINNOM SILVER AMULETS

In a tomb just outside the walls of Jerusalem, archaeologist Gabriel Barkay excavated two small silver amulets, or charms, which were finely engraved with more than twenty lines.[34] The amulets were in a burial depository within a tomb complex located on the western shoulder of the Hinnom Valley, on the old road that would have led from Jerusalem toward Bethlehem. The archaeological context requires that these amulets be dated to the late seventh century B.C.E.[35] The text of the amulets paraphrases two well-known biblical passages. The first is the priestly blessing known from Numbers 6:24–26, "May YHWH bless you and keep you. May YHWH make his face to shine upon you and give you peace! May he be gracious to you. May YHWH lift up his face upon you." The second passage is the well-known text from Deuteronomy 7:9: "Know, therefore, that only YHWH your God is God, the steadfast God who keeps His covenant faithfully to the thousandth generation of those who love Him and keep His commandments." This latter text continued to be an important text in the Second Temple period (see Dan. 9:4; Neh. 1:5).[36] The use of these biblical texts in amulets, furthermore, seems to be an attempt to literally carry out the injunction of the *shema*, namely, "Bind them [the teaching] as a sign on your hand and let them serve as a symbol on your forehead; *inscribe* them on the doorposts of your house and on your gates" (Deut. 6:8–9). Indeed, writing on the doorposts (the *mezuzot*) became a Jewish tradition practiced even today. The use of these amulets might be regarded as an early expression of the later practice of using phylacteries (or tefillin; see Matt. 25:3; *m. Shevu'ot* 3:8, 11). Wisdom literature mentions the wearing of words of wisdom around the neck, on the fingers, or on the chest (see Prov. 1:9; 3:3; 6:21; 7:3); however, usually this is understood metaphorically. What is notable about the development of this tradition is that it is the text from a particular book, the Torah, that is to be written on the doorposts, in the phylacteries, or—in the present case—on amulets.

These two amulets would not have been unique. They were not one-of-a-kind objects. We must assume that these chance finds represent a much larger phenomenon in the late monarchic period. People would use inscribed texts as amulets that were worn around the neck. We also have examples of writing used on doors, gates, and even in the foundations of buildings as protection. Although such writing was not intended to be read, it speaks to the religious power that *written* texts came to have in the late Judean monarchy.

The Use of Vowel Letters in Standard Biblical Hebrew

The generally accepted view of the history of vowel letters is that they were first introduced in Aramaic by the ninth century and subsequently Hebrew borrowed this spelling convention.[37] This influence of Aramaic upon Hebrew is seen as developing from the Assyrians' use of Aramaic as a lingua franca for their dealings with the west, with the most well-known example in the biblical account of the Assyrians at the gates of Jerusalem in 701 B.C.E. At that time, the Assyrian king Sennacherib was campaigning in the southern Levant in response to Hezekiah's carefully planned rebellion against Assyrian hegemony, and the Assyrians came to Jerusalem, where negotiations for surrender took place. The Judean officials requested that Aramaic be spoken rather than Hebrew, which indicates that Judean scribes had transnational training (see 2 Kings 18:26; Isa. 36:11). The Assyrians apparently sent administrators with training in Aramaic, namely the LÚA.BA scribes (*sepīru*), who spread Assyrian administration and ideology into the new provinces of the empire.[38] Judean scribes—those responsible for the composition and editing of the Hebrew Bible—would likely have learned Aramaic from Assyrian administrators, so it is hardly surprising that Aramaic influence creeps into biblical texts as well as Epigraphic Hebrew of the late Iron II period. One major contribution to Hebrew from the ^{LÚ}A.BA, or Aramaic-writing, scribes may have been the introduction of vowel letters. It is also through the use of vowel letters that both Hebrew and Aramaic distinguish themselves from Phoenician writing during the eighth and seventh centuries B.C.E.

For decades, the classic study of orthography in ancient Hebrew was the monograph *Early Hebrew Orthography: A Study of the Epigraphic Evidence* by Frank Moore Cross and David Noel Freedman. They argued that "orthographic patterns followed rigid laws."[39] Yet orthographic patterns only follow rigid laws when there are official standards and standard keepers to enforce them. In our own times, social media (for example, texting, instant messaging, e-mail) all demonstrate that rigid laws of spelling and grammar can quickly disintegrate without the social structures to enforce the standards. Moreover, the neogrammarian approach that has dominated historical Hebrew linguistics has largely focused on the reconstruction of phonology—that is, vernacular—even though the evidence is exclusively textual. It now needs to be rethought in the context of the linguistics of writing systems. Modern linguistic studies of spelling and writing systems would tend to support the basic line of Cross and Freedman's argumentation, namely, that spelling conventions tend to be fixed and show extraordinary conservatism. Changes in spelling, however, follow social and political changes, particularly as they affect the training of scribes, and do not necessarily closely mirror dialect geography. For example, we know from later Punic inscriptions that vernacular Phoenician probably had the most aggressive implementation of the so-called Canaanite shift—that is, /ā/ to /ō/—extending even to the shift of short-*a* vowels; at the same time, written Phoenician was the most conservative, even though the Phoenician spoken language underwent dramatic phonetic changes that only appear beginning in the fifth century B.C.E. in Punic (that is, the writing of Phoenician with Greek letters). The case of Phoenician demonstrates how radical changes in speech forms often do not show up in written texts until major political or social changes occur—in the Phoenician case, the rise of Hellenism and the use of the Greek alphabetic writing system to write Phoenician (which we then call "Punic"). Whereas the Phoenician orthography remained quite stable between the tenth and fifth centuries B.C.E., the Hebrew writing system showed significant innovations, particularly in its use of vowel letters.

To be sure, the introduction of vowel letters into West Semitic writing systems appears already with the Ugaritic *cuneiform* alphabet by the fourteenth century B.C.E. Whereas the later Phoenician *linear* alphabet had no vowel letters whatsoever, Ugaritic had already introduced three vowel letters—*ʾa*, *ʾi*, and *ʾu*—in conjunction with the presumed "glottal stop" (that is, the Semitic letter *ʾaleph*). Presumably, this innovation in Ugaritic was influenced by the cuneiform (Akkadian) writing system, which was the primary writing system for West Semitic scribes during the second millennium B.C.E. The Phoenician linear alphabet itself, however, was an adaptation of the vowel-less Egyptian hieroglyphic writing system; therefore, any introduction of vowels into the system was a further step in its innovation. Phoenician did not make this innovation until the language began to be written in Greek letters. Aramaic, by contrast, already began to show this innovation by the ninth century B.C.E. We may posit that the introduction of vowel letters in Aramaic was also an influence of bilingual Akkadian-Aramaic scribes who saw the utility of vowel letters. Once the concept was introduced among scribes who worked transnationally, the innovation spread and was adapted locally for Hebrew. Vowel letters already appeared in Hebrew inscriptions of the late eighth century and became quite prominent by the seventh century B.C.E. Yet, no standardized use of vowel letters can be discerned in Hebrew during the Iron Age.

Scribal Schools for Standard Biblical Hebrew

Linguistic standardization requires strict political or social control of writing. This might be accomplished either within strong government political structures or within narrowly circumscribed scribal schools. Though there was movement toward a much more urbanized society in Judah and a stronger centralized government in Jerusalem, these trends were apparently accompanied by the breakdown of narrowly controlled writing in scribal schools. And, as a result, it is worth recognizing that there is no strict standardization of Hebrew during the Iron Age, especially after we begin to see the proliferation of writing and its use outside of scribal classes.

There is little evidence for the equivalent of the Mesopotmian *edubba*, or scribal school, in ancient Judah. There may be a variety of explanations for this, but it is probably not ideal to simply argue that an elaborate scribal school system existed but we have not found the evidence yet. To begin with, Mesopotamian and Egyptian were different cultures with much larger and richer bureaucracies than ancient Judah had. As a result, it is not surprising that far more elaborate structures for the education of scribes developed in those places. Writing had a rather circumscribed role as an administrative and communicative tool in the Levant in the second millennium and into the first millennium B.C.E. In addition, based on comparative evidence, we may assume that scribal schools were based on a family apprenticeship system. The clients for their skills were primarily the palace and, to a lesser extent, the temple, but in the small and relatively poor kingdoms of the Levant, there was only a limited need for writing.

Writing is fundamentally a luxury good, and the spread of writing and growth of the scribal profession was likewise a reflex of the economic realities of the Near East. David Jamieson-Drake in his book *Scribes and Schools in Monarchic Judah* reminds us of some aspects required for luxury items.[40] These include the ability of elites to provide them with support, regional trade, technology, and the evidence of economic control systems (for example, standardized weights, seals). The elite support of scribes is nicely underscored by the Egyptian Papyrus Anastasi when it urges, "Be a scribe. It saves you from toil and protects you from all manner of work."[41] The larger and more wealthy the economy, the more scribes it could support. On the one hand, archaeologists have noted the lack of imported pottery in Judah before the seventh century B.C.E., and on the other hand, there is significant evidence of economic control systems in the Iron IIB–C period (725–586 B.C.E.). It is hardly surprising then that the flourishing of writing—a luxury item—coincided with the economic development of the late monarchy. It is within this context that scribes must have begun to proliferate. Yet, there was no background for a large, well-developed system of scribal schools for the late Judean monarchy.

Even in Mesopotamia, the location of scribal schools was in small family settings and not under direct state control. In the Levant, scribal schools developed in a wider regional context, as is evidenced by the use of the Phoenician alphabet from the southern Levant, along the coast, and up into Asia Minor and Syria. The localization of scribal schools had to be predicated on the growth of local economies and bureaucracy that we see in the late Iron Age, but the growing number of Judean scribes was not under direct institutional direction or control. Ironically then, the growth of writing did not necessarily result in either a higher quality of writing or a rigid standardization in writing.

The best example of the lack of standardization is in the variable-spelling practices that we see in Hebrew inscriptions dating to the late monarchy. Perhaps not surprisingly, this variable spelling continues into the Hebrew Bible itself and has been the subject of more than one monograph.[42] James Barr, in particular, vividly illustrates the variable spelling that we find in the Hebrew Bible. He lists, for example, different spellings of *ephod* (*ʾpd* and *ʾpwd*) and the word for "generations," *toledot* (*tldt*, *twldt*, *tldwt*, and *twldwt*). Indeed, as Barr notes, "the variability of the biblical spelling is one of its fundamental characteristics."[43] Barr raises the question of whether these differences should be understood as resulting at a linguistic level or at a scribal level. Both of Barr's categories actually refer to ways of relating the transcription of speech into text; however, this is not the best way to understand spelling practices, since (as we have discussed in the opening chapter) writing is not a transcription system. Rather, learned spelling practices are usually related to social and ideological conventions rather than the scribe's attempt to reproduce a precise linguistic transcription of speech. Indeed, while the introduction of vowels does bring us one step closer to transcription, the intermittent use of vowel letters in Hebrew hardly makes ancient Hebrew writing a real attempt at transcription.

The variable spelling of Hebrew should hardly be surprising, and it is actually the expected orthographic practice. In English, for example, variable spellings were quite common in Old and Middle English, even in writings from the same scribe.[44] Furthermore, Alan Millard has pointed out that variable spelling is quite typical for the Near East in antiquity.[45] Indeed, the cuneiform and hieroglyphic writing systems certainly lent themselves to variable spelling practices. In contrast, Phoenician was quite standardized in its orthography. Standard Phoenician spelling changed very little from the tenth century through the fifth century B.C.E. However, Phoenician was also an austere writing system that used only consonants; in this respect, it was certainly not a transcription system. To be sure, there were dialectal varieties of Phoenician, particularly from Byblos, that had their own orthography, but these too seem to be quite stable.[46] Likewise, Ugaritic has a relatively stable orthography. The introduction of vowel letters, however, introduces an extraordinary opportunity for variability in spelling. The spread of writing outside of a small and narrow cadre of scribal schools further exacerbated the variability of spelling that we witness in Hebrew inscriptions from the late monarchy as well as in the Hebrew Bible.

The employ of the scribal profession within the palace is well known from biblical texts from the late Iron Age.[47] For example, the book of Jeremiah mentioned that a "scribal chamber" was located within the palace (36:12), and the scribe Baruch was familiar in the halls of the palace (vv. 11–20). Scribes were part of the royal bureaucracy, and some even had the title Scribe of the King; moreover, royal scribes were also involved with matters related to the temple and the temple economy (for example, 2 Kings 12:11; 22:3). One scribe named Jonathan has his house converted by the government officials into a prison (Jer. 37:15–20). There were military scribes (2 Kings 18:18; 25:19; Jer. 52:25), and scribes were associated with the keeping of royal chronicles (for example 1 Kings 11:41; 14:19, 29). Judean scribes were apparently bilingual—knowing both Hebrew and Aramaic (2 Kings 18:26). The Assyrians used Aramaic as an imperial lingua franca for their administration. As a result, there is little evidence to suggest Judean scribes would have had a direct knowledge of Akkadian; there is, for example, little evidence of cuneiform found in excavations in Israel dating to the Neo-Assyrian period.[48] The burgeoning palace and the government bureaucracy were, not surprisingly, main employers for the scribes. Yet, in spite of this, there is no direct evidence for a royal scribal school or the institutionalization of the scribal profession in Judah.

Democratization of Hebrew Writing in Judah

Writing was democratized in Judah during the late monarchy. What do we mean by *democratization*? The term describes the spread of writing through a variety of social classes in Judah during the late eighth through early sixth centuries B.C.E. Imperialism and urbanization were the critical social processes that would enable writing as a technology of communication to break free of the closed circles of the scribal elite. These social processes were precipitated, first of all, by the Assyrian conquests in the Levant. For the Assyrians, urbanization was a political strategy that allowed the Assyrians to utilize the periphery of their empire for the greatest benefit to the center.[49] Urbanization led to the increased use of writing in government bureaucracy and the economy. Writing would thus become a more common technology throughout Judah in the late monarchic period.

The sudden and precipitous increase in both the quantity and variety of texts in the late Iron Age also raises interesting comparative issues. The changes in Judean society beginning in the late eighth century can account for the remarkable increase in the epigraphic evidence. And as Joachim Latacz notes in his study of ancient Greece, "the beginning of textuality in early literate cultures can regularly be deduced from a sudden increase in the quantity of texts."[50] This increase in the number and type of texts also speaks to the beginning of textuality in ancient Judah. Textuality, however, is not simply a scribal phenomenon. Rather, what makes this emerging textuality interesting is the spread of writing among nonscribal classes. For example, a significant number of Hebrew seals are written rather crudely, reflecting writing among nonelites. Texts like the Letter of a Literate Soldier, the judicial plea from Mesad Hashavyahu, and the graffiti from Khirbet el-Qôm and Khirbet Beit-Lei only serve to further suggest that Hebrew writing had spread outside of scribal classes. It should hardly be surprising that the religious reforms of Josiah were predicated on a written text found in the temple (see

1 Kings 22–23), whereas prophets like Isaiah or Hosea never quote texts to prove their cases. Jeremiah revealingly complains that the *torah*—that is, "teaching"—had become a text in the late Judean monarchy (Jer. 8:8). Indeed, texts like the Ketef Hinnom amulets certainly confirm that Hebrew as a written language became religiously important during the late monarchy.

The democratization of writing raises the question of literacy rates in ancient Judah. The question of literacy in turn raises the problem of defining literacy and then quantifying literacy. For example, the Assyrians developed a two-tier system of literacy among scribes and bureaucrats. There is evidence from seals, seal impressions, and administrative texts for a higher rate of mundane literacy, but it is almost impossible to quantify literacy rates. The arguments for widespread literacy have followed several paths. Some have argued for literacy even in the premonarchic period, as illustrated by a commonly cited story about the "young lad of Sukkoth" who could read and write (Judg. 9:14). Biblical texts thus become a basis for the argument for early and widespread literacy in Israel. Such arguments beg several questions. Foremost, there is debate about the dating of the biblical stories and then about the historical value of such anecdotal tales. For this reason scholars have increasingly looked to epigraphic and archaeological evidence. The sharp increase in the number and variety of inscriptions in the late eighth century B.C.E. makes it a more likely setting for broadening of literacy. Likewise, the societal changes (urbanization, globalization) accompanying the rise of the Assyrian Empire point to the late Judean monarchy as a more plausible setting for the spread of literacy. Naysayers, however, are quick to point out that such archaeological and epigraphic evidence "cannot lead to secure results."[51] The evidence, however, does point to a decisive shift toward increasing literacy, even if the extent will be impossible to measure precisely. More important, the evidence points to a more central role that writing had in Judean society.

The necessary ambiguities in interpreting the evidence have naturally (and correctly) urged investigation into theoretical frameworks for literacy. Indeed, ancient literacy has been a hotly debated topic among social theorists from many disciplines. Some scholars, such as Jack Goody, Walter Ong, and Eric Havelock, have argued for early literacy, especially in ancient Greece.[52] Others, such as William Harris, have been quite critical of exaggerated claims for widespread literacy and its cultural implications.[53] Harris, for example, argues that the printing press was necessary in order to produce inexpensive texts and that there was only "a rather low level of craftsman's literacy without the printing press."[54] Harris also points out that extensive school systems are necessary to achieve majority literacy and that "rural patterns of living are inimical to the spread of literacy."[55] Harris sees the Industrial Revolution as a turning point in economic complexity, wherein education was held to be indispensable to the state's economic well-being. Finally, there must be a widespread ideology that values reading and writing. Harris downplays the substantive shift on the orality-literacy continuum, namely, the shift from widespread illiteracy toward widespread yet mundane literacy. If modern standards of literacy are applied to the ancient world, then it will come up short. Yet, there were technological advances in writing technology, changes toward a more urban society, and movement toward a more global and complex economy in the late Iron Age that set the stage for a seminal shift along the orality-literacy continuum. Moreover, recent studies have noted that the spread of literacy need not be unidirectional—that is, from the public to the private sector.[56] Additionally, the shift from oral authority toward textual authority can also serve ideological causes. In Judah, the numerous seal impressions, jar inscriptions, and graffiti make it clear that writing was widely employed for economic reasons and outside of the government administration or the temple cult. Although an extensive school system might be necessary for advanced literacy, it was not for mundane literacy. In sum, Harris defines literacy too narrowly and along modern standards. As Susan Niditch has emphasized, orality and literacy exist along a continuum.[57] For the present purposes, it is important to note the decisive shift that takes place along this continuum. This shift is marked by the large number of epigraphic remains in Hebrew during the late Iron Age that point to a process of democratization of Hebrew writing.

"Distinctiveness" in Language and Literature

One reflex of the nationalistic sentiments that emerged in ancient Israel is the obsession in biblical literature with Israel's distinctiveness. Not surprisingly, this topic of distinctiveness has been the subject of some reflection by biblical scholars.[58] By *distinctiveness*, I refer to the self-perception of Israel as a chosen people that is reflected in the Bible. It is, of course, quite typical of ancient peoples to think of themselves as special or chosen, and examples can certainly be cited from ancient Egypt or Mesopotamia. Moreover, I should hasten to add that we are *not* interested in the problem of Israel's actual distinctiveness within her Near Eastern context. Scholars have long debated the extent of ancient Israel's distinctiveness, and much of the recent quest for Israel's distinctiveness stems from modern religious and ideological sensibilities.[59] Or scholars have tended to diminish the unique aspects of ancient

Israel. The present issue then is not Israel's actual distinctiveness but rather how Israel perceived itself.

The scholarly discussion may be understood, to some extent, as also arising from the Bible's own obsession with Israel's distinctiveness. Peter Machinist has adroitly suggested that it was Israel's comparative "newness," especially when seen against her Near Eastern neighbors like Egypt or Babylon, whose histories stretched back into the prehistoric periods, that motivated the biblical attempts to highlight Israel's uniqueness and distinctiveness.[60] The rulers in Jerusalem could not compete with Babylon or Thebes in grandeur or antiquity, but their scribes were involved in forging an identity of distinctiveness in religion, land, and language. In the words of the Deuteronomist:

> It was not because you were more numerous than any other people that Yahweh set his heart on you and chose you—for you were the fewest of all peoples. It was because Yahweh loved you and kept the oath that he swore to your ancestors, that Yahweh has brought you out with a mighty hand, and redeemed you from the house of slavery, from the hand of Pharaoh king of Egypt. (Deut. 7:7–8)

Not merely were the people chosen, but also the land, as the Deuteronomist makes clear:

> . . . the land that Yahweh swore to your ancestors to give them and to their descendants, a land flowing with milk and honey. For the land that you are about to enter to occupy is not like the land of Egypt, from which you have come, where you sow your seed and irrigate by foot like a vegetable garden. But the land that you are crossing over to occupy is a land of hills and valleys, watered by rain from the sky, a land that Yahweh your God looks after . . . (Deut. 11:9–12)

In the Bible, the Hebrew word *Judah* refers to the territory (Judah), the people (Judeans), and the language (Judean) of the small kingdom in the southern hills of Palestine. As linguistic anthropologists have pointed out, the multiple applications of this term imply a certain conceptual universe. Judeans were part of an ethnic group ("Judeans"), spoke a distinct language ("Judean"), and lived within distinct borders ("Judah").

With regard to a distinct national dialect (as mentioned earlier), the language of the kingdom of Judah is first called "Judean" in a story set in the late eighth century B.C.E.[61] Judean officials plead with an Assyrian emissary of Sennacherib to speak Aramaic rather than Judean: "Please speak to your servants in the Aramaic language, for we understand it; do not speak to us in the Judean language within the hearing of the people who are on the wall" (2 Kings 18:26, compare Isa. 36:11; also see 2 Chron. 32:18).

In contrast, the term *Hebrew* (*ʿbryt*, עברית) does not appear as a linguistic description in the Bible.[62] Perhaps the earliest biblical reference to the Hebrew language, in Isaiah 19:18, refers to speaking "the language of Canaan" (*śpt knʿn*) in the land of Egypt; in this case, the use of the term *Canaan* probably reflects a more general population as well as the literary contrast with Egypt. In Jewish literature of late antiquity, Hebrew is usually called "the holy language," with reference to the biblical corpus, and the "language of the sages," when referring to the language of the oral tradition—what is called Mishnaic or Rabbinic Hebrew. When the term *Hebrew* first appears in the Bible (for example, Gen. 14:13; 39:14; 41:12; Exod. 2:11; Jon. 1:9), it refers not to a language but rather to an ethnicity. It occurs almost always as a synonym of the more commonly encountered "sons of Israel" when the in-group came in contact with the out-group; that is, *Hebrew* often seems to be a pejorative description of the Israelites used by foreigners. Only with reference to the categorization of native-born versus foreign slaves does it appear as an in-group ethnic term (Exod. 21:2; Deut. 15:12). Though the term *Hebrew* as a language reference appears in the Talmud, it rarely refers to what we call the Hebrew language. In one citation, most opinions assert that *Hebrew* refers to some Aramaic dialect (*b. Megillah* 18a). The designation *Hebrew* appears in the Talmud in one other linguistic context, referring to the old Canaanite alphabet, which is called "Hebrew writing" as contrasted with "Assyrian writing" (*b. Megillah* 3a). The newer alphabetic style, at least in the shape of its letters, replaced the older one throughout the Near East during the early Persian period, evolving into the "square character" and its cursive derivatives that are in use today. The term *Hebrew* becomes common as a linguistic term only during the last thousand years. Apparently, the term *Hebrew* as the in-group reference among Jews to their own language borrows from Arabic and was first introduced by Saadia Gaon (882–942 C.E.) in his grammatical writings.[63] This new designation for the Hebrew language spread only when Jews began to write their grammatical studies in their own language a few centuries later. The self-description of Hebrew in the Bible is "Judean," which referred to the language spoken in Judah.

Commonly Proposed Features of Epigraphic Hebrew

Epigraphic Hebrew is primarily represented by the corpus of Hebrew inscriptions from the late Iron Age, that is, from about 725 to 586 B.C.E. Though there are important inscriptions from the earlier Iron Age (discussed in chapter 3), it is best to characterize Epigraphic Hebrew by the bulk of Hebrew inscriptions from the late Judean monarchy.

Some commonly proposed features of Epigraphic Hebrew include the following:

1. Use of *-h* as the 3ms suffix (instead of SBH *-w*). For example, we find *ʿbḏh*, "his servant" (עבדה, Mesad Hashavyahu 1:2), and *-w* on plural nouns, e.g., *ʾnšw* "his men" (אנשו, Lachish 2.3:18) versus SBH *ʾnšyw* (אנשיו).
2. Standardized use of the *lamed of ownership*. This form is used on inscribed objects to designate the owner of the object, e.g., לפקח·סמדר *lpqḥ•smdr̠*, "Belonging to Pekah, SMDR-wine" (Hazor 7:1); see also the *lmlk*, "belonging to the king," jar handles.
3. Developed system for accounting and record keeping (note Jer. 32:10). This consisted of standardized use of columns, hieratic numbers, and abbreviations for measurements and quantities, e.g., use of columns and hieratic numbers in Kadesh Barnea 6; the use of *b-* in Arad 2:2 as an abbreviation for the measurement *bt*, "bath."
4. Use of *matres lectionis*. The *waw* represents a /u/ vowel, *yod* represents an /i/ vowel, and final *heh* can represent the vowels /a/, /e/, and /o/, e.g., *ʾḥyʾl*, "Achiel" (אחיאל, Jerusalem 25:1), and *ʾḥyʾb*, "Achiab" (אחיאב, Seal B 37); though, often defective spelling is employed, e.g., *ʿt* (as opposed to *ʿth*) "now" (עת), in the Arad and Lachish ostraca, and *brkt (*as opposed to *brkty*), "I bless" (ברכת, Arad 21:2; Kuntillet ʿAjrud 18:1).
5. *Plene* spelling resulting in elongated verbal forms, e.g., *šlḥth* (as opposed to SBH *šlḥt*), "you sent" (שלחתה, Lachish 3:6), *yḏʿth̠*, "you [do not] know" (ידעתה, Lachish 3:8), and *ktbth*, "you wrote" (כתבתה, Arad 7:6).
6. Use of the *waw* consecutive in narratives, e.g., *wyqḥ•ʾt bgd ʿbdk*, "And he took your servant's cloak" (ויקח·את בגד עבדכ, Mesad Hashavyahu 1:8).
7. Use of the infinitive absolute as an imperative, e.g., *ʿt•ntn•lktym*, "now give to the Kittim" (עת·נתנ·לכתימ, Arad 1:2).
8. Use of the periphrastic construction to denote ongoing events set in the past, e.g., *qṣr•hyh•ʿbdk*, "your servant was harvesting" (קצר·היה·עבדכ, Mesad Hashavyahu 1:3).
9. Regular usage of both the definite article *h-* and the accusative particle *ʾt* (את), e.g., *qrʾty•ʾth*, "I read it" (קראתי·אתה, Lachish 3:12).

6

Hebrew in Exile

Linguistic subjugation (or unification, depending on one's point of view) is an important strategy in implementing political subjugation (or unification).

—Peter Trudgill

The Babylonian exile is where the waters part in the history of the Hebrew language. It marks major changes to take place in the Hebrew speech and scribal communities during the sixth century B.C.E. In a series of military campaigns, the Babylonian armies decimated Judah, burned the city of Jerusalem, and ravaged the economy of the region. The first campaign came in 597 B.C.E. At that time the Babylonians deported a large number of Judeans, including the royal family of Jehoiachin. A second campaign in 586 B.C.E. resulted in the burning of Jerusalem and the countryside. The Babylonians set up a provisional government, and in 581 the Babylonians returned and took another group of Judeans into exile. The vernacular language was not unscathed by the conquest of the land, yet it would survive. The standard Hebrew literary dialect develops in the late eighth century, and it disappears by the end of the sixth century B.C.E.

The Babylonian invasions affected the spoken and the written Hebrew languages differently. A spoken vernacular survived along with the remnant of the Judeans who remained in the land. Vernacular languages tend to survive as long as there is no physical displacement of the *speech community*.[1] Demographic upheaval would mark the beginnings of a major disruption of the Hebrew speech communities, but some Judean villages did remain in the land, and such villages continued to speak their own Hebrew vernacular. Written languages, however, require social, economic, and political infrastructures to survive. War, exile, dispersion, and economic blight signaled an end to Hebrew scribal schools. The writing of the Hebrew language lost its social location and institutional support—that is, the palace, the temple, and the marketplaces of ancient Judah. Although the infrastructure for Hebrew scribes in Judah was decimated by the Babylonians, Hebrew writing did survive in exile. In the archaeological record, Hebrew written artifacts disappear in Judah during the early sixth century B.C.E. Yet, Hebrew scribes were deported to Babylon along with the royal family, and scribes resided among the Judean royal family and its entourage in comfort in the royal citadel of Babylon while being supplied generous rations by the Babylonian government. Although the Babylonian conquests and exiles decimated the Judean people, some remnant of the scribal infrastructure of the royal family remained intact through the end of the sixth century B.C.E.

Ironically, the exile is sometimes considered the period of a great flourishing of Hebrew writing—the birth of the Bible as literature. Yet the circumstances hardly allow for such an interpretation.[2] The epigraphic evidence yields little indication that Hebrew even continued to be written. The exile supposedly provoked a creative burst of literary energy, and the destruction of Jerusalem led Judeans to preserve their traditions through writing. Indeed, Axel Knauf has attempted to read the town of Bethel as key to the formulation of biblical texts and the shaping of the Hebrew language. He observes that the town of Bethel is repeatedly mentioned in the Bible and argues that Bethel is an exilic and postexilic town and that its prominent mention in the Bible can only reflect the exilic and postexilic production of the Bible.[3] However, this reading is based on a misunderstanding of the archaeology of Bethel. As Israel Finkelstein has pointed out, Bethel was actually destroyed in the late eighth century B.C.E. and was sparsely occupied thereafter.[4] Therefore, Knauf's main biblical argument based on the prominence of Bethel in biblical narratives actually fits best in the late eighth century as opposed to the Babylonian and Persian periods, when the site had essentially disappeared. More generally, it should be noted that war and exile actually invite retrenchment rather than intense literary activity. The suggestion that writing was a natural response to the attempt to preserve culture is a modern text-centric response—the reaction of our post-Gutenberg world. Ancient Israel, however, was a society of emerging textuality at the end of the Judean monarchy. Textual creation was not a natural cultural response to war, exile, economic blight, and slavery. The written Hebrew language would survive in spite of the Babylonian exile, not because of it!

Hebrew in the Land

Archaeological excavations and surveys have increasingly pointed to drastic changes in the demographics of the southern Levant, which underscore the impact of the Babylonian exile. The population of Judah decreased markedly during the Babylonian period because of war, exile, and flight. Yet, some people certainly remained in the land. The question remains only about the extent of demographic changes. How many villages remained unscathed by the Babylonian invasions? How many people remained in the land? The answers to these questions are critical to understanding the extent to which Hebrew would have continued to be spoken in the Babylonian (and later Persian) province of Yehud.

Recent archaeological investigations have increasingly laid bare the fury of the Babylonian destruction of Jerusalem, Judah, and the entire Levant. Ephraim Stern, for example, contrasts the Babylonian and Assyrian presence in Judah: "The Babylonians waged far fewer military campaigns for the domination of Palestine than the Assyrians, and the number of written sources at our disposal describing these is likewise much smaller. However, the results of the Babylonian conquest were, by all measures, far more destructive, and brought the once-flourishing country to one of the lowest ebbs in its long history."[5] On the one hand, the scope and ferocity of the Babylonian conquest is becoming increasingly clear with each new archaeological investigation. On the other hand, the destruction was not complete.

There was also some continuity after the Babylonian exiles. We know, for example, that the Babylonians appointed a provisional governor over the province in the town of Mizpah (five miles north of Jerusalem), which—unlike the rest of Judah—was largely unscathed by the Babylonian military campaigns.[6] Even the Bible testifies, according to 2 Kings 25:12, that the Babylonians left "the poorest of the land to be vinedressers and tillers of the soil." Mizpah apparently continued to serve as a regional capital, and when the Persians overthrew the Babylonian Empire, many returnees settled in this region (for example, Ezra 2:21–28; note Neh. 3:7). Some scholars have argued that too much is made of the exile as a historical event. For example, C. C. Torrey, in his work *Ezra Studies*, published in 1910, argued that the exile was essentially a fiction created by Jewish scribes of the late Persian period: "The terms 'exilic,' 'pre-exilic,' and 'post-exilic' ought to be banished forever from usage, for they are merely misleading, and correspond to nothing that is real in Hebrew literature and life."[7] The Irish biblical scholar Robert Carroll wrote that he would like to have this sentence of Torrey's "emblazoned on all biblical history textbooks."[8] Carroll minimized the importance of the exile: "At this juncture in history the land lost some people; very much a minority of people, even important people of status were deported. *Most people lived on in the land as if nothing, except the burning of Jerusalem, had happened.*"[9] Hans Barstad, in his book *The Myth of the Empty Land*, has particularly emphasized the continuity in the material culture of Judah during the Babylonian period (ca. 586–538 B.C.E.).[10] Though it is true that the conventional nomenclature of our academic disciplines has been framed by a biblical metanarrative that was fostered in the postexilic (or Second Temple) period, ironically, biblical narratives do not isolate the exile as a discrete historical period, nor do they actually promote the notion of the "empty land."[11] The biblical metanarrative would telescope the Babylonian exile into a moment in time and portray it as a watershed of historical memory. Though this metanarrative served an important rhetorical purpose for the postexilic community, it also oversimplified and even overlooked the Babylonian period (namely, the sixth century B.C.E.). More important, an overemphasis on the exile can obscure the fate of the Hebrew language. In light of these views, we need to explore the consequences of the Babylonian conquest and exiles for the demographics and social institutions of Judah in the sixth century B.C.E.

There are two assumptions behind critiques of the exile as a major historical event. The first assumption is that the majority of the people were left in the country at the end of the Babylonian period. In other words, the demographic picture changed very little. The second assumption is that the life of the Judean people continued in much the same way. Neither of these propositions stands up to scrutiny. In fact, the demographic changes in Judah were quite profound, reflecting a substantial depopulation,[12] and Daniel Smith-Christopher has shown in his comparative sociological studies of the exile just how far-reaching and profound the experience of exile was for ancient Israel.[13] The land was not empty, but it was depopulated. This is a critical observation for any hypothesis regarding the continuity of vernacular Hebrew. Moreover, every cultural institution of Judean life changed. There was no more Davidic king. There was no temple. The marketplaces changed. Most important for our purposes, the scribal infrastructure was dispersed. Both the written and spoken language would be fundamentally influenced by the lingua franca of these times, namely, Aramaic.

We may assume that Hebrew continued to be spoken in the Judean villages that persisted into the Babylonian and Persian periods. But just how many villages were there? And, how many new villages appeared? These questions have great bearing on the nature of the speech communities of the sixth through fourth centuries. The land was considerably more empty by the end of the Babylonian period than recent critics of the exile have realized. From archaeological surveys, a relative assessment of the population demographics can be made. For example, between the seventh century (at the end of the monarchy) and the mid-fifth century B.C.E. (mid-Persian period), there is an 83.5 percent decline in the number of settlements in the region around Jerusalem.[14] This data is punctuated by evidence from tomb excavations that suggests an abrupt end to family tombs at the end of the Iron II period. The demographic decline in the number of settlements is reinforced by a similar decline in the total settled area (from 1,000 dunams at the end of the Iron Age to about 110 dunams in the Persian period)—a nearly 90 percent decline.[15] The Negev region, which had flourished in the late Iron Age, experienced a similar decline, with most of the fortresses in the region destroyed and a settlement gap that lasted until the fifth century (at the earliest) and as late as the Hellenistic period at some sites.[16] The Judean desert region east of Jerusalem was even harder hit, experiencing a 95 percent decline in settlement.[17] Even the foothills west of Jerusalem experienced about an 80 percent decline in settlement, along with the conspicuous destruction of major cities like Lachish and Timnah, and most towns did not recover until the Hellenistic period.[18] Not only was Jerusalem burned, but large cities disappeared from Judah proper. In general, there was a shift from cities to villages; excavations of cities such as Jerusalem, Lachish, and Gezer testify to great conflagrations ignited by the Babylonians in Judah.[19] These results are also confirmed by the pottery assemblages and distribution patterns that changed dramatically at the beginning of the Babylonian period.[20] The Babylonians then largely abandoned the ravaged lands.[21] It took centuries to recover. Resettlement began in the Persian period, but the flourishing of sites like Jerusalem would not take place until the Hellenistic and Roman periods.

Though the Babylonian invasions obviously marked a catastrophic change in the demographics, and consequently the speech communities, we must also be careful to acknowledge aspects of continuity. The most important area of continuity was the region of Benjamin and the town of Mizpah, the seat of the Babylonian provincial government. There was also continuity to the west of Jerusalem, where 20 percent of the villages in the foothills show continued settlement into the Persian period. Such continuity in settlement would be accompanied by linguistic continuity in speech communities. That is, these small villages would have continued to speak local Hebrew dialects even if they also might have become bilingual—Hebrew and Aramaic—through contact with the Babylonian (and later Persian) administration of the region.

The scribal transition from Hebrew to Aramaic was immediate. As David Vanderhooft has pointed out, "Scribes in regional chanceries adjusted very rapidly to master the technology, including morphology and ductus, of new scripts in whatever language dominated the administrative and commercial spheres of the region."[22] He illustrates this with a couple of examples. First, one of the earliest Yehud stamp seals (dating to the late sixth or early fifth century B.C.E.) reads, *lʾḥyb // pḥwʾ*, "belonging to Achiab, the governor." The seal is marked as Aramaic by the use of the word for "governor" with the distinctive morphology of the Aramaic definite article, the suffixed *ʾaleph*. The Aramaic script of this stamp has some archaic letter shapes (particularly the *ʾaleph*, *mem*, and *resh*) that point to a sixth-century B.C.E. date for the transition from Hebrew to Aramaic. The use of the double divider line, //, is a stylistic feature of late Iron Age Hebrew seals. Still, there is no epigraphic evidence indicating that Hebrew script was still being used during the Babylonian period. Moreover, when we begin to see paleo-Hebrew utilized again during the fourth century B.C.E., it is a revival of the Hebrew script and "not part of the organic process of continuous usage and production that initially pushed Hebrew aside in favor of Aramaic."[23] Aramaic script had completely replaced Hebrew in the Babylonian period.

Hebrew in the Babylonian Court

The fate of the Hebrew scribal infrastructure follows the monarchy into exile. According to the biblical account, "King Jehoiachin of Judah gave himself up to the king of Babylon, himself, his mother, his servants, his officers, and his palace officials" (2 Kings 25:12), and he was taken to Babylon in about 597 B.C.E. The book of Kings ends by narrating the eventual release of Jehoiachin:

> In the thirty-seventh year of the exile of King Jehoiachin of Judah, in the twelfth month, on the twenty-seventh day of the month, King Evil-merodach of Babylon, in the year that he began to reign, released King

> Jehoiachin of Judah from prison; he spoke kindly to him, and gave him a seat above the other seats of the kings who were with him in Babylon. So Jehoiachin put aside his prison clothes. Every day of his life he dined regularly in the king's presence. For his allowance, a regular allowance was given him by the king, a portion every day, as long as he lived. (2 Kings 25:27–30)

The biblical account of the fate of Jehoiachin and the royal family was essentially corroborated by an archive of 290 clay tablets discovered in the 1930s during excavations of the ancient city of Babylon.[24] These tablets date from the years 595 to 570 B.C.E. and list payments of rations in oil and barley to prominent political prisoners of Nebuchadnezzar's military campaigns. One implication of the payments "to Jehoiachin, king of Judah" (*ana* ^{I}*yaʾukinu šarri ša* ^{KUR}*yaḫudu*) described in the cuneiform tablets excavated in the Ishtar Gate is that the royal scribes of Judah worked within the Babylonian administration. Jehoiachin was treated as royalty, even though he was under house arrest by the Babylonians. Rations were supplied to Jehoiachin, the princes of Judah, and the royal Judean entourage. One representative text (Babylon 28178) may be translated as follows:

> 6 liters (of oil) for J[eh]oiachin, king of the land of Judah
> 2½ liters for the five princes of Judah
> 4 liters for the eight men of Judah

According to the Babylonian lists, the five young Judean princes had an attendant named Keniah, who received the supplies for them. The royal entourage included "eight men of Judah." Presumably, some of these were the servants, officers, and palace officials who surrendered to Nebuchadnezzar and were placed under house arrest in Babylon along with Jehoiachin. This royal entourage may have lived in the southern citadel of Babylon.[25] Jehoiachin and his exiled administration probably served as royal counsel, providing information as required about their homeland, which was in a remote region of the Babylonian Empire. We may assume that the support afforded by the royal administration in the Babylonian court allowed some Judean scribes to perpetuate their craft.

The exile thus represented both continuity and change for the written Hebrew language. There was continuity in the royal court along with its scribes who were brought into exile. Indeed, these royal scribes must have been responsible for the composition and preservation of biblical literature. There are telltale signs of scribal activity during the exilic period; for example, the fate of the exiled king Jehoiachin is the central theme of the end of the book of

Kings: 2 Kings 24–25 is essentially an exilic appendix to the book of Kings. The ending focuses on the fate of the two last Judean kings—Jehoiachin and Zedekiah—beginning with Jehoiachin's exile to Babylon and ending in the last verse with the king of Judah dining at the table of the Babylonian kings. This appendix has the exiled royal scribes telling Jehoiachin's story. This is just one example, but it illustrates the continuity of the royal scribes in writing and preserving Hebrew literature.

The exile, however, also marks the beginning of change for the Hebrew language. Hebrew was not one of the languages of the Babylonian or Persian administrations. Akkadian was the prestige language of the Babylonian court, and Aramaic would serve as an administrative language for both the Babylonian and Persian kingdoms. Not surprisingly, the Judean scribes that are said to have worked as Persian administrators were trained in Aramaic. In the court of Babylon, the Hebrew language was a cultural legacy; it was not an administrative language. Eventually, when the exiles began to return to Jerusalem, Hebrew would continue to be written—but written with dramatic changes. First of all, Hebrew would be written with Aramaic script. Indeed, this change might be compared to later Jewish languages like Yiddish, Ladino, or Dzhidi—namely, languages that mix script and grammar. In each of these cases, however, we have a dialect that is essentially local—German for Yiddish, Spanish for Ladino, and Persian for Dzhidi—using the Hebrew alphabet. After the exile, in contrast, we have Hebrew written with Aramaic letters. The mixture of language and script nevertheless creates an inevitable linguistic influence.

Akkadian Influence

During the Babylonian period there was the possibility of direct and extended contact between Hebrew scribes and the Mesopotamian "scribal school" (that is, the *edubba*). Hebrew scribes were actually living in the Babylonian court, as we can surmise from cuneiform documents. The most telling example of this contact was the borrowing into Hebrew of the Neo-Babylonian month names, which became the standard names in the Jewish calendar.[26] Indeed, according to the Jerusalem Talmud, the Jews "carried the names of the months back with them from Babylonia" (*y. Rosh HaShanah* 1:56d).

Earlier and later periods were not nearly as conducive to direct Akkadian linguistic influence. For example, the Judeans were under Assyrian influence for more than a century (from the mid-eighth through the late seventh centuries B.C.E.); however, there is little to suggest direct contact with the *edubba*.

Rather, the Assyrians sent scribes and administrators who utilized Aramaic as a scribal language. Mankowski, in his study *Akkadian Loanwords in Biblical Hebrew*, points to a large number of apparent loanwords in biblical Hebrew that are mediated through Aramaic, which he calls *trans-Akkadian* loans.[27] These are not Akkadian loanwords into Hebrew, even though their origin is Akkadian. Moreover, the Judeans would also have come to know Assyrian literary forms, such as Assyrian vassal treaties, through the Aramaic language rather than from Akkadian cuneiform. By the Persian period, Akkadian was no longer the language of the empire, since the Achaemenid Empire used Aramaic as its administrative language. Old Persian was the language of the Achaemenid rulers, and Akkadian was relegated to the status of a scholastic language of little interest to the Jews. Much earlier, in the second millennium B.C.E., Akkadian was the main writing system used in Canaan, but this predates the formation of the Judean and Israelite kingdoms and the development of the alphabetic writing system. It seems unlikely that much scribal or literary tradition can be traced to this very early period. Rather, the primary period for direct contact between Hebrew and Akkadian scribes was the sixth century B.C.E.

How should we categorize the dozens and dozens of Akkadian loanwords in Hebrew? Direct influence of Akkadian on Hebrew began in the Neo-Assyrian period. The most obvious linguistic reflex of Akkadian on Hebrew was in the use of loanwords and calques. Terms for the calendar, for example, are *culture words* (*Kulturwörter*), namely, words with high degrees of mobility that can transcend a specific time and place. Several words come to Akkadian from Sumerian and then make their way into Canaanite and Hebrew. One example of this is the word for "palace," from Sumerian É.GAL to Akkadian *ekallu* to Hebrew *hykl* /hêkāl/ [הֵיכָל], although in Hebrew *hykl* also has a semantic shift from "palace" to "temple," with the former typical of SBH and the latter typical of LBH. For the present purposes, however, we are interested not in etymological origins but rather in the language from which the term is borrowed, namely, Akkadian. Most of these terms (for example, *ekallu*) were borrowed from Akkadian into Aramaic, so that Aramaic became the vehicle through which they were transmitted. Even though a number of items on this list (adapted from Rabin) may be regarded as doubtful, the sheer number is nevertheless impressive. It testifies to the pervasive influence of Akkadian, especially in the realm of scribal traditions (for example, technical terms, treaty forms, and traditional texts used for education, like Gilgamesh or *Enuma Elish*). Another form of linguistic influence may be discerned in the adoption of Assyrian literary genres. Most prominently, the use of the treaty genre to structure the book of Deuteronomy has long been recognized as borrowing from Assyrian vassal treaties.[28] Derivative to the adoption of the Assyrian vassal treaty was the borrowing of legal concepts that were calqued into Hebrew. As William Moran has pointed out, the concepts of the "knowing God" and "loving God" in Deuteronomy borrow from Assyrian treaty language.[29] The influence of Akkadian upon SBH suggests contact between Mesopotamian and Canaanite scribal schools.

There are historical limits to the influence of Akkadian on Hebrew. Although Akkadian did not completely disappear as a language until well into the Hellenistic-Roman period, it was already being supplanted as a diplomatic language by Aramaic in the eighth century B.C.E. After the Persian conquest of the Babylonian Empire, Akkadian was merely a scholastic language, and Aramaic was the administrative language. Akkadian texts were copied and passed on, but little literature was written in Akkadian. In sum, Akkadian could no longer directly influence Hebrew in the Persian and Hellenistic periods. Rather, Akkadian influence was confined to the context of the Assyrian and Babylonian Empires' administrations. Indeed, it was the Assyrians who established an elaborate administrative and economic infrastructure throughout the Levant, which would have been the necessary mechanism through which Akkadian influenced the Hebrew language. And it was the Babylonians who hosted Judean scribes in their capital city. As a result, Akkadian loanwords are essentially part of the SBH strata of Hebrew. In contrast to Akkadian, Persian loanwords are limited to LBH; that is, they are found in biblical books composed in the postexilic period (fifth to second centuries B.C.E.; see further discussion in chapter 8). Aramaic influence, in contrast to Akkadian and Persian, is much more difficult to pinpoint chronologically.[30]

Was There an "Exilic" Hebrew?

The traditional periodization of Hebrew has been divided according to the Babylonian exile. Some scholars have even added an "Exilic Hebrew" as an intermediate stage. The sixth century did bring an end to Standard Biblical Hebrew. Yet, languages do not disappear overnight. It is a process. It usually takes about two generations for a language to die out. For Standard Biblical Hebrew, this process began in the sixth century with the Babylonian invasions. Two generations would take the process until the end of the sixth century B.C.E.

Standard Biblical Hebrew continued to be used through the sixth century B.C.E. For example, several biblical texts were likely composed or edited in the late sixth century—parts of the books of Kings, Jeremiah, Zechariah, and

Haggai—and these texts continue the tradition of Standard Biblical Hebrew. As for Ezekiel, it seems better to ascribe its idiosyncratic aspects to linguistic register (for example, priestly language) rather than diachronic development (namely, so-called exilic Hebrew). There is a limited continuation of the Hebrew scribal tradition that went into exile with the royal family. Some scribes apparently also fled to Egypt. The urban centers in Judah, however, were decimated. Although a center for Babylonian administration would survive north of Jerusalem in Mizpah, its focus would be on imperial administration, where Aramaic would have been the writing system. Though some Hebrew writing survived after the Babylonian conquest of 586 B.C.E., it was a much more circumscribed scribal tradition, as the infrastructure for Hebrew writing in the exile was quite restricted.

The evidence for an exilic, or "transitional," Hebrew is particularly associated with the book of Ezekiel and has been gathered in two books by Avi Hurvitz and his protégé, Mark Rooker.[31] Rooker points to thirty-seven linguistic features of Ezekiel that may be described as more typical of Late Biblical Hebrew; however, this is far fewer late features than Persian/Hellenistic works like Chronicles or Esther. Certainly, there are transitional and idiosyncratic aspects to the language of Ezekiel, but it is not necessary to understand them as purely diachronic. Other sixth-century works, such as Isaiah 40–66 or Zechariah, do not exhibit the same transitional aspects to their language. From a diachronic point of view, the Babylonian period is a problematic linguistic period, because it technically lasts less than fifty years (586–539 B.C.E.). Fifty years is too short a period to be linguistically meaningful based on the type of sources that we have. To be sure, there are transitional elements of the language of Ezekiel, but given the limited corpus, it is difficult to accede to the argument that the exilic period constitutes its own stage in the history of the Hebrew language.

Hebrew writing does seem to survive through the sixth century, beginning with the scribes who went into exile with the Judean court. Some of these scribes presumably returned to Jerusalem with the Judean leaders in the late sixth century B.C.E. Indeed, scholars have pointed to the postexilic prophetic books of Zechariah, Haggai, and Malachi as undermining the traditional periodization of SBH and LBH. This analysis can be furthered to include texts like the so-called Second and Third Isaiah (that is, chapters 40–66), which are widely thought to be late exilic or early postexilic in date.[32] These books are written in Standard Biblical Hebrew. Such studies point to the flawed nature of a linguistic classification that creates periodization according to the Babylonian exile, that is, a classification that would end SBH in

586 B.C.E. The end of SBH is not straightforwardly tied to the Babylonian exile, because Hebrew scribes survived the exile and continued to transmit and even create Hebrew literature.[33] Languages, or in this case, scribal traditions, do not abruptly end. The Babylonian exile marked the beginning of the end of the SBH scribal tradition, but the tradition lasted through the sixth century B.C.E.

The spoken Hebrew language would not have disappeared with the destruction of the temple, and the revival of written Hebrew would not necessarily correlate with the Edict of Cyrus or a rebuilding of the temple in the early Persian period. What would be the turning points in the history of classical Hebrew during this period of social, political, and demographic upheaval? The fate of SBH lies with the fate of its scribes and the social institutions that propagated Hebrew. Standard Biblical Hebrew saw a slow demise that began with the Babylonian invasions of Jerusalem. The scribes who created SBH did not disappear with the Babylonian invasions, but these events meant that the SBH scribal institutions were not sustainable. Hebrew scribes were carried into exile. Some perhaps fled to Egypt. By the end of the sixth century B.C.E., SBH had disappeared.

Standard Biblical Hebrew

Scholars have observed both the homogeneity and the diversity of biblical Hebrew. Grammars of biblical Hebrew essentially describe Standard Biblical Hebrew. The degree of homogeneity allows us to speak about "biblical Hebrew" and to write useful introductory grammars. However, scholars have also noted elements in the diversity of biblical Hebrew and have developed categories like "late," "early," or "northern" to account for aspects of this diversity.

Despite these categories, it has been observed that biblical Hebrew is not diverse enough to account for a millennium of linguistic history—that is, from 1200 to 200 B.C.E. Perhaps the most radical assessment was made by Fredrick Cryer, who argued that "the OT was *written* more or less at one go, or at least over a relatively short period of time, so that the texts quite naturally do not reveal signs of significant historical differentiation."[34] This is overstating the homogeneity of biblical Hebrew.[35] At the same time, there is some homogeneity in biblical Hebrew. This reflects a horizon for the collecting and editing of many biblical traditions, one that seems to span from 725 to 500 B.C.E., and the language of these texts may be described as SBH. To be sure, there were literary traditions that preceded this period—written in Archaic Biblical Hebrew—but these are preserved only in a few poetic texts. Likewise, there are some texts (for example, Chron., Ezra, Neh., Esther, Dan., Eccles.) that were written and edited in the Persian and Hellenistic periods (presumably after 400 B.C.E.), and these make up the corpus of Late Biblical Hebrew, but the largest portion of biblical literature belongs to SBH. As a result, descriptions of SBH can be found in the standard grammars of biblical Hebrew.

7

Hebrew under Imperialism

. . . to every province in its own script and to every people in its own language.

—*Esther 1:22; 3:12; 8:9*

The Hebrew language evolved under the long shadow cast by the Aramaic of the Achaemenid Empire. Imperial presence would have demanded that the Hebrew speech community become bilingual, using Aramaic alongside Hebrew. The fate of the Hebrew scribal tradition was even more precarious. The Aramaic writing system and imperial scribal infrastructure supplanted Hebrew within the empire. By the end of the Babylonian period, it is unclear what, if any, infrastructure was available in the region for the continued study of written texts and language. Yet, the Hebrew language and writing would reemerge, in part as an expression of political and religious nationalism.

The Hebrew language survived in spite of political (and linguistic) subjugation. Vernacular Hebrew continued to be spoken in isolated villages of Judah, and written Hebrew survived as a symbol of ethnicity, political legitimacy, and national autonomy. The Achaemenid involvement in the Levant can be divided into two distinct periods. During the first period, from 539 to 450 B.C.E., Persia was occupied with an unsuccessful attempt to extend its empire into Greece. Persian armies were defeated at Thermopylae and Marathon, and their fleet sank in the Gulf of Salamis. During this period, Yehud floundered in both poverty and relative obscurity. After King Xerxes died in the 460s, a major revolt broke out in Egypt, aided by the Athenians. Artaxerxes I responded in force and quelled the Egyptian revolt by 450 B.C.E. However, the revolt signaled a shift in the policy of the Persian Empire toward their satrapy, *Eber-Nari*, "Beyond the River." The Persian rulers built a series of fortresses along the Levantine coast, and the Philistine coastal plain became the staging area for Persian control of Egypt. With the additional imperial presence in the southern Levant also came administration and writing—but not Hebrew writing. Aramaic was the lingua franca of the empire, and its dominant role is reflected in the epigraphic record.

Aramaic: The Language of the Persian Empire

The Persians used the Aramaic language to administer their vast kingdom. Within this empire, Yehud was a tiny and impoverished province in the satrapy called "Beyond the River." With the rise of the Persian Empire, the use of Aramaic spread to its farthest reaches, from Iran to Egypt. An imperial standard, Official Aramaic, had already displaced Hebrew in the local administration of the province of Yehud in the Babylonian period. Jews living in Yehud adopted the Aramaic script as their own (displacing the Paleo-Hebrew script), so much so that it even came to be called the "Jewish script."[1] Indeed, the imposition of the Aramaic writing system and language as a lingua franca threatened the very existence of Hebrew.

The use of Aramaic as a lingua franca in the Near East had already begun in the eighth century B.C.E. (see discussion in chapter 4). The Assyrian Empire adopted Aramaic as an imperial language in their political strategy for integrating the western provinces into their empire.[2] In the Dûr-Sharrukîn Cylinder inscription, for example, the Assyrian monarch Sargon II (r. 722–705 B.C.E.) articulates the goal of unification, cloaked in linguistic jargon. The inscription mentions "one mouth" as a metaphor for allegiance to the Assyrian overlord, but the linguistic vehicle for this imposed allegiance was the Aramaic language. The Assyrians sent "scribes and overseers" to teach their conquered states, and in the east they utilized the Aramaic writing system to implement imperial policy. To carry out their plan, they built new administrative centers (such as Megiddo, Ekron, and Tell Jemmeh in Israel).

Vernacularization—that is, literary communication aimed at the masses—was critical to the emergence of empire in the ancient Near East.[3] Referring to the formation of European and Indian societies, Sheldon Pollock observes that "using a new language for communicating literarily to a community of readers and listeners can consolidate if not create that very community, as both a sociotextual and a political formation."[4] In the case of the ancient Near East, the simplicity of the alphabet as opposed to the cumbersome cuneiform writing system likely informed this choice. More than this, as a result of the spread of Aramaic, cuneiform itself became a restricted and esoteric writing system in the Persian and Hellenistic periods,[5] being supplanted by Aramaic in the administration of far-reaching parts of the empire. To perform its new functions, a literary standard was created, which scholars have called Official Aramaic (or Imperial Aramaic, or *Reichsaramäisch*).[6] Hitherto, Aramaic had been a cacophony of different dialects. The standardization and concomitant simplification of Aramaic was a natural consequence of its wide diffusion under imperial authority. Such tendencies are also evident in the Greek language in the wake of Alexander's conquest and in Arabic in the aftermath of the advent of Islam.[7] For this reason sociolinguists point to Aramaic as "a classic case of imperialism utilizing a foreign language instead of trying to impose its own."[8]

During the Persian period (538–333 B.C.E.), Aramaic was adopted as the language of the empire. From Egypt to Iran, we find ample written evidence for Aramaic that reflects the effectiveness of the empire in training scribes in the literary standard. This literary standard is even found in the Hebrew Bible, where sections of the books of Ezra and Daniel are written in Official Aramaic. Not incidentally, the literary characters of Ezra and Daniel are both officials of the imperial government and, hence, trained by its scribal chancellery. One indicator of authors' training is the use of the verb *mprš*, "to translate" (Ezra 4:18), which was equivalent to the Persian term *(h)uzvarišn*, which describes the unique method invented in the Persian chancelleries for translating a document.[9] Thus, when the *torah* (that is, the Hebrew word meaning "teaching," which was beginning to be used for the text of the Pentateuch) was read aloud in Jerusalem during the Persian period, it apparently needed to be translated into Aramaic to be understood (Neh. 8:7–8): "The Levites explained the *torah* to the people, while the people stood in their places. They read from the scroll of the *torah* of God, translating it and giving the sense; so they understood the reading." Clearly, Hebrew was no longer understood by the majority of people, and this is also reflected in the epigraphic record. Although the province of Yehud was economically poor and demographically depopulated, we still find hundreds of inscriptions in Aramaic, reflecting the penetration of the imperial bureaucracy in virtually all aspects of economic, political, and domestic life.

Aramaic was already used as a lingua franca in the Neo-Assyrian period, but it was only the elites who understood it. By the time we reach the Persian period, Aramaic is being used by both scribes and common people. Appropriately enough, the letters written between the political leaders in Yehud and the Persian king Artaxerxes are written in Aramaic. More than this, even the narrative surrounding the correspondence between political leaders is written in Aramaic (Ezra 4:9–6:18), and undoubtedly the use of Aramaic reflected the scribal training even of the leaders of the community in Yehud. Letters written from the Egyptian Jewish community at Elephantine to Jerusalem are also written in Imperial Aramaic. Although the use of Aramaic in portions of the book of Daniel serves as a literary device (Dan. 2–7), it also reflects the degree to which the Aramaic language was increasingly used by Jews in the Second Temple period, even to the extent that it was allowed to displace Hebrew.

The epigraphic evidence for Aramaic during the fifth through fourth centuries in the southern Levant is quite impressive.[10] There are almost no Greek inscriptions from this period, and very few Hebrew inscriptions. Only on the northern coast, in places like Dor, Akko, and Sidon, do Greek inscriptions begin to appear, probably evidence of traders beginning in the fourth century B.C.E. As Israel Eph'al notes, "The overwhelming majority, however, is written in Aramaic, the lingua franca of the age."[11] Beginning in the 1960s, archaeological excavations began to uncover impressive evidence of the Aramaic administration in the region. Dozens of Aramaic ostraca have been excavated at a variety of sites. These include sixty-seven fourth-century Aramaic ostraca excavated at Beersheba, one hundred ostraca from Arad, and smaller numbers from Tell el-Kheliefeh (biblical Ezion-Geber) on the Red Sea and from Tell Jemmeh. Israel Eph'al and Joseph Naveh published a large cache of administrative ostraca from Idumea dated 363–311 B.C.E. Add to this evidence the famous papyri from Wadi el-Daliyeh and the hundreds of seals and seal impressions, as well as coins. In sum, the evidence for the use of Aramaic in Yehud is quite overwhelming, yet the evidence for Hebrew is almost completely lacking in the epigraphic record.

Hebrew as a Living Language

To what extent did Hebrew continue as a living language after the Babylonian exile? The standard answer was articulated by the eminent Semitic scholar Chaim Rabin: "The Jewish community in the Persian period was thus, it appears, trilingual, using Aramaic for purposes of outside communication and for limited literary composition; Biblical Hebrew for normal literary composition; and in all probability an older form of Mishnaic Hebrew as a purely spoken vernacular."[12] This answer was based on a set of assumptions that are no longer valid. They do not stand up to more-recent literary, epigraphic, and archaeological discoveries.

First, Rabin had suggested that Aramaic was restricted to outside communication and had only limited literary use. Yet, epigraphic discoveries demonstrate that Aramaic was used widely throughout the Levant for both local and international purposes. These discoveries include mundane uses of Aramaic for record keeping, marriage contracts, and economic transactions. To be sure, Aramaic literature is relatively limited until the end of the Persian period (that is, until 330 B.C.E.). The most well-known early Aramaic literary text is the Proverbs of Ahiqar, which was apparently a widely known scribal and school text.[13] According to this tale, Ahiqar is a wise scribe of the Neo-Assyrian kings. The earliest known versions of the tale date to the fifth century B.C.E. and were found at Elephantine in Egypt. The lack of a more-developed Neo-Assyrian or Persian literary corpus suggests that the primary role of Aramaic writing was largely administrative in the early periods. In contrast, Aramaic literary production flourishes in the Hellenistic and Roman periods. Although some Qumran Aramaic texts (such as Enoch) were conceivably written in the late Persian period, most date to the Hellenistic period.[14] The Aramaic stories in the book of Daniel also seem to come from the Persian period, though the shaping of the book as a whole dates to the Hellenistic or Hasmonean period. In sum, there is meager evidence for the writing of literature in Aramaic during the Persian period.

The proposition that biblical Hebrew (instead of Aramaic) was used for normal literary composition during the Persian period is based on the assumption that this was the period when the composition of biblical literature flourished. I have dealt with this widely held assumption in earlier works,[15] but it is worthwhile to make a couple of observations in this context. There is no external evidence for this presumption, and the explicit internal biblical evidence is quite limited. That is, few biblical texts situate themselves as Persian compositions, so the argument must be made on external criteria that are either limited or equivocal.

Rabin thought that most of the common people would have continued to speak some form of vernacular Hebrew, a precursor to Rabbinic Hebrew. To be sure, it seems unlikely that vernacular Hebrew would have completely disappeared, especially given that it continued to be spoken (although it is difficult to be sure how widely) until the third or fourth century C.E. Joachim Schaper nuanced Rabin's position, arguing, "The use of Aramaic and Hebrew respectively was a matter of social division, not literary genre."[16] At the heart of Schaper's argument is this assumption: "The majority of the inhabitants of Judaea had not been abducted by the Babylonians and had thus remained virtually unaffected by Aramaic linguistic influences."[17] To be sure, continuity and change in the Hebrew language would be greatly shaped by changes in the demographic situation in Judah. It is often asserted that the demographic situation in Judah remained largely unchanged after the Babylonian conquests; however, archaeological investigation tells a different story.

Demographics and Language Shift in Persian Yehud

The evidence for vernacular languages spoken in ancient Yehud must necessarily begin with demographics. In his monumental work *Principles of Linguistic Change*, William Labov stressed that changes in the demographic composition of a community are a central factor determining the course of linguistic change.[18] Thus, the continuity of linguistic communities (that is, Hebrew speaking) as well as the introduction of new linguistic communities (namely, Aramaic speaking) can be directly correlated to the impact of the Babylonians and Persians in Yehud. Archaeological excavations and surveys indicate both continuity and significant disjunction in communities from the end of the Iron Age (586 B.C.E.) until the Hellenistic period (333 B.C.E.).

As discussed in the previous chapter, the Babylonian military campaigns to Judah resulted in a massive demographic disruption. Perhaps even more important than the overall decline in population is the disjunction and displacement in individual cities, towns, and villages. Archaeologists have estimated that at least 65 percent of Persian towns were new foundations—they have no continuity from the late Iron Age into the period of Persian control. This type of demographic disjunction resulted in a significant language shift in southern Yehud during this period. In sum, the majority of Hebrew speakers were actually displaced by the events surrounding the Babylonian invasions and administration of Judah in the sixth century B.C.E. Further, most Persian towns and villages were not simply continuations of their Iron Age predecessors but rather new foundations. What language would these new settlements speak? Aramaic. New towns and villages—that is, new speech communities—appeared throughout the Persian province of Yehud, and their language was Aramaic.

There was also some continuity in Hebrew speech communities. Although most Iron Age towns and villages show a disjunction between the seventh and fifth centuries B.C.E., there are certainly many examples of continuity of settlement. According to *Principles of Linguistic Change*, we may expect continuity in the vernacular of these speech communities. The most striking modern example of this in the modern Middle East is the stubborn persistence of Aramaic speakers in Iraq. Indeed, my UCLA colleague Yona Sabar is a native Neo-Aramaic speaker, though his children no longer speak Aramaic because his village was displaced in 1950.[19] Speech communities can demonstrate quite striking continuity, as long as the community is not physically displaced. Likewise, Hebrew speech communities persisted in Judah after the Babylonian invasions, into the Persian, Hellenistic, and Roman periods.

By the end of the Persian period in the fourth century B.C.E., the demographic landscape of the southern Levant again began to shift, as the Persian administration extended inland. Up until the fourth century, Persian interest in the southern Levant was largely confined to the establishment of coastal centers for the control of maritime trade. Oded Lipschits notes, "In contrast to the rich, well-developed cities found along the coast, very few building remains dating to the Persian Period have been uncovered in the hill country—that is, within the province of Yehud."[20] Not surprisingly, Persian interest in the region was limited to its strategic commercial and military position, which meant that their interest in the southern Levant was largely confined to the coastal plain. The changing political landscape explains the changing Persian interests in the southern Levant, beginning with Egyptian revolts headed by Pharaoh Amyrteus (404–399 B.C.E.), which resulted in sixty years of Egyptian independence (until 343 B.C.E.).[21] The Persians responded by strengthening their hold on the southern Levant, until they were finally able to regain control of Egypt. Only with this unrest did the Persian administration begin to take more interest in the hill country, and we begin to see significantly expanding settlements.

The Survival of Hebrew

There are competing linguistic issues that we must consider as we assess the extent to which Hebrew continued to be spoken in ancient Palestine during the Persian, Hellenistic, and Roman periods. On the one hand, the use of Aramaic writing reigned supreme in the Persian Empire and seriously curtailed the use of Hebrew. On the other hand, the survival of the Hebrew language was closely related to the survival of the Jewish people. That is, the survival of the language was tied to the role that it came to play in ethnic identity.

The use of Aramaic as lingua franca challenged the very existence of the Hebrew language. We began this chapter by pointing out that linguistic unification is an important strategy in implementing political subjugation. Aramaic certainly served this role in the empire. It was the language of commerce and administration. As Joachim Schaper noted, it would certainly have been the language of political elites, even Jewish elites.[22] Yet it was the role of Aramaic in commerce that would have an impact on everyday life in Yehud. For example, all the economic records that we have from the Persian and Hellenistic periods are written in Aramaic, and as such there could not have been a simple social separation in the use of Aramaic by elites and the common man. Since most towns and villages even in the Judean hill country during the Persian period were new foundations, these communities would have spoken Aramaic. The coastal plain and northern areas were Aramaic speech communities. Only a few isolated villages remained as Hebrew speech communities.

The Aramaic-speaking communities surrounding and interspersing Yehud exerted an enormous pressure on the very survival of Hebrew speech communities. Not surprisingly, the Hebrew language that survived was heavily colored by Aramaic.[23] The Hebrew-speaking community from the late Persian period through the early Roman period (ca. 400 B.C.E.–200 C.E.) was largely bilingual, needing to speak both Hebrew and Aramaic. Only in the hill country around Jerusalem were there old villages where Hebrew would have continued to be spoken, while the new villages used the lingua franca. Indeed, Aramaic was becoming a Jewish language. For example, linguistic descriptions of Judean languages from Roman-period literary sources in Greek are ambiguous about the difference between Hebrew and Aramaic. In this context, the survival of Hebrew-speaking communities was seriously threatened. Thus, we can understand the above-quoted episode in Nehemiah 13: 23–25: "I saw Judeans who had married women of Ashdod, Ammon, and Moab; and half of their children spoke the language of Ashdod, and they could not speak the language of Judah." It was the Judeans—that is, the indigenous population—who had married various surrounding peoples. The Hebrew-speaking community was already threatened by the fact that it was a demographic minority for three centuries under foreign political domination. At the same time, language maintenance is important for preserving ethnic boundaries.[24] In other words, Hebrew became integral to Judean identity. This is the undercurrent of Nehemiah's observation that "they could not speak the language of Judah"; the statement is driven by the perceived loss of ethnic identity.

Language death is often equated with the complete assimilation of ethnic identity. Thus, the preservation of Hebrew, even if the Hebrew language was threatened, was important to the preservation and emergence of identity in the Second Temple period. Peter Trudgill points out, "Where language is a defining characteristic of a minority ethnic group wanting independence, particularly where other (for example physical) characteristics are not significant (as in the case of Welsh), linguistic factors are likely to play an important role in any separatist movement they might undertake."[25] Leaders in the Judean community during the Persian and Hellenistic periods would fight for the survival of Hebrew because the survival of the language was tied to the survival of their identity.

The ongoing study of the biblical literature would be critical to the survival of the Hebrew language. Yet, it is difficult to find evidence for such study during the Persian period. Joachim Schaper takes up this important topic in an essay entitled "Hebrew and Its Study in the Persian Period."[26] However, Schaper grasps at the proverbial straws trying to find evidence for the study of Hebrew during this period. Everything always begins with the assumption that this period was critical for the composition and editing of the Bible. For example, Anthony Saldarini writes, "Scribal activity by a variety of groups (priests, prophets, visionaries, scribes, and other community leaders) must be postulated in order to account for the composition and editing of the biblical collection during the exilic and postexilic periods."[27] As an extension of this, Schaper (following the comments of Joseph Naveh and Jonas Greenfield) points out that it must have required considerable erudition to produce literary texts with the "antique flavour" of classical Hebrew.[28] This, of course, begs the question of exactly when biblical literature was composed. If, as I have argued, biblical literature was largely composed from the eighth until the end of the sixth centuries under the auspices of scribal institutions of ancient Judah, then the need to posit a great variety of scribal schools with "considerable erudition" during the Persian period becomes unnecessary. No one had to give most of biblical literature its "antique flavour" because most of the literature had already been written. Rather, it took fewer scribes to preserve, copy, and edit existing literature than to create a body of literature in a language that was not spoken by many people nor utilized by the government bureaucracy.

Biblical literature itself suggests a profound loss in the knowledge of Hebrew during the Persian period. For example, when the *torah* is read aloud, it must be translated into Aramaic to be understood; thus, "They read from the scroll of the *torah* of God, translating it and giving the sense; so they understood the reading" (Neh. 8:8). Schaper suggests that such texts refer to "the Jewish élite, not the common man."[29] But is this anything more than an assumption? A main support for schools and the study of Hebrew in the Persian period is the book of Chronicles. Since it is widely acknowledged that Chronicles is a prime example of LBH, it is often read as a source for understanding the Persian period. Schaper is particularly interested in 1 Chronicles 2:55, which speaks of "families/guilds of scribes (*mšpḥwt swprym*) dwelling in Jabez" that Schaper feels were "the single most important institution conducting and furthering the study of Hebrew in the Persian period."[30] However, this verse has been notoriously difficult to interpret, and it is rather precarious to place this much weight on such a shaky foundation.[31] Many scholars (myself included) believe that this verse derives from a preexilic genealogical list and, therefore, would tell us nothing about the Persian period. A further difficulty with 1 Chronicles 2:55 is that we have no idea where these families of scribes lived: The town of Jabez has never been identified, although contextually it seems to be in the vicinity of Bethlehem. The town must also have been close to Jerusalem, as the main employer of scribes would have been the royal administration and secondarily the temple. If Jabez were a Persian-period town of scribal guilds, it seems exceedingly unlikely that the many scribes from this town would have left no written remnant regarding its location. Indeed, the location of the town is unknown from any Persian, Hellenistic, or Roman textual record! It has essentially vanished in history. Most likely, Jabez was an Iron Age town located between Bethlehem and Jerusalem that disappeared after the Babylonian invasions (like so many other towns) and, consequently, disappeared from the historical record.[32] With this, the evidence for Hebrew scribal guilds in Yehud also vanishes.

The Gap in the Hebrew Scribal Tradition

The Hebrew scribal tradition was broken in the Babylonian and Persian periods. The disruption began with the Babylonian conquest and developed in the context of Babylonian and Persian rule. As long as the Hebrew scribal tradition had remained unbroken, new generations of students learned the meaning of older texts even as the vernacular Hebrew language underwent continual change. A gap in the scribal tradition, however, would result in a gap in the understanding of Hebrew. There is evidence for an unbroken chain of scribes from the Hellenistic period (that is, fourth century B.C.E.) through the Roman period and into the medieval period.[33] In other words, there is an unbroken chain of scribal tradition from the Hellenistic period up through the creation of the Masoretic Text of the Hebrew Bible (and from then up to the present day). It is also easy to provide evidence for Hebrew scribal schools in the Iron Age, beginning as early as the beginning of the first millennium and becoming particularly robust during the period of scribal standardization of Hebrew in the late Iron Age (ca. 750–586 B.C.E.). What is difficult to account for in the historical, archaeological, and epigraphic record is evidence for Hebrew scribes in the late sixth through early fourth centuries B.C.E. There is a gap. The silence is especially deafening in the epigraphic record, but it can even be traced in biblical literature.

How many, if any, Hebrew scribes were there in the fifth century in Persian Yehud, in Egypt, or in Mesopotamia? Were there any? It is difficult to know. It is clear that there was little infrastructure for Hebrew scribes and that Hebrew scribal traditions must have languished, even if they did not completely disappear. Hebrew and Aramaic are not so completely different that the Aramaic scribal chancellery could not have given some ancillary support for the preservation of Hebrew literature. Nevertheless, the disjunction in the Hebrew scribal institutions from the sixth century until the revival of schools in the Hellenistic period meant that archaic linguistic structures and uncommon words were no longer precisely understood by later scribes. There is a gap in the understanding of Hebrew that later scribes needed to address, and they did so with a variety of devices.

One illustration of the gap in Hebrew scribal tradition is pseudoclassicisms. This phenomenon has been studied in particular by Jan Joosten, who has identified a number of examples. He notes, "Pseudoclassicisms are less frequent in the LBH corpus than in the Qumran Scrolls. But they are not rare. Several other examples have been identified in Chronicles, Nehemiah and Daniel."[34] They show that later authors studied earlier texts diligently and tried to match their language and style in their own writing. They also illustrate that biblical Hebrew had become, to some degree, a dead language by the time the late biblical books were composed. Joosten notes, for example, that the book of Chronicles uses the SBH expression "to fill one's hand" (x + *ʾt yd* + *piʿel mlʾ*). In SBH, however, the expression means "to ordain to a sacred office" (for example, Exod. 28:41; Lev. 8:33; Num. 3:3; Judg. 17:5, 12; 1 Kings 13:33), and in LBH it means "to bring an offering" (for example, 2 Chron. 13:9).[35] This use of an apparently classical expression is really a pseudoclassicism. It shows that later authors were studying the earlier texts but that the meanings of certain words and expressions from SBH were no longer understood. Indeed, SBH was a dead language, even though a vernacular Hebrew continued to be spoken and would inform the writing of Hebrew in the postexilic period.

The phenomenon of hapax legomena (that is, words that appear only once in a textual corpus) illustrates the gap in Hebrew scribal tradition. Oftentimes a word appears only once by chance, and it is not necessarily a rare or difficult word. More generally, hapax legomena are associated with rare and difficult words. There are about thirteen hundred hapax legomena in the Hebrew Bible, but only about four hundred are difficult to interpret.[36] These difficult words derive primarily from biblical texts from the sixth century

B.C.E. or earlier. The disjunction in the Hebrew scribal tradition after the Babylonian destruction of Jerusalem created a significant number of problematic words (as well as other linguistic features) because the meaning of many words was lost during the exilic and early postexilic periods.

It is not surprising that the Bible has hapax legomena, since it is a characteristic of all literary works, but the question is how to explain the difficult words. The first tool is simply literary context, but the other main tools are etymology and linguistic cognates. The linguistic cognates of hapax legomena reflect the scribal contexts out of which they arise. The best comparative Semitic resources for understanding most hapax legomena in the Hebrew Bible are Akkadian and Ugaritic—that is, linguistic resources dating from the thirteenth through the sixth centuries B.C.E.

Not surprisingly, the languages prevalent in the Near East during the Persian and Hellenistic periods—namely, Aramaic, Persian, and Greek—play little role in the philological problems related to the difficult hapax legomena in the Hebrew Bible. To illustrate, we may begin with examples of hapax legomena in Esther, Daniel, Ezra, Nehemiah, and Chronicles—that is, books that have internal claims that date them in the later Persian or Hellenistic periods. In Esther, for example, we immediately come upon the hapax word *ʾns* (אנס), whose meaning, "to press, force, violate," is well known from Rabbinic Hebrew. In Esther 7:4, we find the word *nzq* (נזק), "damage," which is again well known in Rabbinic Hebrew as well as Jewish Aramaic. In Esther 8:10, there is the unusual word *rmkh* (רמכה), whose etymology is unknown, though it seems like a loanword, yet its meaning of "mule, racing mare" is well established by its use in Rabbinic Hebrew and Jewish Aramaic. Turning to Ezra-Nehemiah, we find examples like *gzbr* (גזבר) in Ezra 1:8, which is a Persian loanword meaning "treasurer" and which continued to be used in Rabbinic Hebrew. In Ezra 4:7 we find *knt* (כנת), which is an Aramaic loanword meaning "companion," well known in contemporary texts like the Jewish Aramaic texts from Elephantine. In Daniel 9:24 we find the word *ḥtk* (חתך), "to determine, impose," which is well known in later rabbinic texts, and in Daniel 10:21 the word *ršm* (רשם), "to record," is likely an Aramaic loan that becomes quite common in later Hebrew texts. The book of Chronicles yields similar examples; thus, in 1 Chronicles 28:11 we find the hapax word *gnzk* (גנזך), "treasury," a loan from Persian, and in 2 Chronicles 36:16 we find the word *lʿb* (לעב), "to deride, mock," which is well known in later Jewish texts. Examples such as these could be multiplied, but the observation is simply that the hapax legomena from LBH texts can be easily understood as loans from Persian or Aramaic or from their use in later Jewish texts.[37]

They are accessible in their contemporary contexts, and they are well known from the continuity of the scribal and linguistic tradition in later centuries.

The case is much different when we survey hapax legomena from the main corpus of biblical literature (that is, texts composed in the sixth century B.C.E. or earlier). To be sure, it is sometimes merely happenstance that a word occurs only one time in a given corpus. It is a feature of all literary corpora that a certain percentage of the lexemes will occur only one time in the corpus. What is telling, however, is the number of difficult words that appear in the pre–sixth-century B.C.E. texts. Chaim Cohen, in his book *Biblical Hapax Legomena in the Light of Akkadian and Ugaritic*, has nicely summarized the evidence that clarifies the meaning of twenty-eight hapax legomena.[38] The use of ancient Semitic languages to decipher the meaning of these rare words is quite striking. Akkadian was essentially unknown outside of scholastic circles by the fifth century B.C.E., and Ugaritic disappeared as a language around 1200 B.C.E. The hapax legomena were words whose meanings were presumably understood by ancient Hebrew scribes down through the sixth century, but these meanings were lost when the scribal tradition of Hebrew suffered a disjunction by the end of the sixth century B.C.E. It is noteworthy that not a single one of these difficult hapax legomena is found in the corpus of LBH texts (for example, Esther, Dan., Ezra, Neh., Chron.). At the same time, several terms do come from the corpus of texts deriving from the Babylonian period, that is, Isaiah 40–66, Jeremiah 26–52, and Ezekiel. These terms include *štʿ* (שתע), "to be afraid" (Isa. 41:10); *qbʿt* (קבעת), "cup" (Isa. 51:22); *zyz* (זיז), "nipple" (Isa. 66:11); *ʾšyh* (אשיה), "tower" (Jer. 50:15); *lbh* (לבה), "rage" (Ezek. 16:30); *swgr* (סוגר), "collar" (Ezek. 19:9); and *brmym* (ברמים), "two-colored fabric" (Ezek. 27:24). The phenomenon of hapax legomena in exilic texts further underscores the continuity in the Hebrew scribal tradition through the sixth century, as is suggested by Babylonian documents (and discussed in chapter 6). More generally, the substantial number of hapax legomena in SBH texts elucidated only by Ugaritic and Akkadian further demonstrates the periodization of Hebrew into SBH and LBH corpora. The absence of difficult hapax legomena in postexilic texts or LBH, on the other hand, indicates the continuity in Hebrew scribal tradition after a major break.

The philological problems created by linguistic change coupled with a gap in scribal tradition are not limited to hapax legomena. There were also older words and constructions that had gone out of use during the monarchic period but were preserved in the textual record. An interesting example of this is the asseverative *lamed*.[39] Originally, there were two separate terms in West Semitic: a negative particle /lā/, "no, not," and an asseverative /lū/, "indeed, surely." These two particles can be illustrated through Ugaritic as well as the Amarna letters.[40] The Canaanite shift caused the negative /lā/ to be pronounced as /lō/; as a result, this negative particle sounded similar to the positive asseverative particle /lū/. A prosthetic *ʾaleph* was added in Hebrew /lōʾ/ (לֹא), and this gave a graphemic distinction between the negative and the asseverative, but the asseverative nevertheless eventually disappeared in Hebrew and other Canaanite dialects. An excellent example of the problems that this disjunction created for later scribes, as well as the ways they attempted to resolve them, may be seen in Genesis 23, the story of Abraham's purchase of a burial plot for Sarah. The repeated use of the asseverative *lamed* in this narrative, employed four times in verses 5, 11, 13, and 14, has resulted in the variety of readings suggested by the *Qere-Kethib*, the versions, and modern exegetes.[41] The Masoretes also misdivided the text. For instance, verses 5–6 in the Masoretic Text (MT) read:

> *And the Hittites answered Abraham saying, "Indeed, listen to us my lord* (MT, וַיַּעֲנוּ בְנֵי־חֵת אֶת־אַבְרָהָם לֵאמֹר לוֹ שְׁמָעֵנוּ אֲדֹנִי), you are a prince of God in our midst, bury your dead in our best burial plot. None of us will withhold his burial plot from you for burying your dead."

The MT has vocalized an original asseverative *l* as a prepositional phrase + suffix, *lw*, "to him" (also in v. 14), even though this possibility is precluded by the fact that the preceding word, *lʾmr* (לֵאמֹר), invariably introduces a direct quote in Hebrew.[42] The interpretive problem is repeated in verses 10–11, 13, and 14–15 with slight variations resulting from a misunderstanding of the asseverative *lamed*. In verses 10–11 we read:

> Now Ephron was sitting in the midst of the Hittites and he answered Abraham in the hearing of the Hittites, all who came in the gate of the city saying, "Indeed (MT, לֵאמֹר לֹא־אֲדֹנִי), my lord, listen to me. I give you the field and I give you the cave which is in it; I give it to you before my people. Bury your dead."

The later scribes understood the asseverative *lamed* as a simple negation, *lʾ* (לֹא), "No, my lord!"; this was made easier by the fact that the following word began with the letter *ʾaleph* and simple scribal dittography of the *ʾaleph* produced the negative. The dittography, however, was not a scribal mistake but rather a correction or clarification that gave sense to a text that the scribes no longer understood. However, the similarity between verses 10–11 and 5–6 indicates that this was merely a scribal device to create an intelligible text for later readers. The asseverative sense of *lʾ* in verse 11 is borne out by verse 13, where the emphatic particle *ʾk* (אך) follows the marker of direct quotation *lʾmr*. In verses 13–15 the scribe also faced additional problems with the asseverative *l*:

> And Abraham spoke to Ephron in the hearing of the people of the land, saying, "Surely, if you would certainly listen to me (MT, לֵאמֹר אַךְ אִם־אַתָּה שְׁמָעֵנִי). I give the price of the land; accept it from me, so that I may bury my dead there." And Ephron replied to Abraham, saying, "Indeed, hear me (MT, לֵאמֹר לוֹ אֲדֹנִי שְׁמָעֵנִי), the land is worth four hundred shekels of silver—what is that between you and me? Bury your dead."

In verse 13 the Masoretic scribes make the asseverative *lamed* into a conditional *lû* (לוּ); however, this is an extremely problematic reading. On the basis of the Septuagint, scholars sometimes emend *lû* (לוּ) to *ly* (לִי), "to me";[43] however, this is no better, as it recreates a repetition of the pronoun *me* attached to both the verb and the preposition. When we recognize that this is merely the old asseverative *lamed* that is no longer understood by postexilic scribes (and modern commentators), then all the difficulties are resolved.

In other cases, the asseverative *lamed* must have created such difficulties for later scribes that the text needed to be changed in some way in order for it to be understood. In some cases no doubt the asseverative *lamed* would have simply dropped out of the text. We have some nice examples, however, of the creative changes that scribes could make to the text to render it intelligible. For example, by simply affixing an interrogative *heh*, the asseverative *lamed* could be made into a rhetorical question; thus, in Jeremiah 49:9 we find an apparent asseverative *lamed* in the statement "If grape gatherers came to you, surely [*lʾ*] they would leave gleanings," but Obadiah 5 clarifies this traditional saying by making it a rhetorical question: "would they not [*hlwʾ*] leave gleanings?"[44] Such examples illustrate the devices that scribes could use to make outdated language intelligible for themselves and to a later generation.

Enclitic *mem* is another well-known linguistic feature of Semitic languages of the Bronze and Iron Ages that had disappeared by the Persian period. The phenomenon in biblical Hebrew has been documented in a classic article by Horace Hummel published in 1957.[45] Hummel demonstrated a variety of ways in which enclitic *mem* was used in Akkadian, Canaano-Akkadian, Ugaritic, and even Egyptian. One of the first identifications of the enclitic *mem* was in Psalm 29, which was sometimes thought to be a Hebraized

Canaanite hymn.[46] Though this claim was overstated, the possible enclitic *mem* in verse 6 is instructive:

> וַיַּרְקִידֵם כְּמוֹ־עֵגֶל לְבָנוֹן וְשִׂרְיֹן כְּמוֹ בֶן־רְאֵמִים, "He made Lebanon dance like a calf, and Sirion like a wild ox."

The Masoretes vocalized the enclitic *mem* as if it were an anticipatory suffix, which is not uncommon in Aramaic from the Persian period. However, the suffix would be plural and the noun that it anticipates, "Lebanon," is singular; moreover, the anticipatory suffix is not a SBH linguistic feature. Still, the existence of the anticipatory suffix in the language of the Persian-period (and later) scribes allowed them to make sense of the enclitic *mem*—that is to say, it was not necessary to delete it in order for later scribes to make some sense of it, even though its original meaning had been lost. In the Septuagint, for example, the enclitic is simply translated with a 3mp pronoun, αὐτάς, "them."[47] In sum, Hummel offered seventy-six possible examples of the enclitic *mem*, and although many of these may be explained in other ways, it was precisely because they could be understood in other ways that many of these examples were preserved by later scribes.

Another way to illustrate the gap in the Hebrew scribal tradition is through the Septuagint translation of SBH texts. A classical example is the locative *heh* (ה-) affixed to the end of words to indicate direction. This feature of Hebrew is found regularly in SBH texts as well as Epigraphic Hebrew but becomes increasingly rare in LBH and QH and exists only in frozen expressions in Rabbinic Hebrew (for example, *ḥwṣh*, "to the outside"; *mʿlh*, "upward"). The Hellenistic Greek translators were unaccustomed in the vernacular Hebrew of their day to seeing the locative *heh* as a generative grammatical form and as a result often understood it as part of a proper name.[48] Jan Joosten summarizes the situation as follows:

> The locative *heh* is attached to a common noun defined by the article 140 times in Classical Biblical Hebrew [i.e., SBH], but only 7 times in Late Biblical Hebrew (20 times more cases in Classical Biblical Hebrew than in Late Biblical Hebrew). The locative *heh* is attached to a noun in the construct state 25 times in Classical Biblical Hebrew and not even once in Late Biblical Hebrew. This means that a form like הָעִירָה ["to the city"] (2 Kgs 20:20) is rare in Late Biblical Hebrew, and a syntagm like בֵּיתָה בְתוּאֵל ["to the house of Bethuel"] (Gen 28:2) is unattested. In light of this distribution, it is interesting to note that in the small corpus of inscriptions we find both העירה ["to the city"] (Lak 4:7) and ביתה·אלישב ["to the house of Eliashib"] (Arad 17:2). The latter expres-

> sions show that in the Hebrew of the inscriptions, as in Classical Biblical Hebrew, locative *heh* is a living feature that can be freely attached to any nominal form to express direction.[49]

Again, the later scribes preserved the older linguistic feature, but only by understanding it in a different way, that is, as part of the geographical name.

The scribes described in the late biblical texts were trained in the Persian courts. The scribe par excellence was Ezra, who had training in the Achaemenid scribal chancellery in the royal court and then brought these skills back to Jerusalem and used them in the service of the temple and the administration of Yehud. Likewise, Nehemiah is an imperial administrator who applied his training to the administration of Jerusalem. Another literary figure is Daniel, who is depicted as having trained in the Babylonian courts and served the Persian kings. These examples undoubtedly reflect the real experiences of Jews during the fifth and fourth centuries B.C.E. It is no coincidence that the scribes mentioned in late biblical literature were trained in Aramaic.

The first account of training in Hebrew after the Babylonian exile is in the Wisdom of Ben Sira—but this example brings us well into the Hellenistic period. To be sure, Hebrew and Aramaic are closely related languages; and, theoretically, the skills of the Aramaic scribal chancellery would have been transferable to the copying, editing, and even composing of Hebrew texts. At the same time, we must not forget that Hebrew came to be written in Aramaic script during this period, another sign of the role of the imperial scribal chancellery. The very letters that scholars came to label "Jewish script" are Aramaic, reflecting the training of scribes during the Persian period. The scribes of the Persian period were trained in the imperial language and tradition—not in Hebrew—and then these skills could have been transferred to the copying, editing, and (to a limited extent) composing of Hebrew literature. Moreover, we should not merely attribute this gap to the misunderstanding of Masoretic scribes. As we pointed out above, there is a continuous scribal tradition from the Hellenistic period to the Masoretes. The break in the scribal tradition is in the fifth century B.C.E. (not the fifth century C.E.).

Land, Ethnicity, and Language

The religious reforms of the Persian period began with a return to ancestral lands and an attempt to revive the Hebrew language. From a general linguistic, anthropological perspective, language is inextricably tied to land. This is nicely expressed in Genesis 10:5: "These are the descendants of Japheth, in their lands, each one according to its language (*llšnw*)" (also Gen. 10:20, 31). When the book of Esther describes Persian linguistic policy, it also makes the tight connection between ethnicity, land, and language:

> Dispatches were sent to all the provinces of the king, to every province in its own script and *to every nation in its own language*, that every man should wield authority in his home and *speak the language of his own people*. (Esther 1:22; also see 3:12; 8:9)

In our particular case, those who returned to Yehud from Babylon placed a premium on the nexus between locale and language. As we can see in Nehemiah 13:23–25, languages are associated with places like Ashdod, Ammon, Moab, and most important, Judah. The language of Ashdod during the Persian period was already Aramaic, but they could not label it as "Aramaic" because that would have located the language within Syria (that is, the homeland of the Aramaeans). Languages also define in-groups and out-groups. Nehemiah 13 connects intermarriage with the inability to speak the paternal language, whereas Ezra 9 associates intermarriage with a plea for ethnic purity. Injunctions about intermarriage play a central role in the religious reforms described in the book of Ezra:

> The people of Israel, the priests, and the Levites have not separated themselves from the peoples of the lands with their abominations, from the Canaanites, the Hittites, the Perizzites, the Jebusites, the Ammonites, the Moabites, the Egyptians, and the Amorites. For they have taken some of their daughters as wives for themselves and for their sons. Thus the holy seed has mixed itself with the peoples of the lands, and in this faithlessness the officials and leaders have led the way. (Ezra 9:1–2)

The "peoples of the lands" may speak their own languages, but for Ezra the people of Judah must speak Hebrew. Intermarriage resulted in an inability to speak Hebrew. It seems reasonable to infer that speaking Hebrew was deemed by the religious and political leaders (that is, Ezra and Nehemiah) to be part of living in the land of the ancestors. The Hebrew language was associated with the homeland, which is why the Hebrew language was called "Yehudit," from the geographic term Judah. In contrast, the use of the nongeographic term *ʿbryt* (עברית) "Hebrew" to describe the language would become particularly conspicuous when the Jewish people were living in the Diaspora (that is, after the two revolts against Rome in the first centuries C.E.). For Ezra-Nehemiah, speaking the languages of other peoples while living in the land of Judah was like mixing the holy seed with the peoples of other lands.

Ezra 9 depends on the Deuteronomic ideology that framed the nationalistic movements of the late monarchy in Judah. The book of Deuteronomy evidences a highly developed land theology, and this becomes a source for postexilic nationalism and religious ideology.[50] It is expressed, for example, by the emphasis on the *land* as given by God to Israel forever.[51] We can illustrate this with the following three passages from Deuteronomy:

> See, *I place the land at your disposal*. Go, take possession of *the land that the Lord swore to your fathers*, Abraham, Isaac, and Jacob, to assign to them and to their heirs after them. (Deut. 1:8; emphasis added)
>
> Observe His laws and commandments, which I enjoin upon you this day, that it may go well with you and your children after you, and *that you may long remain in the land that the Lord your God is assigning to you for all time*. (Deut. 4:40; emphasis added)
>
> When you cross the Jordan and *settle in the land that the Lord your God is allotting to you*, and He grants you safety from all your enemies around you and you live in security. (Deut. 12:10; emphasis added)

Nationalism is also expressed by the radical exclusivity of Israelite religious ideology, particularly in the fanaticism for holy war. This fanaticism began with extermination of the foreign nations, as we see in Deuteronomy 7:1–2:

> When the Lord your God brings you to the land that you are about to enter and possess, and He dislodges many nations before you—the Hittites, Girgashites, Amorites, Canaanites, Perizzites, Hivites, and Jebusites, seven nations much larger than you—and the Lord your God delivers them to you and you defeat them, you must utterly destroy them. Make no covenant with them and show them no mercy.

Deuteronomy goes on to forbid intermarriage (7:3–4) and then enjoins Israel to destroy the foreign nations' religious shrines and images (v. 5). The Mosaic voice then explains that Israel is a holy nation (v. 6). Nehemiah picks up this land ideology and makes a very typical association with linguistic nationalism.

The Revival of "Biblical" Hebrew: Late Biblical Hebrew

Although the epigraphic evidence from the fifth and fourth centuries B.C.E. is almost exclusively written in Aramaic, vernacular Hebrew still played a role in the villages of Yehud during the Persian period. Moreover, written Hebrew had a symbolic role in the emergence of a new political and religious identity.

After the Babylonian destruction of Jerusalem in the early sixth century, until the rise of Hellenism in the third century B.C.E., the epigraphic evidence for Hebrew is "very slight."[52] The earliest evidence includes a few seal impressions dating to the early fifth century (that is, the beginning of Persian rule in Yehud), which were published by Nahman Avigad.[53] Avigad suggested that they were written in an archaizing Aramaic script but noted that the seals used Hebrew words such as *bn* (בן), "son of," and *ʾmt* (אמת), "maidservant of," and the Hebrew prefixed definite article *h-* (-ה). The use of the Hebrew word *ben* instead of the Aramaic *bar*, "son," is telling, even if there is the admixture of Aramaic script with these Hebrew words, because words such as *son* are ethnic markers. The use of the Hebrew prefixed definite article *h-*, as opposed to the suffixed Aramaic -ʾ (א-), is also a revealing linguistic marker. Even though the overall epigraphic record points to the overwhelming use of Aramaic, the use of Hebrew on a few coins and seals indicates that Hebrew continued to have an important place in Jewish cultural identity.[54]

Beginning in the fourth century B.C.E., coinage was introduced into the economy of ancient Yehud. The first coins bearing the imprint *yhd*, "Yehud," written in Aramaic script seem to appear just after 400 B.C.E., and coins actually minted in Jerusalem also seem to appear by the early to mid-fourth century B.C.E. There are also a few coins dating to the mid-fourth century B.C.E. that use the Hebrew words *khn* (כהן), "priest," or *pḥh* (פחה), "governor," written in Paleo-Hebrew letters. Coins in particular are symbols of political identity, and the use of the old Hebrew script on these symbols of political power are revealing of the role that Hebrew continued to have in the political ideology. The use of officially minted coins allowed merchants to conduct business without having to use stone weights or metal rings and bars. The use of coins spread increasingly throughout the region; they were especially used for the collection of taxes, and this no doubt facilitated their more general acceptance. Indeed, according to the book of Ezra, the Jews collected donations for the rebuilding of the temple measured in coins: "61,000 gold darics [*drkmwnym*], 5,000 minas of silver, and 100 priestly tunics" (2:69). *Daric* was a Persian word for a gold coin introduced by the Persian king Darius in the late sixth century B.C.E. The word appears in LBH spelled either *ʾdrknym* or *drkmwnym* (Ezra 2:69; 8:27; 1 Chron. 29:7; Neh. 7:66–71), and its description as a "gold" coin points to its Persian origin.[55] All the coins minted under the aegis of the Persians used Aramaic script and the inscription "Yehud" (*yhwd*), the name of the Persian province.[56]

From the late fourth century, there are two Samaritan seal impressions written with Paleo-Hebrew letters—a script that would come to be known as "Samaritan" script.[57] These include the impression from "[xxx]-yahu, son of Sanballat, governor of Samaria." These types of inscriptions—coins and seal impressions—were official symbols of the Jewish and Samaritan governments. They point to the ideological role of Hebrew for both the Jewish and Samaritan linguistic communities in the late Persian period. The Samaritan seal impressions illustrate the complexity of using seals and coins as evidence of the linguistic situation. The seals were part of the discoveries at Wadi Daliyeh just north of Jericho. The most important finds were Aramaic legal papyri, including slave conveyances, property deeds, and marriage contracts. The inscriptions also included some seal impressions used to seal the documents. Although the seal impression of the son of Sanballat, governor of Samaria, was inscribed in the Hebrew language and script, it was affixed to an Aramaic legal papyrus. The use of the Hebrew language on the seal of a Samaritan governor most certainly acknowledges the ideological value of Hebrew as the old language of the Israelite and Judean monarchy, and its use on a Samaritan governor's seal can be understood as asserting the antiquity of the Samaritan people and their roots in ancient Israel.

Literary sources from the Second Temple period point to the competing claims of leaders in Jerusalem and Samaria to antiquity and legitimacy. Seals and coins were two vehicles for asserting such claims. As such, they certainly reflect the important role that Hebrew would play in ideologies of linguistic communities in Judah during the Second Temple period. However, they are poor evidence for assessing the extent of the vernacular use of Hebrew. We must assess the role of all textual artifacts "in modeling the cultural phenomenology of nationalism."[58] Letters, marriage contracts, or economic texts are more valuable in assessing vernacular than are seals and coins. Seals and coins, however, are important indicators of the ideological import of language. In the present case, it is telling for the vernacular language that all legal and economic texts dating to the Persian and early Hellenistic periods, whether from the government or from the rural population, were written in Aramaic.

Persian control of the Levant, however, began to break down in the mid-fourth century B.C.E., and the "Yehud" coins reflect this political unrest. Two different types of Yehud coins include inscriptions in Paleo-Hebrew letters instead of the standard script of the empire—Aramaic. Most striking is a coin probably minted in Jerusalem in the early fourth century B.C.E. bearing the inscription *ywḥnn hkwhn*, "Yochanan, the priest," which points to a certain autonomy as well as leadership by the Jerusalem temple and priests in the late Persian period.[59] The use of the Hebrew definite article *h-* (as opposed to the Aramaic -ʾ) differentiates the language from the Aramaic of the Persian administration. We also find examples of coins with the Paleo-Hebrew imprint, for example, "Yehezkiah, the governor" (*yḥzqyh/hpḥh*). The importance of language and script in the coins is underscored by later changes in the Hellenistic period. Betlyon observes, "The coin series then continues under Ptolemaic sponsorship after Alexander. Old dies were initially reused, with the inscription 'Yehud' (in Aramaic) replaced by 'Yehudah' (in Hebrew)."[60] The choice of language and script on coins thus closely mirrored the ebb and flow of political events in the fourth century B.C.E., with the old Hebrew script and language being tied to aspirations of political autonomy.

The Use of Paleo-Hebrew Script

Apart from a few coins, the Paleo-Hebrew script is largely unknown in the Persian period. Aramaic script eclipsed Hebrew during this period. Angel Sáenz-Badillos suggests that this limited evidence of Hebrew writing is enough to confirm that "Hebrew continued to be spoken and understood in Jerusalem and Judaea."[61] Although I agree with his conclusion, the epigraphic evidence is insufficient to support it. Rather, the evidence of Hebrew script exclusively on seals and coins suggests that the Hebrew script was largely symbolic in the Persian period. We must look instead to the limited demographic continuity of villages between the Iron Age and Persian period to find evidence for cultural and, presumably, linguistic continuity.

Even when Hebrew literature began to flourish again in the late Hellenistic and Roman periods (for example, the Dead Sea Scrolls), Hebrew was usually written with Aramaic script. Linguistic anthropologists have noted the important role of script and orthography for linguistic communities,[62] and the relative development of the Hebrew and Aramaic scripts and their roles in the linguistic community certainly points to the shift from Hebrew to Aramaic that took place during the Persian period. However, the use of Hebrew script on coins and seals indicates that Hebrew script was associated with political autonomy and legitimacy. The Paleo-Hebrew script made claims to antiquity and legitimacy; it connected governments (for example, Samaritan, Hasmonean, Bar Kokhba) and religious groups (for example, the Qumran sect) with the golden age of ancient Israel.

The Aramaic script underwent enormous development from the seventh through the second centuries B.C.E., whereas the Hebrew script saw very little development. The enormous change in the Aramaic script reflects the constant use and adaptation of a living language. It is as if the Hebrew writing system was frozen in time, and in a manner of speaking it was.[63] The contrast reflects the different fates of these two writing systems. Aramaic was actively used, whereas the old Hebrew script was lightly used and served a largely ideological purpose. The revival of the Hebrew language during the late Persian and Hellenistic periods, however, would utilize the Aramaic writing system—a change that would underscore a major transition in the history of the Hebrew language.

Commonly Proposed Features of Late Biblical Hebrew

Late Biblical Hebrew (LBH) designates biblical and inscriptional Hebrew of the Persian and early Hellenistic periods—that is, the fifth through the third centuries B.C.E. This dating highlights a gap in Hebrew scribal tradition and written literary production.[64] The main corpus of postexilic biblical texts includes Chronicles, Ezra, Nehemiah, Esther, and Daniel. Other partial works that can be included in LBH include books like Job (the prologue and epilogue, chapters 1–2, 42) and certain psalms.[65] In addition to the aforementioned works, we should include the book of Ecclesiastes as well as the Song of Songs, which are among the few biblical texts that include Persian (or Greek) loanwords.[66] Unfortunately, there is much debate about the dating of biblical literature, and it is best to base descriptions of LBH on this primary corpus. For example, many scholars have traditionally dated the priestly source of the Pentateuch (for example, much of the books of Leviticus and Numbers) to the postexilic period, following the evolutionary theory of the Wellhausian Documentary Hypothesis, but other scholars have pointed out that there is nothing in the language itself to indicate a postexilic origin or composition.[67]

Some commonly proposed features of Late Biblical Hebrew include the following:

1. Increased use of vowel letters (i.e., *plene* spelling). This is particularly evident in passages in Chronicles that parallel Samuel and Kings; for example, the most prominent example of *plene* spelling is *dwyd*, "David."
2. Nominal patterns influenced by Aramaic. For example, the use of the Aramaic morpheme *–wn*, as in *ḥsrwn*, "lacking" (Eccles. 1:15); *šlṭwn*, "power" (Eccles. 8:4); *rṣwn*, "desire" (Esther 1:8); and *–wn* as in *sklwt*, "folly" (Eccles. 1:17), or *mlkwt*, "kingdom" (2 Chron. 1:1).

3. Use of plural nominal forms to denote collectives. For example, *psḥym* for *psḥ*, "passover," and *dmym* for SBH *dm*, "blood." Double plural constructions, for example, *ʾnšy šmwt*, "men of renown" (1 Chron. 5:24), for SBH *ʾnšy šm* (Num. 16:2). Doubly marked plural nouns, for example, *byrnywt*, "fortresses" (2 Chron. 17:12).
4. Changes in directional particles. For example, *l-*, "to," is preferred over *ʾl*. The directional *heh* begins to disappear, for example, *lyrwšlm*, "to Jerusalem," instead of SBH *yršlmh*.
5. Particles that are rare or not found in SBH. For example, *ʾlw*, "if only" (Esther 7:4).
6. Shifting meaning in particles. For example, *ʾbl* shifts from being an asseverative particle, "truly," in SBH to a negation particle, "however, but"; *hrbh*, "very" (Neh. 2:2; 3:33) as opposed to SBH substantive, "much, many."
7. The relative particle *š-*, "of, which, that," begins to replace *ʾšr*. Note the appearance of the compound genitive *šl*, "belonging to" (formed from the relative *š* and the preposition *l-*), as in *šly*, "mine" (Song 1:6), or *šlšlmh*, "belonging to Solomon" (Song 3:7).
8. Changing verbal system. This includes: (i) gradual disappearance of the *waw* consecutive; for example, a decrease in use of *wyhy*, "and it came to pass" (the standard formula beginning narratives in SBH); (ii) development of the active participle as a present tense; (iii) development of the periphrastic construction *hyh* + participle to denote ongoing or habitual action, as in *hyw ʾmrym*, "they used to speak" (Neh. 6:19); (iv) preference for active verbal constructions, for example, *qrʾw lw ʿyr dwyd*, "they called it the City of David" (1 Chron. 11:7), as opposed to the more typical SBH, "was called"; (v) use of the particle *ʾz* (אָז) followed by the perfect, as in *ʾz ʾmr dwyd*, "then David said" (1 Chron. 15:2), as opposed to the short imperfect or archaic preterite in SBH (1 Kings 8:1); (vi) avoidance of infinitive absolute as an imperative; compare "Go and say to David" (1 Chron. 21:10) and SBH (2 Sam. 24:12); (vii) *nipʿal* has replaced the *qal* passive; and (viii) longer imperfect forms that resemble the cohortative morphologically but not semantically, as in *wʾṯʾblh*, "I mourned" (Neh. 1:4).
9. Changes in word order. For example, "Solomon, the king" (2 Chron. 10:2) instead of SBH "King Solomon" (1 Kings 1:34), and cardinal numbers follow (instead of precede) the noun they are describing.
10. Preference for *ʾny* as opposed to *ʾnky*, "I."

11. Vocabulary and idioms that become common in Rabbinic Hebrew are first attested in LBH.
12. LBH is characterized by a proliferation of loanwords. Especially notable are Persian loanwords such as *dt*, "law" (Esther 1:13), which appear in LBH but never in SBH. Aramaic loanwords and idioms are especially common, including Aramaic calques derived from official language, that is, expressions such as "may the king live forever" (Neh. 2:3) or "if it pleases the king" (Neh. 2:7).

8

Hebrew in the Hellenistic World

They spoke the language of various peoples.

—*Nehemiah 13:24*

The ideological role of language came to the fore in the Hellenistic world. Language became essential in defining Hellenistic culture and citizenship. Indeed, the word *Hellenism* itself derives from the Greek word ἑλληνιζειν, meaning "to speak Greek." The knowledge of Greek became a distinguishing criterion of this elite culture. For example, a letter dating to the mid-third century B.C.E. illustrates linguistic ideology, as an Egyptian complains that the Greeks "have treated me with contempt because I am a barbarian" and asks to be paid regularly "so that I do not die of hunger because I do not know how to speak Greek (ἑλληνιζειν)."[1] Language both united *and* divided the Hellenistic world. On the one hand, the Greek language was used to create group identity; on the other hand, it was used to justify oppression and discrimination. Hellenism elevated language ideology, so it is hardly surprising that this context saw the emergence of Hebrew as a language of Jewish cultural and religious identity.

With the end of the Persian imperial administration came the end of scribal training in Aramaic chancellery. Out of the shadow of the Persian Empire,

Hebrew schools and writing emerged, and Hellenism even encouraged the establishment of Hebrew schools in Jerusalem. Although Paleo-Hebrew script had given way to Aramaic in everyday use, it reemerged as a national script on seals and coins. In addition, Hebrew took a special role in religious ideology. Debates between the various groups of Jews in the Hellenistic period would be played out in their differing attitudes toward the Hebrew language. The Greek translation of Nehemiah 13:23–24 is telling in this regard:

> In those days also I saw Jews who had married women of Ashdod, Ammon, and Moab; and half of their children spoke the language of Ashdod, and they could not speak the language of Judah, *but they spoke the language of various peoples*. [underlined text omitted in the Greek]

As pointed out in the previous chapter, this text reflects the growing use of Aramaic as a native language among Jews in Yehud during the Persian period. It also reflects an ideological commitment by some Jews toward the Hebrew language that would be taken up in the Hasmonean period. By eliding the final clause, the Greek translator omits precisely the statement that would implicitly critique the Diaspora Jewish community, which used Greek—a language of "various peoples"—as its native tongue. The translation of the Bible into Greek fundamentally challenged the emergent linguistic nationalism that was trying to revive the Hebrew language. When we survey the use of Hebrew in the Hellenistic and Roman periods, most scholars think that spoken Hebrew continued to survive—at least in some isolated communities—as a vernacular language in Palestine until the second century C.E.[2] Although there were major demographic changes in the Babylonian and Persian periods, there were a number of villages and towns where Hebrew continued to be spoken that survived. One expression of the reassertion of Jewish autonomy in the fourth, third, and second centuries would be the revival of Hebrew scribal institutions. The Hebrew of these institutions drew upon the contemporary vernacular Hebrew as well as the deeply entrenched legacy of the Persian scribal chancellery.

Hebrew and Aramaic after the Persian Period

Hebrew and Aramaic competed for ascendancy after the collapse of the Persian Empire. With its use by successive empires beginning in the eighth century B.C.E., Aramaic had gained a foothold—not only as an administrative language but also as a vernacular language—in the eastern Mediterranean world. After the collapse of the Persian Empire, however, Aramaic no longer had the privileged support of the state. Indeed, a new language was introduced as the imperial language in the fourth century B.C.E.: Greek. Greek, however, was a foreign language in Yehud. It was a non-Semitic language. This left Hebrew and Aramaic as the local languages of people in the region that would come to be known as "Palestine"—a Greek term derived from the Hebrew word *Philistine*.

The resurgence of Hebrew in Jerusalem had already begun in the fourth and third centuries B.C.E. This is expressed first of all in the minting of coins with inscriptions in the Hebrew language and script.[3] The use of Hebrew language and script on the Yehezkiah coins in the fourth century B.C.E. is the first expression of this new autonomy. With the emergence of a Jewish state in the second century B.C.E., Hebrew language and Paleo-Hebrew script were then used on the coins of the Hasmonean dynasty as an expression of early Jewish nationalism. And the Hebrew language and script was later used on the Bar Kokhba coins (132–135 C.E.), although by this time the coins actually reflected a poor knowledge of Hebrew. Outside of coins, most "Hebrew" inscriptions of this period were written using the Aramaic script. The inscriptional evidence for Hebrew—apart from the Dead Sea Scrolls—is actually still rather meager.[4] Of course, Hebrew figures prominently on coins during the Hellenistic and early Roman periods.

Inscriptions can illustrate the complex relationship between Hebrew and Aramaic engendered by the Aramaic chancellery. For example, an inscription (IN 17) discovered in Jerusalem, dating to about 300 B.C.E., has indications of both Hebrew and Aramaic.[5] The ostracon is written in Aramaic script and has been deciphered as follows:

ככרן [1] לף חנניה	"Loaves (of bread): [1] thousand for Hananiah
בצק	dough"

The language is mixed. Naveh points out that the word for "dough," *bṣq* (בצק), is typical of Hebrew, as opposed to Aramaic *lyšʾ* (לישא), and the word *kkr* (ככר), if we take its meaning as "loaf," is also a Hebrew word. Yet the morphology of *kkrn* with the plural spelling *-n* is Aramaic. Of course, Rabbinic Hebrew would also adopt this Aramaic spelling, but this is an early third-century B.C.E. inscription. Naveh suggests that "this ostracon served as a label in a public (perhaps military) bakery, where Hebrew was presumably the spoken language."[6] Although Hebrew may have been the vernacular, as suggested by the distinctive vocabulary, the writing system was Aramaic, as indicated by the script as well as the Aramaic morphology of the plural word *kkrn*, "loaves." How do we classify such a text? It uses distinctly Hebrew vocabulary but writes with an Aramaic morphology and script. The use of distinctly Hebrew vocabulary indicates the continuation of some type of vernacular Hebrew, whereas the Aramaic script and morpheme would seem to represent the continuing influence of an Aramaic scribal chancellery.

The resurgence of the Hebrew language was also rooted in religion.[7] This is certainly illustrated by the centrality of reading the Hebrew text highlighted by the book of Nehemiah (see 8:1–5). Though it is difficult to date the composition of late biblical literature precisely, the Dead Sea Scrolls give evidence for the copying of biblical manuscripts by the mid-third century B.C.E. Although the sectarian community itself seems not to have written in Aramaic, the Qumran "library" includes nonsectarian Aramaic works such as Enoch and the Genesis Apocryphon. Such Aramaic literature from the Dead Sea Scrolls corpus reflects the ongoing legacy—at least in part—of the Aramaic scribal training of the Persian period, but it also reflects the continuing use of Aramaic by Jews in Palestine. Although the Hebrew language begins to flourish again in the third century B.C.E., it continues to be written with Aramaic letters, with the exception of a few Dead Sea Scrolls, Samaritan literature, and coins.

The Wisdom of Ben Sira is attributed to an author who wrote in Jerusalem during the early second century B.C.E. and modeled his work on the book of Proverbs. Although the book is known mostly in its Greek version, fragments of the Hebrew original were first discovered in the Cairo Geniza between 1896 and 1900 and then more recently at Masada.[8] The prologue to the Wisdom of Ben Sira describes the translation of the work into Greek and suggests that by the end of the third century B.C.E., a Jewish school had been established in Jerusalem for studying biblical and Hebrew literature. Ben Sira, in fact, uses the term for "house of instruction" (οἴκῳ παιδείας), which translates the Hebrew *beth midrash* "house of study" (51:23). This seems to allude to an emerging Jewish social institution dedicated to the study of biblical literature. By the second century B.C.E., manuscript discoveries from the region of the Dead Sea point to a new flourishing of Hebrew religious literature (for example, postbiblical compositions such as Ben Sira, Jubilees, and Tobit).

Although there was a resurgence of Hebrew literature, the shift from Hebrew to Aramaic was profound and irreversible. Often the linguistic changes would hardly have been perceptible to ancient speakers. So, for example, Hebrew increasingly uses periphrastic constructions—that is, the verb for "to be" (*hyh*) plus a participle. Thus, we find a variety of periphrastic constructions in postexilic literature, and they become normative in Rabbinic Hebrew:

היו ישבים בעפל, "they were living (*hyw yšbym*) in the Ophel" (Neh. 3:26)
יהיו מריעים בחצוצרות, "they shall be blowing (*yhyw mryʿym*) on the trumpets" (1QM 16:19)
והיית בויש באמת, "and you will be ashamed (*whyyt bwyš*) by the truth" (Sirach 42:1/Mas1h 4:5)

The periphrastic construction, however, is a syntagm (linguistic unit) borrowed from Aramaic.

Another example of Aramaic influence is the syntax of the Hebrew relative particle *š* (ש), "that, which." On the surface, the word *š* appears to be merely a replacement for the SBH *ʾšr* (אשר). However, the syntax of the relative particle *d*-, "that, which," in Aramaic is much more pliable and more frequent than its Hebrew counterpart, *š*. By way of illustration, the relative particle *ʾšr* (אשר) occurs 411 times in the Hebrew text of Genesis, but the Aramaic relative particle *d*- (-ד) occurs 1,176 times in the Aramaic translation of Genesis in Targum Onqelos. This demonstrates the much broader and more pliable use of Aramaic *d*- as opposed to Hebrew *š*- or *ʾšr*. The Aramaic particle *d*-, for example, routinely introduces causal clauses, whereas *ʾšr* (אשר) generally does not do this in SBH. Even Qumran Hebrew, which studiously avoids Aramaisms, is unaware of the influence of Aramaic on Hebrew syntax and frequently uses the relative particle in syntactically similar ways to Aramaic. To the casual observer of language, Qumran Hebrew is using classical forms like the relative pronoun *ʾšr*, but it frequently employs the SBH lexicon with typical Aramaic syntax. Thus, even when there was a linguistic ideology that resulted in the avoidance of Aramaic, the influence of Aramaic can still be detected in subtle (and sometimes not-so-subtle) ways.

Hebrew was revived as a literary language and gave voice to the political and religious aspirations of Jewish groups in the Hellenistic period. Still, the progressive shift from Hebrew toward Aramaic was not halted by the ebb and flow of Jewish autonomy in the Persian through Roman periods. By the third century C.E., the language shift from Hebrew to Aramaic was complete (as a result of the Roman displacement of Hebrew-speaking villages), and Hebrew essentially disappeared as a vernacular language in Roman Palestine. Even as Hebrew was receding as a vernacular and written language, it was also being preserved as an icon of political legitimacy and national identity, as a liturgical language, and as a sacred tongue. Hebrew was the official language of the Hasmonean state. This is best illustrated by the use of Paleo-Hebrew script on Hasmonean coins. The Hasmonean kings undoubtedly associated the Paleo-Hebrew writing with the golden age of ancient Israel—

that is, "David, Solomon and the kings following them" (Josephus, *War*, 5.143). Second Maccabees repeatedly speaks about "the ancestral language" of the Jewish people (2 Macc. 7:8, 21, 27; 12:37; 15:29).

One Hellenistic Jewish tradition suggested that Nehemiah founded a library in Jerusalem. Libraries were icons of political power in the Hellenistic world. Note, for example, the description in 2 Maccabees 2:13:

> The same things are reported in the records and in the memoirs of Nehemiah, and also that he founded a library and collected the books about the kings and prophets, and the writings of David, and letters of kings about votive offerings.

Nehemiah's library is associated with royal writing from the golden age of ancient Israel. The cultural importance of mentioning a Jewish library in Jerusalem can be nicely contextualized in the Hellenistic world. Namely, 2 Maccabees is likely a late second-century B.C.E. Greek composition written in Alexandria, which was the location of the largest library of the ancient world. The library was a creation of the early Ptolemaic rulers, probably founded by Ptolemy I Soter (323–283 B.C.E.) or his son Ptolemy II Philadelphus (283–246 B.C.E.). Tradition places the initial translation of the Pentateuch into Greek under Ptolemy II. Thus, Nehemiah's supposed establishment of a library in Jerusalem paralleled and even preceded the foundation of the Great Library of Alexandria. Unfortunately, external confirmation for the founding of a library by Nehemiah is wanting. It is not mentioned in the books of Ezra and Nehemiah and appears only in a later Hellenistic context; thus, it seems likely that this is a later projection back into an earlier period (Nehemiah's) to connect it with the golden age (that is, the time of King David).

The earliest mention of the famous Library of Alexandria is actually in the *Letter of Aristeas*, a Jewish Hellenistic work from the second century B.C.E. The letter purports to be a letter from Aristeas to Philocrates and describes the translation of the Jewish law into Greek by seventy-two interpreters—six men from each of the twelve tribes—who manage to translate the law in seventy-two days.[9] The letter makes a clear distinction between the use of Hebrew and Aramaic among the Jews. In the letter, Demetrius is quoted as saying:

> For in the country of the Jews they use a peculiar alphabet (just as the Egyptians, too, have a special form of letters) and speak a peculiar dialect. They are supposed to use the Aramaic (or "Syriac"; Greek, Συριακῆ) language, but this is not the case; their language is quite different. (§11)

In contrast, the letter emphasizes that the Jewish law is "written *in the Hebrew characters and language* [Ἑβραϊκοῖς γράμμασι καὶ φωνῇ]" (§30). The letter also underscores the distinction between writing (γράμμασι) and speech (φωνῇ) in the text. When the letter speaks of the translation process, it explicitly ties it with writing (§38): "to translate to Greek text/writing from the Hebrew text/writing that is used among you" (μεθερμηνευθῆναι γράμμασιν Ἑλληνικοῖς ἐκ τῶν παρ' ὑμῶν λεγομένων Ἑβραϊκῶν γραμμάτων). Indeed, this underscores the exceptional situation of the Hebrew language in the Hellenistic period, namely, the fact that it could be written in two different scripts—Paleo-Hebrew or Aramaic.

Hebrew as the Language of the Golden Age

Hebrew had a special religious and ideological role in the Hellenistic period. No doubt its prestige owed much to the role of Hebrew in the golden age of Jewish history and literature. Hebrew was the language of the old Judean monarchy and of their works of classical antiquity—namely, biblical literature. It was the language of the lawgiver, Moses, as well as the patriarchs. In this respect, Hebrew fits easily into one general and deeply held belief about language, namely, the Golden Age Principle. The linguist William Labov observed that people generally believe that at some time in the past, language was in a state of perfection.[10] Every linguistic change therefore represents a movement away from perfection. Not surprisingly, language ideology may try to recapture the golden age of a particular language.

Hebrew was understood to be the language of the Jewish golden age. Indeed, it was the language of God himself. This might be inferred from the first chapter of Genesis, where God creates the world *in Hebrew*, speaking the words *y^e^hî ʾôr* (יהי אור), that is, "Let there be light." This belief is explicitly expressed in the well-known rabbinic idea that Hebrew was the language of creation. This idea, however, is already evident in the book of Jubilees—that is, in a Hellenistic work originally written in Hebrew by the early second century B.C.E.[11] In Jubilees 12:25–26, God speaks with Abraham in Hebrew, and Abraham studies books written in Hebrew:

> And the Lord God said: "Open his mouth and his ears, that he may hear and speak with his mouth, with the language which has been revealed"; for it had ceased from the mouths of all the children of men from the day of the overthrow (of Babel). And I opened his mouth, and his ears and his lips, and I began to speak with him *in Hebrew in the tongue of the creation.* (emphasis added)

In Jubilees, the author makes a point that Hebrew was God's language. The fact that this point is so explicitly developed by this Hellenistic writer suggests that the knowledge and the use of Hebrew were socially and even politically charged issues.

Not only is Hebrew the vernacular of God's creative acts, but also *books* are *written* in this same Hebrew language. The ideology of Jubilees implicitly identifies God's spoken language of creation with the written:

> And he [Abraham] took the books of his fathers, *and these were written in Hebrew*, and he transcribed them, and he began from henceforth to study them, and I made known to him that which he could not understand, and he studied them during the six rainy months. (Jub. 12:27; emphasis added)

According to Jubilees, Hebrew was the language originally spoken by both humankind and animals, and more important, it was the language of heaven. However, after God confused the languages at the Tower of Babel, Hebrew was forgotten. The divine language of creation was later revived when the patriarch Abraham was taught Hebrew by the angels (Jub. 12:26). Enoch was the first man initiated by the angels in the art of writing and wrote down the secrets of astronomy and chronology.

What were the implications of such beliefs about the antiquity of Hebrew as the language of the Jewish ancestors and of God himself? The ideological importance of the Hebrew script is most evident in the Hasmonean (and later in the Bar Kokhba period, and even in the contemporary Israeli) adoption of the Paleo-Hebrew script on their coins. The relative rarity of the Hebrew script also made it a much more powerful religious and political symbol. The religious role is well illustrated in the Dead Sea Scrolls. The political role can be demonstrated by the role of Hebrew in the Hasmonean state.

Samaritan Hebrew

Hebrew was also the sacred language among the Samaritan community. The Samaritans were an ethnic group who claimed their ancestry from the Israelite descendants of the tribes of Ephraim and Manasseh and resided in the region of Samaria.[12] The ideological value of Hebrew among the Samaritans is indicated, first of all, by the use of a Paleo-Hebrew script for Samaritan inscriptions. James Purvis has argued that the so-called Samaritan script can be traced back to the sixth century B.C.E. and the Hebrew scribal tradition known from inscriptions dating to the late Judean monarchy. The immediate parallels for the Samaritan script are the contemporary scripts of the Hasmonean period.[13] Most tellingly, the Samaritans also used this Paleo-Hebrew script on seals and coins—that is, the administrative and political symbols of the state.[14] Finally, the Samaritan Pentateuch reflects the centrality of Hebrew in Samaritan culture. The manuscripts from the Judean desert (near Qumran) have only further solidified the antiquity of the Samaritan tradition. The scholarly view is that the Samaritan Pentateuch was based on an old Judahite version of the Pentateuch, probably dating to the fourth century B.C.E.

The Samaritan community itself developed a strong linguistic ideology. According to their beliefs, "the precise recitation of the Torah in accordance with the rules of grammar, as Moses spoke it from God's own mouth, is a basic commandment."[15] Unfortunately, the Samaritan recitation tradition is only known from a much later period. Nevertheless, it is clear that the textual tradition for the Samaritan Pentateuch reaches back at least into the Hellenistic period, and its antiquity is well supported in the Dead Sea Scrolls. Outside of the Samaritan Pentateuch, we have very few textual sources for Samaritan Hebrew dating to the Second Temple period.

The Paleo-Hebrew script played a particularly prominent role in Samaritan written culture. It continued to be the primary script of the Samaritans' written language, even when writing in Aramaic, and the Samaritan Paleo-Hebrew script was even used later by the Samaritans in Arabic inscriptions.[16] In contrast, Paleo-Hebrew script had already lost its sacredness for the Jewish community by the second century C.E., as noted in *m. Yadayim* 4:5–6. According to the Pharisaic opinion expressed there, only sacred books written in Aramaic script impart uncleanness; thus, the works of Homer—just like biblical texts written in Paleo-Hebrew—do *not* impart uncleanness. Writing the Scriptures in Aramaic script makes the texts sacred, whereas writing in Paleo-Hebrew, according to the Pharisaic tradition, renders the Scriptures profane! This turns on its head the principle that we see, for example, in the use of Paleo-Hebrew from Qumran, where the divine name is frequently written in Paleo-Hebrew instead of regular Aramaic script in order to demonstrate the sacredness of the divine name. In the Dead Sea Scrolls, writing in Paleo-Hebrew was even more sacred than Aramaic script. Indeed, it was precisely this special meaning given to the Paleo-Hebrew script by groups like the Samaritans and the Essenes that must have encouraged the Pharisaic tradition (as reflected in the Mishnah) to reject the special nature of the Paleo-Hebrew script.

The Samaritan reading tradition, as it is preserved from the Middle Ages, postdates the Second Jewish revolt. This is most clear in the treatment of the guttural, as Ze'ev Ben-Hayyim has pointed out. Medieval Samaritan grammarians saw the gutturals as "models for shaping the vowel signs."[17] For the Samaritan reading tradition, the nonpronunciation of gutturals actually was thought to reflect the antiquity of the reading tradition (as opposed to the Masoretic tradition). Nevertheless, the evidence for the pronunciation of gutturals in transcriptions, including Akkadian and Greek, indicate otherwise. Although it is clear that the Samaritan use of Hebrew dates back into the early Second Temple period (and probably into the late Iron Age), the preserved evidence for the Samaritan Hebrew reading tradition is mostly from much later periods.

Qumran Hebrew

The largest repository of Hebrew texts from the Hellenistic world is the Dead Sea Scrolls. First discovered in 1947, these texts have been primarily associated with the sectarian religious site at Khirbet Qumran, although the term *Dead Sea Scrolls* often is used to refer to all texts found near the Dead Sea dating from the fourth century B.C.E. until the fourth century C.E., not just those associated with Khirbet Qumran. For the most part, previous studies have dealt with the formal linguistic aspects of the Dead Sea Scrolls using the methods of historical, comparative, structural, and generative linguistics.[18] These approaches have yet to account for the idiosyncrasies in the scrolls. The scrolls include sectarian texts that represent the language of an isolationist religious sect, often referred to by the untranslated term *yaḥad*, "community," in scholarly literature or sometimes equated with the Essenes based on correlation of internal and external evidence. The language has usually been called Qumran Hebrew, which closely associates the language with the settlement of Khirbet Qumran. However, the language could more accurately be called Essene Hebrew, which acknowledges that the language belongs to a larger religious movement than the settlement at Khirbet Qumran and that not all the sectarian texts were copied or composed at Qumran. Still, we shall retain the traditional terminology Qumran Hebrew (QH), which identifies the language with the location of the discovery rather than the neologism Essene Hebrew, which has the distinct advantage of identifying the language with the religious group (or, in linguistic jargon, "speech community") most likely to have authored, compiled, and copied the sectarian manuscripts.

To be sure, the association of the scrolls with the Essenes described by Pliny, Philo, or Josephus has been the subject of some heated debate. Nonetheless, a consensus still holds that the Essenes described in the classical sources can be associated with the religious sectarian literature of the Dead Sea Scrolls.

I find the argument for this association still cogent and the alternative—namely, that the sectarian scrolls should be related to a yet-unidentified Jewish sectarian group(s)—not particularly useful. Although labels such as "Essene" or "Pharisee" are oversimplifications of the social history of Judaism in the Second Temple period, they are also useful heuristic terms. I will refrain from using the term *Qumran community* because it too-narrowly identifies the sectarian texts with the site of Khirbet Qumran. The term *Essene community*, which I believe is a most plausible designation, is the subject of too much controversy that is outside the scope of this book. As a result, I adopt the more neutral term *yaḥad community*, which derives from the sectarian literature itself.

There are a number of caveats that must be acknowledged when trying to characterize the language of the Dead Sea Scrolls. To begin with, the scrolls derive from a religious community (or communities) that existed for at least two hundred years in disparate places. The dates of various scrolls actually span three hundred years, though most were copied between 100 B.C.E. and 68 C.E. Not every scroll found in the caves near Khirbet Qumran was composed by the religious sect that inhabited the site; hence, every scroll does not necessarily reflect the community's particular use of language. Moreover, it has been cogently argued that the settlement of Khirbet Qumran may not even have been the center of the religious community.[19] The scrolls also describe a religious group located in many different places (or "camps," as they are called in the scrolls). Although Qumran may have been an important religious center for the group, it would not have been the only locale of the group. Indeed, Josephus describes an "Essene Gate" in Jerusalem, which suggests a presence in the capital of Judea. Josephus also speaks of different kinds of Essenes (marrying and celibate), varying locations, and numbers that were at least as large as the Pharisees. Our description of QH is further complicated by the fact that biblical Hebrew is a literary register, whereas Rabbinic Hebrew (RH) arose from the textualization of a colloquial linguistic register. For these reasons, QH should not be expected to fit neatly on a historical continuum from LBH to RH. Such problems underscore the sociolinguistic premise that "language is a complex social fact,"[20] and QH is a particularly rich example of this. The complex character of QH can only be appreciated by reference to its social function within an evolving sectarian religious community located in a variety of places in ancient Palestine.

One of the sectarian characteristics of Qumran Hebrew is its use of secret-code terminology as well as ideologically laden references to language. For example, the sectarian documents typically use opaque language like "the man of the lie," "the lion of Judah," "the seekers of smooth things," or "the wicked priest," rather than directly identifying people.[21] The ideological role of language can be illustrated by the many references to language in the *yaḥad* literature.[22] The most important term for language in Hebrew is *lšwn* (לשון), "language, tongue"; other important words in the semantic field include *śph* (שפה), "lip, speech, language," and *dbr* (דבר), "word." Chaim Rabin suggested that the scrolls allude to vernacular Hebrew, which the *yaḥad* community regarded as *lšwn ʾḥrt*, "another language" (לשון אחרת, 1QH[a] 10:19; 12:16); *lwʿg śph*, "a halting language" (לועג שפה, 1QH 12:16); *lšwn gdwpym*, "a blasphemous language" (לשון גדופים, CD 5:11–12; 1QS 4:12); and *ʿrwl śph*, "an uncircumcised language" (ערול שפה, 1QH[a] 10:7, 18–19).[23] In the *Damascus Document* we find the following apparent critique of the oral law: "Also they have corrupted their holy spirit, and with blasphemous language they have reviled the statutes of God's covenant, saying, 'They are not fixed'" (5:11–12). The idea that the law was not fixed must refer to the oral law, which was favored by the opponents of the *yaḥad*. More specifically, the critique refers to the way the Pharisees interpreted the law of intermarriage. The *Damascus Document* here cites Leviticus 18:13, emphasizing what Moses *spoke* (CD[a] 5:8). Certainly, the authority of the oral versus the written *law* was a hot topic in the late Second Temple period. The criticism that language as reflected in a particular interpretation of the law was "not fixed" arises out of the Qumran doctrine of predestination, which apparently opposed the fluidity of the oral law.[24]

The *Thanksgiving Hymns* are additional sectarian texts that are particularly rich in language ideology. They reveal a belief that the community's language was unique and divinely inspired. For example, 1QH 9:27–29 reads:

> You created breath for the tongue (לשון), and You know its words (דבריה). You determined the fruit of the lips (פרי שפתים) before they came about. You appointed words by archetype (דברים על קו) and the utterance of the breath of the lips (ומבעי רוחות שפתים) by calculation. You sent forth archetypes (קוים) for their mysteries (לרזיהם), and the utterances of spirits (ומבעי רוחות) for their plan (לחשבונם).

From such liturgical ruminations it is clear that the *yaḥad* community had a highly loaded ideology of language that inevitably shaped its linguistic choices. One particularly significant relexicalization in Qumran Hebrew is the term *qw* (קו), which becomes the pattern or archetype for language and speech. This may already be inferred from the statement quoted above: "You appointed words by archetype" (1QH 9:28). The translation of *qw* as "pattern" would be sufficient, except that it is clear that the sectarian theology of predestination colors its use of the term. For example, in sectarian literature the term *qw* is engraved (חקק): "You engraved according to the archetype" (1QH 23:11; cf. 1QpHab 7:13–14). It is paralleled with a "secret" (סוד) etched in stone (1QH 14:26), and it is a metaphorical source (מקור) from which proper judgment derives (1QH 16:21).[25]

The *yaḥad* community undoubtedly drew upon the enigmatic use of the term *qw* in the book of Isaiah, where several possible interpretations of its meaning have been offered, including incoherent speech, foreign speech, and children's babbling (18:2, 7; 28:10, 13; also see Ps. 19:5).[26] The Teacher instructs according to the "archetype of his justice" (1QS 10:9). This rigidity extended to other areas of *yaḥad* life and thought. The *Community Rule* speaks of the "law that is determined by the archetype of the ages" (1QS 10:26). Everything was fixed before creation itself. It applies, for instance, to liturgy at Qumran, which was fixed in contrast to the fluid liturgy of rabbinic Judaism (*m. Berakhot* 4:4; *b. Berakhot* 29).[27] This issue also underlies code terminology applied disparagingly to the sect's opponents—phrases like "those who move the boundary" (מסיגי הגבול, CD[a] 1:16; 5:20; 19:15), or "seekers of easy interpretations" (דורשי החלקות, CD[a] 1:18; 1QH 10:32). The ideology seems to be that both the oral law and its linguistic register—that is, vernacular Hebrew—were blasphemous.

The linguistic character of the sectarian scrolls must be related to their ideology, both social and linguistic. The strong social ideology would work its way into the linguistic features of the sectarian scrolls. One strong indication of the separatist nature of the group was the use of a solar calendar (as opposed to the Jewish lunisolar calendar).[28] Most Jewish communities as well as the Jerusalem temple used a lunisolar calendar in the Second Temple period. Since a year is not evenly divisible by an exact number of lunar months, the addition of intercalary months is necessary to prevent the agricultural seasons and festivals from drifting each year (as they do in the Islamic calendar). This results in a thirteen-month year every two or three years. Jewish groups debated the intercalation, but they still celebrated the same calendar, which defined them as a group. However, the solar calendar separated the *yaḥad* community, who intentionally would *not* have celebrated any holidays with the general Palestinian Jewish community using the lunisolar calendar as calculated by the Jerusalem temple aristocracy. This obviously was a point of contention between the *yaḥad* community and the Jerusalem temple; for example, we find the well-known description in the Habakkuk Pesher, column 11:

> This refers to the Wicked Priest, who pursued the Teacher of Righteousness to destroy him in the heat of his anger at his place of exile. At the appointed time of the festival, *the rest of the Day of Atonement*, he appeared to them to destroy them and to cause them to stumble on the fast day, the Sabbath intended for their rest. (emphasis added)

The solar calendar intentionally separated this religious sect, just as their language would separate them.

The analysis of Qumran Hebrew can be aided by setting the *yaḥad* community within the process of iconization that indexes social groups. The sociolinguists Judith Irvine and Susan Gal write, "Linguistic features that index social groups or activities appear to be iconic representations of them, as if a linguistic feature somehow depicted or displayed a social group's inherent nature or essence."[29] This small, isolated religious community on the north shore of the Dead Sea used language ideologically as a means of differentiating and further insulating themselves. In this instance, this iconization seems to have become a proactive means of differentiation. Linguistic ideology takes on exaggerated importance among groups that are exclusive and sharply bounded, as the *yaḥad* community was. Confronted with anomalous forms like the long spellings of the personal pronouns *hwʾh, hyʾh* (הואה, היאה), "he, she," scholars have sometimes turned to historical and comparative linguistics for explanations.[30] Although this is a valuable preliminary step, it is a questionable approach for explaining such anomalous forms. Are we to believe that the *yaḥad* scribes used these forms as a result of a direct development of an earlier, yet-unknown Hebrew dialect? Or, is it more likely that these peculiar forms result from the artificial and ideological creation of an idiolect for the community?[31] The evidence seems to support the latter. Spelling is a way to create identity in the written registers of language; thus, the British spelling *centre* does not reflect pronunciation but does index social identity. Moreover, as the sociolinguist Suzanne Romaine observes, "Due to the social significance of personal reference, pronouns are particularly susceptible to modification in response to social and ideological change."[32] In other words, rather than understanding the long forms of these personal pronouns as primarily preserving either an archaic form or a different dialect, we must also anticipate them as arising from social and ideological aspects of the religious community.

Qumran Hebrew can be characterized by the sociolinguistic category of an *antilanguage*.[33] Michael Halliday describes the principle of an antilanguage as "that of same grammar, different vocabulary; but different vocabulary only in certain areas, typically those that are central to the activities of the subculture and that set it off most sharply from the established society."[34] Small, weak, and marginal religious communities such as the *yaḥad* community typically cultivate linguistic idiosyncrasies in order to enhance group identity. For example, Hugh Ormsby-Lennon points out that dissenting religious sects like the Quakers in Puritan England actually cultivated both verbal and written idiosyncrasies.[35] Judith Irvine writes, "The [linguistic] code's origin in *counter-societies* is reflected in many aspects of their linguistic form, for instance in their elaboration of lexicon and metaphor relevant to their special activities and their attitudes toward the normative society. . . . Also significant is their conspicuous avoidance and violation of forms recognized as 'standard.' . . . The anti-language is not, and has never been, anyone's native tongue, nor are all its formal characteristics simply arbitrary. Both functionally and formally it is derived from the normative code, just as its speakers define their social role in opposition to the normative society."[36] These sociolinguistic observations seem especially apt for understanding the language of the *yaḥad* community.

Several lines of evidence point to the conscious creation of an antilanguage by scribes within the *yaḥad* community. These include the use of code and symbolic terminology, the avoidance of Aramaic and popular language (for example, RH), pseudoclassicizing tendencies, and orthography and paleography. Taken together, this evidence points to the use of language within the *yaḥad* community as another vehicle for differentiating the group from other Jewish groups in the late Second Temple period.

Antilanguages both relexicalize and overlexicalize, and they betray a familiarity with the native and colloquial languages through grammar. Applying these observations to Qumran Hebrew, we should expect that it was at the same time a continuation of LBH and a reaction against the colloquial languages spoken in Palestine—both Aramaic and Rabbinic Hebrew. In this regard, we should expect new uses of SBH vocabulary (such as *qw*) alongside a framework of LBH and RH syntax. It is important to remember, as William Labov pointed out, "The great majority of linguistic rules are quite remote from any social value," and consequently they are "well below the level of social affect." Though he warns against overestimating the role of social factors, Labov continues, "Variables *closer to the surface structure* frequently are the focus of social affect."[37] The attempt to form an antilanguage is most apparent in the surface structure of language (for example, terminology, lexicon), whereas the deep structure (for example, syntax) is less affected. Group ideology finds its reflex in a linguistic ideology that transforms the surface structures of a language. This is the situation we confront in the sectarian literature of the Dead Sea Scrolls.[38]

Emanuel Tov has emphasized an orthographic distinction in Qumran Hebrew by isolating what he describes as "Qumran scribal practice," arguing that scrolls not written in the peculiar orthography of the community were not written by the community's scribes.[39] Tov was able to isolate 140 texts that exhibit features of the scribal practice. However, just because a document was *copied* by a *yaḥad* scribe does not mean it was *authored* within the *yaḥad* community or at the site of Qumran itself. Biblical scrolls are a good example of this. Even though the Great Isaiah Scroll (1QIs[a]) was copied in "Qumran scribal practice," it was not composed by *yaḥad* scribes. Scrolls such as the biblical Samuel Scroll, which was copied in the third century B.C.E., predate the site of Qumran and were obviously brought to the site. At the same time, although some scrolls were copied elsewhere and brought to the site, archaeological and scientific evidence also proves that some scrolls were copied at Khirbet Qumran.[40] For this reason, Qumran Hebrew must be distinguished from the corpus of Dead Sea Scrolls Hebrew, and the Hebrew of the scrolls should not be simply identified with the site of Khirbet Qumran.[41]

Orthography is a surface structure of language, and it was easy for *yaḥad* scribes to exploit orthography in creating their distinctive scribal tradition. The most characteristic feature of sectarian orthography is the use of *scriptio plena* (or "full writing"). This is particularly true of the use of *waw*, which is used where we find long and short *ḥolem, shureq, qibbutz, qametz ḥatuf, ḥaṭef qametz,* and even sometimes *vocal shewa* in the Masoretic vocalization tradition.[42] Also characteristic is the use of *heh* and *ʾaleph* as final vowel letters. Some orthographic peculiarities reflect the diachronic situation of QH. So, for example, the occasional use of *samekh* where *śin* is expected may be understood within the context of a general tendency reflected also in RH.[43] Yet, on the whole, sectarian orthography is unique and unexpected. Emanuel Tov has argued that the sectarian orthography reflects a unique system.[44] According to Tov, notable features of this system include the following:

1. Writing of the vowel /o/ by the *waw* (e.g., כוה, זאות/זואת/זות, כול, לוא),
2. lengthened independent pronouns (e.g., הואה, היאה, אתמה, אתנה),
3. lengthened pronominal suffixes for second- and third-person plural (e.g., -כה, -מה),
4. use of pausal forms (e.g., ויקטולו as well as the pronouns המה, הנה),
5. form כיא,
6. forms מאודה/מואדה/מודה,
7. use of initial-medial letters in final position, and

8. writing of divine names *ʾl* and *yhwh* (יהוה and אל) using Paleo-Hebrew characters.

Although the general characteristics of this system are clear, Tov admits that the implementation is inconsistent. In fact, he remarks that "in only a few cases do all the features appear together in one scroll, such as 4Q174 (Florilegium)."[45] Moreover, Tov also acknowledges that certain clearly sectarian manuscripts such as the *Community Rule* (for example, 4Q258) and the *Damascus Document* (for example, 4Q270) are not written in sectarian orthography.[46] The inconsistency of the system would be particularly troubling *if all the sectarian documents were copied at Qumran*; however, the realization that the sectarian scrolls were copied by a variety of *yaḥad* scribes in a variety of places over a two-hundred-year period accounts for the inconsistencies in sectarian orthography. Indeed, the lack of complete standardization points to a loose social structure of the group, with some members living in the desert at Khirbet Qumran and others living in "camps" throughout the land. Still, even though Tov's "Qumran scribal practice" is not completely standardized, the features of the system are nevertheless quite circumscribed.

Eugene Ulrich questioned Tov's idea of a distinctly Qumran scribal practice, asking "whether the principles and practices of the scribes at Qumran differed significantly from those of other contemporary Jewish scribes."[47] Ulrich's objections, however, are not convincing. He points specifically to the problem of *plene* spelling using vowel letters, but this is not the real crux of *yaḥad* scribal practices. The unique features of *yaḥad* orthography are items such as *hwʾh* for personal pronouns, the use of pausal verbal forms like *yqtwlw*, or the writing of divine names with Paleo-Hebrew characters. Ulrich's objections could be further contextualized by noting the use of the cryptic scripts—texts that now number as many as eighty manuscripts.[48] Clearly, script as well as orthography was being used for ideological purposes in the sectarian manuscripts from Qumran. As anthropological linguists have pointed out, script and spelling are often the subject of ideological manipulation.[49] The very character of the radical religious sect reflected in the documents from Khirbet Qumran, as well as their staunch ideological opposition to the Jerusalem temple, provides a typical motivation for the ideological manipulation of orthography, script, and language.

A slightly different explanation of the Dead Sea Scrolls orthography is hinted at by E. Y. Kutscher's study of 1QIsa. Kutscher argues that the use of full spelling in the scrolls arises from an attempt to avoid Aramaisms. He notes the natural tendency for homographs in Hebrew and Aramaic—for example, *lʾ*, *yʾmr*, *rʾš*—to be pronounced according to their Aramaic rather than Hebrew pronunciation in RH. He argues then that "for both nationalistic and religious reasons" the pronunciation was made clear through *plene* spelling, that is, *lwʾ*, *ywʾmr* or *yʾwmr*, *rwʾs* or *rʾws* (לוא, יואמר or יאומר, רואש or ראוש) in QH.[50] There is probably some truth in Kutscher's analysis; however, as he himself admits, it does not account for all the anomalies in the sectarian orthography. More than this, it is hard to believe that the readers of the scrolls, namely, the community itself, needed to be reminded that in Hebrew *lʾ* was pronounced /lōʾ/ and not /lāʾ/. No. The purpose of orthography is to mark identity more than pronunciation, as illustrated by the British spelling *colour* instead of *color*. Indeed, I recall inquiring of a British publisher of one of my books whether I should use British spelling and being told that this was not allowed because I was an American. Moreover, it is worth pointing out that spellings such as *centre* or *labour* do not indicate any special difference between British and American pronunciation. Likewise, with Qumran scribal practice, we should be careful not to equate spelling with pronunciation. Indeed, the pronunciation of common words like "not" (*lwʾ* or *lʾ*) and "that" (*kyʾ* or *ky*) was already clear. Furthermore, the scrolls themselves indicate that there may have been religious reasons that caused the *yaḥad* community to distinguish the language not only from Aramaic but also from the colloquial Hebrew of their contemporaries.

For the most part, *yaḥad* orthography has not been found outside of the Qumran scrolls. The nearest parallels are with the Samaritan tradition that uses lengthened second- and third-person plurals, *ʾtmh* and *hmh* (אתמה and המה), lengthened suffixes, and the verbal form *yqṭwlw* (יקטולו).[51] The Samaritan tradition, however, also diverges in many important ways. On the one hand, it does not have many important features of *yaḥad* orthography, such as the lengthened 3s forms *hwʾh* and *hyʾh* (הואה and היאה) or the general tendency toward *plene* spelling. On the other hand, the Samaritan tradition incorporates features unknown in either *yaḥad* or standard orthography, such as the 2fs pronoun *ʾty* (אתי). Other similarities to *yaḥad* orthography may be found in the Severus Scroll, which is known through fragmentary rabbinic sources, though these should not be overstated. The Severus Scroll uses nonfinal letters in final position (that is, כ for ך, מ for ם, נ for ן, צ for ץ), as we find in some of the early Qumran manuscripts, and it also uses *plene* spelling, but these are not distinct Qumran scribal practice.[52] Emanuel Tov was quite conservative in his conclusions regarding the peculiarity of Qumran scribal practice, as it is possible that "new documents may be discovered which would undermine the uniqueness of the Qumran Scrolls."[53] Parallels with other scribal traditions such as Samaritan orthography warrant a cautious approach. Yet Tov's conclusion that the scrolls written in Qumran scribal practice were copied at Qumran, whereas those in standard orthography were brought from outside, can no longer be sustained.[54] It has become increasingly clear that the Qumran settlement itself had ties with the outside world. The variability in the "Qumran scribal practice" itself suggests that the sectarian scrolls arose not in a narrowly circumscribed setting but rather "among the camps" throughout ancient Palestine.

The inconsistency of *yaḥad* orthography indicates that Qumran scribal practice was not "standard" scribal practice, even for many of the *yaḥad* scribes. William Labov observes that "overt correction tends to be rather unsystematic when it occurs late in life, and it focuses on individual words rather than general rules."[55] The many orthographic inconsistencies in QH indicate that the system consciously went against well-entrenched scribal practice. This is perhaps most clear in the use of supralinear corrections, which bring orthography in line with the *yaḥad* system, as well as the use of final letters in medial position (for example, ומנחתםה, "their offering," 11QT^{b} frag. 14+15 7; מרעיתךה, "your pasture," 4Q266 frag. 18 5:13; בריתךה, "your covenant," 1QH 10:22).[56] The appearance of scrolls in *yaḥad* orthography (for example, 1QIs^{a}) alongside those in standard (or "Proto-Masoretic") orthography (for example, 1QIs^{b}) itself indicates that the *yaḥad* scribes were well aware of the standard orthography. The frequent slips that resulted in final letters placed in medial position or that had to be corrected with supralinear notations also indicate a conscious departure from the standard orthography. The scribes were used to the standard Hebrew orthography, but they were also aware of the special Qumran scribal practice and tried to correct toward it. At the same time, there was no tightly controlled scribal community strictly enforcing "Qumran scribal practice." This fact also argues strongly in favor of a model of dispersed groups living in a variety of places—that is, a *yaḥad* community living in camps throughout the land, as is suggested both by the scrolls themselves and by Josephus's and Philo's descriptions of the Essenes.

The orthography and scripts used in the Dead Sea Scrolls also point to strong linguistic ideology. Anthropological linguists have shown that orthography and script are ideologically loaded.[57] Experimentation with Paleo-Hebrew and cryptic scripts in the Second Temple period were also socially marked uses of script. A modern example of this was the decision to write Turkish using the Roman instead of the Arabic script. It is noteworthy that the revival of Paleo-Hebrew script appears on Jewish coins of the Second Temple period, reflecting nationalistic movements. The use of cryptic scripts now appears to be much more extensive than initially thought, with perhaps more than eighty fragmentary manuscripts.[58] One can only speculate concerning the rationale for the use of cryptic script. It may have arisen from a rejection of the "foreign" Aramaic script or the "Samaritan" (that is, Paleo-Hebrew type) script, or it might have been an attempt to recover the written alphabet from creation. It certainly speaks to the highly charged linguistic ideology of the *yaḥad* community.

The *yaḥad* community also used paleography to differentiate the community. The most obvious example of the special use of paleography is in the cryptic texts (for example, 4Q186, 4Q249, 4Q250, 4Q298, 4Q313, 4Q317, and 4Q324c). An analysis of the script (labeled "Cryptic A") shows an eclectic assortment of influences.[59] Cryptic A script is clearly an artificial creation. Stephen Pfann observes that "the contents of this short scroll [4Q298] wouldn't seem to warrant such careful protection" using a cryptic script; yet Pfann concludes that use of the Cryptic A script suggests that "all Essene teaching, even the foundational principles, was treated as crucial, even mystical knowledge, and hence was worthy of concealment from non-members."[60] If we understand QH as an antilanguage, however, this need not be the case. Halliday points out that antilanguages do not merely arise from the desire for secrecy, but they help to form group boundaries and reflect the subjective reality of the group.[61]

One feature of antilanguages, as Irvine noted earlier, is "their elaboration of lexicon and metaphor relevant to their special activities and their attitudes toward the normative society." This feature is reflected in the *yaḥad* community's use of code terminology and metaphor and in the development of a peculiar lexicon. The use of code (or "typological") terminology in the scrolls is well known. Code terminology is used for people, such as the Teacher of Righteousness (for example, 1QpHab 1:13; 8:3; CD 1:11; 4QpPs[a] frags. 1–10 3:15), the Wicked Priest (for example, 1QpHab 1:13; 4QpPs[a] frags. 1–10 4:8), the Man of the Lie (for example, CD 20:15; 1QpHab 5:11), and the Lion of Wrath (for example, 4QpNah frags. 3–4 1:5–6). It is used for concepts like Damascus (for example, CD 6:5, 19), the Kittim (for example, 1QpHab 2:12; 1QM 1:2; 4QpNah frags. 3–4 1:3), or the house of Judah (for example, CD 4:11; 4QpPs[a] frags. 1–10 2:13). Lexicon is developed to describe the community's interpretative activities (for example, the *pesher* genre) and to set it against the establishment that is described as "the seekers of smooth things" (for example, CD 1:18; 1QH 10:32; 4QpNah frags. 3–4 1:2) or "those who move the boundary" (for example, CD 1:16; 5:20).

Another feature of antilanguages, according to Irvine, is "their conspicuous avoidance and violation of forms recognized as 'standard.'" Qumran Hebrew displays just such a studied avoidance of both Aramaisms and popular language on the surface level of language. Indeed, it seems that none of the

Aramaic scrolls found among the Qumran texts derive from the *yaḥad* community, as is indicated by the lack of distinctively Qumran terminology or orthography among the Aramaic scrolls. The very fact that none of the Aramaic scrolls appear to have been composed by the *yaḥad* community already suggests a conscious avoidance of the Aramaic language.[62] This is not to say that the standard language did not influence the antilanguage developed among the *yaḥad* community; after all, the creation of the antilanguage arises out of the standard language. Nevertheless, antilanguages are a conscious reaction to the standard language, particularly in some of its most recognizable features (for example, the spelling of personal pronouns like הוא vs. הואה in QH).

Qumran Hebrew is conspicuous in its paucity of loanwords. Kutscher, for example, writes, "It is astonishing that the DSS should contain so few new foreign loans except for Aramaic and those that are already part and parcel of BH."[63] This contrasts with RH, which is replete with loanwords not only from Aramaic and Greek but also from Latin.[64] It is noteworthy that the Copper Scroll and MMT (Halakhic Letter)—two decidedly sectarian texts—both indicate that the scribes at Qumran could write in RH. The Copper Scroll itself was first described as being written in "colloquial Mishnaic Hebrew."[65] J. T. Milik's official publication of the Copper Scroll included an extensive discussion of its language. Among other things, Milik noted the exclusive use of the RH relative particle *š* (-שׁ), as opposed to the regular biblical term *ʾšr* (אשׁר), and the typical RH plural morpheme *-yn* (-ין) instead of the SBH *-ym* (-ים). These RH forms occur elsewhere in the scrolls, but only irregularly.[66] The avoidance of typically RH forms of language must thus be considered a studied avoidance.

The *yaḥad* scribes were not entirely successful in their avoidance of Aramaisms. Bar-Asher offers examples of what he terms "involuntary" Aramaisms in the sectarian literature, which seem to stem from knowledge of the targumic traditions.[67] Kutscher notes, "In spite of the strong desire . . . to preserve the purity of the Hebrew language, it was impossible to avoid the absorption—both conscious and unconscious—of elements from the rival tongue."[68] Kutscher assumes that the mother tongue of the scribe for the Great Isaiah Scroll was Aramaic and consequently that the scribe "inadvertently grafted Aramaic forms upon the Hebrew text."[69] Such examples include the defective spelling *mwznym*, "balances, scales" (מוזנים), which follows Aramaic as against the SBH form *mʾznym* (מאזנים; Isa. 40:12; see also v. 15) that derives from a popular etymology relating to the root *ʾzn* (אזן), "ear."

The area in which the *yaḥad* scribes had the most difficulty avoiding popular language was the deep structure of language, namely, syntax. It is particularly unfortunate then to focus overly on vocabulary when analyzing the differences between QH and SBH.[70] A paradigmatic example of changes in the deep structures of language in QH is the use of the relative particle *ʾšr*, "that, which." We have discussed this term earlier as an Aramaism, but from the perspective of lexicon it might be called a classicism. In fact, the feature becomes the first argument for Shelomo Morag's argument that QH "is neither Biblical nor Mishnaic, but rather an independent entity."[71] However, the syntax of *ʾšr* in the sectarian scrolls approximates *š* in RH as well as *d-* in Aramaic. This is apparent first of all in the fact that *ʾšr* is employed more frequently in QH than in SBH—a tendency that begins already in LBH, which eschews asyndetic syntax. More important, *ʾšr* is employed in ways more typical of *š* in RH; for example, *ʾšr* begins to replace *ky*, "because," introducing a causal clause, just as we see in RH.[72] We may take as one example of this phenomenon the phrase "they shall receive judgments of fire *because* [*ʾšr*] they blasphemed and insulted the chosen ones of God" (1QpHab 10:13); in this example, *ʾšr* has become like the Aramaic particle *dy* or RH *š*, introducing a causal clause, much like the use of *ky* in SBH.

Rabin provides examples that he terms "involuntary Mishnaisms."[73] He gives a number of examples of lexical items, including *prwš* (פרוש), "exact" (for example, CD 2:13; 4:8); *msr* (מסר), "to pass over" (CD 3:3); *ḥrbn* (חרבן), "destruction" (CD 5:20); *htʿnyt* (התענית), "fast" (CD 6:19); and *srk* (סרך), "rule" (for example, 1QS 1:1; CD 7:6; 10:4). A prime example of RH morphology in QH would be the infinitive *lyrwš* (לירוש), "to inherit" (CD 1:7);[74] elsewhere QH invariably uses the SBH form *lršt* (לרשת; for example, CD 8:4; 19:27; 1QpHab 2:15; 3:2; 11QT 51:16). The scribes obviously know both forms, but they do not (and probably could not) consistently employ the SBH form as against the contemporary RH form. This example confirms Rabin's labeling of such forms as "involuntary." The involuntary label also accords with the nature of antilanguages and emphasizes the impact of language ideology on QH.

Further examples readily demonstrate that the use of Mishnaic or Aramaic syntax is frequent in QH. For instance, the use of the prohibitive construction *lʾ* + *l-* with the infinitive is quite common (for example, 1QS 1:6, ולוא ללכת, "and he shall not walk").[75] This construction is exceedingly rare in biblical literature, with only ten occurrences, many from late contexts or in biblical Aramaic texts.[76] This syntactical construction is a regular feature of Jewish Palestinian Aramaic and likely comes into Hebrew through Aramaic influence.[77] Likewise, the use of periphrastic constructions (that is, *hyh* + participle) in QH reflects a transition from LBH, where such constructions are relatively infrequent but attested, to RH, where these constructions become a regular feature of the language.[78] Thus, we find both similarity and distinction between QH and RH. Even where scribes could replace RH lexemes with their more classical counterparts, they were not consistently able to eliminate the influence of contemporary syntax from RH.

It is impossible to fully account for the linguistic peculiarities of QH by supposing that it was simply an attempt to imitate biblical Hebrew. We must dismiss the idea that QH is simply archaizing. There is something more going on. There is no evidence, for example, that distinctive Qumran forms like the long pronouns *hwʾh* and *hyʾh* are archaic, other than fanciful historical linguistic imagination. These are anomalous forms, yet they are the most recognizable feature of QH. This is certainly not archaizing based on any orthography known from the Masoretic tradition or ancient Hebrew inscriptions.[79] In this respect, it is not even a pseudoclassicism. In contrast, it could be argued that forms such as the elongated *hmh* and *hnh* are based on biblical forms—that is, they are archaisms or pseudoclassicisms. Likewise, the so-called long imperfect (for example, *ʾdʿh*, "I shall know," 1QH[a] 7:26) found in sectarian texts could be understood as a pseudoclassicism. The form apparently occurs only in the first-person imperfect.[80] Such elongated forms in SBH are cohortatives (for example, Gen. 18:29); however, already in LBH such forms are sometimes used as simple indicatives, and the cohortative (along with the jussive) will completely disappear in RH.[81] Undoubtedly, the cohortative as a unique morphological form no longer existed in the vernacular of the late Second Temple period. The *yaḥad* scribes employ what may only be understood as an attempt to use the cohortative form, but often without an understanding of the grammatical form. A particularly instructive example of the eclipse of the cohortative may be found in 11QT 56:13, where a scribe makes a supralinear correction, ואמרתה אשיםה עלי מלך ככול הגואים, in order to correct 11QT according to Deuteronomy 17:14 (אשׂימה), "and you shall say, '*Let me set* a king over me like all the nations.'" The 11QT manuscript uses the final *mem* for the verb, indicating that it is morphologically a simple imperfect. Although the correction above the line might be construed as morphologically correcting this to a cohortative, in fact, this elongated form is a typical form for the simple imperfect in QH. This error and correction exhibits the natural tendency for the cohortative forms to disappear. The frequent misuse of the cohortative suggests that the use of these long forms reflects the classicizing tendency of *yaḥad* scribes.

Another apparent example of an attempt to imitate biblical style is the regular use of SBH "pausal" forms. For example, the penultimate accentuation of the *qal* imperfect forms, that is, *yqtwlw* (for example, 1QS 6:4, 7, 17, 21, 22), which is one of the characteristics of Qumran scribal practice, is widely known in biblical Hebrew as a pausal form resulting from the accent on a final syllable. Another example of a pausal form in Qumran scribal practice is the 3m and 3f pronouns, *hmh* and *hnh*. It has been argued that "the pausal forms [in biblical Hebrew] act as punctuation, reflecting a logical system of text division."[82] The pausal forms are well known in biblical literature but especially common in prophetic speech and poetry (for example, Pss. 10:8; 56:7; Isa. 1:18; 5:11; 9:18; 11:10; 13:17; Jer. 3:16; 5:26; Ezek. 23:47; Hosea 4:10; 8:7). This is partly because pausal forms mark syntactic units, and poetry naturally tends to be broken into smaller syntactical units than prose. As a result, pausal forms are much more dense in poetry (for example, psalms, prophetic literature) than in prose. Moreover, poetry also exhibits irregular word order, so that verbs (for example, *yqtwlw*) and pronouns (for example, *hmh*) are more likely to appear as the last word of a syntactical unit and therefore in pause. If these pausal forms in biblical literature are a form of punctuation, as has been suggested, then the use of pausal forms as regular scribal practice obviates their biblical meaning. They can no longer serve as a form of punctuation, because they are used indiscriminately. What were the *yaḥad* scribes trying to do by making these pausal forms a feature of Qumran scribal practice? They are not precisely trying to imitate biblical style, because they would have known quite well that these were not regular forms.

The changing meaning and use of the *waw* consecutive (that is, the *waw* + prefix conjugation) also illustrates the use of biblical form (surface structure) without understanding the biblical meaning (deep structure). In SBH, the *waw* consecutive is a narrative tense, whereas in QH it becomes a tense converter without regard to syntax (as the medieval grammarians understood it—*waw ha-hipukh*, "converting waw").[83] The SBH use of the *waw* consecutive as a narrative preterite was already in decline in LBH and completely disappeared by RH. For example, a staple of SBH prose is the narrative formula *wyhy*, "and it came to pass"—a feature no longer present in QH. Qumran Hebrew used the *waw* consecutive as a converted tense in imitation of classical style but did not capture the nuances of its narrative syntax.

By way of concluding the discussion of QH, it is worthwhile to reflect on how the Halakhic Letter (or MMT) as well as the Temple Scroll fit into our description of QH as an antilanguage.[84] MMT was written using an epistolary expression: "we have written to you" (אנחנו כתבנו, 4Q398 frag. 14–17 2:2). Many scholars think this is rhetorical, that is, it was not legal correspondence addressed from the community to the Jerusalem temple leadership. Nevertheless, it is couched in such terms, and the linguistic register must be contextualized as part of this rhetoric. In their publications, Elisha Qimron and

John Strugnell have emphasized some of the striking differences between the Hebrew of MMT and the rest of the sectarian literature. In a word, MMT is more "Mishnaic." It uses, for instance, the usual RH relative pronoun *š* (שׁ), "that, which," as opposed to the more typical Qumran use of SBH *ʾšr* (אשר). Qimron and Strugnell summarize the situation as follows: "A close examination of the linguistic components proves that the similarity to RH is restricted to vocabulary and to the use of the particle שׁ, whereas in areas of grammar (spelling, phonology, morphology, and syntax) there is very great similarity to the Hebrew of other Dead Sea Scrolls."[85] Two factors account for these differences. First of all, MMT was rhetorically couched as a letter sent to the Jerusalem aristocracy; hence, it used the common vernacular. Second, as indicated by the content of MMT, it is couched as a rapprochement to the Jerusalem aristocracy and therefore uses a common rather than sectarian language. As Halliday points out, antilanguages arise as "a counter-reality, set up in opposition to some established norm."[86] The attempt at rapprochement in MMT would not have been conducive to the use of an antilanguage.

The Temple Scroll is another Dead Sea text that illustrates a strong language ideology. First it needs to be acknowledged that the Temple Scroll seems to be an early text, with fragments dating to 125 B.C.E. It dates to an early period in the formation of the *yaḥad*—certainly a very early period in the development of Qumran scribal practice—and predates the Qumran sectarian settlement.[87] As previously mentioned, the classicizing tendencies in QH generally follow the lines of biblical poetry known primarily from the Psalter but also from the prophets. More specifically, the elongated forms of the Temple Scroll follow classical Hebrew poetry. Second, poetic texts such as the Psalms and prophetic books were believed to be the speech of God. The prophetic speeches are explicitly introduced as the speech of God, for example, "Thus says the Lord" (כה אמר יהוה), and texts such as the Psalms Scroll show the Psalms were "prophecy" as well (note 11Q5 27:11). Third, the Temple Scroll rewrites the voice of the Torah (especially Deuteronomy) so that the book frames itself as the direct speech of God. In keeping with this direct speech, the language used idiosyncrasies in Hebrew known especially from biblical poetry and prophetic speech, for example, forms like המה, אחיהו, or יקטולו. The peculiar language of the Temple Scroll is a reflex of the change in voice. In other words, now the Torah is a direct revelation of God, and God's speech is different from human speech. The linguistic register of the Temple Scroll reflects this. We get glimpses of this divine language in biblical poetry or prophetic speech, both considered by the sectarians as more directly divine speech than the canonical Pentateuch. The penultimate accentuation of the *qal* imperfect forms, that is, יקטולו, is also considered a classicism. Such forms are known in biblical poetry but especially in the prophetic speech of God (for example, Pss. 10:8; 56:7; Isa. 1:18; 5:11; 9:18; 11:10; 13:17; Jer. 3:16; 5:26; Ezek. 23:47; Hosea 4:10; 8:7). The reasonable inference is that these forms are used as a reflex of the *genre* of the Temple Scroll. The Temple Scroll is the speech of God; its language is the language of God. In this respect, the Temple Scroll is quite similar to the theology of the *yaḥad* poet who writes: "my language is as one of your disciples" (1QH 15:10). It is quite typical for religious sectarians to develop such strong religious ideology with regard to language.

In sum, it is important to create a systemic analysis of Qumran Hebrew. Typical analyses of QH have labored under the neogrammarian approaches to language with assumptions about the immutability of linguistic rules and the isolation of language from the rest of the cultural system. In the case of QH, however, the very obvious linguistic ideology of the speakers—which was, moreover, a more general issue of Jewish culture in the late Second Temple period—begs for a sociolinguistic approach that tries to account for a whole array of linguistic data with the theory that language (and linguistic data) must be explained within a cultural system.

Commonly Proposed Features of Qumran Hebrew

The corpus of sectarian religious texts from the region of Khirbet Qumran begins with the characteristic texts and genres found in multiple copies. These include the *Damascus Document*, the *Community Rule*, the pesher texts, and the *War Scroll*. More fragmentary texts as well as texts that include only a single exemplar must be approached more cautiously in describing the sectarian speech community, though they are a valuable resource for describing the broader phenomenon of Hebrew in the late Hellenistic and early Roman periods.

Some commonly proposed features of Qumran Hebrew include the following:

1. Increased use of vowel letters (i.e., *plene* spelling). For example, the negative particle *lwʾ*, "not" (compare SBH *lʾ*); *kwh*, "thus" (compare SBH *kh*); or *rwʾš*, "head" (compare SBH *rʾš*).
2. Elongated forms. Some of these are merely new spelling conventions based on vernacular phonology, such as nominal and verbal suffixes like –*kh*, "you" (compare SBH -*k*). Others seem to be partially formed on the basis of biblical pausal forms; hence, pronouns like *hmh*, "they"; the suffix –*mh*, "their" (compare SBH -*m*); or the

3mp verbal form *yšmwrw*, "they shall guard," have clear antecedents in biblical pausal forms. In contrast, elongated forms like the pronouns *hwʾh*, "he" (compare SBH *hwʾ*); *ʾtmh*, "you [plural]" (compare SBH *ʾtm*); or the adverb *mʾwdh*, "very" (compare SBH *mʾd*) seem to be analogical.

3. Spelling with final *aleph*. New spellings for words add a final *aleph* with no apparent historical antecedent, as in *kyʾ*, "because" (compare SBH *ky*), or *myʾ*, "who?" (compare SBH *my*).
4. Changes in the verbal system. The decreasing use of forms such as the *waw* consecutive, the infinitive absolute, and infinitive constructs with *b*- or *k*-. The archaic passive *qal* is replaced by the *niphal*. The periphrastic verbal syntax (the verb *hyh*, "to be," coordinated with a participle) becomes more common.
5. Use of classical Hebrew lexemes with later Hebrew and Aramaic syntax. The most notable example is the relative *ʾšr*, "that, which, because," in a manner similar to RH *š*- and Aramaic *dy, d*-.
6. The use of asyndetic syntax (typical of SBH) almost disappears. Relative particles, especially *ʾšr* and sometimes *š*-, coordinate clauses.

9

The End and the Beginning of Hebrew

The language of the Torah is a language by itself, and the language of the sages is a language by itself.

—*Babylonian Talmud*

Our account of the social history of classical Hebrew comes to an end in about 200 C.E., after the two Jewish revolts in the first and second centuries. It was an end for Hebrew, but it was also a new beginning for the Hebrew language. The revolts against Rome resulted in the displacement of the Hebrew speech communities of Roman Palestine. With the displacement of most Hebrew speakers, vernacular Hebrew waned. In a manner of speaking, this was the end of Hebrew as a living language. Yet, this was not the end of the Hebrew language: Hebrew continued as a secondary vernacular among disparate Jewish communities as well as continuing as a religious and literary language. But it was an end to the continuity of Hebrew as a living language in the land. It was the end of the continuous speech communities that stretched back more than a thousand years, from when the Israelites first settled in Canaan and then later developed a writing system for their language. At the same time, this also marked the rise of Rabbinic Hebrew

(RH) as a literary language and as a language of Jewish culture. It was this preservation and even flourishing of Hebrew as a literary language that paved the way for the rebirth of the Hebrew language as a living language almost two thousand years later.

The seminal events of the final stage of Hebrew as a living language spoken in Palestine were the two Jewish revolts. The first revolt, or Great Revolt, against Rome began in 66 C.E. and lasted until the fall of Masada in 74 C.E. The Roman quashing of this revolt was punctuated by the destruction of the Jerusalem temple, after which point Jews were no longer permitted to live in Jerusalem but did remain in Judea. A second revolt—the Bar Kokhba revolt—lasted from 132 until 135 C.E. This revolt emanated from the villages of Judea, and it also resulted in the destruction and displacement of most Judean villages.

With respect to the history of vernacular Hebrew, the decisive break was not the Babylonian exile but rather the Bar Kokhba revolt. Although the Babylonian exile was a milestone in the history of Hebrew, particularly in the literary dialect and the scribal schools, it was not a turning point. The Babylonian campaigns resulted in more than 80 percent of the towns and villages around Judah being destroyed, but a remnant of the Hebrew speech community survived. Though such minority speech communities struggle against their environment, they do survive and even thrive. Striking examples include modern Aramaic speech communities in West Asia, which have continued until this very day;[1] according to the Summer Institute of Linguistics' *Ethnologue*, about 550,000 native speakers of Neo-Aramaic dialects were living in 1994. Thus, the survival of speech communities that are not displaced is a well-known phenomenon, and we may confidently posit the survival of Hebrew speech communities into the first centuries of the Common Era. The Second Jewish revolt, however, resulted in the systematic displacement of Jewish villages in Judea. It would be a turning point for the social history of Hebrew.

The revolts were also pivotal for the writing down of the major texts in Rabbinic Hebrew. The codification of the Mishnah is usually dated to about 220 C.E. and ascribed to Rabbi Judah "the Prince" (or Judah Ha-Nasi). The Mishnah is the codification of the *Oral* Torah—literally, the "*torah* in the mouth" (תורת שבעל פה). According to the Sayings of the Fathers, "Moses received the [oral] *torah* from Sinai and passed it on to Joshua, and Joshua to the elders, and the elders to the prophets, and the prophets passed it on to the men of the great assembly" (*m. Avot* 1:1). The oral transmission is highlighted by the verbal expressions, and scholars have regarded the oral heritage of the Mishnah as the defining linguistic character of the corpus. As such, the linguistic differences between biblical Hebrew and RH are often described as relating to a type of diglossia—namely, the distance between the written language and vernacular speech. A standard work on the history of Hebrew by Angel Sáenz-Badillos, for example, suggests that "whereas BH was the language of literature and administration, the spoken language even before the exile might have been an early version of what would later become RH."[2] The demographic shift of the Jewish population from Judea to Galilee in late antiquity no doubt further encouraged the rising prominence of Aramaic. The Talmud (ca. 500 C.E.), for example, would be written primarily in Aramaic. Aramaic eventually completely replaced Hebrew as both a literary and a vernacular language.

One of the consequences of the Jewish revolts was the diminishing knowledge of Hebrew. On the one hand, this gave impetus to the writing down of Jewish oral tradition, beginning with the Mishnah. On the other hand, this also gave rise to allowances for those who no longer spoke or understood Hebrew. For example, according to *m. Megillah 2:1*, those who do not know Hebrew are permitted to read the scroll of Esther "in a foreign language." The foreign language here is probably Greek, but allowances are made especially for Aramaic, which becomes an increasingly important Jewish language. Exceptions are given for the reading and translation of the Scriptures into Aramaic in the synagogue (for example, *t. Megillah* 3:41). The reading of the Aramaic translations of the Torah (that is, the Targums) in the synagogue is a practice that dates back into the Second Temple period in Galilee, but it became especially prominent after the two Jewish revolts.[3]

How is it that *written* texts such as the Mishnah or the Mekilta are characterized as vernacular? Indeed, we should be uneasy with *oral* characterization of *written* artifacts. In the case of RH, however, this oral description may in part be justified by the linguistic ideology of rabbinic literature. The authority of the Mishnah lay precisely in the oral character of its origin and transmission; that is, "Moses received the [oral] *torah* from Sinai and passed it on" (*m. Avot* 1:1). The authority of the Oral Torah had to compete with the written Torah—the Pentateuch—which in biblical accounts is variously penned by Moses (for example, Exod. 24:4; Deut. 31:9) or engraved on the tablets by the finger of God himself (for example, Exod. 31:18; Deut. 9:10). The Pentateuch was the quintessential written text, and the Mishnah had little room to claim authority as a written artifact. The Mishnah therefore had to claim its authority in oral tradition, and it purposefully represented itself as vernacular. The textualization of the Mishnah was a turning point for the transition of RH from a living language into a literary language.

Rabbinic Hebrew: From a Living to a Literary Language

Hebrew in late antiquity is usually called either *Rabbinic* Hebrew or *Mishnaic* Hebrew (MH). The term *RH* corresponds to the social group most closely associated with the literary preservation of the language, whereas the term *MH* relates to the major literary corpus. Rabbinic Hebrew has been divided into two periods, 70–200 C.E. and 200–500 C.E., corresponding to the Tannaim and the Amoraim. The Tannaim were rabbinic sages who flourished between 70 C.E. and 200 C.E., and the Amoraim were later sages conventionally dated between 200 C.E. and 500 C.E. This distinction divides RH into two substrata, reflecting the eclipse of Hebrew as a living language. The seminal event for this division was the Bar Kokhba revolt, which was pivotal to the fate of Hebrew as a living language. As Angel Sáenz-Badillos writes, "The decisive incident separating the two periods is the collapse of the Bar-Kochba revolt in 135 C.E., which led to the dispersal of the people of Judaea."[4] As sociolinguistic studies have shown, the geographic continuity of speech communities is critical to the continuation of the vernacular. Few Hebrew speech communities survived the two Jewish revolts. It usually takes two generations for language death in a displaced speech community. In the present case, the Bar Kokhba revolt meant the final displacement of most Hebrew speech communities and with it the demise of vernacular Hebrew, which is usually given a terminus of about 200 C.E. Such dates, of course, are merely approximations that bookmark the transition.

The First Jewish revolt (66–73 C.E.) had already resulted in significant displacements of Hebrew speech communities, but the Roman destruction and displacement seems to have been primarily focused on Jerusalem. Some Hebrew-speaking villages in Judea survived and continued to preserve Hebrew as a living language. However, the Second Jewish revolt emanated from Judean villages such as Bethar (modern Battir; also spelled Betar or Beitar), whose history stretched back into the First Temple period. Bethar was the last settlement to fall, marking the end of the Bar Kokhba revolt. Few Hebrew-speaking villages survived to perpetuate the indigenous speech communities after the Bar Kokhba revolt. There are indications that a small number of Hebrew-speaking communities may have existed through the fourth century C.E. For example, Rabbi Jonathan from Eleutheropolis—a town in the southern foothills of Judah—could still encourage speaking Hebrew as a vernacular (*y. Megillah* 71b). Already in the late second century C.E., Rabbi Judah the Prince had to rely on his housekeeper as an informant for Hebrew (*b. Hullin* 137b)![5] Vernacular Hebrew was dying, and Hebrew would have to survive as a secondary language.

The evidence for the continuity of vernacular Hebrew until the Second Jewish revolt comes in varied forms. For example, the Qumran documents show continuity with LBH (often in distinction from SBH) and RH.[6] This suggests a continuity in vernacular Hebrew into the last century B.C.E. and first century C.E. To be sure, the Hebrew-speaking communities were pressured by the other socially and politically dominant speech communities—first Aramaic, then Greek, and finally Latin. The common belief is that Hebrew was most widely used as a vernacular in Judea, whereas Aramaic was used in Galilee. It is also possible that Greek became a vernacular for Jewish communities in Greco-Roman cities like Joppa or Caesarea Maritima; however, the Greek loanwords in RH are largely confined to aspects of the marketplace and Roman administration, suggesting that Greek functioned as a secondary language rather than a primary vernacular for Jewish communities.

What about written Hebrew? Hebrew was no longer an administrative language after the first centuries of the Common Era. Written Hebrew had served as a religious language—the "holy language"—as well as an expression of political ideology (for example, in the coins of the First and Second Jewish revolts). Whereas vernacular Hebrew struggled to survive the First Jewish revolt, written Hebrew struggled to survive the Roman destruction of Jerusalem in 70 C.E.

A primary social location for scribes was the Jerusalem temple, and the First Jewish revolt dealt a devastating blow to the Hebrew scribal communities. One alternative for Jewish scribal activity was the sectarian religious community—the Essenes—associated with Khirbet Qumran, but the site of Qumran was destroyed by the Romans in 68 C.E., and the sectarian movement seems to have ended with the destruction of the site. This sectarian religious movement was priestly in background. Both the social context of the scribes and the economic support for the scribal community would have been disenfranchised by the Jewish revolts. Scribes were primarily drawn from the priestly classes in the Second Temple period. This begins paradigmatically with the figure of the priest Ezra. Likewise, the leader and founder of the Dead Sea community, the Teacher of Righteousness, is a priestly figure. The scribal role of the priests in teaching and writing perhaps reaches its apex in the messianic figure of the priestly *Doresh Ha-torah*, the Interpreter of the Law, as described in the Dead Sea Scrolls. In contrast, the Pharisees were not known as scribes, and it is not surprising that there are no Pharisaic texts from the Second Temple period. The Jewish revolts, however, destroyed the temple and must have shifted the social location of scribes. This began a process that eventually resulted in written texts (for example, the Mishnah) produced by the rabbis (that is, nonpriests).

There are many references to the importance of education in ancient Jewish culture.[7] For example, Josephus writes that Jews were commanded "to bring those children up in learning"—literally, the *instruction in letters* (γράμματα παιδεύειν).[8] However, most of the allusions to early Jewish education mention not reading and writing but rather knowledge of the Torah, often acquired by hearing the recitation of texts. Thus, for example, in his *Antiquities*, Josephus relates as follows: "Let the high priest stand upon a high desk, whence he may be heard, and let him read the laws to all the people; and let neither the women nor the children be hindered from hearing" (*Ant.* 4.214). This seems to be the more typical manner of acquiring knowledge of the Torah, namely, that a priest or scribe recited it, and children memorized and repeated. Philo states hyperbolically that Jews were taught "from their very swaddling-clothes by their parents, and teachers, and instructors, and even before that by their holy laws, and also by their unwritten maxims and customs, to believe that there was but one God, their Father and the Creator of the world" (*Gaius* 115). This instruction of very young children in the Torah was aimed not at reading and writing but at memorizing and reciting. Yet there was also an emphasis on the formal and public reading of the Torah, as in the well-known example in which Jesus visited a synagogue, was given a scroll of Isaiah, and performed a public reading (Luke 4:16–24).

Private ownership and study of texts was quite limited. For example, the cost of scrolls in antiquity meant that private ownership was prohibitive; even synagogues may not have owned an entire collection of the biblical scrolls. It is no coincidence that the most commonly quoted books in the New Testament are Deuteronomy, Psalms, and Isaiah and that they are also found in the most copies in the Qumran caves. Education involved the reading of these scrolls by a teacher and memorization by students. Limited education in "letters," namely, the ability to do public recitation along with memorization of the Torah, was part of the general education of Jewish boys. As a result, Hebrew would survive its demise as an everyday vernacular. It would continue as a religious language and could serve as a trade language within the Jewish Diaspora.

Tannaitic Hebrew (RH_1) is mainly known from literature that records the words of the Tannaim as well as the last of the *zugot* (Hebrew, "pairs"). The *zugot* refer especially to five pairs of rabbis at the end of the Second Temple period, culminating with Hillel and Shammai (that is, the period from 150 B.C.E. to 30 C.E.). They are followed by the Tannaim, that is, the sages who lived between 70 and 200 C.E. Tannaitic literary texts include the Mishnah, the Tosefta, and the Tannaitic midrashim (including Mekilta, Sifra, and Sifre). Still, it is an oversimplification to label RH_1 as a vernacular. First of all, the corpus consists of literary texts. Second, the compilers of these rabbinic texts were educated elites who studied in schools.

The problem of describing literary texts like the Mishnah is highlighted when we compare it to epigraphic discoveries like the Bar Kokhba texts. Such epigraphic discoveries represent a closer representation of aspects of vernacular Hebrew in late antiquity. To be sure, they are still texts, but they are not generated by educated elites, and they reflect the more mundane interactions of daily life. Textual artifacts represent a less standardized form of RH_1, but for this reason they are also an important control for the description of the Hebrew of late antiquity. Perhaps the best illustration of the vernacular influence in the Bar Kokhba texts is assimilation and syncopation. In the Bar Kokhba documents, we find assimilated forms such as *ʿnpšh* (ענפשה), instead of *ʿl npšh* (על נפשה), "on his own behalf," which is known from both SBH and RH. This is simply a reflection of the speech patterns. Likewise, syncopated forms such as *mmrh* (ממרה), instead of SBH *mʾmrh* (מאמרה), "his statement," reflect vernacular speech more than standardized spellings found in literary texts. Such examples remind us that although RH_1 may draw upon vernacular, it comes to us as a textualized and standardized vernacular.

The displacement of Hebrew speech communities after the Bar Kokhba revolt eventually led into a second stage of Rabbinic Hebrew, namely, Amoraic Hebrew (RH_2). As RH_2 represents a stage when Hebrew was no longer a living language in Palestine, it stands outside the scope of this study, which has been framed by the social history of Hebrew as a daily language in the land of Palestine. Amoraic Hebrew covers the sages of the Talmud who flourished from the time when the Mishnah was codified until the codification of the Talmud (about 500 C.E.). The Amoraic rabbis were active in both Palestine and Babylon. In addition to the Babylonian and Palestinian Talmuds, their writings included midrashim such as Midrash Rabba. These writings reflect the eclipse of Hebrew as a vernacular language and the increasing influence of Aramaic upon the written Hebrew literary language. Hebrew remained important for the Jewish Diaspora, but it was important as the language of the Torah, the (former) temple, and the Jewish liturgical tradition. Hebrew was the "holy language," but it was no longer the everyday language.

Language and Jewish Identity in the Roman World

The Hebrew language continued to be a flashpoint for Jewish identity in the Roman world. Although Aramaic was the dominant language in Jewish Palestine during the first centuries C.E., Hebrew continued to be used and even predominated in certain contexts. In the Jewish Diaspora, Greek would become a Jewish language. Indeed, Greek translations of the Bible were even found among the Dead Sea Scrolls. Nevertheless, Hebrew was still a cornerstone of Jewish identity. For example, the brief inscriptions from Masada dealing with "priestly shares" are predominantly written with Hebrew morphology, especially using the Hebrew definite article *h-*.

Hebrew was emblematic of the Jewish revolts, as can be seen in a variety of ways. The most well known, of course, are on artifacts of the incipient Jewish state, namely, the use of Paleo-Hebrew script and Hebrew language on Bar Kokhba coins.

Especially revealing is the shifting emphasis toward Hebrew in textual artifacts. It is generally acknowledged that Aramaic was increasingly important in Jewish Palestine during the first centuries C.E. Yet, in certain contexts, Hebrew reasserted its ideological importance to Jewish identity. This is striking in the textual artifacts from the Bar Kokhba revolt. As Yigael Yadin observed, "It is interesting that the earlier documents are written in Aramaic while the later ones are in Hebrew. Possibly the change was made by a special decree of Bar-Kokhba who wanted to restore Hebrew as the official language of the state."[9] This is especially striking because the main language at the end of the Second Temple period was Aramaic. For example, the three letters from Masada are all written in Aramaic, which is also the language of the administrative dockets.[10] Because of the similarity between Hebrew and Aramaic, certain linguistic features serve as markers for the Hebrew or Aramaic language. The interchangeability of Hebrew and Aramaic is nicely illustrated by the telltale use of definite articles—Hebrew with the prefix *h-* and Aramaic with a suffix *-ʾ*; although the Aramaic suffixed *ʾaleph* is most common, the Hebrew prefixed *heh* occurs six times. Another linguistic marker is the word for "son"; both the Hebrew *bn* and the Aramaic *br* are used in personal names, even though the Aramaic is dominant. Aramaic had become the vernacular and administrative language, but Hebrew was being revived under the auspices of the Bar Kokhba administration.

Already in the Mishnah, Aramaic received an equal footing with Hebrew as a sacred language. For example, we read in *m. Yadayim* 4:5:

> The Aramaic (passages) that are in Ezra and Daniel impart uncleanness to hands. The Aramaic (passages contained in Scriptures) written in Hebrew, or a Hebrew (passage) written in Aramaic or (passages written in Paleo-) Hebrew letters do not impart uncleanness to hands. (Holy Scriptures) impart uncleanness to hands only if written in (square) Assyrian characters, on parchment, and with ink.

Scriptural texts were believed to impart uncleanness because they were sacred. In the above passage, the critical issue is not the language (Hebrew or Aramaic) or the writing system (Paleo-Hebrew or square Assyrian—that is, the typical Aramaic Jewish script) but rather the language in which the text was originally written. The archaic Hebrew script (which at that time was being used by the Samaritans) actually disqualified a text from being sacred. In Qumran manuscripts, the Paleo-Hebrew script (for example, contrast ʾ, *b*, *d* in Paleo-Hebrew 𐤀 𐤁 𐤃 with square script א ב ד) was employed especially to write the sacred name of God. This is in contrast to the rabbinic viewpoint, where Paleo-Hebrew actually becomes profane. The Aramaic (or Assyrian) script is the sacred script, and the Aramaic language is sacred for those passages (Gen. 31:47; Dan. 2:4b–7:28; Ezra 4:8–6:18; 7:12–26; Jer. 10:11) that were written in Aramaic. In fact, the very presence of Aramaic in the Hebrew Bible proved to the rabbis that it too was a sacred language. The Amoraic phase of RH would be much more heavily influenced by Aramaic.

After the Jewish revolts, symbols of Jewish nationalism were regarded with great contempt. Consequently, the speaking of Hebrew, even among speech communities that might have survived the two Jewish revolts intact, would have been greatly discouraged. The speech communities in Jerusalem and in Judea more generally were most disrupted by the Jewish revolts. Doron Bar notes that the uprisings were local and had an impact on "Judaean sites such as Kiryat Sefer, Hurvat Zikhrin, or Horvat Itri, villages that were inhabited by Jews until the second century and destroyed during the Bar Kokhba revolt."[11] In contrast, the number of settlements in Galilee actually increased during this time, many new settlements appeared, and others saw an expansion, "with farms extending into villages, and villages into small towns."[12] Some part of this growth and expansion must be seen as a direct result of the Jewish uprisings. The shifting demographics also meant a significant disjunction for the Hebrew speech communities that had remained in Judea.

The autonomy of Judea had a direct impact on language usage and language change. As Catherine Hezser points out, "In places with relatively clear cut geographical boundaries inhabited by people who all share the same mother tongue, a phenomenon which is especially prevalent in rural communities, contact with native speakers of another language tends to be very limited and is often restricted to trade situations only."[13] The autonomy of Judea before the Jewish revolts of the first and second centuries C.E. resulted in limited interaction between Jewish Palestine and the greater Roman world. Autonomy lent itself to the preservation of Hebrew-speaking communities. The Jewish wars dispersed the Hebrew speech communities, and Hebrew had to survive outside of autonomous Hebrew-speaking communities. From these changes to the Jewish communities of Roman Palestine sprang a textualization of vernacular Hebrew and the rise of Aramaic as a sacred language for the Jewish people.

History of the Study of Rabbinic Hebrew

The study of Rabbinic Hebrew itself has an interesting history, reflecting a deep-seated language ideology within the Jewish community through the ages. During the incipient stages of the study of Hebrew grammar in the Middle Ages, Jewish scholars first began the scientific study of Hebrew grammar, usually focusing on biblical Hebrew. Important early Jewish scholars, such as Saadia Gaon and Ibn Janaḥ, often cited rabbinic textual examples in expounding Hebrew grammar; however, RH was not an object of study itself but a means to understand the biblical text. The important medieval grammarian Menahem ben Saruq even argued that RH was an entirely different language.[14] Ben Saruq and his disciples argued that RH was a faulty and incomplete language that was inferior to biblical Hebrew, and they reserved the description of "holy tongue" for the Bible. Still, their position was a minority position. Most medieval grammarians had a more positive view of the grammatical and especially lexicographical contributions that RH could make to the study of Hebrew. The focus of medieval grammarians was the Bible itself, and the debate was merely over the role of RH in the grammatical description of biblical Hebrew.

The critical study of Rabbinic Hebrew began only in the eighteenth century. The primary questions were about the character of RH, its relationship with biblical Hebrew, and its nature as a living language. The classic work of Avraham Geiger, *Lehr- und Lesebuch zur Sprache der Mischnah*, published in 1845, set the agenda for the study of RH for the next century. Geiger believed that RH was a continuation of biblical Hebrew, but he also argued that RH was *not* a spoken language but rather an artificial creation. His oft-quoted conclusion was that "Hebrew had accordingly ceased to be a living language. It remained, however, like Latin in the medieval ages, a religious vernacular of scholars during the period of the Temple."[15] Geiger thought that Aramaic was the vernacular language of Palestine and that RH was invented by the rabbis based on both Aramaic and biblical Hebrew. This touched off a rather heated debate among Jewish scholars in the nineteenth and early twentieth centuries. The lines of this debate were largely drawn ideologically, between the Reform and Conservative Jewish communities. The work of Moshe Segal, *A Grammar of Mishnaic Hebrew*, first published in 1927, was a watershed in the debate. Segal began with a long introduction defending MH as a living language and downplaying its reliance on Aramaic, and this viewpoint eventually won general acceptance. Segal's arguments were further confirmed by Hebrew documents subsequently discovered in the region of the Dead Sea. The most well known of these new documents were the Dead Sea Scrolls. Perhaps most critical to our understanding of vernacular Hebrew were the Bar Kokhba letters, which concern matters of everyday life. Although Segal's argument that MH was a living language has become the consensus, he understated the influence of Aramaic.[16] Aramaic had a profound influence on the evolution of the living Hebrew vernacular during the Second Temple period and into late antiquity.

The sources for Rabbinic Hebrew present some difficulties. These begin with the fact that printed texts reflect a tendency to harmonize RH toward biblical Hebrew.[17] For example, printed texts invariably spell the word for "man" according to its biblical orthography *ʾdm* (אדם), whereas early manuscripts indicate that the spelling was *ʾdn* (אדן), reflecting the Aramaic influence on Hebrew that exchanged final *m* for *n*. Another example of this tendency is the personal name Lazarus, known from the New Testament and spelled in first-century inscriptions without the initial *ʾaleph*, *lʿzr* (לעזר), instead of the SBH form *ʾlʿzr* (אלעזר), "Eliezer"; all the printed early rabbinic texts, however, harmonize the spelling with biblical Hebrew. Such examples could be multiplied. They reflect the language ideology of the later Masoretic scribes and grammarians that generally regarded biblical Hebrew as the more "correct" form. More generally, it reflects the golden-age fallacy that assumes that older forms of language are better and more correct.

The scientific study of biblical Hebrew flourished in the medieval period, yet the opinion of medieval Jewish grammarians about Rabbinic Hebrew was the subject of some debate. Some, such as Menachem ben Saruq, regarded RH as a completely different language. Others, for example Saadia Gaon, emphasized the importance of RH as a source for clarifying the Bible, especially hapax legomena. For the most part, however, medieval grammarians did not consider RH a topic worthy of study, and the scientific study of RH began only in the early nineteenth century C.E. Rabbinic Hebrew was associated with Jewish life outside of the land and the nation, whereas biblical Hebrew was idealized as the language of the Jewish nation and state. In this respect, language ideology had an important role in shaping the history of the study of Hebrew long after the destruction of Jerusalem and the dispersal of the Hebrew-speaking communities in the land.

Commonly Proposed Features of Tannaitic Hebrew

The typical corpus for early Rabbinic or Tannaitic Hebrew (RH_1) would begin with the Mishnah. In addition, the Tosefta and the Tannaitic midrashim (including Mekilta, Sifra, and Sifre) are usually included in the corpus of Tannaitic texts. Inscriptions are an important external control to this description of RH_1, and the Bar Kokhba texts in particular bring a new perspective to late-antique Hebrew. Typically, features of RH_1 would be limited to Mishnaic texts, but here we have included some features found particularly in late-antique-Hebrew inscriptions. The inscriptional material gives a richer perspective on Hebrew in late antiquity.

Some commonly proposed linguistic features of Tannaitic Hebrew (RH_1) include the following:

1. Changes to the verbal system. As E. Y. Kutscher noted, "The most revolutionary change between BH and MH occurred in the area of tenses and moods."[18] In general, the verbal system shifts from being primarily aspectual (as in SBH) to being more tense oriented.[19] The beginnings of these changes can already be observed in LBH (as noted in chapter 7). Notable aspects include: (i) the SBH active participle is used with personal pronouns to generate a simple present tense and is regularly spelled *plene*, as in *qwrʾ* (קורא), "read," or *ʾwmr* (אומר), "say"; (ii) the word for "future," *ʿtyd*, is used in the verbal construction *ʿtyd l*-VERB (VERB-עתיד ל) to create the future tense; (iii) increased use of auxiliary verbs such as *hyh* (היה), "to be"; *htḥyl* (התחיל), "to begin"; *hlk* (הלך), "to go"; (iv) regular use of periphrastics, namely, the use of the verb *hyh* (היה), "to be," + active participle to express habitual action; (v) adverbs are used with auxiliary verbs followed by the preposition *l*-, "to," and infinitive verbs such as *ršyy* (רשיי), "permitted"; *ḥyyb* (חייב), "bound"; *ṣryk* (צריך), "need" (e.g., *ṣryk lqrwʾ* "need to designate" or *ṣryk lhpryš* "need to separate," Dem. 4:3); and (vi) disappearance of SBH verbal forms such as the *waw* consecutive, infinitive constructs with *b*- and *k*-, and special forms for the jussive and cohortative. At the same time, we have the appearance of new conjugations like the *Nitpa'al* and the *Nuf'al*.
2. *Plene* spelling. Standardized use of *waw*, *yod*, *ʾaleph*, and *heh* as vowel letters. The letters *waw* and *yod* are frequently doubled when they represent the consonants.

3. Final *mem* and *nun* appear to be almost interchangeable. This results, e.g., in the conflation of independent pronouns that were differentiated in SBH by a final *mem* on the masculine and *nun* on feminine forms, e.g., the masculine and feminine forms *ʾtm*/*ʾtn* (אתן/אתם), "you," and *hm*/*hn* (הן/הם), "they."
4. Irregular orthography. Gradual weakening of the Semitic gutturals whereby the laryngeal and pharyngeal graphemes are interchanged; the confusion of *bgdkpt* letters; interchange of sibilants, e.g., the interchange of *šin* and *samekh* in words like *sbr* (סבר/שׂ), "break."
5. Drift between *h* (ה) and *ʾ* (א). For example, in the Bar Kokhba texts we find the verbal forms *nqrh* (נקרה) instead of SBH *nqrʾ* (נקרא), "called"; *mwdʾ* (מודא) instead of SBH *mwdh* (מודה), "acknowledge"; and *mṣwʾ* (מצוא) instead of SBH *mṣwh* (מצוה), "command." The appearance of the *ʾapʿel* verbal stem (with preformative *ʾaleph*) instead of the typical SBH *hipʿil* is also noteworthy in this respect. Nonverbal forms include *mhrʾ* (מהרא) instead of SBH *mhrh* (מהרה), "quickly," and *špynʾ* (שפינא) instead of SBH *spynh* (ספינה), "ship."[20]
6. Assimilation and syncopation. In the Bar Kokhba documents, we find assimilated forms such as *ʿnpšh* (ענפשה) instead of SBH *ʿl npšh* (על נפשה), "on his own behalf," and syncopated forms such as *mmrh* (ממרה) instead of SBH *mʾmrh* (מאמרה), "his statement." This seems to reflect vernacular speech more than the standardized spellings found in the Mishnah.
7. Several SBH pronominal forms—1cs *ʾnky* (אנכי) and 1cp *ʾnḥnw* (אנחנו)—are no longer attested; instead, we find 1cs *ʾny* (אני) and 1cp *ʾnw* (אנו).
8. Aramaic influence in the 2ms and 2fs pronominal suffixes, spelled *-k*, presumably pronounced /*-āk/ (2ms) and /*-îk/ (2fs); e.g., *mnk* (מנך), "from you," and *bʿlyk* (בעליך), "your husband," instead of SBH *-k(h)* and *-k(y)*.
9. Increased use of the relative pronouns, particularly *š-* (-ש), "that, which." In addition, the genitive particle *šl* (של) to form genitival constructions; the demonstrative pronouns; masculine singular *zh* (זה); feminine singular *zw* (זו), "this"; and plural *ʾlw* (אלו), "these"; and the demonstratives *hlh* (הלה), "this," and *hll* (הלל), "these."
10. Use of the noun *ʿṣm* (עצם), "bone" + pronominal suffix as a reflexive pronoun, e.g., *ʿṣmy* (עצמי), "myself," or *ʿṣmw* (עצמו), "himself."
11. Increase in loanwords from Greek and Latin.

10

Epilogue

The Hebrew language can live only if we revive the nation and return it to the fatherland.

—*Eliezer ben Yehuda*

Hebrew survived and even flourished, despite its disappearance in Palestine for almost two millennia. On the one hand, the limits of this study have been defined by the demise of the use of Hebrew as a vernacular language in the land. On the other hand, we have emphasized that our knowledge and description of Hebrew is dependent on the texts *written* in ancient Israel, Judah, Yehud, and Roman Palestina. The Hebrew language would survive the displacement of Hebrew speech communities by becoming a language of religion, piety, poetry, and trade. It survived primarily as a written language that served to bind together the Jewish Diaspora for almost two thousand years. The survival of Hebrew as a religious, literary, and trade language enabled its revival as a vernacular language in the Zionist movement of the nineteenth century and its adoption as the language of the new Jewish state of Israel in 1948. Yet, the survival and rebirth of Hebrew is, in a real sense, its second rebirth. The first challenge to Hebrew occurred with the Babylonian invasions and destruction of Jerusalem in 586 B.C.E. The Hebrew language showed resilience, surviving in spite of the widespread dispersal of the early Judean speech communities and in spite of the destruction of a social infrastructure for writing. In this respect, the Hebrew language demonstrated its strong connection to its speakers and writers.

Language death is not a new phenomenon. Many languages, ancient and more recent, have disappeared in the course of human history. The Hebrew language, however, had a near-death experience and survived—twice. This curious fact demands some investigation. This book has examined the first part of the story of the Hebrew language. It has followed the history of Hebrew from its beginnings in the land of Canaan even before David, Solomon, and the kings who came after them arrived in the land and established a nation. It has followed the language through the vicissitudes of war and peace, prosperity and poverty. The end of this story is also the beginning of another story, which ends with the second resurrection of Hebrew along with the reestablishment of a Jewish state in Israel. This second rebirth of Hebrew is certainly not unaware of the first; indeed, the coins of the new Israeli state consciously utilize the Paleo-Hebrew letters and symbols depicted on the coins of the ancient Hasmonean state. This anecdotal example serves to remind us that language survival is closely tied to group identity—in this case, both ancient and modern Jewish identity.

Throughout this book, we have emphasized the close relationship between social history and linguistic history, between society and language, and particularly between the ancient Jews and the Hebrew language. In the first chapter, we recalled the words of the early linguistic anthropologist Edward Sapir, who suggested that the history of language and culture move along parallel lines. This has proven quite true for the history of classical Hebrew. The language was shaped by the emergence of a state, by the centralization of political power, and by the rise of empires, beginning with Assyria. Hebrew was also shaped by the tragedies of ancient Judah, by the destruction of the central place of scribal activity—Jerusalem—and by the dispersal of its speech communities to the far corners of the known world. Hebrew was shaped by the languages of the foreigners who dominated the land—first the Egyptians, later the Assyrians and Babylonians, and finally the Persians, Greeks, and Romans.

Our survey has also emphasized the limited and special nature of the early history of Hebrew, namely, that it is the history of a *written* language. Grammars of ancient Hebrew have tended to focus on the linguistics of speech, even though we have no direct evidence of ancient vernacular. Of course, we may piece together glimpses of the everyday Hebrew of ancient times from all kinds of sources—the (later) Masoretic traditions, foreign translations (like the Greek Septuagint), cognate and contemporary languages, and even archaeology. Yet this study has chosen to focus not on the phonology of ancient Hebrew speech but rather on the role of language in the social life of the Jewish people in antiquity. As it happened, it was this preservation of written Hebrew—in the Bible, in the Mishnah, and especially in Jewish prayer—that helped the Hebrew language survive the Roman destruction of Jerusalem and the dispersal of ancient Hebrew speech communities.

In the post-Roman Jewish Diaspora, Hebrew became the language of prayer and the language of the Bible. Prayer would replace the temple and sacrifice in Jewish religious life, and Jewish tradition would require males to pray three times a day and to read Torah portions weekly. In the Middle Ages, it became customary to read the Bible with commentary. Often the Torah portion would be read twice in Hebrew and then once in Aramaic, using the Targum Onqelos. Commentary included the Hebrew midrashim, and Jews were also expected to learn the Hebrew oral law (or Mishnah). In addition, the more-educated Jews would have also studied the Talmud, which is mostly written in Aramaic but requires a strong knowledge of biblical and Rabbinic Hebrew. As a result, Hebrew literacy remained unusually high in Jewish communities in spite of the fact that Hebrew was no longer an everyday vernacular. The knowledge of Hebrew was certainly important to the continuing group identity of the Jewish community in the Diaspora. One of the normal features of group identity, namely geographical location, could no longer serve as a facilitator of Jewish identity in the Diaspora, and as a result language played an even more important role for Jewish identity after the Jewish revolts in the first and second centuries of the Common Era.

The embodiment of the ideological role of Hebrew in Jewish history culminated with Eliezer Ben-Yehuda. Ben-Yehuda was a Lithuanian Jew, born in 1858, who grew up (like most Jewish children) learning Hebrew as part of his religious upbringing. He also grew up in the context of the rise of European nationalisms that began in the early nineteenth century. In the wake of the French Revolution in 1814, waves of romantic nationalism rolled across the European continent, and new countries were formed along with new national languages. Classical languages were revived in Greece and Italy. In Italy, for example, only 2.5 percent of the population could speak the standard Tuscan Italian dialect when the nation was unified in 1861. These contemporary examples gave Ben-Yehuda hope that the Hebrew vernacular could be revived and, along with it, a Jewish state.[1] Ben-Yehuda, inspired by these events, immigrated to Palestine and resolved to revive the Hebrew language. In 1880, he wrote in the journal *HaShahar*, "The Hebrew language can live only if we revive the nation and return it to the fatherland." He began with his own son, whom he named Ben-Zion (meaning "son of Zion") and with whom he spoke only Hebrew from his infancy. Many people could speak Hebrew in Ben-Yehuda's social circles, but none of them were monolingual. Ben-Zion Ben-Yehuda grew up monolingual, speaking only Hebrew, and became the symbol of the revival of the Hebrew language and of a new Hebrew speech community in Palestine. The events following World War II resulted in the establishment of Ben-Yehuda's dream, the creation of both a modern Jewish state and an official language, modern Hebrew.

Notes

Chapter 1. Language, Land, and People

1. Duranti, *Linguistic Anthropology*, 162.
2. Ibid., 7.
3. Sapir, *Language*, 219.
4. See Duranti, *Linguistic Anthropology*, 23–50; Duranti is informed by Claude Lévi-Strauss, Roman Jakobson, and especially Geertz, *Interpretation of Cultures*.
5. Coulmas, *Writing Systems*, 113.
6. See, e.g., Morgan, "Speech Community," 3–22.
7. Sáenz-Badillos, *History of the Hebrew Language*; Hadas-Lebel, *Histoire de la langue Hébraïque*; and Kutscher, *History of the Hebrew Language*. Kutscher passed away before completing his book, and it was constructed from his notes by his son Raphael Kutscher and published posthumously.
8. C. Rabin, *Short History*.
9. Horowitz, *How the Hebrew Language Grew*, and Hoffman, *In the Beginning*.
10. The scope of this study is similar to Clines (ed.), *The Dictionary of Classical Hebrew*, which covers the Hebrew language up to 200 C.E., that is, preceding the editing of the Mishnah. Although the 200 C.E. delimitation is a convenient practical terminus, I am employing the social and demographic terminus—namely, the use of Hebrew in ancient Palestine.
11. Sáenz-Badillos, *History of the Hebrew Language*, 51–52. I take exception to Sáenz-Badillos's contention that the revitalization of Israeli Hebrew "breaks the pattern of the language's natural development" (52). If anything, it is the gradual disuse of Hebrew as a spoken language during the rabbinic period (second to sixth centuries C.E.) that breaks its natural development, hence the eclectic nature of medieval Hebrew. The revitalization of the language—at least from a sociolinguistic perspective—is a much more natural process.

12. See, e.g., Fishman (ed.), *Readings in the Sociology of Jewish Languages*, and the literature cited therein.
13. A variety of scholars have wrestled with the notion of Jewishness; see, e.g., S. Cohen, *Beginnings of Jewishness: Boundaries, Varieties, Uncertainties*.
14. Clines (ed.), *Dictionary of Classical Hebrew*, 1:7.
15. See Trudgill, *Sociolinguistics*, 119–46.
16. Irvine and Gal, "Language Ideology and Linguistic Differentiation," 35–36.
17. See, e.g., the entry in Danker, *A Greek-English Lexicon of the New Testament*, which defines Ἑβραϊστί as "Hebrew/Aramaic."
18. For a general discussion, see Rogers, *Writing Systems*, 13–17.
19. Coulmas (and citing Saussure), *Writing Systems*, 16.
20. For the use of this term with respect to Hebrew, see Rendsburg, *Diglossia*.
21. This term was coined by P. Daniels to distinguish alphabets like Greek, which include consonants and vowels, from systems like Hebrew, Phoenician, or Arabic, which do not regularly write vowels. See Daniels, "Study of Writing Systems," 3–17.
22. See, e.g., Hendel, "Sibilants and *šibbōlet*," 69–76, or Woodhouse, "Biblical Shibboleth Story," 271–90.
23. Ullendorff, "Is Biblical Hebrew a Language?" 3–17.
24. Coulmas, *Writing Systems*, 89.
25. Prince, "Segments," 384–87. See the discussion by Coulmas, *Writing Systems*, 89–108.
26. Coulmas, *Writing Systems*, 184.
27. Webster, *Essay on the Necessity*.
28. Specifically on script choice, see Unseth, "Sociolinguistics of Script Choice," 1–4.
29. For a convenient summary, see Rendsburg, "Linguistic Variation," 177–90.
30. Ibid., 179.
31. As quoted by Sampson, *Writing Systems*, 11.
32. Ibid., 13.
33. Derrida, *Of Grammatology*, 44.
34. Coulmas, *Writing Systems*, 184.
35. Ibid., 292.
36. Ullendorff, "Is Biblical Hebrew a Language?" 7.
37. See Humboldt, *Über die Verschiedenheit des menschlichen Sprachbaues*, 26.
38. Peter Daniels even questioned whether the Phoenician alphabet should be characterized as a true alphabet because it lacked vowels, but Coulmas's critique of Daniels is well taken—namely, that all alphabets are incomplete representations of the sounds of a language. See Coulmas, *Writing Systems*, 113–14. Note further the study of Faber, "Phonemic Segmentation," 111–34, which calls into question the primacy of the alphabet itself as a transcription system for speech.
39. See Diakonoff, "Ancient Writing," 99–121.
40. Gumperz and Cook-Gumperz, "Studying Language, Culture, and Society," 532–45.
41. Trudgill, *Sociolinguistics*, 23. Also see Gumperz and Cook-Gumperz, "Studying Language, Culture, and Society," 532–45.
42. Labov, *Sociolinguistic Patterns*, 183.
43. Saussure, *Course in General Linguistics*, 33.
44. Ibid., 9.
45. A summary of their contributions may be found in Lucy, *Language Diversity and Thought*, 11–68.
46. Sapir, *Language*, 8.
47. Lucy, *Language Diversity and Thought*, 66.
48. Ibid., 127–87.

49. More recently, the approach of "generative grammar" has dominated the American academy. The Saussurian revolution paved the way for the concept of language universals and generative grammar advocated by Noam Chomsky. Chomskian linguists have emphasized that language is innate in the human brain. Consequently, they find language universals that generate linguistic phenomena across the whole spectrum of languages, although their work has tended to focus on a few European languages. This approach to linguistics, usually called "generative grammar," has limited application to classical Hebrew because it emphasizes language universals. If language systems are universal, there is little reason to focus on Hebrew in particular. Although "universal grammar" maintains a stranglehold on the American linguistic academy (less so on the European academy), there have been challenges and even cracks in the consensus. Perhaps most notable is the work of Daniel Everett, "Cultural Constraints," 621–46. Steven Pinker, perhaps the most articulate defender of Chomsky's theory of language, argues that language (or more precisely, grammar) is part of the circuitry of the human brain, but Pinker also admits that language is partly social: "Language inherently involves sharing a code with other people" (Pinker, *Language Instinct*, 243).
50. Grimm's Law was the first law of systematic sound change to be discovered in linguistics and, as such, was a turning point for historical and comparative linguistics. It is illustrated, e.g., in the changes from /p > f > ph/, /t > th/, / k > ch/, /b > p/, which may be seen by comparing words like Greek *pous* with English *foot* or Latin *tertius* with English *third*. See further the discussion and examples in Bloomfield, *Language*, 347–55.
51. Bloomfield, *Language*. Bloomfield writes, "Writing is not language, but merely a way of recording language by means of visible marks" (21). For a review and critique of Bloomfield's postulates for linguistic science, see Silverstein, review of Hockett's *View from Language*, 235–53.
52. Labov, *Sociolinguistic Patterns*, 252.
53. See Nichols, "Functional Theories of Grammar," 97–117.
54. See the observations of Labov, "Study of Language in Its Social Context," 152–56.
55. Kroskrity, "Regimenting Languages," 5; emphasis added.
56. Romaine, *Language in Society*, ix.
57. See Toubouret-Keller, "Language and Identity," 315; contra Schwartz, "Hebrew and Imperialism in Jewish Palestine," 54.
58. Ibid., 58.
59. From "Why Can't the English?" in *My Fair Lady*, Alan J. Lerner and Frederick Loewe's musical adaptation of George Bernard Shaw's play *Pygmalion*.
60. Labov, *Sociolinguistic Patterns*, 260.
61. Joüon, *Grammar of Biblical Hebrew*; Brockelmann, *Hebräische Syntax*.
62. Waltke and O'Connor, *Introduction to Biblical Hebrew Syntax*.
63. Harris, *Development*.
64. C. Rabin, "Historical Background," 144–61.
65. C. Rabin describes it as follows: "The tendency of this book is sociological, and approaches somewhat the methods of the science of sociolinguistics, without any pretense at either sociological profundity or the scientific evaluation of detailed facts as practiced by that science" (*Short History*, 5).
66. C. Rabin, "Emergence," 71–78.
67. Garr, *Dialect Geography*.
68. Rendsburg, *Diglossia*, 166.
69. Ibid., 166–67. Rendsburg points here to the work of Saussure, though Saussure is by no means the main proponent of sociolinguistic analysis.
70. Young, *Diversity*.

71. Labov, *Sociolinguistic Patterns*, 275.
72. Titunik, "Formal Method," 181.
73. Polak, "Sociolinguistics," 115–62; Polak, "Style Is More Than the Person," 38–103.
74. Also see Sanders's own book, *Invention.*
75. See Cross, "History of the Biblical Text," 177–95.
76. Kutscher, *Language and Linguistic Background of the Isaiah Scroll.*
77. Gianto, "Historical Linguistics and the Hebrew Bible," 1553–71.
78. See Saussure, *Writings in General Linguistics* and the original, *Écrits de linguistique générale*; see also Saussure, *Course in General Linguistics (Cours de linguistique générale).*
79. The ḫābiru-Hebrew connection was already raised by F. J. Chabas in 1862. After the discovery of the Amarna letters in 1887, this identification became quite commonplace. Note the classic studies by Bottéro, *Le Problème des Ḫābiru*, and Greenberg, *Ḫāb/piru.*
80. See *CAD* Ḫ, 84.
81. See Na'aman, "Ḫābiru and Hebrews," 271–88.
82. Trudgill, *Sociolinguistics*, 33.
83. Labov, *Sociolinguistic Patterns*, 274.
84. Ibid., 275.
85. Labov, *Principles of Linguistic Change*, 514.
86. Ibid., 516.
87. Ibid.
88. Ibid., 34.
89. Trudgill, *Sociolinguistics*, 83.
90. Voloshinov, *Marxism and the Philosophy of Language*, 19. V. Ivanov argued that Voloshinov's works were actually authored by his colleague Mikhail Bakhtin (*Marxism and the Philosophy of Language* , ix). Bakhtin himself never denied the attribution.

Chapter 2. The Origins of Hebrew

1. For discussion and examples, see Schniedewind, *How the Bible Became a Book*, 24–34.
2. Although the Amarna letters reflect, for the most part, a unified grammar, there are some indications of local dialects, most notably in the tablets from Gezer; see Izre'el, "Gezer Letters," 13–90.
3. See Huffmon, *Amorite Personal Names*; also note Izre'el's analysis of the Amurru Amarna letters, *Amurru Akkadian*, 11–14.
4. Huffmon, *Amorite Personal Names.*
5. It is worth pointing out that Ezek. 16:3 must be understood as more than mere polemic. The polemicizing aspect of the text is the mention of the Canaanites, which obviously carried a strong negative connotation. The Amorites and the Hittites are irrelevant to exilic/postexilic audiences. The Amorites, e.g., disappear from the biblical narrative in the premonarchic period, and they are essentially unknown in Neo-Babylonian and Persian literature. The Hittites do not fare much better, though at least they last into the David/Solomon stories and then disappear (appropriately enough). In order for something to work as a polemic, it has to resonate with something that is known to the writer's or speaker's contemporary audience. The core of Ezek. 16:3 is a neutral proverb reflecting cultural memory with specific details that had little meaning to Ezekiel's contemporary audience, namely, "Your father was an Amorite, and your mother a Hittite." The prophet then takes this, contemporizes it, and offers a polemical interpretation: "Your origin and your birth were in the land of the Canaanites."
6. Houston, "Archaeology of Communication Technologies," 235.
7. The Middle Bronze (MB) Age extends from ca. 2200 to 1530 B.C.E. and is divided into two parts, an "interlude" period called MB I, extending from 2200 to 1900 B.C.E., and MB II,

from 1900 to 1530 B.C.E. Scholars quibble about the precise dates for the transitions between the Early, Middle, and Late Bronze Ages. There is also discussion about the correct label for the MB I period; see, e.g., Mazar, *Archaeology,* 152.

8. Horowitz and Oshima, *Cuneiform in Canaan.*
9. See the summary in Pedersén, *Archives.*
10. Malamat, "Mari and Hazor," 66–70.
11. Horowitz and Oshima, *Cuneiform in Canaan,* 12.
12. See the corpus of texts from Hazor in ibid., 65–87.
13. See the discussion by Daniels, "Scripts of the Semitic Languages," 16–45.
14. Coulmas, *Writing Systems,* 113–14.
15. Ibid., 89–108.
16. See the summary of these classical sources by Lemaire, "Spread of the Alphabetic Scripts," 46.
17. See the *editio princeps* by Darnell et al., "Two Early Alphabetic Inscriptions from the Wadi el-Hôl," 73–124.
18. Houston, "Archaeology of Communication Technologies," 239.
19. See J. Allen, *Middle Egyptian,* 224.
20. See Hamilton, *Origins of the West Semitic Alphabet.*
21. See Goldwasser, "Canaanites Reading Hieroglyphs," 151–53; contra the hypothesis of Hamilton in *Origins of the West Semitic Alphabet.*
22. For a convenient catalog of early alphabetic inscriptions, see Hamilton, *Origins of the West Semitic Alphabet,* 323–400.
23. Cross, "Invention and Development of the Alphabet," 77–78. See the critique of this position by Rollston ("Scribal Education in Ancient Israel," 47–74), who downplays the differences between learning the cuneiform writing system and learning the linear alphabet.
24. See Allen, *Middle Egyptian,* 26.
25. See Lambdin, "Egyptian Loanwords," 145–55.
26. For a summary of the scribes' curriculum, see the Sumerian text "The Dialogue between an Examiner and a Student" (*COS* 1.186), and the edition by Civil, "Sur les 'livres d'écolier,'" 67–78.
27. See Goldwasser, "Egyptian Scribe from Lachish," 248–53; Aharoni, "Use of Hieratic Numerals," 13–19.
28. Goldwasser and Wimmer, "Hieratic Fragments," 39–42, and the bibliography cited there.
29. See Allen, "Craft of the Scribe," 9–14 (§3.2); note especially lines 18:7–22:2.
30. See, e.g., Overland, "Structure in the Wisdom of Amenemope," 275–91; Ray, "Egyptian Wisdom Literature," 17–29; N. Shupak, *Where Can Wisdom Be Found?* 297–311.
31. On the Ugaritic script, see Dietrich and Loretz "Ugaritic Script," 81–89, and Stieglitz, "Ugaritic Cuneiform and Canaanite Linear Alphabets," 135–39.
32. Albright, cited in the discussion section of Kraeling and Adams, *City Invincible,* 123 (critically cited by Rollston, "Scribal Education in Ancient Israel," 48).
33. See Seymour, "Early Reading Development," 296–315; Share and Levine, "Learning to Read and Write," 89–111.
34. See the useful general discussion by Rollston, "Scribal Education in Ancient Israel," 48–50; and see the modern theoretical discussion by Ehri, "Phases of Acquisition," 7–28.
35. This example may be found in *KTU* 5.6. There is also evidence for another order, best known in Old South Arabian but also in alphabetic cuneiform; see Dietrich and Loretz, "Ugaritic Script," 81–90.
36. Curiously, however, Ugaritic uses the *h* for its pronouns, whereas in all other Semitic languages the causative prefix and the pronoun are related; e.g., Akkadian *šafel* and 3ms

pronoun *šuati*. This leads us to question whether the use of the *shin* causative prefix is an Akkadianism and does not reflect the actual phonetic realization.

37. Cassuto, *Biblical and Oriental Studies*, 17.
38. Kaufman, "Classification," 41–57.
39. Rainey, "Kingdom of Ugarit," 102–25.
40. Romaine, *Language in Society*, 1–32.
41. Ginsberg, "Phoenician Hymn," 472–76; see also Avishur, *Studies in Hebrew and Ugaritic Psalms*, 39–110.
42. Albright, review of Gordon's *Ugaritic Grammar*, 438. Albright returned to this topic repeatedly in his own writings; see, e.g., "Old Testament and Canaanite Language," 5–31; "Psalm of Habakkuk," 1–20; and *Yahweh and the Gods of Canaan*.
43. For example, Dahood, *Psalms 101–150*.
44. See the discussion of Dahood's approach in the review of literature by Avishur, *Studies in Hebrew and Ugaritic Psalms*, 21–24.
45. See Gevirtz, *Patterns*; Freedman, "Counting Formulae," 65–81; Roth, "Numerical Sequence," 300–311.
46. See Polak, "Epic Formulas," 437–89. Polak cites the classic work of Cassuto, *Biblical and Oriental Studies*, as first calling attention to these parallels, as well as Frank Moore Cross's seminal work, *Canaanite Myth and Hebrew Epic*. See most recently Polak, "Linguistic and Stylistic Aspects," 285–304.
47. On the language of the Amarna letters, see the comprehensive treatment of Rainey, *Canaanite in the Amarna Tablets*. See further the approach of Von Dassow, "Canaanite in Cuneiform," 641–74.
48. Izre'el, *Canaano-Akkadian*, 20–23 (page numbers refer to electronic version).
49. See ibid.
50. See further Rainey, "Ancient Hebrew Prefix Conjugation," 1–19, and Rainey, "Prefix Conjugation Patterns," 407–20; Van de Sande, *Nouvelle perspective*.
51. It is a mistake to reduce the Hebrew verbal system to the issue of either tense or aspect. Most languages have verbal systems that are a combination of both. Hebrew undergoes a transition from an aspectual system in West Semitic toward a tense system in Rabbinic Hebrew.
52. See Rainey, *Canaanite in the Amarna Tablets*, 2:181–94.
53. Von Dassow, "Canaanite in Cuneiform," 641.
54. Izre'el, *Canaano-Akkadian*, 16.
55. See Rainey, "Whence Came the Israelites?" 41–64; Rainey, "Redefining Hebrew," 37–56; Rainey, "Inside, Outside," 45–50, 84.
56. See Emerton, "New Evidence," 255–58; Muraoka, "Linguistic Notes," 19–21; and Sasson, "Some Observations," 111–27.
57. See Killebrew, *Biblical Peoples and Ethnicity*, and Faust, *Israel's Ethnogenesis*.

Chapter 3. Early Hebrew Writing

1. C. Rabin, "Emergence," 73.
2. See, e.g., the popular work by Finkelstein and Silberman, *David and Solomon*. For a more radical critique, see Whitelam, *Invention of Ancient Israel*.
3. See Halpern, "Two Views," 77–83.
4. I first developed this in my 1999 book, *Society and the Promise to David*, but I discuss it more fully in *How the Bible Became a Book*, 64–117. Finkelstein and Silberman borrow the concept in "Temple and Dynasty," 259–85.
5. For this dating see Mazar, "Debate," 15–30; Bruins et al., "Groningen Radiocarbon Series," 271–93; Bruins and Mazar, "End of the 2nd Millennium BCE," 77–99.

6. Particularly useful is the analysis of Byrne, "Refuge of Scribalism," 1–31. Byrne summarizes this transitional period as follows: "Unlike the Late Bronze and Iron II epigraphic corpora, which reflect the dimensions of state interests, the Iron I evidence suggests a culture of scribalism that survived largely through circumstantial appeal to elite patronage" (3).
7. See Blau, *On Polyphony*, and Blau, *Phonology*, 73–76.
8. The problem of Hebrew homographs is further compounded by the lack of vowel letters in ancient Hebrew. There are more than seventeen hundred examples of homographs in Hebrew, representing about 20 percent of biblical Hebrew vocabulary. Most of these are the result of the lack of vowels in the earlier stages of Hebrew writing that began to be remedied with the introduction of vowel letters by the eighth century B.C.E. and continued much later with the introduction of vowel pointing.
9. This point is made quite eloquently by Sanders, *Invention*, 36–75.
10. Garr, *Dialect Geography*, 231.
11. See, e.g., Trudgill's observations on spelling in various European languages (*Sociolinguistics*, 135–46); and, more generally, Eira, "Authority and Discourse," 171–224.
12. For a general account of the use of cuneiform in the Levant during the second millennium B.C.E., see Horowitz and Oshima, *Cuneiform in Canaan*, 10–19.
13. Ibid., 15–22.
14. On Egyptian administration in the Levant at the end of the second millennium B.C.E. (particularly during the Nineteenth Dynasty), see Morris, *Architecture of Imperialism*, 386–504.
15. See Allen, "Craft of the Scribe," *COS* §3.2.
16. See, e.g., Goldwasser and Wimmer, "Hieratic Fragments," 39–42; Wimmer, "Prince of Safit?" 37–48.
17. Scholars have usually argued that there was a major break in Egyptian scribal culture, presumably in the early twelfth century B.C.E., and then a resumption of Egyptian scribal influence again in the tenth century B.C.E. This scenario is quite unlikely given the archaeological evidence of cultural continuity from the Bronze Age into the Iron Age.
18. See Lambdin, "Egyptian Loanwords," 149. The spelling of the Hebrew word apparently reflects the orthographic interchange between *dalet* and *resh*.
19. Goldwasser, "Egyptian Scribe from Lachish," 248–53.
20. Contra Kletter, *Economic Keystones*, 146. My thanks to Professor Jacco Dieleman for his insights into the development of hieratic and demotic scripts and numerals.
21. See Lambdin, "Egyptian Loanwords," 145–55.
22. Possible Egyptian influence on ancient Israelite scribes has also been suggested for biblical wisdom literature, particularly Ps. 104 and Prov. 22:17–24:22; however, it is difficult to date such general traditions, as it is clear that there was a revival of Egyptian influence in Judah during the late eighth and seventh centuries B.C.E.; see Ash, *David, Solomon and Egypt*.
23. See de Vaux, "Titres et fonctionnaires," 394–405. A wide variety of alternative suggestions has been offered, but none have the simplicity and elegance of the Egyptian explanation, especially when viewed in the context of other Egyptian loanwords, the use of hieratic numerals, and the history of Egyptian administration in the region.
24. It has been suggested that Shisha be derived from the Hurrian name Šawa-šarri, but this derivation is quite fanciful and begins with the presumption that this figure was originally part of the old Hurrian/Jebusite administration (see Cogan, *1 Kings*, 200–201). See also Cody, "Le titre égyptien," 381–93.
25. As suggested by Mettinger, *Solomonic State Officials*, 29–30. Mettinger also argued that the name Elihoreph is a Hebraized Egyptian name, in which *ḥp* represents the god Apis (note that the Greek transliterations show no evidence of a *resh*).
26. See Goldwasser, "How the Alphabet Was Born," 36–50, 74.

27. See especially the arguments by Hamilton, *Origins of the West Semitic Alphabet.*
28. Mendenhall, "Hebrew Conquest," 66–87.
29. Compare the situation with Latin; see Pulgram, "Spoken and Written Latin," 458–66.
30. Brent, "Problem of the Placement," 105–6.
31. See Moran, "Hebrew Language," 59–84.
32. Jamieson-Drake, *Scribes*, 76–77.
33. See Mendenhall, "Hebrew Conquest," 66–87; Gottwald, *Tribes of Yahweh.*
34. See Dever, *Who Were the Israelites . . . ?* 101–28.
35. Mendenhall, "Social Organization," 132–51.
36. Collections of ancient Hebrew inscriptions may be found in Renz and Röllig, *Die althebräischen Inschriften*, and Dobbs-Allsopp et al., *Hebrew Inscriptions.*
37. For an overview of the stele and the secondary literature, see Hasel, "Israel in the Merneptah Stele," 45–61.
38. It is also important to note that many early inscriptions were not discovered in controlled excavations, and their authenticity is therefore open to question. See especially the general observations of Rollston, "Non-Provenanced Epigraphs I," 135–93; Rollston, "Non-Provenanced Epigraphs II," 57–79.
39. Sanders calls these inscriptions "an unstandardized Canaanite" (*Invention*, 105).
40. See Kochavi, "Ostracon," 1–13; Cross, "Newly Found Inscriptions," 1–20.
41. Grant, "Découverte épigraphique," 401–2, pl. xv.
42. Maeir et al., "Late Iron Age I / Early Iron Age II Old Canaanite Inscription," 39–71.
43. Stager, "Inscribed Potsherd," 45–52.
44. See the discussion and literature cited by Garfinkel and Ganor, "Khirbet Qeiyafa," 67–78. The initial report was published in Garfinkel and Ganor, *Khirbet Qeiyafa.* The reconstructions by Galil and Puech require much imagination; see Puech, "L'Ostracon de Khirbet Qeyafa," 162–84; Galil, "Hebrew Inscription," 193–242.
45. I concur here with the opinion of Rollston; see especially his article "Scribal Education in Ancient Israel," 47–74.
46. For the original publication, see H. Misgav, Y. Garfinkel, and S. Ganor, "The Khirbet Qeiyafa Ostracon," in *New Studies in the Archaeology of Jerusalem and Its Region*, ed. D. Amit, G. D. Stiebel, and O. Peleg-Barkat (Jerusalem: Israel Antiquities Authority and the Institute of Archaeology, the Hebrew University of Jerusalem, 2009), 111–23 (Hebrew).
47. See Dobbs-Allsopp et al., *Hebrew Inscriptions*, 156–65.
48. It has even been suggested that this written sign was borrowed from Egyptian; see J. B. Segal, "YRH in the Gezer 'Calendar,'" 212–21.
49. Tappy et al., "Abecedary," 5–46.
50. Mazar, "Three 10th–9th Century B.C.E. Inscriptions," 171–84.
51. See Schniedewind, "Problems in the Paleographic Dating," 405–12.
52. Sanders, *Invention*, 49.
53. The most extensive recent study is the example from the city of Emar studied by Y. Cohen, *Scribes and Scholars.* More generally, see Rollston, *Writing and Literacy*, 115–26.
54. See, e.g., A. George, "In Search of the é.dub.ba.a," 127–37.
55. See van Soldt, "Written Sources," 40–41.
56. See, e.g., Robertson, *Linguistic Evidence.*
57. See Kutscher, *History of the Hebrew Language*, §§53–56, 111.
58. See the classic study of Hummel, "Enclitic Mem," 85–107, which gives a comprehensive, though overstated, list of possible enclitic *mems* in the biblical corpus. See also Waltke and O'Connor, *Introduction to Biblical Hebrew Syntax*, §9.8.
59. Note, e.g., the interesting mixed forms of the passive √*yld*, "to be born," in the LBH text of 1 Chron. 3:5 and 20:8, reflecting both the old passive *qal/puʿal* and contemporary use

of the *nipʿal* conjugation. The existence of a *qal* passive is indicated wherever a verb exists in the *qal* and *puʿal*, but not the *piʿel* conjugation, as is the case with √*yld*.

60. See Waltke and O'Connor, *Introduction to Biblical Hebrew Syntax*, §11.2.10i. A related phenomenon is the asseverative *l*-; see Schniedewind and Sivan, "Letting Your 'Yes' Be 'No,'" 209–26.
61. See lists of vocabulary in Kutscher, *History of the Hebrew Language*, §§115–16; Sáenz-Badillos, *History of the Hebrew Language*, 56–61.
62. Greenfield, "Amurrite, Ugaritic and Canaanite," 99–100.
63. See Waltke and O'Connor, *Introduction to Biblical Hebrew Syntax*, §8.2e.

Chapter 4. Linguistic Nationalism and the Emergence of Hebrew

1. This point is nicely developed by Sanders, *Invention*.
2. See Trudgill, *Sociolinguistics*, 127–46.
3. Fishman, *Language and Nationalism*, 44.
4. In particular, see Rendsburg, "Linguistic Variation," 177–90.
5. See the discussion of Samr 119 by Dobbs-Allsopp et al., *Hebrew Inscriptions*, 496–97.
6. The term *Israelian* was coined by H. L. Ginsberg in *The Israelian Heritage of Judaism*. The term was adopted and has become mainstream because of the writings of Gary Rendsburg (e.g., *Israelian Hebrew in the Book of Kings*).
7. Knauf suggests, "The main problem of Israelite Hebrew is its bad attestation and, secondarily, that more than one language was spoken in the Kingdom of Israel" ("Bethel," 312). The former is certainly a limitation. The latter, though certainly true, does not pose as much of a problem, as we really must limit our inquiry to the written language, and dialectal differences do not necessarily translate directly into writing systems. Rather, it is likely that a uniform writing system for IH was circumscribed by the administrative and political centers of Israel (namely, Shechem and then Samaria). Influence of the Israelian vernaculars would have followed the wave of refugees from the north—that is, in the late eighth century B.C.E. (and not the sixth century B.C.E., as Knauf proposes).
8. See the classic study by Burney, *Notes on the Hebrew Text*. Rendsburg, *Israelian Hebrew*, adopts a larger corpus to include all the northern narratives in the book of Kings.
9. For a more maximalist list, see Rendsburg, "Comprehensive Guide," 8.
10. See Rendsburg, "Linguistic Variation," 177–90.
11. It is noteworthy that Shalmaneser III (r. 858–824 B.C.E.) fought frequently in the open field, which suggests a perceived parity between opponents. By the time we reach the end of the eighth century, in contrast, Assyrian monarchs are more usually involved with siege warfare, suggesting their relative superiority; see Eph'al, "On Warfare," 88–106; Kühne, "Urbanization," 55–84.
12. The original publication on this topic was Broshi, "Expansion," 21. I developed this argument further in several places (see "Jerusalem," 375–93, and most recently, *How the Bible Became a Book*, 64–90). Although this position was critiqued by Na'aman, "When and How . . . ?" 21–56, a thorough rejoinder was made by Finkelstein, "Settlement History," 499–515.
13. Finkelstein, "Archaeology of the Days of Manasseh," 173.
14. See the chapter "Hezekiah and the Beginning of Biblical Literature" in Schniedewind, *How the Bible Became a Book*, 64–90.
15. Rendsburg, "Comprehensive Guide," 8–9.
16. I have discussed this at length in *How the Bible Became a Book*, 64–117, but also see my review of van der Toorn's *Scribal Culture and the Making of the Hebrew Bible*.
17. Harper, *A Critical and Exegetical Commentary*, clxxiii.
18. Note the observation by Y. Kutscher, *Words and Their History*, 34.

19. See, in general, Grosby, *Biblical Ideas.*
20. These periods are conceptualized with a view to the archaeology, changes in material culture, and changes in scribal institutions.
21. On the Assyrian alphabetic scribes, see Pearce, "Sepîru," 355–68.
22. See the articles by Hurvitz, "Chronological Significance," 234–40; Hurvitz, "Hebrew and Aramaic in the Bible," 79–94.
23. This point is made by C. Rabin, "Foreign Words," *EM* 4:1075 (Hebrew).
24. See Schwartz, "Language, Power and Identity," 3–47.
25. Ibid., 10.
26. Ibid., 12.
27. See Myers-Scotton, "Code-Switching," 217–37. The study of code-switching is especially associated with John J. Gumperz; see his *Discourse Strategies.* Also note the work of M. Heller, e.g., *Codeswitching.*
28. See Schürer, *History*, 1:603–5.
29. Rollston, *Writing and Literacy*, 35.
30. See Cross, "Paleography," 393–409.
31. Rollston, *Writing and Literacy*, 37–41.
32. Ibid., 42–46.
33. Rollston does acknowledge "the pronounced elongation present in the Phoenician script of subsequent centuries," and he goes on to say that "it is very difficult to consider elongation to be a distinctive feature of Old Hebrew" (ibid., 33).
34. See Cogan, *Imperialism and Religion.*
35. Trudgill, *Sociolinguistics*, 118–46.
36. Porter, "Language, Audience and Impact," 60.
37. Fales, "Use and Function," 118; emphasis added.
38. The old translation by Luckenbill (*Ancient Records*, 2:65–66) is cited prominently in Sparks, *Ethnicity and Identity*, 35. See also the more recent edition of the inscription in Fuchs, *Die Inschriften Sargons II.*
39. *CAD* A, 1:189–92.
40. Unfortunately, there are some minor problems with Luckenbill's translation. To begin with, Luckenbill translates the Akkadian word *aklu* as "scribes," but the word never has this nuance. Rather, *aklu* means "overseer," usually one in charge of a group of soldiers, workers, or craftsmen (see *CAD* A, 1:277–80). In the original publication of the cylinder, D. G. Lyon suggested that the Akkadian term *šāpiru*, which Luckenbill translated as "sheriff or superintendent," actually referred to a "Schriftgelehrte," that is, some sort of scribe. Lyon thought that the word was connected with the Aramaic term for scribe, *sāprāʾ* (e.g., Ezra 4:8).
41. Cited in *CAD* Ṭ, 152.
42. Tadmor, "Aramaization," 451.
43. Fales, "Use and Function," 89–124.
44. It is noteworthy that the term *sepīru* does not appear until the Neo-Babyonian period, whereas the logogram A.BA is common in the Neo-Assyrian period. More generally, the Neo-Babylonian scribes routinely wrote out logograms syllabically, in this case giving us a syllabic rendering for the neologism that the Neo-Assyrian administrative bureaucracy created for Aramaic/alphabetic scribes.
45. See the edition by Lindenberger, *Aramaic Proverbs*, and the general discussion by Greenfield, "Wisdom of Ahiqar," 43–52.
46. Tadmor, "Aramaization," 459; Pearce, "Sepîru," 361.
47. Deller, "Das Siegel," 151.
48. *PRU* 3, 212:12–14 (see Pearce, "Sepîru," 361).
49. See Kiernan, "Languages and Conquerors," 191–210.

50. Trudgill, *Sociolinguistics*, 127.
51. On the anthropology of refugees and its application to the study of ancient Israel, see Burke, "Anthropological Model," 41–56.
52. See most recently Finkelstein, "Settlement History," 499–515.
53. Bethel itself diminished in the wake of the Assyrian invasions and did not revive until the Hellenistic period; see Finkelstein and Singer-Avitz, "Reevaluating Bethel," 33–48; contra Knauf, "Bethel," 291–349.
54. Finkelstein and Silberman, "Temple and Dynasty," 268, citing Finkelstein, Lederman, and Bunimovitz, *Highlands*, 898–909.
55. See Burke, "Coping with the Effects," 263–87.
56. The most extensive work on the northern dialect of Hebrew had been done by Gary Rendsburg; see, e.g., Rendsburg, *Israelian Hebrew*, and Rendsburg, "Comprehensive Guide," 5–35.
57. For a discussion of the unique case of the Elijah-Elisha narratives as well as some methodological caveats for discerning Israelian Hebrew, see Schniedewind and Sivan, "Elijah-Elisha Narratives," 303–37.
58. Northern immigrants are also indicated by the appearance of *yw-* prefixes, which are also northern (e.g., used frequently in the Samaria ostraca), in a few Judean seals (note particularly the seven impressions of the seal of "Menachem, (son of) Jobana," excavated at Lachish, Ramat Rahel, Gibeon, and Jerusalem; see Avigad and Sass, *Corpus*, no. 678; also note another Judean seal [*Corpus*, no. 663] as well as names in the Samaria ostraca 36:3, 45:3, 111:1 (see Dobbs-Allsop, *Hebrew Inscriptions*, 423–97).
59. The historical and linguistic features are discussed in detail in Rendsburg and Schniedewind, "Siloam Tunnel Inscription," 188–203.
60. It should be noted that the term *mwzh* does have a more typically Judean spelling, which would usually be read as a contracted diphthong /*môzâ < *mawzâ/.
61. Cross and Freedman, *Early Hebrew Orthography*, 42–43. Garr argues, "Although the Mesha inscription reflects a dialect in which diphthongs had, for the most part, contracted, vestigial uncontracted forms do appear" (*Dialect Geography*, 38).
62. Dearman, *Studies in the Mesha Inscription*, 119.
63. Labov, *Sociolinguistic Patterns*, 299.
64. Ibid., 300.
65. See Rendsburg, *Diglossia*, 20, citing Malamed, "Conversation," 28.
66. Rendsburg, *Diglossia*, 20–21.
67. Linguists now recognize that writing is not merely a system for the representation of speech but has its own logic that differs from speech; see, e.g., Coulmas, *Writing Systems*, 16–17.
68. See Grosby's discussion of the application of nationalism to antiquity, *Biblical Ideas*, 13–51.
69. A most helpful study of nationalism in Hasmonean Israel is provided by Mendels, *Rise and Fall*. Mendels is careful to acknowledge the problems of applying modern definitions to ancient societies but rightly sees the utility in many of the categories.
70. Trudgill, *Sociolinguistics*, 44.
71. See Woolard, "Language Ideology as a Field," 16–17.
72. See Grosby, "Religion and Nationality," 229–65.
73. Tigay, *You Shall Have No Other Gods*; Tigay, "Israelite Religion," 157–94. Tigay probably overstates the religious implications of the onomasticon for monotheism; see e.g., Binger, *Asherah*, 30–35.
74. The data is available in Avigad and Sass, *Corpus*.
75. Grosby, "Borders," 6.
76. Grosby, "Kinship," 3–18.
77. See Aharoni, *Land of the Bible*, 64–80.

78. For the original publication, see Biran and Naveh, "Tel Dan Inscription," 1–18; for a discussion of the meaning of the expression "house of David" in the historical and linguistic context, see Rendsburg, "On the Writing ביתדוד," 22–25.
79. Although the phrase "house of David" must be partially restored, the reading is quite convincing; see Lemaire, "'House of David,'" 30–37.
80. See *COS* 2:113A.
81. See Williamson, *Israel in the Book of Chronicles.*
82. See *COS* 2:117D.
83. See *COS* 2:119B.
84. See the essays in Carsten, *Cultures of Relatedness.*
85. E.g., G. Rendsburg, "Geographical and Historical Background," 105–15.
86. A comprehensive list of possible northernisms in biblical literature may be found in Rendsburg, "Comprehensive Guide," 10–31.
87. Rendsburg and Schniedewind, "Siloam Tunnel Inscription," 188–203.

Chapter 5. The Democratization of Hebrew

1. E. Stern, *Archaeology*, 169.
2. See Kletter, *Economic Keystones.*
3. Shoham, "Hebrew Bullae," 29–57.
4. Ibid., seals B1, 11, 12, 15, 18, 19, 23, 33, 34, 37, 41, and 44.
5. See discussion and literature cited by Shoham, "Hebrew Bullae," 33.
6. Avigad, *Hebrew Bullae*, 121.
7. See ibid., 122; Crowfoot and Crowfoot, *Early Ivories*, 2, 88.
8. Reich, Shukron, and Lernau, "Recent Discoveries," 156–60.
9. Millard, "Uses," 106.
10. Shoham, "Hebrew Bullae," 47–48.
11. Ibid., 53.
12. Rollston, *Writing and Literacy*, 92–94.
13. Deutsch and Heltzer, *New Epigraphic Evidence*, 92–103.
14. The *editio princeps* was done by H. Torczyner (*Lachish I*). The present discussion draws upon my article "Sociolinguistic Reflections," 157–67.
15. Translation by Parpola, "Man without a Scribe," 315–24. Also see Fuchs and Parpola, *Correspondence*, 17.
16. Charpin, *Reading and Writing*, 63.
17. This text is frequently mistranslated, e.g., NRSV, "he shall have a copy of this law written for him." However, the Hebrew verb *ktb*, "to write," is clearly active, not passive, and the king, who is the implied subject of the verb, is writing. See, e.g., Tigay, *Deuteronomy*, 168; however, I do not agree that this active verb can have the meaning "have written" (168 n. 76). This is a case of special pleading based on a targumic translation.
18. Brettler, "Structure," 87–97.
19. Isserlin, "Epigraphically Attested Judean Hebrew," 197; Young, *Diversity*, 110.
20. Schniedewind, "Sociolinguistic Reflections," 157–67.
21. E.g., Cross, "Literate Soldier," 45. He reads it as a *casus pendens*. This assumes that a subject + verb + objective (SVO) sentence is (in Cross's words) "unusual." What is especially unusual is not the SVO order but the nonstandard epistolary opening.
22. Pardee et al., *Handbook*, 85.
23. Barr, *Variable Spellings*, 114–27.
24. Cross, "Literate Soldier," 45.
25. E.g., Lehman, "Forgotten Principle," 93–101. Dahood applied this example to extensively rewrite the psalter in his commentary; see *Psalms 101–150*, 371–72.

26. Pardee, *Handbook*, 86.
27. See Judg. 20:28; Ezek. 31:11; Ps. 89:28; 2 Chron. 7:20.
28. The original publication was Naveh, "Hebrew Letter," 129–39. Also see Naveh, "Some Notes," 158–59; Talmon, "New Hebrew Letter," 29–38; Dobbs-Allsopp, "Genre of the Mesad Hashavyahu Ostracon," 49–55.
29. An example of this type of verbal construction in SBH also appears in direct speech, 1 Sam. 17:34, *rōʿeh hāyâ* (רֹעֶה הָיָה), "But David said to Saul, 'Your servant was shepherding.'" See discussion by Ahituv, *Echoes*, 160. In RH, the periphrastic is more typically *hyh* followed by the participle, as opposed to the participle followed by *hyh*, although both constructions are attested (see *b. Pe'ah* 2:4; *b. Shevu'ot* 8:10; *b. Shabbat* 1:9).
30. Note, e.g., the common expression in RH, *ʾwmr hyh* (אומר היה), or more commonly, *hyh ʾwmr* (היה אומר), "he used to say." See further Greenfield, "'Periphrastic Imperative,'" 199–210; Muraoka, "Participle," 188–204.
31. This inscription was initially published by Dever, "Iron Age Epigraphic Material," 139–204. There have been several attempts to understand these inscriptions, and a good summary may be found in Dobbs-Allsopp et al., *Hebrew Inscriptions*, 405–20. Note also the treatment by Ahituv, which includes several other inscriptions from the antiquities market that allegedly come from the vicinity (*Echoes*, 220–33).
32. The tombs date to the end of the Judean monarchy, in spite of some suggestions that they might be later; see Naveh, "Old Hebrew Inscriptions," 74–92; Lemaire, "Prières," 558–68.
33. The inscriptions were originally published by Naveh, "Old Hebrew Inscriptions," 74–92. Ahituv summarizes the three major attempts to decipher the five inscriptions (*Echoes*, 233–36).
34. Originally published by Barkay, "Priestly Benediction," 139–91.
35. The paleographic dating of the amulets has been the subject of some discussion. Unfortunately, much of the earlier discussion was based on early photographs and consequently inaccurate drawings; see Barkay et al., "Amulets," 41–71.
36. See also Fishbane, "Form and Reformulation," 115–21.
37. See the survey of the discussion by Gogel, *Grammar of Epigraphic Hebrew*, 49–74.
38. On the Assyrian alphabetic scribes, see Pearce, "Sepîru," 355–68.
39. Cross and Freedman, *Early Hebrew Orthography*, 58–59.
40. Jamieson-Drake, *Scribes*, 107–10.
41. Lichtheim, *Ancient Egyptian Literature*, 185
42. See Barr, *Variable Spellings*, and Andersen and Forbes, *Spelling*.
43. Barr, *Variable Spellings*, 2.
44. Van Gelderen, *History*, 13.
45. Millard, "Variable Spelling," 106–15.
46. See Krahmalkov, *Phoenician-Punic Grammar*, 8–9.
47. Rollston, *Writing and Literacy*, 85–89; Crenshaw, *Education in Ancient Israel*, 85–114; also see the classic work by A. Lemaire, *Les Écoles et la Formation de la Bible dans L'ancien Israël*.
48. See Horowitz and Oshima, *Cuneiform in Canaan*, 19–22.
49. See Parker, *Mechanics*; Kühne, "Urbanization," 55–84.
50. Latacz, *Homer*, 18.
51. Young, "Israelite Literacy," 240.
52. See Goody and Watt, "Consequences of Literacy," 304–45; Goody, *Domestication of the Savage Mind*; Goody, *Logic of Writing*; Ong, *Orality and Literacy*; Ong, "Writing Is a Technology," 23–50; Havelock, *Literate Revolution*.
53. Harris, *Ancient Literacy*.
54. Ibid., 15.

55. Ibid., 17.
56. Bowman and Woolf, "Literacy and Power in the Ancient World," 9–10.
57. This point is nicely made in Niditch's recent work, *Oral World*.
58. See, e.g., Machinist, "Question of Distinctiveness," 196–212.
59. Ibid., 196–97. See, e.g., Snaith, *Distinctive Ideas*, or Wright, *Old Testament*.
60. Machinist, "Question of Distinctiveness," 210–11.
61. There is considerable debate among scholars as to the dating of the book of Kings as well as of Isaiah. I regard this text as dating to the Hezekian (i.e., late eighth century B.C.E.) redaction of the book of Kings favored by several scholars. See Schniedewind, *How the Bible Became a Book*, 73–90, and my summary in "Problem with Kings," 22–27.
62. See the general discussion by G. Schramm, "Hebrew," *ABD* 4:203–14.
63. Skoss, *Saadia Gaon*.

Chapter 6. Hebrew in Exile

1. For the definition of a speech community, see Duranti, *Linguistic Anthropology*, 72–83.
2. I discussed this at length in an earlier work; see Schniedewind, *How the Bible Became a Book*, 139–64.
3. Knauf, "Bethel," 291–349.
4. Finkelstein and Singer-Avitz, "Reevaluating Bethel," 33–48. Early archaeological work had postulated 597 and 586 B.C.E. destruction levels (with Bethel supposedly conquered in 597 B.C.E.), but more-recent work has confirmed that the Assyrians were responsible for the earlier destruction (usually assigned to Sennacherib in 701 B.C.E., although earlier Neo-Assyrian campaigns [e.g., 721, 712 B.C.E.] are possible, depending on the site).
5. E. Stern, *Archaeology*, 303. See also E. Stern, "Babylonian Gap," 45–51, 76.
6. Zorn, "Mizpah," 28–38, 66; Stipp, "Gedalja," 155–71. On the Babylonian administration of Judah, see Vanderhooft, *Neo-Babylonian Empire*, 104–10.
7. Torrey, *Ezra Studies*, 289.
8. Torrey's work also resurfaced in the volume of essays from the European Seminar in Historical Methodology: Torrey, *Leading Captivity Captive*. See Carroll, "Exile!" 77.
9. R. Carroll, "Israel, History of: Post-Monarchic Period," *ABD* 3:567–76; emphasis added.
10. Barstad, *Myth*, 18–19; also see Barstad, "On the History," 25–36.
11. See the essays by Oded, "Where Is the 'Myth . . . '?" 55–74, and Japhet, "Periodization," 75–89.
12. See, e.g., Jamieson-Drake, *Scribes*, 321–26.
13. See D. Smith, *Religion*; Smith-Christopher, "Reassessing the Historical and Sociological Impact," 7–36, and Smith-Christopher, *Biblical Theology*.
14. Lipschits, "Demographic Changes," 332.
15. Ibid., 333. These statistics actually suggest an even more precipitous decline than the older statistics in studies by Jamieson-Drake, *Scribes*, 62, and Carter, *Emergence*, 114–213.
16. Lipschits, "Demographic Changes," 334–38.
17. Ibid., 338–41.
18. Ibid., 341–45.
19. See the summary by Mazar, *Archaeology*, 458–60.
20. Lehmann, "Trends," 21–32. Lehmann's work utilizes the new archaeological data to update Ephraim Stern's classic work that had pointed to some continuity in the material culture between the Iron and Persian periods; see E. Stern, *Material Culture*, 229.
21. See Vanderhooft, *Neo-Babylonian Empire*, 61–114.
22. Vanderhooft, "Scribes and Scripts," 535.
23. Ibid., 539.

24. Weidner, "Jojachin," 923–28; Albright, "King Jehoiachin," 49–55. The Neo-Babylonian archives, including this particular archive, are discussed in Pedersén, *Archives*, 183–84.
25. As suggested by J. Berridge, "Jehoiachin," *ABD* 3:661–63; also see Albright, "King Jehoiachin," 49–55.
26. On the Babylonian linguistic influence, see the classic work by Zimmern, *Akkadische Fremdwörter*. Although Zimmern's book represents an early period of the field of Assyriology, and certainly overstates the extent of Akkadian influence, it remains a valuable resource.
27. Mankowski, *Akkadian Loanwords*, 9; also see the earlier works by Kaufman, *Akkadian Influences*; Ellenbogen, *Foreign Words*; C. Rabin, "Foreign Words," *EM* 4:1070–80. Finally, the lexicon edited by Koehler and Baumgartner, *Hebrew and Aramaic Lexicon*, is an essential resource for historical etymology.
28. See Weinfeld, *Deuteronomy*, 59–178.
29. Moran, "Ancient Near Eastern Background," 77–87.
30. Hurvitz, "Hebrew and Aramaic in the Biblical Period," 24–37.
31. See Hurvitz, *Linguistic Study*; Rooker, *Biblical Hebrew*.
32. E.g., Rooker, "Dating Isaiah 40–66," 303–12.
33. See especially the analysis by Talshir, "Habitat and History of Hebrew," 251–75.
34. See especially Cryer, *Divination*, 192. Cited by Young and Rezetko, *Linguistic Dating*, 1:47.
35. Contrast, e.g., Young, *Diversity*. Some of the leveling of Hebrew may also be ascribed to the transmission process, however this too is uneven; note, e.g., the Great Isaiah Scroll from Qumran with the Masoretic text (see Kutscher, *Language and Linguistic Background of the Isaiah Scroll*).

Chapter 7. Hebrew under Imperialism

1. This is the term that Naveh uses in his *Early History of the Alphabet*, 162–74.
2. Tadmor, "Aramaization," 449–70.
3. Vernacularization was also a dialectic in the formation of the Hebrew Bible, particularly books like Deuteronomy (see my discussion, *How the Bible Became a Book*, 111–17).
4. Pollock, "Cosmopolitan," 592.
5. For an account of the demise of cuneiform, see Geller, "Last Wedge," 43–95.
6. Fitzmyer, "Phases," 57–84.
7. See Kiernan, "Languages and Conquerors," 191–210.
8. Ibid., 195.
9. Naveh and Greenfield, "Hebrew and Aramaic in the Persian Period," 116.
10. See summary by Eph'al, *Archaeology*, 360–66, 535–70. Also see Eph'al and Naveh, *Aramaic Ostraca*.
11. Eph'al, *Archaeology*, 362.
12. C. Rabin, "Historical Background," 152.
13. Lindenberger, *Aramaic Proverbs*. More generally, see Beyer, *Die aramaischen Inschriften*.
14. See Berthelot and Stökl Ben Ezra, *Aramaica*.
15. See Schniedewind, *How the Bible Became a Book*, and Schniedewind, "Aramaic, the Death of Written Hebrew," 137–48.
16. Schaper, "Hebrew," 17.
17. Ibid., 16.
18. Labov, *Principles of Linguistic Change*, 503.
19. See Kahn, "Neo-Aramaic Dialect," 213–25; also see the anecdotal account in Sabar, *My Father's Paradise*.
20. Lipschits, "Achaemenid Imperial Policy," 27.
21. See E. Stern, *Archaeology*, 353–60; Briant, *From Cyrus to Alexander*, 645–87.

22. This is also the position of Sáenz-Badillos, *History of the Hebrew Language*, 112–13.
23. In his defense of MH as a living language, M. Segal underplayed the significance of Aramaic influence on MH (see especially the introduction to *A Grammar of Mishnaic Hebrew*, 1–20). Segal's point, namely, that Mishnaic Hebrew was based on a living language, was well taken; however, his minimizing of the impact of Aramaic should be understood in retrospect as merely a rhetorical device of his argument.
24. See, e.g., P. Kroskrity's study of the Arizona Tewa Indians, "Arizona Tewa Kiva Speech."
25. Trudgill, *Sociolinguistics*, 128.
26. Schaper, "Hebrew," 15–26.
27. A. Saldarini, "Scribes," *ABD* 5:1013, cited by Schaper, "Hebrew," 18.
28. Ibid.; also see Naveh and Greenfield, "Hebrew and Aramaic in the Persian Period," 115–29. Contrast Schniedewind, "Aramaic, the Death of Written Hebrew," 137–48.
29. Schaper, "Hebrew," 17.
30. Ibid., 22.
31. See Williamson, *1 and 2 Chronicles*, 55–56; Japhet, *I & II Chronicles*, 89–90.
32. I regard the site of Ramat Rahel, a royal administrative site located between Jerusalem and Bethlehem, as an ideal candidate for the site of Jabez. A town of "scribal families" should be associated with the royal administration in Jerusalem, and Ramat Rahel would be a plausible candidate.
33. This is underscored by the close relationship between the Proto-Masoretic text known from the Dead Sea Scrolls and the later Masoretic tradition; see, e.g., Tov, *Textual Criticism*, 21–79. For an exhaustive analysis of the Masoretic tradition, see Yeivin, *Introduction to the Tiberian Masorah*, and Yeivin, *Hebrew Language*.
34. Joosten, "Pseudoclassicisms in Late Biblical Hebrew," 146–59.
35. Joosten, "Evolution of Literary Hebrew."
36. See J. Blau, "Hapax Legomena," *EncJud* 8:337.
37. On the importance of loanwords for dating biblical texts, see Eshkult, "Importance," 8–23.
38. C. Cohen, *Biblical Hapax Legomena*; also see Greenspahn, *Hapax Legomena*.
39. See further Schniedewind and Sivan, "Letting Your 'Yes' Be 'No,'" 209–26.
40. See Rainey, *Canaanite in the Amarna Tablets*, 3:195–200 (esp. 200); also Brown, "*HL* in Northwest Semitic," 218–19.
41. For a comparison of the versions, see Grill, "Die alten Versionen," 277–78. Note the emendations proposed by Skinner, *Genesis*, 336–38.
42. This is the only example of the word לאמר not being immediately followed by a direct quote in the entire Hebrew Bible. לאמר is commonly employed in the phrases ויקרא . . . לאמר, ויצו . . . לאמר, וידבר . . . לאמר, ויאמר . . . לאמר, and many other variations to introduce direct quotes. The direct quote invariably follows the use of לאמר.
43. See, e.g., Skinner, *Genesis*, 337.
44. For more examples, see Schniedewind and Sivan, "Letting Your 'Yes' Be 'No,'" 213–26.
45. Hummel, "Enclitic Mem," 85–107.
46. See the lengthy discussion by Avishur, *Studies in Hebrew and Ugaritic Psalms*, 39–110 (esp. 91–95). The original observation was made by H. L. Ginsberg; see generally Ginsberg, "Phoenician Hymn," 472–76, and specifically his Hebrew book, *Kitve Ugarit*, 130.
47. Still, the Greek translator struggled with the meaning, translating "Lebanon" as a part of a construct phrase, "like the calf of Lebanon."
48. See Joosten, "Distinction between Classical and Late Biblical Hebrew" 337–38. This phenomenon was already pointed out by Frankel, *Vorstudien*, 197–99.
49. Joosten, "Distinction between Classical and Late Biblical Hebrew," 337–38.
50. See Heaton, *School Tradition*, 107–14.
51. See also Deut. 8:1; 11:9; 16:20; 19:10, 14; 21:23; 24:4.

52. Naveh and Greenfield, "Hebrew and Aramaic in the Persian Period," 119.
53. Avigad, *Bullae and Seals.*
54. S. Schwartz argued that vernacular Hebrew disappeared in the Persian period, citing inscriptional evidence that points primarily to Aramaic (see "Hebrew and Imperialism in Jewish Palestine," 53–84). Yet, the survival of vernacular Hebrew during the Second Temple period would have been in speech communities that were not necessarily literate. Moreover, his suggestion that shared language as a component of group identity is "simplistic" (54) flies in the face of basic sociolinguistic theory. In the words of the sociolinguist Peter Trudgill, "Language is a signal of group identity" (*Sociolinguistics*, 130). Schwartz seems to want to make a special case for ancient Jews, suggesting that language (and especially Hebrew) was not critical for their group identity. Yet the use of Hebrew in *symbolic* ways (coins, religious ceremonies) indicates otherwise. The problem of how pervasive Hebrew was as a vernacular is a different problem, but its importance for group identity cannot be dismissed.
55. The word is sometimes associated with the Greek for drachma.
56. For a comprehensive study and catalog of the Yehud inscriptions, see Lipschits and Vanderhooft, *Yehud Stamp Impressions.*
57. The initial publication was by Cross, "Papyri of the Fourth Century B.C.," 41–62; also see Avigad, *Bullae and Seals.*
58. See Silverstein's critique of Benedict Anderson's *Imagined Communities* in "Worfianism and the Linguistic Imagination," 85–138.
59. See Fried, "Silver Coin," 65–85; Barag, "Some Notes on a Silver Coin," 166–68; Betlyon, "Provincial Government," 633–42; Root, "Coinage, War, and Peace," 131–34.
60. Betlyon, "Provincial Government," 641.
61. Sáenz-Badillos, *History of the Hebrew Language*, 129.
62. Trudgill, *Sociolinguistics*, 136–44; Eira, "Authority and Discourse," 171–224.
63. The small changes in the Hebrew script between the seventh and first centuries B.C.E. makes the differences almost imperceptible to all but trained epigraphers. This became clear when two biblical scholars (Rogerson and Davies, "Was the Siloam Tunnel Built . . . ?" 138–49) suggested redating a late eighth-century B.C.E. Hebrew inscription (the Siloam Tunnel inscription) to the second century B.C.E. Although trained epigraphers (see, e.g., Hackett, "Defusing Pseudo-Scholarship," and the other articles in *Biblical Archaeology Review* 23, no. 2 [1997]) quickly corrected this mistake, it illustrated how little the Hebrew script had changed over the centuries.
64. This follows the observations of Talshir, "Habitat and History of Hebrew," 251–75. See also E. Axel Knauf, who notes, "400 becomes a more likely date for the BH/LBH divide than 586 ("Bethel," 311).
65. See Hurvitz, "Date of the Prose Tale of Job," 17–34.
66. Although the poetic aspects of these latter works have suggested to some scholars that they are Israelian Hebrew, it seems more likely that the idiosyncrasies of this literature result from its register (i.e., poetry) rather than its origin (i.e., Samaria).
67. See, e.g., Hurvitz, "Once Again," 180–91. This work has been critiqued in recent works (e.g., Young and Rezetko, *Linguistic Dating*), but the critiques are not entirely convincing (see, e.g., the review by Joosten in *Bibel und Babel*).

Chapter 8. Hebrew in the Hellenistic World

1. As cited by Bowman and Woolf, *Literacy and Power in the Ancient World*, 11.
2. See Sáenz-Badillos, *History of the Hebrew Language*, 112–210; Alexander, "How Did the Rabbis Learn Hebrew?" 72–89.
3. See Meshorer, *Ancient Jewish Coinage.*

4. C. Rabin claimed that fragments of Hebrew literature from the later Second Temple period have been preserved in rabbinic literature, including the Account of King Yannai (*b. Qiddushin* 66a) and the Account of Simeon the Just (Sifre for Num. 22); see Saénz-Badillos, *History of the Hebrew Language*, 128 n. 51. However, these are short and problematic linguistic sources.
5. Naveh, "Hebrew and Aramaic Inscriptions," 9–10.
6. Ibid., 10.
7. See, e.g., Weitzman, "Why Did the Qumran Community Write in Hebrew?" 35–45; Schniedewind, "Linguistic Ideology in Qumran Hebrew," 245–55.
8. See Beentjes, *Book of Ben Sira in Hebrew*.
9. Later tradition suggests that all seventy-two translators came up with precisely identical translations, thus proving the inspiration of the Greek Bible (e.g., Irenaeus, *Against Heresies* §3.21.2).
10. Labov, *Principles of Linguistic Change*, 514.
11. The idea that Hebrew was a divine and even primordial language is especially developed in some of the literature from the Dead Sea Scrolls. Of course, the book of Jubilees itself seems to have been an important text in the sectarian literature, with at least fifteen copies found in the Qumran caves. Note the inclusion of Jubilees in Abegg, Flint, and Ulrich, *Dead Sea Scrolls Bible*, 196–98.
12. Purvis, *Samaritan Pentateuch*.
13. Ibid., 50–52.
14. Meshorer, *Ancient Jewish Coinage*, 31–32; Meshorer and Qedar, *Samarian Coinage*.
15. Ben-Hayyim, *Grammar of Samaritan Hebrew*, 1.
16. Ibid., 23–28.
17. Ibid., 335.
18. See Qimron, *Hebrew of the Dead Sea Scrolls*. Qimron's volume, alongside Kutscher's masterful *Language and Linguistic Background of the Isaiah Scroll*, provides a serviceable description of QH. For a survey of QH, see Sáenz-Badillos, *History of the Hebrew Language*, 130–46, and the literature cited there.
19. See Collins, *Beyond the Qumran Community*, and Schofield, *From Qumran to the Yahad*.
20. In the words of Judith Irvine ("When Talk Isn't Cheap," 250), who obviously borrows from Durkheim.
21. Devorah Dimant has distinguished between "documents employing terminology connected to the Qumran Community" and "works not containing such terminology." She estimates that approximately 40 percent of the Cave 4 manuscripts should be classified among those "not containing terminology connected to the Qumran Community" ("Qumran Manuscripts," 32).
22. For a survey of recent studies on language ideology, see Woolard and Schieffelin, "Language Ideology," 55–82.
23. C. Rabin, "Historical Background," 146.
24. Such a belief would lend more support to Schiffman's argument for the Proto-Sadduccean origins of the Qumran community; see Schiffman, *Reclaiming the Dead Sea Scrolls*, 83–89.
25. The reference to a metaphorical source (מקור) suggests that the Qumran sectarians associated this term with the verb √קוה in its meaning "to gather water," and the related noun מקוה (e.g., Gen. 1:9–10, where God gathers the primordial waters). It might be fruitful to pursue the relationship between this concept and the "well" motif; see Fishbane, "Well of Living Water," 3–16.
26. See Clements, *Isaiah 1–39*, 165, 228, and the literature cited there.
27. Talmon, "Emergence of Institutionalized Prayer in Israel," 200–43.
28. Talmon, "What's in a Calendar?" 25–58; see S. Stern, "Qumran Calendars," 179–86.

29. This is a term used by Irvine and Gal in their methodologically important study "Language Ideology and Linguistic Differentiation," 35–83.
30. Frank Moore Cross, for instance, characterizes these as a "survival of Old Canaanite"; Cross, "Some Notes on a Generation of Qumran Studies," 4.
31. This issue has been particularly important in recent studies in sociolinguistics; e.g., Gal, "Codeswitching and Consciousness," 637–53; Irvine, "When Talk Isn't Cheap," 248–67; Heller, *Codeswitching*. Also see the classic study by Voloshinov, *Marxism and the Philosophy of Language*, 9–15.
32. Romaine, *Language in Society*, 148.
33. See Schniedewind, "Qumran Hebrew as an Antilanguage," 235–52, and the further comments by Rendsburg, "Qumran Hebrew," 217–46.
34. Halliday, "Anti-Languages," 571. Notably, Halliday considers the early Christian community an antisociety and to a certain degree its language an antilanguage (575). All the more so the *yaḥad* community.
35. Ormsby-Lennon, "From Shibboleth to Apocalypse," 72–112; also see N. Smith, "Uses of Hebrew in the English Revolution," 51–71.
36. Irvine, "When Talk Isn't Cheap," 253. The principle is actually a general sociolinguistic pattern, as Labov observes (*Sociolinguistic Patterns*, 314), but it appears to be exaggerated in sharply bounded groups.
37. Labov, *Sociolinguistic Patterns*, 251; emphasis added.
38. Linguistic diversity among the scrolls also becomes an occasion to argue that Qumran Hebrew is an "artificial" language, independent from both LBH and RH. See, e.g., Meyer, "Das Problem der Dialektmischung," 139–48, and Meyer, "Bemerkungen zu den hebräischen Aussprachetraditionen," 39–48. Antilanguages, however, are not artificial. From sociolinguistic and functionalist perspectives, there is no such thing as an artificial language. Qumran Hebrew is not artificial, but it does arise out of a countersociety.
39. Tov, "Orthography and Language of the Hebrew Scrolls," 31–57; Tov, "Hebrew Biblical Manuscripts from the Judaean Desert," 5–37; Tov, *Scribal Practices*.
40. Indeed, the proximity of the site to the scroll caves had always made this an obvious inference, and the discovery of three inkwells in the excavations at Khirbet Qumran further solidified the argument. The scientific tests showing that the ink on some scrolls was made using water from the Dead Sea should put an end to this question; see I. Rabin et al., "On the Origin of the Ink of the Thanksgiving Scroll," 97–106.
41. Note the critique of Kim, "Free Orthography in a Strict Society," 72–81, as well as Tov's response, "Reply to Dong-Hyuk Kim's Paper," 360–61.
42. See Kutscher, *Language and Linguistic Background of the Isaiah Scroll*, 5–8; Qimron, *Hebrew of the Dead Sea Scrolls*, §100.
43. M. Segal, *Grammar of Mishnaic Hebrew*, 32; Qimron, *Hebrew of the Dead Sea Scrolls*, §200.15.
44. See Tov, "Orthography and Language of the Hebrew Scrolls," 31–57, and Tov, "Hebrew Biblical Manuscripts from the Judaean Desert," 5–37.
45. Tov, "Orthography and Language of the Hebrew Scrolls," 36.
46. See especially Tov, "Reply to Dong-Hyuk Kim's Paper," 360–61.
47. Ulrich, *Dead Sea Scrolls and the Origins of the Bible*, 88.
48. Pfann, "Cryptic Texts," 515–74.
49. See Eira, "Authority and Discourse," 171–224.
50. Kutscher, *Language and Linguistic Background of the Isaiah Scroll*, 19.
51. See Ben-Hayyim, "Traditions in the Hebrew Language," 200–214.
52. See Tov's critique ("Orthography and Language of the Hebrew Scrolls," 38–39) of Siegel, *Severus Scroll and 1QIsa*.
53. Tov, "Orthography and Language of the Hebrew Scrolls," 39.

54. Neither can we accept Norman Golb's argument that all the scrolls came from outside the community, because there are too many scribal hands evidenced in the scrolls; see Golb, "Problem of Origin and Identification," 1–24.
55. Labov, *Sociolinguistic Patterns*, 292.
56. Other clear examples include 1QH 15:29; 4Q175 5, 6, 18; 4Q185 5; 4Q378 frag. 3 1:8; 4Q417 frag. 1 2:7; 4Q504 frag. 1–2R 5:5; 11QT 34:9; 59:10. I wish to express thanks to Martin Abegg for supplying me a complete list of supralinear letters and final letters in medial position in the Qumran texts.
57. See Eira, "Authority and Discourse," 171–224.
58. See Pfann, "Writings in Esoteric Script from Qumran," 177–90.
59. Pfann, "4Q298," 216–21.
60. Ibid., 225.
61. Halliday writes, "An anti-language is the means of realization of a subjective reality: not merely expressing it, but actively creating and maintaining it" ("Anti-Languages," 576).
62. See Weitzman, "Why Did the Qumran Community Write in Hebrew?" 35–45.
63. Kutscher, *History of the Hebrew Language*, 100.
64. Ibid., 135–41.
65. C. Rabin, "Historical Background," 146.
66. Morag, "Qumran Hebrew," 149.
67. Bar-Asher, "Mishnaic Hebrew and Aramaic in Qumran Hebrew," 15–19.
68. Kutscher, *Language and Linguistic Background of the Isaiah Scroll*, 23.
69. Ibid., 24.
70. For this reason, the analysis of I. Young is particularly misguided, focusing as it does on lexical items that are largely generated by the language ideology of QH (Young, "Late Biblical Hebrew and the Qumran Pesher Habakkuk").
71. Morag, "Qumran Hebrew," 149.
72. See M. Segal, *Grammar of Mishnaic Hebrew*, 146. See examples cited in Clines (ed.), *Dictionary of Classical Hebrew*, 1:432–33.
73. C. Rabin, "Historical Background," 146–48.
74. See M. Segal, *Grammar of Mishnaic Hebrew*, §169.
75. Other examples include 1QS 1:13, 14, 15, 17; 3:10; 6:11; 9:16; CD 2:16; 7:2; 1QH 15:15; 18:15; 20:24; 1QH frag. 2 1:12; 1QH frag. 5 1:14; 4Q287 frag. 8 1:13; 4Q396 frags. 1–2 4:6, 7; 4Q397 frags. 6–13 1:12; 11QT 50:2.
76. See Judg. 1:19; Isa. 30:5; Jer. 4:11; Amos 6:10; Dan. 6:9, 16; Ezra 6:8; 1 Chron. 5:1; 15:2; 2 Chron. 12:12.
77. See Stevenson, *Grammar of Palestinian Jewish Aramaic*, 20.
78. In spite of M. Segal's objections (*Grammar of Mishnaic Hebrew*, 164–65), it seems obvious that the use of the periphrastic construction in Mishnaic Hebrew is the result of Aramaic influence. Even Segal concedes that the periphrastic construction occurs mainly in LBH, not SBH. On its use in biblical Hebrew, see Waltke and O'Connor, *Introduction to Biblical Hebrew Syntax*, §37.7; Joüon, *Grammaire de l'Hébreu biblique*, §121g; there are substantive differences between Joüon's original discussion and Muraoka's translation and revision in *Grammar of Biblical Hebrew*.
79. The elongated form *hwʾh* is known from Dead Sea Scrolls biblical manuscripts copied using Qumran scribal practice (e.g., 1QIs[a], 1Q4, 2Q13, 4Q27, 4Q128, 4Q138).
80. Some examples include 1QS 10:12, 16, 25; 1QpHab 6:12; 1QM 13:12, 13; 14:13; 1QH 5:26; 7:13; 9:23; 10:30; 12:39; 14:6, 7; 17:8, 9, 13, 14; 18:16, 20, 31, 34; 19:6, 20, 23; 20:2, 3; 22:9, 10; 1Q34bis frag. 2+1 i, 3; 4Q427 frag. 1 1:3, 4; 2:4; frag. 4 1:1; frag. 8 1:2; 4Q491 frags. 8–10 1:10; 4Q503 frags. 7–9 4:3; 11QT 29:8; 30:1; 54:10; 55:4; 56:13.
81. See M. Segal, *Grammar of Mishnaic Hebrew*, 72, 153–55.
82. Revell, "Pausal Forms in Biblical Hebrew," 168.

83. See, e.g., 1QS 3:18; 4:17; 11:7; 1QpHab 6:1; 7:1. My observations here are first of all indebted to a graduate seminar paper at UCLA by Roger Good, entitled "Changes in the Use of the Prefix and Suffix Conjugation of the Verb in the Different Types of Qumran Literature." Also see M. Smith, "Converted and Unconverted Perfect and Imperfect Forms," 1–16; Thorion-Vardi, "Use of the Tenses in the Zadokite Documents," 65–88; Montaner, "Some Features of the Hebrew Verbal Syntax," 273–86.
84. See Qimron and Strugnell, "Unpublished Halakhic Letter from Qumran," 400–407.
85. Ibid., 405.
86. Halliday, "Anti-Languages," 576.
87. See Collins, *Beyond the Qumran Community*, 43–46.

Chapter 9. The End and the Beginning of Hebrew

1. See, e.g., Heinrichs, *Studies in Neo-Aramaic*, xi–xv.
2. Sáenz-Badillos, *History of the Hebrew Language*, 56.
3. See, e.g., Shinan, "Aramaic Targum as a Mirror of Galilean Jewry," 244–45.
4. Sáenz-Badillos, *History of the Hebrew Language*, 171.
5. See E. Y. Kutscher, "Hebrew," *EncJud* 8:640.
6. This point is made by Alexander, "How Did the Rabbis Learn Hebrew?" 74–75.
7. Unfortunately, most references to Jewish education come from much later texts, such as the Talmud, and cannot be relied upon for understanding education in the first couple of centuries C.E. Citations here will be limited to earlier (i.e., contemporary) sources.
8. Josephus, *Against Apion*, 2.204.
9. Yadin, *Bar-Kokhba*, 181.
10. See Yadin and Naveh, *Masada I*, 8–9.
11. Bar, "Population, Settlement and Economy," 311.
12. Ibid.
13. Hezser, *Jewish Literacy in Roman Palestine*, 244; emphasis added.
14. Sáenz-Badillos, *History of the Hebrew Language*, 161–62.
15. Cited, e.g., by Chomsky, "What Was the Jewish Vernacular . . . ?" 194.
16. As was pointed out by E. Y. Kutscher, "Hebrew Language, Mishnaic," *EncJud* 8:639–50.
17. See ibid., 640–42.
18. Kutscher, *History of the Hebrew Language*, 75.
19. See the discussions by Blau, *Phonology and Morphology*, 3–4; Pérez Fernández, *Introductory Grammar of Rabbinic Hebrew*, 104–10; Mishor, "Tense System in Tannaitic Hebrew."
20. Yadin et al., *Documents from the Bar Kokhba Period*, 14–15.

Chapter 10. Epilogue

1. See the account by J. Fellman, *Revival of a Classical Tongue*.

Bibliography

Abegg, Martin, Peter Flint, and Eugene Ulrich. *The Dead Sea Scrolls Bible*. New York: Harper Collins, 1999.

Aharoni, Yohanan. *The Land of the Bible*. Translated by A. F. Rainey. Rev. ed. Philadelphia: Westminster, 1979.

———. "The Use of Hieratic Numerals in Hebrew Ostraca and the Shekel Weights." *Bulletin of the American Schools of Oriental Research* 184 (1966): 13–19.

Ahituv, Shmuel. *Echoes from the Past: Hebrew and Cognate Inscriptions from the Biblical Period*. Translated by A. F. Rainey. Jerusalem: Carta, 2008.

Albright, William F. "King Jehoiachin in Exile." *Biblical Archaeologist* 5 (1942): 49–55.

———. "The Old Testament and Canaanite Language and Literature." *Catholic Biblical Quarterly* 7 (1945): 5–31.

———. "The Psalm of Habakkuk." In *Studies in Old Testament Prophecy*, edited by H. H. Rowley, 1–20. Edinburgh: T&T Clark, 1950.

———. Review of *Ugaritic Grammar*, by C. H. Gordon. *Journal of Biblical Literature* 60 (1941): 438.

———. *Yahweh and the Gods of Canaan: A Historical Analysis of Two Contrasting Faiths*. London: University of London Press, 1968.

Alexander, Philip S. "How Did the Rabbis Learn Hebrew?" In *Hebrew Study from Ezra to Ben-Yehuda*, edited by W. Horbury, 72–89. Edinburgh: T&T Clark, 1999.

Allen, James P. "The Craft of the Scribe (Papyrus Anastasi I)." In *Archival Documents from the Biblical World*. Vol. 3 of *The Context of Scripture*, edited by W. W. Hallo, §3.2. Leiden, Netherlands: Brill, 2000.

———. *Middle Egyptian: An Introduction to the Language and Culture of Hieroglyphs*. Cambridge, UK: Cambridge University Press, 2000.

Andersen, Francis I., and A. Dean Forbes. *Spelling in the Hebrew Bible*. Rome: Pontifical Biblical Institute Press, 1986.

Ash, Paul S. *David, Solomon and Egypt: A Reassessment*. Journal for the Study of the Old Testament Supplement Series 297. Sheffield, UK: Sheffield Academic Press, 1999.

Austin, Michel M. *The Hellenistic World from Alexander to the Roman Conquest*. Cambridge, UK: Cambridge University Press, 1981.

Avigad, Nahman. *Bullae and Seals from a Post-Exilic Judean Archive*. Qedem 4. Jerusalem: Hebrew University Press, 1976.

———. *Hebrew Bullae from the Time of Jeremiah*. Jerusalem: Society for the Land of Israel and Its Antiquities, 1986. Hebrew.

Avigad, Nahman, and Benjamin Sass. *Corpus of West Semitic Stamp Seals*. Jerusalem: Jerusalem Academy of Sciences and Humanities, 1998.

Avishur, Yitzhak. *Studies in Hebrew and Ugaritic Psalms*. Jerusalem: Magnes, 1994.

Bar, Doron. "Population, Settlement and Economy in Late Roman and Byzantine Palestine (70–641 AD)." *Bulletin of the School of Oriental and African Studies, University of London* 67 (2004): 307–20.

Barag, Dan. "Some Notes on a Silver Coin of Jonathan the High Priest." *Biblical Archaeologist* 48, no. 3 (1985): 166–68.

Bar-Asher, Moshe. "Mishnaic Hebrew and Aramaic in Qumran Hebrew." In *Diggers at the Well: Proceedings of a Third International Symposium on the Hebrew of the Dead Sea Scrolls and Ben Sira*, edited by T. Muraoka and J. Elwolde, 25–52. Leiden, Netherlands: Brill, 2000.

———. "Mishnaic Hebrew: An Introductory Survey." *Hebrew Studies* 40 (1999): 115–51.

Barkay, Gabriel. "The Priestly Benediction on Silver Plaques from Ketef Hinnom in Jerusalem." *Tel Aviv* 19 (1992): 139–91.

Barkay, Gabriel, et al. "The Amulets from Ketef Hinnom: A New Edition and Evaluation." *Bulletin of the American Schools of Oriental Research* 334 (2004): 41–71.

Barr, James. *The Variable Spellings of the Hebrew Bible*. Oxford, UK: Oxford University Press, 1989.

Barstad, Hans. *The Myth of the Empty Land: A Study in the History and Archaeology of Judah During the "Exilic" Period*. Oslo: Scandinavian University Press, 1996.

———. "On the History and Archeology of Judah during the Exilic Period: A Reminder." *Orientalia lovaniensia Periodica* 19 (1988): 25–36.

Bauer, Hans, Pontus Leander, and Paul Kahle. *Historische Grammatik der hebräischen Sprache des Alten Testaments*. Hildesheim, Germany: Olms, 1962.

Beentjes, Pancratius. *The Book of Ben Sira in Hebrew: A Text Edition of All Extant Hebrew Manuscripts and a Synopsis of All Parallel Hebrew Ben Sira Texts*. Leiden, Netherlands: Brill, 1997.

Ben-Hayyim, Ze'ev. *A Grammar of Samaritan Hebrew*. With the assistance of Abraham Tal. Jerusalem: Magnes, 2000.

———. "Traditions in the Hebrew Language, with Reference to the Dead Sea Scrolls." *Scripta Hierosolymitana* 4 (1958): 200–214.

Berthelot, Katell, and Daniel Stökl Ben Ezra, eds. *Aramaica Qumranica: Proceedings of the Conference on the Aramaic Texts from Qumran at Aix-en-Provence (June 30–July 2, 2008)*. Studies on the Texts of the Desert of Judah 94. Leiden, Netherlands: Brill, 2010.

Betlyon, John. "The Provincial Government of Persian Period Judea and the Yehud Coins." *Journal of Biblical Literature* 105 (1986): 633–42.

Beyer, Klaus. *Die aramaischen Inschriften aus Assur, Hatra und dem ubrigen Ostmesopotamien*. Göttingen, Germany: Vandenhoeck & Ruprecht, 1998.

Binger, Tilde. *Asherah: Goddesses in Ugarit, Israel and the Old Testament*. Journal for the Study of the Old Testament Supplement Series 232. Sheffield, UK: Sheffield Academic Press, 1997.

Biran, Avraham, and Joseph Naveh. "The Tel Dan Inscription: A New Fragment." *Israel Exploration Journal* 45 (1995): 1–18.

Blau, Joshua. *On Polyphony in Biblical Hebrew*. Proceedings of the Israel Academy of Sciences and Humanities 6/2. Jerusalem: Israel Academy of Sciences, 1982.

———. *Phonology and Morphology of Biblical Hebrew*. Winona Lake, IN: Eisenbrauns, 2010.

Bloomfield, Leonard. *Language*. Chicago: University of Chicago Press, 1984.

Bottéro, Jean. *Le Problème des Ḫābiru à la quartième Recontre Assyriologique Internationale*. Paris: Imprimerie Nationale, 1954.

Bowman, Alan, and Greg Woolf, eds. *Literacy and Power in the Ancient World*. Cambridge, UK: Cambridge University Press, 1994.

Brent, John F. "The Problem of the Placement of Ugaritic among the Semitic Languages." *Westminster Theological Journal* 41 (1978–79): 105–6.

Brettler, Marc Z. "The Structure of 1 Kings 1–11." *Journal for the Study of the Old Testament* 49 (1991): 87–97.

Briant, Pierre. *From Cyrus to Alexander: A History of the Persian Empire*. Winona Lake, IN: Eisenbrauns, 2002.

Brockelmann, Carl. *Hebräische Syntax*. Neukirchen, Germany: Neukirchener Verlag, 1956.

Broshi, Magen. "The Expansion of Jerusalem in the Reigns of Hezekiah and Manasseh." *Israel Exploration Journal* 24 (1974): 21–28.

Brown, Michael. "*HL* in Northwest Semitic." *Maarav* 4 (1987): 201–19.

Bruins, Hendrik J., and Amihai Mazar. "The End of the 2nd Millennium BCE and the Transition from Iron I to Iron IIA: Radiocarbon Dates of Tel Rehov, Israel." In *The Synchronisation of Civilisations in the Eastern Mediterranean in the Second Millennium B.C. III: Proceedings of the SCIEM 2000—2nd EuroConference, Vienna, 28th of May–1st of June 2003*, edited by M. Bietak and E. Czerny, 77–99. Vienna: Verlag der Österreichischen Akademie der Wissenschaften, 2007.

Bruins, Hendrik J., et al. "The Groningen Radiocarbon Series from Tel Rehov: Oxcal Bayesian Computations for the Iron IB–IIA Boundary and Iron IIa Destruction Events." In *The Bible and Radiocarbon Dating: Archeology, Text, and Science*, edited by T. Higham and T. E. Levy, 271–93. London: Equinox, 2005.

Burke, Aaron. "An Anthropological Model for the Investigation of the Archaeology of Refugees in Iron Age Judah and Its Environs." In *Interpreting Exile: Interdisciplinary*

Studies of Displacement and Deportation in Biblical and Modern Contexts, edited by B. E. Kelle and F. R. Ames, 41–56. Atlanta, GA: Society of Biblical Literature, 2011.

———. "Coping with the Effects of War: The Archaeology of Refugees in the Ancient Near East." In *Disaster and Relief Management in Ancient Israel, Egypt and the Ancient Near East*, edited by A. Berlejung, A. Bagg, and G. Lehmann, 263–87. Forschungen zum Alten Testament. Tübingen, Germany: Mohr Siebeck, 2012.

Burney, Charles F. *Notes on the Hebrew Text of the Book of Kings*. Oxford, UK: Clarendon Press, 1903.

Byrne, Ryan. "The Refuge of Scribalism in Iron I Palestine." *Bulletin of the American Schools of Oriental Research* 345 (2007): 1–31.

Carroll, Robert P. "Exile! What Exile?" In *Leading Captivity Captive*, edited by L. Grabbe, 62–79. Sheffield, UK: Sheffield Academic Press, 1998.

Carsten, Janet, ed. *Cultures of Relatedness: New Approaches to the Study of Kinship*. Cambridge, UK: Cambridge University Press, 2000.

Carter, Charles E. *The Emergence of Yehud in the Persian Period: A Social and Demographic Study*. Sheffield, UK: Sheffield Academic Press, 1999.

Cassuto, Umberto. *Biblical and Oriental Studies*. Vol. 2, *Bible and Ancient Oriental Texts*. Translated by I. Abrahams. Jerusalem: Magnes, 1975.

Charpin, Dominique. *Reading and Writing in Babylon*. Cambridge, MA: Harvard University Press, 2010.

Chomsky, William. "What Was the Jewish Vernacular during the Second Commonwealth?" *Jewish Quarterly Review* 42 (1951): 193–212.

Civil, Miguel. "Sur les 'livres d'écolier' à l'époque paléo-babylonienne." In *Miscellanea Babylonica*, edited by J.-M. Durand, 67–78. Paris: Éditions Recherche sur les Civilisations, 1985.

Clements, Ronald E. *Isaiah 1–39*. New Century Bible Commentary. Grand Rapids, MI: Eerdmans, 1980.

Clines, David J. A., ed. *The Dictionary of Classical Hebrew*. 5 vols. Sheffield, UK: Sheffield Academic Press, 1993–.

Cody, Aelred. "Le titre égyptien et le nom propre du scribe de David." *Revue Biblique* 72 (1965): 381–93.

Cogan, Mordechai [Morton]. *Imperialism and Religion: Assyria, Judah and Israel in the Eighth and Seventh Centuries B.C.E.* Missoula, MT: Scholars Press, 1974.

———. *1 Kings: A New Translation with Introduction and Commentary*. Anchor Bible 10. New York: Doubleday, 2001.

Cohen, Chaim. *Biblical Hapax Legomena in the Light of Akkadian and Ugaritic*. Society of Biblical Literature Dissertation Series 37. Missoula, MT: Scholars Press, 1978.

Cohen, Shaye. *The Beginnings of Jewishness: Boundaries, Varieties, Uncertainties*. Berkeley: University of California Press, 1999.

Cohen, Yoram. *The Scribes and Scholars of the City of Emar in the Late Bronze Age*. Harvard Semitic Studies 59. Winona Lake, IN: Eisenbrauns, 2009.

Collins, John J. *Beyond the Qumran Community: The Sectarian Movement of the Dead Sea Scrolls*. Grand Rapids, MI: Eerdmans, 2009.

Coulmas, Florian, ed. *The Handbook of Sociolinguistics.* Oxford, UK: Blackwell, 1997.

———. *Writing Systems: An Introduction to Their Linguistic Analysis.* Cambridge, UK: Cambridge University Press, 2003.

Crenshaw, James L. *Education in Ancient Israel: Across the Deadening Silence.* New York: Doubleday, 1998.

Cross, Frank Moore. *Canaanite Myth and Hebrew Epic.* Cambridge, MA: Harvard University Press, 1973.

———. "The History of the Biblical Text in Light of Discoveries in the Judaean Desert." In *Qumran and the History of the Biblical Text,* edited by F. M. Cross and S. Talmon, 177–95. Cambridge, MA: Harvard University Press, 1975.

———. "The Invention and Development of the Alphabet." In *The Origins of Writing,* edited by W. Senner, 77–90. Lincoln: University of Nebraska Press, 1991.

———. "A Literate Soldier: Lachish Letter III." In *Biblical and Related Studies Presented to Samuel Iwry,* edited by A. Kort and S. Morschauser, 41–47. Winona Lake, IN: Eisenbrauns, 1985.

———. "Newly Found Inscriptions in Old Canaanite and Early Phoenician Scripts." *Bulletin of the American Schools of Oriental Research* 238 (1980): 1–20.

———. "Paleography and the Date of the Tell Fakhariyeh Inscription." In *Solving Riddles and Untying Knots: Biblical, Epigraphic, and Semitic Studies in Honor of Jonas C. Greenfield,* edited by Z. Zevit, S. Gitin, and M. Sokoloff, 393–409. Winona Lake, IN: Eisenbrauns, 1995.

———. "Papyri of the Fourth Century B.C. from Daliyeh." In *New Directions in Biblical Archaeology,* edited by D. N. Freedman and J. C. Greenfield, 41–62. Garden City, NY: Doubleday, 1969.

———. "Some Notes on a Generation of Qumran Studies." In *The Madrid Qumran Congress: Proceedings of the International Congress on the Dead Sea Scrolls, Madrid, 18–21 March, 1991,* edited by J. T. Barrera and L. V. Montaner, 1–14. Leiden, Netherlands: Brill, 1992.

Cross, Frank Moore, and David Noel Freedman. *Early Hebrew Orthography: A Study of the Epigraphic Evidence.* American Oriental Series 36. New Haven, CT: American Oriental Society, 1952.

Crowfoot, John W., and Grace M. Crowfoot. *Early Ivories from Samaria.* London: Palestine Exploration Fund, 1938.

Cryer, Frederick. *Divination in Ancient Israel and Its Near Eastern Environment.* Sheffield, UK: JSOT Press, 1994.

Dahood, Mitchell. *Psalms 101–150.* Anchor Bible 17A. Garden City, NY: Doubleday, 1970.

Daniels, Peter T. "Scripts of the Semitic Languages." In *The Semitic Languages,* edited by R. Hetzron, 16–45. New York: Abingdon, 1997.

———. "The Study of Writing Systems." In *The World's Writing Systems,* edited by P. Daniels and W. Bright, 3–17. Oxford, UK: Oxford University Press, 1996.

Danker, Frederick W., ed. *A Greek-English Lexicon of the New Testament and other Early Christian Literature.* 3rd ed. Chicago: University of Chicago Press, 2000.

Darnell, John, et al. "Two Early Alphabetic Inscriptions from the Wadi el-Hôl." *Annual of the American Schools of Oriental Research* 59, no. 2 (2005): 73–124.

de Vaux, Roland. "Titres et fonctionnaires égyptiens à la cour de David et Solomon." *Revue Biblique* 48 (1939): 394–405.

Dearman, Andrew. *Studies in the Mesha Inscription and Moab*. Atlanta, GA: Scholars Press, 1989.

Deller, Karlheinz. "Das Siegel des Schreibers." *Baghdader Mitteilungen* 13 (1982): 143–54.

Derrida, Jacques. *Of Grammatology*. Translated by G. Chakravorty Spivak. Baltimore, MD: Johns Hopkins University Press, 1976.

Deutsch, Robert, and Michael Heltzer. *New Epigraphic Evidence from the Biblical Period*. Tel Aviv: Archaeological Center, 1995.

Dever, William. "Iron Age Epigraphic Material from the Area of Khirbet el-Kôm." *Hebrew Union College Annual* 40–41 (1970): 139–204.

———. *Who Were the Israelites and Where Did They Come From?* Grand Rapids, MI: Eerdmans, 2003.

Diakonoff, Igor M. "Ancient Writing and Ancient Written Language: Pitfalls and Peculiarities in the Study of Sumerian." In *Sumerological Studies in Honor of Thorkild Jacobsen on his Seventieth Birthday, June 7, 1974*, edited by S. J. Lieberman, 99–121. Assyriological Studies 20. Chicago: University of Chicago Press, 1976.

Dietrich, Manfred. *The Neo-Babylonian Correspondence of Sargon and Sennacherib*. State Archives of Assyria 17. Helsinki, Finland: University of Helsinki Press, 2003.

Dietrich, Manfred, and Oswald Loretz. "The Ugaritic Script." In *Handbook of Ugaritic Studies*, edited by W. G. E. Watson and N. Wyatt, 81–89. Leiden, Netherlands: Brill, 1999.

Dimant, Devorah. "The Qumran Manuscripts: Contents and Significance." In *"Time to Prepare the Way in the Wilderness": Papers on the Qumran Scrolls by Fellows of the Institute for Advanced Studies of the Hebrew University, Jerusalem, 1989–90*, edited by D. Dimant and L. H. Schiffman, 23–58. Leiden, Netherlands: Brill, 1994.

Dobbs-Allsopp, Frederick W. "The Genre of the Mesad Hashavyahu Ostracon," *Bulletin of the American Schools of Oriental Research* 295 (1994): 49–55.

Dobbs-Allsopp, Frederick W., et al., eds. *Hebrew Inscriptions: Texts from the Biblical Period of the Monarchy with Concordance*. New Haven, CT: Yale University Press, 2004.

Duranti, Alessandro. *Linguistic Anthropology*. Cambridge Textbooks in Linguistics. Cambridge, UK: Cambridge University Press, 1997.

Ehri, Linnea. "Phases of Acquisition in Learning to Read Words and Implications for Teaching." In *Learning and Teaching Reading*, edited by R. Stainthorp and P. Thomlinson, 7–28. British Journal of Educational Psychology Monograph Series 1. Leicester, UK: British Psychological Society, 2002.

Eira, Christina. "Authority and Discourse: Towards a Model for Orthography Selection." *Written Language and Literacy* 1 (1998): 171–224.

Ellenbogen, Maximilian. *Foreign Words in the Old Testament: Their Origin and Etymology*. London: Luzac, 1962.

Emerton, John A. "New Evidence for the Use of *Waw* Consecutive in Aramaic." *Vetus Testamentum* 44 (1994): 255–58.

Eph'al, Israel. *Archaeology of the Land of the Bible, Volume II: The Assyrian, Babylonian, and Persian Periods (732–333 B.C.E.)*. New York: Doubleday, 2001.

———. "On Warfare and Military Control in the Ancient Near Eastern Empires: A Research Outline." In *History, Historiography and Interpretation: Studies in Biblical and Cuneiform Literatures*, edited by H. Tadmor and M. Weinfeld, 88–106. Jerusalem: Magnes, 1983.

Eph'al, Israel, and Joseph Naveh. *Aramaic Ostraca of the Fourth Century BC from Idumaea*. Jerusalem: Israel Exploration Society, 1996.

Eshkult, Mats. "The Importance of Loanwords for Dating Biblical Hebrew Texts." In *Biblical Hebrew: Studies in Chronology and Typology*, edited by I. Young, 8–23. Journal for the Study of the Old Testament Supplement Series 369. London: T&T Clark, 2003.

———. "Verbal Syntax in Late Biblical Hebrew." In *Diggers at the Well: Proceedings of a Third International Symposium on the Hebrew of the Dead Sea Scrolls and Ben Sira*, edited by T. Muraoka and J. F. Elwolde, 84–93. Studies on the Texts of the Desert of Judah 36. Leiden, Netherlands: Brill, 2000.

Everett, Daniel. "Cultural Constraints on Grammar and Cognition in Pirahã: Another Look at the Design Feature of Human Language." *Cultural Anthropology* 46 (2005): 621–46.

Faber, Alice. "Phonemic Segmentation as Epiphenomenon: Evidence from the History of Alphabetic Writing." In *The Linguistics of Literacy*, edited by P. Downing, S. Lima, and M. Noonan, 111–34. Amsterdam: John Benjamins, 1992.

Fales, Frederick M. "The Use and Function of Aramaic Tablets." *Ancient Near Eastern Studies Supplement* 7 (2000): 89–124.

Faust, Avraham. *Israel's Ethnogenesis: Settlement, Interaction, Expansion and Resistance*. London/Oakville, CT: Equinox, 2006.

Fellman, Joshua. *The Revival of a Classical Tongue: Eliezer Ben Yehuda and the Modern Hebrew Language*. The Hague, Netherlands: Mouton, 1973.

Finkelstein, Israel. "Archaeology and the List of Returnees in the Books of Ezra and Nehemiah." *Palestine Exploration Quarterly* 140 (2008): 7–16.

———. "The Archaeology of the Days of Manasseh." In *Scripture and Other Artifacts: Essays on the Bible and Archaeology in Honor of Philip J. King*, edited by M. Coogan, J. Cheryl Exum, and L. Stager, 196–87. Louisville, KY: Westminster John Knox, 1994.

———. "Jerusalem in the Persian (and Early Hellenistic) Period and the Wall of Nehemiah." *Journal for the Study of the Old Testament* 32 (2008): 501–20.

———. "The Settlement History of Jerusalem in the Eighth and Seventh Centuries BC." *Revue Biblique* 115 (2008): 499–515.

Finkelstein, Israel, Zvi Lederman, and Shlomo Bunimovitz. *Highlands of Many Cultures*. Tel Aviv: Tel Aviv University Institute of Archaeology, 1997.

Finkelstein, Israel, and Neil A. Silberman. *David and Solomon: In Search of the Bible's Sacred Kings and the Roots of the Western Tradition*. New York: Free Press, 2006.

———. "Temple and Dynasty: Hezekiah, the Remaking of Judah and the Rise of the Pan-Israelite Ideology." *Journal for the Study of the Old Testament* 30 (2006): 259–85.

Finkelstein, Israel, and Lily Singer-Avitz. "Reevaluating Bethel." *Zeitschrift des deutschen Palästina-Vereins* 125 (2009): 33–48.

Fishbane, Michael. "Form and Reformulation of the Biblical Priestly Blessing." *Journal of the American Oriental Society* 103 (1983): 115–21.

———. "The Well of Living Water: A Biblical Motif and Its Ancient Transformations." In *"Sha'arei Talmon": Studies in the Bible, Qumran, and the Ancient Near East Presented to Shemaryahu Talmon*, edited by M. Fishbane et al., 3–16. Winona Lake, IN: Eisenbrauns, 1992.

Fishman, Joshua. *Language and Nationalism: Two Integrative Essays*. Rowely, MA: Newbury, 1972.

———, ed. *Readings in the Sociology of Jewish Languages*. Leiden, Netherlands: Brill, 1985.

Fitzmyer, Joseph. "The Phases of the Aramaic Language." In *A Wandering Aramean: Collected Aramaic Essays*, 57–84. Society of Biblical Literature Monograph Series 25. Chico, CA: Scholars Press, 1979.

Frankel, Zacharias. *Vorstudien zu der Septuaginta*. Leipzig, Germany: Vogel, 1841.

Freedman, David. "Counting Formulae in the Akkadian Epics." *Journal of the Ancient Near East Society* 3 (1971): 65–81.

Fried, Lisbeth S. "A Silver Coin of Yoḥanan Hakkôhēn." *Transeuphratène* 26 (2003): 65–85.

Fuchs, Andreas. *Die Inschriften Sargons II aus Khorsabad*. Göttingen, Germany: Cuvillier, 1994.

Fuchs, Andreas, and Simo Parpola. *The Correspondence of Sargon II*. Vol. 3, *Letters from Babylonia and the Eastern Provinces*. State Archives of Assyria 15. Helsinki, Finland: Helsinki University Press, 2001.

Gal, Susan. "Codeswitching and Consciousness in the European Periphery." *American Ethnologist* 14 (1987): 637–53.

Galil, Gershon. "The Hebrew Inscription from Khirbet Qeiyafa/Neta'im: Script, Language, Literature and History." *Ugarit Forschungen* 41 (2010): 193–242.

Garfinkel, Yosef, and Saar Ganor. *Khirbet Qeiyafa*. Vol. 1, *Excavation Report, 2007–2008*. Jerusalem: Israel Exploration Society, 2009.

———. "Khirbet Qeiyafa in Survey and Excavations: A Response to Y. Dagan." *Tel Aviv* 37 (2010): 67–78.

Garr, Randall. *Dialect Geography of Syria-Palestine: 1000–586 B.C.E.* Philadelphia: University of Pennsylvania Press, 1985.

Geertz, Clifford. *The Interpretation of Cultures*. New York: Basic Books, 1973.

Geller, Markham. "The Last Wedge." *Zeitschrift für Assyriologie* 87 (1997): 43–95.

George, Andrew. "In Search of the é.dub.ba.a: The Ancient Mesopotamian School in Literature and Reality." In *An Experienced Scribe Who Neglects Nothing: Ancient Near Eastern Studies in Honor of Jacob Klein*, edited by Y. Sefati, et. al, 127–37. Bethesda, MD: CDL Press, 2005.

Gevirtz, Stanley. *Patterns in the Early Poetry of Israel*. Chicago: University of Chicago Press, 1963.

Gianto, Agustinus. "Historical Linguistics and the Hebrew Bible." In *Studi Sul Vicino Oriente Antico dedicati alla memoria di Luigi Cagni*, edited by M. Casaburi and G. Lacerenza, 1553–71. Rome: Herdner, 2000.

Ginsberg, Harold L. *Kitve Ugarit*. Jerusalem: Bialik, 1936. Hebrew.

———. "A Phoenician Hymn in the Psalter." In *Atti del XIX Congresso Internazionale degli Orientalisti*, 472–76. Rome: Bardi, 1935.

Gogel, Sandra. *A Grammar of Epigraphic Hebrew*. Society of Biblical Literature Resources for Biblical Study 23. Atlanta, GA: Scholars Press, 1998.

Golb, Norman. "The Problem of Origin and Identification of the Dead Sea Scrolls." *Proceedings of the American Philosophical Society* 124 (1980): 1–24.

Goldwasser, Orly. "Canaanites Reading Hieroglyphs: Horus Is Hathor? The Invention of the Alphabet in Sinai." *Egypt and the Levant* 16 (2006): 151–53.

———. "An Egyptian Scribe from Lachish and the Hieratic Tradition of the Hebrew Kingdoms." *Tel Aviv* 18 (1991): 248–53.

———. "How the Alphabet Was Born from Hieroglyphs." *Biblical Archaeology Review* 36, no. 2 (2010): 36–50, 74.

Goldwasser, Orly, and Stefan Wimmer. "Hieratic Fragments from Tell el-Far'ah (South)." *Bulletin of the American Schools of Oriental Research* 313 (1999): 39–42.

Goody, Jack. *The Domestication of the Savage Mind*. Cambridge, UK: Cambridge University Press, 1977.

———. *The Logic of Writing and the Organization of Society*. Cambridge, UK: Cambridge University Press, 1986.

———. *The Power of the Written Tradition*. Washington, DC: Smithsonian, 2000.

Goody, Jack, and Ian Watt. "The Consequences of Literacy." *Comparative Studies in Society and History* 5 (1963): 304–45.

Gottwald, Norman. *The Tribes of Yahweh*. New York: Orbis, 1979.

Grant, Elihu. "Découverte épigraphique a Beth SMS." *Revue Biblique* 37 (1930): 401–2, pl. xv.

Greenberg, Moshe. *The Ḫāb/piru*. New Haven, CT: Yale University Press, 1955.

Greenfield, Jonas. "Amurrite, Ugaritic and Canaanite." In *Proceedings of the International Conference on Semitic Studies*, 92–101. Jerusalem: Israel Academy of Sciences and Humanities, 1965.

———. "The 'Periphrastic Imperative' in Aramaic and Hebrew." *Israel Exploration Journal* 19 (1969): 199–210.

———. "The Wisdom of Ahiqar." In *Wisdom in Ancient Israel*, edited by J. Day et al., 43–52. Cambridge, UK: Cambridge University Press, 1997.

Greenspahn, Frederick. *Hapax Legomena in Biblical Hebrew: A Study of the Phenomenon and Its Treatment since Antiquity with Special Reference to Verbal Forms*. Atlanta, GA: Scholars Press, 1985.

Grill, Severin. "Die alten Versionen und die Partikeln lo', lô, lû, lî." *Bibliche Zeitschrift* 1 (1957): 277–78.

Grosby, Stephen. *Biblical Ideas of Nationality: Ancient and Modern*. Winona Lake, IN: Eisenbrauns, 2002.

———. "Borders, Territory and Nationality in the Ancient Near East and Armenia." *Journal of the Economic and Social History of the Orient* 40 (1997): 1–29.

———. "Kinship, Territory, and the Nation in the Historiography of Ancient Israel." *Zeitschrift für die Alttestamentliche Wissenschaft* 105 (1993): 3–18.

———. "Religion and Nationality in Antiquity." *Archives Européennes de Sociologie* 32 (1991): 229–65.

Gumperz, John J. *Discourse Strategies*. Cambridge, UK: Cambridge University Press, 1982.

Gumperz, John J., and Jenny Cook-Gumperz. "Studying Language, Culture and Society: Sociolinguistics or Linguistic Anthropology?" *Journal of Sociolingistics* 12 (2008): 532–45.

Hackett, Jo Ann, et al. "Defusing Pseudo-Scholarship: The Siloam Inscription Ain't Hasmonean." *Biblical Archaeology Review* 23, no. 2 (1997): 41–50.

Hadas-Lebel, Mireille. *Histoire de la langue Hébraïque: Des origines à l'époque de la Mishna*. Paris: Peeters, 1995.

Halliday, Michael. "Anti-Languages." *American Anthropologist* 78 (1976): 570–84.

Halpern, Baruch. "Two Views of a History of Ancient Israel." *Bulletin of the American Schools of Oriental Research* 357 (2010): 77–83.

Hamilton, Gordon. *The Origins of the West Semitic Alphabet in Egyptian Scripts*. Edited by M. Smith. Catholic Biblical Quarterly Monograph Series 40. Washington, DC: Catholic Biblical Association, 2006.

Harper, William R. *A Critical and Exegetical Commentary on Amos and Hosea*. International Critical Commentary. Edinburgh: T&T Clark, 1905.

Harris, William. *Ancient Literacy*. Cambridge, UK: Cambridge University Press, 1989.

———. *Development of the Canaanite Dialects: An Investigation in Linguistic History*. American Oriental Series 16. New Haven, CT: American Oriental Society, 1939.

Hasel, Michael. "Israel in the Merneptah Stele." *Bulletin of the American Schools of Oriental Research* 296 (1994): 45–61.

Havelock, Eric. *The Literate Revolution in Greece and Its Cultural Consequences*. Princeton, NJ: Princeton University Press, 1982.

Heaton, Eric W. *The School Tradition of the Old Testament*. Oxford, UK: Oxford University Press, 1994.

Heinrichs, Wolfhart, ed. *Studies in Neo-Aramaic*. Atlanta, GA: Scholars Press, 1990.

Heller, Monica, ed. *Codeswitching: Anthropological and Sociolinguistic Perspectives*. Contributions to the Sociology of Language 48. Berlin: de Gruyter, 1988.

Hendel, Ron. "Sibilants and *šibbōlet* (Judges 12:6)." *Bulletin of the American Schools of Oriental Research* 301 (1996): 69–76.

Hezser, Catherine. *Jewish Literacy in Roman Palestine*. Tübingen, Germany: Mohr Siebeck, 2001.

Hoffman, Joel. *In the Beginning: A Short History of the Hebrew Language*. New York: New York University Press, 2004.

Hoftijzer, Jacob, and Gerrit van der Kooij, eds. *The Balaam Text from Deir Alla Re-Evaluated: Proceedings of the International Symposium Held at Leiden, 21–24 August 1989*. Leiden, Netherlands: Brill, 1991.

Horowitz, Edward. *How the Hebrew Language Grew*. New York: Ktav, 1960.

Horowitz, Wayne, and Takayoshi Oshima. *Cuneiform in Canaan: Cuneiform Sources from the Land of Israel in Ancient Times*. Jerusalem: Israel Exploration Society, 2006.

Houston, Stephen. "The Archaeology of Communication Technologies." *Annual Review of Anthropology* 33 (2004): 223–50.

Huehnergard, John. "Semitic Languages." In *Civilizations of the Ancient Near East*, edited by J. M. Sasson, 4:2117–34. New York: Charles Scribner's Sons / Macmillan Library Reference, 1995.

Huffmon, Herbert. *Amorite Personal Names in the Mari Texts*. Baltimore, MD: Johns Hopkins University Press, 1965.

Humboldt, Wilhelm. *Über die Verschiedenheit des menschlichen Sprachbaues*. Darmstadt, Germany: Wissenschaftliche Buchgesellschaft, 1949.

Hummel, Horace. "Enclitic *Mem* in Early Northwest Semitic, Especially Hebrew." *Journal of Biblical Literature* 76 (1957): 85–107.

Hurvitz, Avi. "The Chronological Significance of 'Aramaisms' in Biblical Hebrew." *Israel Exploration Journal* 18 (1968): 234–40.

———. "The Date of the Prose Tale of Job Linguistically Reconsidered." *Harvard Theological Review* 67 (1975): 17–34.

———. "Hebrew and Aramaic in the Bible: The Problem of 'Aramaicisms' in the Research of Biblical Hebrew." In *Studies in the Hebrew Language and in Languages of the Jews*, edited by M. Bar-Asher, 79–94. Jerusalem: Bialik, 1996.

———. "Hebrew and Aramaic in the Biblical Period: The Problem of 'Aramaisms' in Linguistic Research on the Hebrew Bible." In *Biblical Hebrew: Studies in Chronology and Typology*, edited by I. Young, 24–37. London: T&T Clark, 2003.

———. *A Linguistic Study of the Relationship between the Priestly Source and the Book of Ezekiel*. Paris: Gabalda, 1981.

———. "Once Again: The Linguistic Profile of the Priestly Material in the Pentateuch and Its Historical Age." *Zeitschrift für die alttestamentliche Wissenschaft* 112 (2000): 180–91.

———. "The Recent Debate on Late Biblical Hebrew: Solid Data, Experts' Opinions, and Inconclusive Arguments." *Hebrew Studies* 47 (2006): 191–210.

———. *The Transition Period in Biblical Hebrew*. Jerusalem: Bialik, 1972. Hebrew.

Irvine, Judith T. "When Talk Isn't Cheap: Language and Political Economy." *American Ethnologist* 16 (1998): 248–67.

Irvine, Judith T., and Susan Gal. "Language Ideology and Linguistic Differentiation." In *Regimes of Language: Ideologies, Polities, and Identities*, edited by P. Kroskrity, 35–83. Santa Fe, NM: School of American Research, 2000.

Isserlin, B. "Epigraphically Attested Judean Hebrew, and the Question of Upper Class (Official) and Popular Speech Variants in Judea during the Eighth–Sixth Centuries B.C." *Australian Journal of Biblical Archeology* 1, no. 5 (1972): 197–203.

Izre'el, Shlomo. *Amurru Akkadian: A Linguistic Study*. Vol. 1. Harvard Semitic Studies 40. Atlanta, GA: Scholars Press, 1991.

———. *Canaano-Akkadian*. Munich: LINCOM, 1998.

———. "The Gezer Letters of the El-Amarna Archive: Linguistic Analysis." *Israel Oriental Studies* 8 (1978): 13–90.

Jamieson-Drake, D. *Scribes and Schools in Monarchic Judah: A Socio-Archeological Approach*. Journal for the Study of the Old Testament Supplement Series 109. Sheffield, UK: Sheffield University Press, 1991.

Japhet, Sara. *I & II Chronicles*. Philadephia: Westminister, 1993.

———. "Periodization: Between History and Ideology; The Neo-Babylonian Period in Biblical Historiography." In *Judah and the Judeans in the Neo-Babylonian Period*, edited by O. Lipschits and J. Blenkinsopp, 75–89. Winona Lake, IN: Eisenbrauns, 2003.

Joosten, Jan. "The Distinction between Classical and Late Biblical Hebrew as Reflected in Syntax." *Hebrew Studies* 46 (2005): 327–39.

———. "The Evolution of Literary Hebrew in Biblical Times: The Evidence of Pseudo-Classicisms." In *Diachrony in Biblical Hebrew*, edited by C. Miller-Naudé and Z. Zevit, 281–92. Winona Lake, IN: Eisenbrauns, 2012.

———. "Pseudoclassicisms in Late Biblical Hebrew, in Ben Sira, and in Qumran Hebrew." In *Sirach, Scrolls, and Sages: Proceedings of a Second International Symposium on the Hebrew of the Dead Sea Scrolls, Ben Sira, and the Mishnah, Held at Leiden University, 15–17 December 1997*, edited by T. Muraoka and J. F. Elwolde, 146–59. Studies on the Texts of the Desert of Judah 33. Leiden, Netherlands: Brill, 1999.

———. Review of *Linguistic Dating of Biblical Texts: An Introduction to Approaches and Problems, vol.* 2, by Ian Young and Robert Rezetko, with the assistance of Martin Ehrensvärd. *Bibel und Babel* 6 (2012): 535–42.

Joüon, Paul. *Grammaire de l'Hébreu biblique*. Rome: Pontifical Biblical Institute, 1923.

———. *A Grammar of Biblical Hebrew*. Translated and revised by T. Muraoka. Rome: Pontifical Biblical Institute, 1991.

Kahn, Geoffrey. "The Neo-Aramaic Dialect Spoken by Jews from the Region of Arbel (Iraqi Kurdistan)." *Bulletin of the School of Oriental and African Studies* 62 (1999): 213–25.

Kaufman, Stephen A. *The Akkadian Influences on Aramaic*. Assyriological Studies 19. Chicago: University of Chicago Press, 1974.

———. "The Classification of the North West Semitic Dialects of the Biblical Period and Some Implications Thereof." Paper presented at the Ninth World Congress of Jewish Studies, Jerusalem, August 1985.

Kiernan, Victor. "Languages and Conquerors." In *Language, Self, and Society: A Social History of Language*, edited by P. Burke and R. Porter, 191–210. Cambridge, UK: Polity Press, 1991.

Killebrew, Anne. *Biblical Peoples and Ethnicity: An Archaeological Study of Egyptians, Canaanites, and Early Israel 1300–1100 B.C.E.* Archaeology and Biblical Studies 9. Leiden, Netherlands: Brill; Atlanta, GA: Society of Biblical Literature, 2005.

Kim, Dong-Hyuk. "Free Orthography in a Strict Society: Reconsidering Tov's 'Qumran Orthography.'" *Dead Sea Discoveries* 11 (2004): 72–81.

Kletter, Raz. *Economic Keystones: The Weight System of the Kingdom of Judah*. Journal for the Study of the Old Testament Supplement Series 276. Sheffield, UK: Sheffield Academic Press, 1998.

Knauf, Ernst Axel. "Bethel: The Israelite Impact on Judean Language and Literature." In *Judah and the Judeans in the Persian Period*, edited by O. Lipschits and M. Oeming, 291–349. Winona Lake, IN: Eisenbrauns, 2006.

Kochavi, Moshe. "An Ostracon of the Period of the Judges from ʾIzbet Ṣarṭah." *Tel Aviv* 4 (1977): 1–13.

Koehler, Ludwig, and Walter Baumgartner. *The Hebrew and Aramaic Lexicon of the Old Testament*. Leiden, Netherlands: Brill, 2000.

Kraeling, Carl H., and Robert M. Adams, eds. *City Invincible: A Symposium on Urbanization and Cultural Development in the Ancient Near East*. Chicago: University of Chicago Press, 1960.

Krahmalkov, Charles. *A Phoenician-Punic Grammar*. Handbuch der Orientalistik 54. Leiden, Netherlands: Brill, 2001.

Kroskrity Paul. "Arizona Tewa Kiva Speech as a Manifestation of a Dominant Language Ideology." In *Language Ideologies: Practice and Theory*, edited by B. Schieffelin, K. Woolard, and P. Kroskrity, 385–400. Oxford Studies in Anthropological Linguistics 16. New York: Oxford University Press, 1998.

———. "Regimenting Languages: Language Ideological Perspectives." In *Regimes of Language: Ideologies, Polities, and Identities*, edited by P. Kroskrity, 1–34. Santa Fe, NM: School of American Research, 2000.

———, ed. *Regimes of Language: Ideologies, Polities, and Identities*. Santa Fe, NM: School of American Research, 2000.

Kühne, Hartmut. "The Urbanization of the Assyrian Provinces." In *Nuove Fondazioni nel Vicino oriente Antico: Realtà e Ideologia*, edited by S. Mazzon, 55–84. Pisa, Italy: Giardini Editori e Stampatori, 1994.

Kutscher, Edward Y. *A History of the Hebrew Language*. Jerusalem: Magnes, 1982.

———. *The Language and Linguistic Background of the Isaiah Scroll (1QIs[a])*. Studies on the Texts of the Desert of Judah 6. Leiden, Netherlands: Brill, 1974.

———. *Words and Their History*. Jerusalem: Kiryath Sefer, 1961.

Labov, William. *Principles of Linguistic Change*. Vol. 2, *Social Factors*. Oxford, UK: Blackwell, 2001.

———. *Sociolinguistic Patterns*. Philadelphia: University of Pennsylvania Press, 1972.

———. "The Study of Language in Its Social Context." In *Advances in the Sociology of Language*. Vol. 1, *The Study of Language in Its Social Context*, edited by J. Fishman, 152–216. The Hague, Netherlands: Mouton, 1971.

Lambdin, Thomas. "Egyptian Loanwords in the Old Testament." *Journal of the American Oriental Society* 73 (1953): 145–55.

Latacz, Homer. *His Art and His World*. Translated by J. Holoka. Ann Arbor. MI: University of Michigan Press, 1996.

Lehman, I. O. "A Forgotten Principle of Biblical Textual Criticism Rediscovered." *Journal of Near Eastern Studies* 26 (1967): 93–101.

Lehmann, Gunnar. "Trends in the Local Pottery Development of the Late Iron Age and Persian Period in Syria and Lebanon, ca. 700 to 300 B.C." *Bulletin of the American Schools of Oriental Research* 311 (1998): 21–32.

Lemaire, André. *Les Écoles et la Formation de la Bible dans L'ancien Israël*. OBO 39. Göttingen, Germany: Vandenhoeck & Ruprecht, 1981.

———."'House of David' Restored in Moabite Inscription." *Biblical Archaeology Review* 20, no. 3 (1994): 30–37.

———."Prières en temps de crise: Les inscriptions de Khirbet Beit Lei." *Revue Biblique* 83 (1976): 558–68.

———. "The Spread of the Alphabetic Scripts (c. 1700–500 BCE)." *Diogenes* 218 (2008): 44–57.

Lichtheim, Miriam. *Ancient Egyptian Literature*. Vol. 1. Berkeley / Los Angeles: University of California Press, 1973.

Lindenberger, James. *The Aramaic Proverbs of Ahiqar*. Baltimore, MD: Johns Hopkins University Press, 1983.

Lipschits, Oded. "Achaemenid Imperial Policy and the Status of Jerusalem, in the Middle of the 5th Century BCE." In *Judah and the Judeans in the Persian Period*, edited by O. Lipschits and M. Oeming, 19–52. Winona Lake, IN: Eisenbrauns, 2003.

———. "Demographic Changes in Judah between the Seventh and the Fifth Centuries B.C.E." In *Judah and the Judeans in the Persian Period*, edited by O. Lipschits and M. Oeming, 323–76. Winona Lake, IN: Eisenbrauns, 2003.

Lipschits, Oded, and David Vanderhooft. *The Yehud Stamp Impressions: A Corpus of Inscribed Impressions from the Persian and Hellenistic Periods in Judah*. Winona Lake, IN: Eisenbrauns, 2011.

Luckenbill, David. *Ancient Records of Assyria and Babylonia*. 2 vols. Chicago: University of Chicago Press, 1926–27.

Lucy, John. *Language Diversity and Thought: A Reformulation of the Linguistic Relativity Hypothesis*. Cambridge, UK: Cambridge University Press, 1992.

Lyon, David G. *Keilschrifttexte Sargons, Königs von Assyrien (722–705 v Chr.): Nach den Originalen*. Leipzig, Germany: Hinrichs Buchhandlung, 1883.

Machinist, Peter. "The Question of Distinctiveness in Ancient Israel: An Essay." In *Ah, Assyria . . . : Studies in Assyrian History and Ancient Near Eastern Historiography Presented to Hayim Tadmor*, edited by M. Cogan and I. Eph'al, 196–212. Jerusalem: Magnes, 1991.

Maeir, Aren, et al. "A Late Iron Age I / Early Iron Age II Old Canaanite Inscription from Tell eṣ-Ṣâfī /Gath, Israel: Palaeography, Dating, and Historical-Cultural Significance." *Bulletin of the American Schools of Oriental Research* 351 (2008): 39–71.

Malamat, Abraham. "Mari and Hazor: Trade Relations in the Old Babylonian Period." In *Biblical Archaeology Today, 1990: Proceedings of the Second International Congress on Biblical Archaeology*. Supp.: *Pre-Congress Symposium: Population, Production and Power*, edited by A. Biran and J. Aviram, 66–70. Jerusalem: Israel Exploration Society, 1993.

Mankowski, Paul. *Akkadian Loanwords in Biblical Hebrew*. Harvard Semitic Studies 47. Winona Lake, IN: Eisenbrauns, 2000.

Mazar, Amihai. *Archaeology of the Land of the Bible, 10,000–586 B.C.E.* Garden City, NY: Doubleday, 1990.

———. "The Debate over the Chronology of the Iron Age in the Southern Levant: Its History, the Current Situation, and a Suggested Resolution." In *The Bible and Radiocarbon Dating: Archaeology, Text and Science*, edited by T. Levy and T. Higham, 15–30. Oakville, CT: Equinox, 2005.

———. "Three 10th–9th Century B.C.E. Inscriptions from Tel Rehov." In *Saxa Loquentur: Studien zur Archäeologie Palästinas/Israels: Festschrift für Volkmar Fritz zum 65. Geburtstag*, edited by C. den Hertog, U. Hübner, and S. Münger, 171–84. Münster, Germany: Ugarit-Verlag, 2003.

Mendels, Doron. *The Rise and Fall of Jewish Nationalism*. 2nd ed. Grand Rapids, MI: Eerdmans, 1992.

Mendenhall, George E. "The Hebrew Conquest of Palestine." *Biblical Archaeologist* 25, no. 3 (1962): 66–87.

———. "Social Organization in Early Israel." In *Magnalia Dei: The Mighty Acts of God; Essays on the Bible and Archaeology in Memory of G. Ernest Wright*, edited by F. M. Cross et al., 132–51. Garden City, NY: Doubleday, 1976.

Meshorer, Ya'akov. *Ancient Jewish Coinage*. Vol. 1, *Persian Period through Hasmoneans*. Dix Hills, NY: Amphora Books, 1982.

Meshorer, Ya'akov, and Shraga Qedar. *Samarian Coinage*. Jerusalem: Israel Numismatic Society, 1999.

Mettinger, Tryggve N. D. *Solomonic State Officials: A Study of the Civil Government Officials of the Israelite Monarchy*. Coniectanea biblica: Old Testament Series 5. Lund, Sweden: Gleerup, 1971.

Meyer, Rudolph. "Bemerkungen zu den hebräischen Aussprachetraditionen von Chirbet Qumrân." *Zeitschrift für die Alttestamentliche Wissenschaft* 70 (1958): 39–48.

———. "Das Problem der Dialektmischung in den hebräischen Texten von Chirbet Qumrân." *Vetus Testamentum* 7 (1957): 139–48.

Millard, Alan. "The Uses of the Early Alphabets." In *Phoinikeia Grammata: Lire et écrire en Méditerranée*, edited by C. Baurain, C. Bonnet, and V. Krings, 101–14. Namur, Belgium: Société des Études Classiques, 1991.

———. "Variable Spelling in Hebrew and Other Ancient Text." *Journal of Theological Studies*, n.s., 42 (1991): 106–15.

Mishor, Mordechay. "The Tense System in Tannaitic Hebrew." Ph.D. dissertation, Hebrew University of Jerusalem, 1983. Hebrew.

Montaner, Luis. "Some Features of the Hebrew Verbal Syntax in the Qumran Hodayot." In *The Madrid Qumran Congress: Proceedings of the International Congress on the Dead Sea Scrolls, Madrid, 18–21 March 1991*, edited by J. T. Barrera and L. V. Montaner, 273–86. Jerusalem: Magnes; Leiden, Netherlands: Brill, 1992.

Mor, Uri. "Language Contact in Judea: How Much Aramaic Is There in the Hebrew Documents from the Judean Desert?" *Hebrew Studies* 52 (2011): 213–20.

Morag, Shelomo. "Qumran Hebrew: Some Typological Observations." *Vetus Testamentum* 38 (1988): 148–64.

Moran, William L. "The Ancient Near Eastern Background of the Love of God in Deuteronomy." *Catholic Biblical Quarterly* 25 (1963): 77–87.

———. "The Hebrew Language in Its Northwest Semitic Background." In *The Bible and the Ancient Near East*, edited by G. E. Wright, 59–84. Garden City, NY: Doubleday: 1961.

Morgan, Marcyliena. "Speech Community." In *A Companion to Linguistic Anthropology*, edited by A. Duranti, 3–22. Oxford, UK: Blackwell, 2004.

Morris, Ellen. *The Architecture of Imperialism: Military Bases and the Evolution of Foreign Policy in Egypt's New Kingdom*. Probleme der Ägyptologie 22. Leiden, Netherlands: Brill, 2005.

Muraoka, Takamitsu. "Linguistic Notes on the Aramaic Inscription from Tel Dan." *Israel Exploration Journal* 45 (1995): 19–21.

———. "The Participle in Qumran Hebrew, with Special Reference to Its Periphrastic Use." In *Sirach, Scrolls, and Sages: Proceedings of a Second International Symposium on the Hebrew of the Dead Sea Scrolls, Ben Sira, and the Mishnah, Held at Leiden University, 15–17 December 1997*, edited by T. Muraoka and J. F. Elwolde, 188–204. Studies on the Texts of the Desert of Judah 33. Leiden, Netherlands: Brill, 1999.

Myers-Scotton, C. "Code-Switching." In *The Handbook of Sociolinguistics*, edited by F. Coulmas, 217–37. Oxford, UK: Blackwell, 1997.

Na'aman, Nadav. "Ḫābiru and Hebrews: The Transfer of a Social Term to the Literary Sphere." *Journal of Near Eastern Studies* 45 (1986): 271–88.

———. "When and How Did Jerusalem Become a Great City? The Rise of Jerusalem as Judah's Premier City in the Eighth–Seventh Centuries B.C.E." *Bulletin of the American Schools of Oriental Research* 347 (2007): 21–56.

Naveh, Joseph. *Early History of the Alphabet*. Jerusalem: Magnes, 1987.

———. "Hebrew and Aramaic Inscriptions." In *Excavations at the City of David*. Vol. 6, *Inscriptions*, ed. A. Belfer Cohen, G. Foerster, E. Stern, and Y. Tsafrir, 1–14. Jerusalem: Hebrew University, 2000.

———. "A Hebrew Letter from the Seventh Century B.C." *Israel Exploration Journal* 10 (1960): 129–39.

———. "Old Hebrew Inscriptions in a Burial Cave." *Israel Exploration Journal* 13 (1963): 74–92.

———. "Some Notes on the Reading of the Meṣad Hashavyahu Letter." *Israel Exploration Journal* 14 (1964): 158–59.

Naveh, Joseph, and Jonas Greenfield. "Hebrew and Aramaic in the Persian Period." In *The Cambridge History of Judaism*. Vol. 1, *Introduction: The Persian Period*, edited by W. D. Davies and L. Finkelstein, 115–29. Cambridge, UK: Cambridge University Press, 1984.

Nichols, Johanna. "Functional Theories of Grammar." *Annual Review of Anthropology* 13 (1984): 97–117.

Niditch, Susan. *Oral World and Written Word: Ancient Israelite Literature*. Library of Ancient Israel. Louisville, KY: Westminster John Knox Press, 1996.

Oded, Bustenay. "Where Is the 'Myth of the Empty Land' to Be Found? History versus Myth." In *Judah and the Judeans in the Neo-Babylonian Period*, edited by O. Lipschits and J. Blenkinsopp, 55–74. Winona Lake, IN: Eisenbrauns, 2003.

Ong, Walter. *Orality and Literacy: The Technologizing of the Word*. Padstow, UK: T. J. Press, 1982.

———. "Writing Is a Technology That Restructures Thought." In *The Written Word: Literacy in Transition*, edited by G. Baumann, 23–50. Oxford, UK: Clarendon Press, 1986.

Ormsby-Lennon, Hugh. "From Shibboleth to Apocalypse: Quaker Speechways during the Puritan Revolution." In *Language, Self, and Society: A Social History of Language*, edited by P. Burke and R. Porter, 72–112. Cambridge, UK: Polity Press, 1991.

Overland, Paul. "Structure in the Wisdom of Amenemope and Proverbs." In *Go to the Land I Will Show You: Studies in Honor of Dwight W. Young*, edited by J. E. Coleson and V. H. Matthews, 275–91. Winona Lake, IN: Eisenbrauns, 1996.

Pardee, Dennis, et al. *Handbook of Ancient Hebrew Letters*. Chico, CA: Scholars Press, 1982.

Parker, Bradley. *The Mechanics of Empire: The Northern Frontier of Assyria as a Case Study in Imperial Dynamics*. Helsinki, Finland: Neo-Assyrian Text Corpus Project, 2001.

Parpola, Simo. "The Man without a Scribe and the Question of Literacy in the Assyrian Empire." In *Ana šadî labnāni lūallik: Beiträge zu altorientalischen und mittelmeerischen Kulturen*, edited by B. Pongratz-Leisten et al., 315–24. Neukirchen-Vluyn, Germany: Neukirchener Verlag, 1997.

Pearce, Laurie. "Sepîru and LÚ A.BA: Scribes of the Late First Millennium." In *Languages and Cultures in Contact*, edited by K. van Lerberghe and G. Voet, 355–68. Leuven, Belgium: Peeters, 1995.

Pedersén, Olof. *Archives and Libraries in the Ancient Near East, 1500–300 B.C.* Bethesda, MD: CDL Press, 1998.

Pérez Fernández, Miguel. *An Introductory Grammar of Rabbinic Hebrew*. Translated by J. Elwolde. Leiden, Netherlands: Brill, 1997.

Pfann, Stephen. "Cryptic Texts." In *Qumran Cave 4: XXVI*, edited by S. Pfann and P. Alexander, 515–74. Discoveries in the Judean Desert 36. Oxford, UK: Clarendon Press, 2000.

———. "4Q298: The Maskîl's Address to All Sons of Dawn." *Jewish Quarterly Review* 85 (1994): 216–21.

———. "The Writings in Esoteric Script from Qumran." In *The Dead Sea Scrolls Fifty Years after Their Discovery: Proceedings of the Jerusalem Congress, July 20–25, 1997*, edited by L. Schiffman, E. Tov, and J. VanderKam, 177–90. Jerusalem: Israel Exploration Society, 2000.

Pinker, Steven. *The Language Instinct: How the Mind Creates Language*. New York: Harper Collins, 1994.

Polak, Frank. "Epic Formulas in Biblical Narrative: Frequency and Distribution." In *Acts du Second Colloque International Bible et Informatique: Méthodes, Outils, Résultats*, edited by R. Poswick et al., 437–89. Paris: Champion, 1989.

———. "Linguistic and Stylistic Aspects of Epic Formulae in Ancient Semitic Poetry and Biblical Narrative." In *Biblical Hebrew in Its Northwest Semitic Setting: Typological and Historical Perspectives*, edited by S. Fassberg and A. Hurvitz, 285–304. Jerusalem: Magnes; Winona Lake, IN: Eisenbrauns, 2006.

———. "Sociolinguistics: A Key to the Typology and the Social Background of Biblical Hebrew." *Hebrew Studies* 47 (2006): 115–62.

———. "Style Is More Than the Person: Sociolinguistics, Literary Culture, and the Distinction between Written and Oral Narrative." In *Biblical Hebrew: Studies in Chronology and Typology*, edited by I. Young, 38–103. London: T&T Clark, 2003.

Pollock, Sheldon. "Cosmopolitan and Vernacular in History." *Public Culture* 12, no. 3 (2000): 591–625.

Polzin, Robert. *Late Biblical Hebrew: Toward an Historical Typology of Biblical Hebrew Prose*. Missoula, MT: Scholars Press, 1976.

Porter, Barbara Nevling. "Language, Audience and Impact in Imperial Assyria." In *Language and Culture in the Near East*, edited by S. Izre'el and R. Drory, 51–72. Leiden, Netherlands: Brill, 1995.

Prince, Alan. "Segments." In *International Encyclopedia of Linguistics*, edited by W. Bright, 384–87. New York: Oxford University Press, 1992.

Pritchard, James B. *Ancient Near Eastern Texts Relating to the Old Testament*. 3rd ed., with supp. Princeton, NJ: Princeton University Press, 1969.

Puech, Emile. "L'Ostracon de Khirbet Qeyafa et les debuts de la royaute en Israel." *Revue Biblique* 117 (2010): 162–84.

Pulgram, Ernst. "Spoken and Written Latin." *Language* 26 (1950): 458–66.

Purvis, James. *The Samaritan Pentateuch and the Origin of the Samaritan Sect*. Cambridge, MA: Harvard University Press, 1968.

Qimron, Elisha. *The Hebrew of the Dead Sea Scrolls*. Harvard Semitic Monographs 29. Atlanta, GA: Scholars Press, 1986.

Qimron, Elisha, and John Strugnell. "An Unpublished Halakhic Letter from Qumran." In *Biblical Archaeology Today: Proceedings of the International Congress on Biblical Archaeology, April 1984*, edited by J. Amitai, 400–407. Jerusalem: Israel Exploration Society, 1985.

Rabin, Chaim. "The Emergence of Classical Hebrew." In *The Age of the Monarchies: Culture and Society*, edited by A. Malamat, 71–78. Jerusalem: Massada, 1979.

———. "The Historical Background of Qumran Hebrew." *Scripta Hiersolymitana* 4 (1958): 144–61.

———. *A Short History of the Hebrew Language*. Jerusalem: Haomanim Press, 1974.

Rabin, Ira, et al. "On the Origin of the Ink of the Thanksgiving Scroll (1QHodayot a)." *Dead Sea Discoveries* 16 (2009): 97–106.

Rainey, Anson. F. "The Ancient Hebrew Prefix Conjugation in the Light of Amarnah Canaanite." *Hebrew Studies* 27 (1986): 1–19.

———. *Canaanite in the Amarna Tablets: A Linguistic Analysis of the Mixed Dialect Used by the Scribes from Canaan*. 4 vols. Leiden, Netherlands: Brill, 1996.

———. "Inside, Outside: Where Did the Early Israelites Come From?" *Biblical Archaeology Review* 34, no. 6 (2008): 45–50, 84.

———. "The Kingdom of Ugarit." *Biblical Archaeologist* 28, no. 4 (1965): 102–25.

———. "The Prefix Conjugation Patterns of Early Northwest Semitic." In *Lingering over Words: Studies in Ancient Near Eastern Literature in Honor of William L. Moran*, edited by T. Abusch, J. Huehnergard, and P. Steinkeller, 407–20. Atlanta, GA: Scholars Press, 1990.

———. "Redefining Hebrew: A Transjordanian Language." *Maarav* 14 (2007): 37–56.

———. "Whence Came the Israelites and Their Language?" *Israel Exploration Journal* 57 (2007): 41–64.

Ray, John D. "Egyptian Wisdom Literature." In *Wisdom in Ancient Israel*, edited by J. Day et al., 17–29. Cambridge, UK: Cambridge University Press, 1997.

Reich, Ronny, Eli Shukron, and Omri Lernau. "Recent Discoveries in the City of David." *Israel Exploration Journal* 57 (2007): 156–60.

Rendsburg, Gary A. "A Comprehensive Guide to Israelian Hebrew: Grammar and Lexicon." *Orient* 38 (2003): 5–35.

———. *Diglossia in Ancient Hebrew*. American Oriental Series 72. New Haven, CT: American Oriental Society, 1990.

———. "The Geographical and Historical Background of the Mishnaic Hebrew Lexicon." *Orient* 38 (2003): 105–15.

———. *Israelian Hebrew in the Book of Kings*. Bethesda, MD: CDL Press, 2002.

———. "Linguistic Variation and the 'Foreign' Factor in the Hebrew Bible." In *Language and Culture in the Near East*, edited by S. Izre'el and R. Drory, 177–90. Israel Oriental Series 15. Leiden, Netherlands: Brill, 1995.

———. "On the Writing ביתדוד in the Aramaic Inscription from Tel Dan." *Israel Exploration Journal* 45 (1995): 22–25.

———. "Qumran Hebrew (with a Trial Cut [1QS])." In *The Dead Sea Scrolls at 60*, edited by L. Schiffman and S. Tzoref, 217–46. Leiden, Netherlands: Brill, 2010.

Rendsburg, Gary A., and William Schniedewind. "The Siloam Tunnel Inscription: Historical and Linguistic Perspectives." *Israel Exploration Journal* 60 (2010): 188–203.

Renz, Johannes, and Wolfgang Röllig, eds. *Die althebräischen Inschriften: Handbuch der althebräischen Epigraphik*. 3 vols. Darmstadt, Germany: Wissenschaftliche Buchgesellschaft, 1995–2003.

Revell, Ernest. "Pausal Forms in Biblical Hebrew: Their Function, Origin and Significance." *Journal of Semitic Studies* 25 (1980): 165–79.

Robertson, David A. *Linguistic Evidence in Dating Early Hebrew Poetry*. Society of Biblical Literature Dissertation Series 3. Missoula, MT: Scholars Press, 1972.

Robinson, Andrew. *The Story of Writing*. 2nd ed. London: Thames & Hudson, 2007.

Rogers, Henry. *Writing Systems: A Linguistic Approach*. Oxford, UK: Blackwell, 2005.

Rogerson, John, and Philip. R. Davies. "Was the Siloam Tunnel Built by Hezekiah?" *Biblical Archaeologist* 59, no. 3 (1996): 138–49.

Rollston, Christopher A. "Non-Provenanced Epigraphs I: Pillaged Antiquities, Northwest Semitic Forgeries, and Protocols for Laboratory Tests." *Maarav* 10 (2003): 135–93.

———. "Non-Provenanced Epigraphs II: The Status of Non-Provenanced Epigraphs within the Broader Corpus of Northwest Semitic." *Maarav* 11 (2004): 57–79.

———. "Scribal Education in Ancient Israel: The Old Hebrew Epigraphic Evidence." *Bulletin of the American Schools of Oriental Research* 344 (2006): 47–74.

———. *Writing and Literacy in the World of Ancient Israel: Epigraphic Evidence from the Iron Age*. Atlanta, GA: Society of Biblical Literature, 2010.

Romaine, Suzanne. *Language in Society: An Introduction to Sociolinguistics*. 2nd ed. Oxford, UK: Oxford University Press, 2001.

Rooker, Mark. *Biblical Hebrew in Transition: The Language of the Book of Ezekiel*. Journal for the Study of the Old Testament Supplement Series 90. Sheffield, UK: JSOT Press, 1990.

———. "Dating Isaiah 40–66: What Does the Linguistic Evidence Say?" *Westminster Theological Journal* 58 (1996): 303–12.

Root, Bradley. "Coinage, War, and Peace in Fourth-Century Yehud." *Near Eastern Archaeology* 68, no. 3 (2005): 131–34.

Roth, Wolfgang. "The Numerical Sequence x/x + 1 in the Old Testament." *Vetus Testamentum* 12 (1962): 300–311.

Sabar, Ariel. *My Father's Paradise*. Chapel Hill, NC: Algonquin, 2009.

Sáenz-Badillos, Angel. "Hebrew as the Language of Judaism." In *The Semitic Languages*, edited by S. Weninger et al., 537–45. Berlin: de Gruyter, 2011.

———. *A History of the Hebrew Language*. Cambridge, UK: Cambridge University Press, 1993.

Safrai, Shmuel. "Education and the Study of the Torah." In *The Jewish People in the First Century: Historical Geography, Political History, Social, Cultural and Religious Life and Institutions*, edited by S. Safrai and M. Stern, 945–70. Assen, Netherlands: Van Gorcum; Philadelphia: Fortress, 1976.

Sampson, Geoffrey. *Writing Systems: A Linguistic Introduction*. Palo Alto, CA: Stanford University Press, 1990.

Sanders, Seth. *The Invention of Hebrew*. Chicago: University of Illinois Press, 2009.

———, ed. *Margins of Writing, Origins of Culture*. Chicago: Oriental Institute of the University of Chicago, 2006.

Sapir, Edward. *Language: An Introduction to the Study of Speech*. New York: Harcourt, Brace, 1921.

Sasson, Victor. "Some Observations on the Use and Original Purpose of the 'Waw' Consecutive in Old Aramaic and Biblical Hebrew." *Vetus Testamentum* 47 (1997): 111–27.

Saussure, Ferdinand de. *Course in General Linguistics*. Edited by C. Bally and A. Sechehaye. Translated by R. Harris. 3rd ed. New York: Open Court, 1983.

———. *Writings in General Linguistics*. Oxford, UK: Oxford University Press, 2006.

Schaper, Joachim. "Hebrew and Its Study in the Persian Period." In *Hebrew Study from Ezra to Ben-Yehuda*, edited by W. Horbury, 15–26. Edinburgh: T&T Clark, 1999.

Schiffman, Lawrence. *Reclaiming the Dead Sea Scrolls*. Philadelphia: Jewish Publication Society, 1994.

Schniedewind, William. "Aramaic, the Death of Written Hebrew, and Language Shift in the Persian Period." In *Margins of Writing, Origins of Culture*, edited by S. Sanders, 137–48. Chicago: Oriental Institute of the University of Chicago, 2006.

———. *How the Bible Became a Book*. Cambridge, UK: Cambridge University Press, 2004.

———. "Jerusalem, the Late Judaean Monarchy, and the Composition of Biblical Texts." In *Jerusalem in Bible and Archaeology*, edited by A. Killebrew and A. Vaughn, 375–93. Atlanta, GA: Society of Biblical Literature, 2003.

———. "Linguistic Ideology in Qumran Hebrew." In *Diggers at the Well: Proceedings of a Third International Symposium on the Hebrew of the Dead Sea Scrolls and Ben Sira*, edited by T. Muraoka and J. F. Elwolde, 245–55. Leiden, Netherlands: Brill, 2000.

———. "The Problem with Kings: Recent Study of the Deuteronomistic History." *Religious Studies Review* 22, no. 1 (1995): 22–27.

———. "Problems in the Paleographic Dating of Inscriptions." In *The Bible and Radiocarbon Dating: Archaeology, Text and Science*, edited by T. Levy and T. Higham, 405–12. Oakville, CT: Equinox, 2005.

———. "Prolegomena for the Sociolinguistics of Classical Hebrew." *Journal of Hebrew Scriptures* 5, no. 6 (2004) [online journal].

———. "Qumran Hebrew as an Antilanguage." *Journal of Biblical Literature* 118 (1999): 235–52.

———. Review of *Scribal Culture and the Making of the Hebrew Bible* by Karel van der Toorn. *Journal of Hebrew Scriptures* 10 (2010): r.29 [electronic journal].

———. *Society and the Promise to David*. New York: Oxford University Press, 1999.

———. "Sociolinguistic Reflections on the Letter of a Literate Soldier (Lachish 3)." *Zeitschrift für Althebräistik* 13 (2000): 157–67.

Schniedewind, William, and Daniel Sivan. "The Elijah-Elisha Narratives: A Test Case for the Northern Dialect of Hebrew." *Jewish Quarterly Review* 87 (1997): 303–37.

———. "Letting Your 'Yes' Be 'No' in Ancient Israel: A Study of the Asseverative לא and הלא in Hebrew." *Journal of Semitic Studies* 38 (1993): 209–26.

Schofield, Alison. *From Qumran to the Yahad*. Leiden, Netherlands: Brill, 2009.

Schürer, Emil. *The History of the Jewish People in the Age of Jesus Christ (175 B.C.–A.D. 135)*. Revised and edited by G. Vermes and F. Millar. Edinburgh: T&T Clark, 1973.

Schwartz, Seth. "Hebrew and Imperialism in Jewish Palestine." In *Ancient Judaism in Its Hellenistic Context*, edited by C. Bakhos, 53–84. Leiden, Netherlands: Brill, 2005.

———. "Language, Power and Identity in Ancient Palestine." *Past and Present* 148 (1995): 3–47.

Segal, J. B. "YRH in the Gezer 'Calendar.'" *Journal of Semitic Studies* 7 (1962): 212–21.

Segal, Moshe H. *A Grammar of Mishnaic Hebrew*. Oxford, UK: Clarendon Press, 1927.

Seymour, Philip. "Early Reading Development in European Orthographies." In *The Science of Reading: A Handbook*, edited by M. Snowling and C. Hulme, 296–315. Oxford, UK: Blackwell, 2005.

Share, David, and Iris Levine. "Learning to Read and Write in Hebrew." In *Learning to Read and Write: A Cross-Linguistic Perspective*, edited by M. Harris and G. Hatano, 89–111. Cambridge, UK: Cambridge University Press, 1999.

Shinan, Avigdor. "The Aramaic Targum as a Mirror of Galilean Jewry." In *The Galilee in Late Antiquity*, edited by L. Levine, 241–51. New York: Jewish Theological Seminary, 1992.

Shoham, Yair. "Hebrew Bullae." In *Excavations at the City of David, 1978–1985, Directed by Yigal Shiloh*. Vol. 6, *Inscriptions*, edited by D. Ariel, 29–57. Qedem 41. Jerusalem: Hebrew University Press, 2000.

Shupak, Nili. *Where Can Wisdom Be Found? The Sage's Language in the Bible and in Ancient Egyptian Literature*. Orbis biblicus et orientalis 130. Fribourg,

Switzerland: University Press; Göttingen, Germany: Vandenhoeck & Ruprecht, 1993.

Siegel, John Paul. *The Severus Scroll and 1QIs[a]*. Missoula, MT: Scholars Press, 1975.

Silverstein, Michael. Review of *The View from Language: Selected Essays, 1948–1974*, by Charles Hockett. *International Journal of American Linguistics* 44 (1978): 235–53.

———. "Worfianism and the Linguistic Imagination of Nationalism." In *Regimes of Language: Ideologies, Polities, and Identities*, edited by P. Kroskrity, 85–138. Santa Fe, NM: School of American Research, 2000.

Skinner, John. *Genesis*. International Critical Commentary. 2nd ed. Edinburgh: T&T Clark, 1930.

Skoss, Solomon L. *Saadia Gaon: The Earliest Hebrew Grammarian*. Philadelphia: Dropsie College Press, 1955.

Smith, Daniel. *The Religion of the Landless: The Social Context of the Babylonian Exile*. Bloomington, IN: Meyer-Stone, 1989.

Smith, Mark. "Converted and Unconverted Perfect and Imperfect Forms in the Literature of Qumran." *Bulletin of the American Schools of Oriental Research* 284 (1991): 1–16.

Smith, Nigel. "The Uses of Hebrew in the English Revolution." In *Language, Self, and Society: A Social History of Language*, edited by P. Burke and R. Porter, 51–71. Cambridge, UK: Polity Press, 1992.

Smith-Christopher, Daniel. *A Biblical Theology of Exile*. Minneapolis, MN: Fortress, 2002.

———. "Reassessing the Historical and Sociological Impact of the Babylonian Exile (597/587–539 BCE)." In *Exile: Old Testament, Jewish, and Christian Conceptions*, edited by J. M. Scott, 7–36. Leiden, Netherlands: Brill, 1997.

Snaith, Norman H. *The Distinctive Ideas of the Old Testament*. New York: Schocken, 1964.

Sparks, Kenton. *Ethnicity and Identity in Ancient Israel: Prolegomena to the Study of Ethnic Sentiments and Their Expression in the Hebrew Bible*. Winona Lake, IN: Eisenbrauns, 1998.

Sperber, Alexander. *A Historical Grammar of Biblical Hebrew*. Leiden: Brill, 1966.

Stager, Lawrence. "An Inscribed Potsherd from the Eleventh Century B.C." *Bulletin of the American Schools of Oriental Research* 194 (1969): 45–52.

Stavans, Ilan. *Resurrecting Hebrew*. New York: Schocken, 2008.

Stern, Ephraim. *Archaeology of the Land of the Bible*. Vol. 2, *The Assyrian, Babylonian, and Persian Periods (732–333 B.C.E.)*. New York: Doubleday, 2001.

———. "The Babylonian Gap." *Biblical Archaeology Review* 26, no. 6 (2000): 45–51, 76.

———. *Material Culture of the Land of the Bible in the Persian Period, 538–332 B.C.* Warminster, UK: Aris and Phillips, 1982.

Stern, Sacha. "Qumran Calendars: Theory and Practice." In *The Dead Sea Scrolls in Their Historical Context*, edited by T. Lim, 179–86. Edinburgh: T&T Clark, 2000.

Stevenson, William. *Grammar of Palestinian Jewish Aramaic*. 2nd ed. Oxford, UK: Clarendon Press, 1962.

Stieglitz, Robert. "The Ugaritic Cuneiform and Canaanite Linear Alphabets." *Journal of Near Eastern Studies* 30 (1971): 135–39.

Stipp, Hermann-Josef. "Gedalja und die Kolonie von Mizpa." *Zeitschrift für Altorientalische und Biblische Rechtsgeschichte* 6 (2000): 155–71.

Tadmor, Hayim. "The Aramaization of Assyria: Aspects of Western Impact." In *Mesopotamien und seine Nachbarn*, edited by H.-J. Nissen and J. Renger, 2:449–70. Berlin: Dietrich Reimer, 1982.

———. "On the Role of Aramaic in the Assyrian Empire." In *Near Eastern Studies Dedicated to H. I. H. Prince Takahito Mikasa on the Occasion of His Seventy-Fifth Birthday*, edited by M. Mori, H. Ogawa, and M. Yoshikawa, 419–23. Bulletin of the Middle Eastern Studies Center in Japan. Wiesbaden, Germany: Harrassowitz, 1991.

Talmon, Shemaryahu. "The Emergence of Institutionalized Prayer in Israel in Light of Qumran Literature." In *The World of Qumran from Within*, edited by S. Talmon, 200–43. Jerusalem: Magnes, 1989.

———. "The New Hebrew Letter from the Seventh Century B.C. in Historical Perspective." *Bulletin of the American Schools of Oriental Research* 176 (1964): 29–38.

———. "What's in a Calendar? Calendar Conformity and Calendar Controversy in Ancient Judaism: The Case of the 'Community of the Renewed Covenant.'" In *The Bible and the Dead Sea Scrolls*, edited by J. Charlesworth, 2:25–58. Waco, TX: Baylor University Press, 2006.

Talshir, David. "The Habitat and History of Hebrew during the Second Temple Period." In *Biblical Hebrew: Studies in Chronology and Typology*, edited by I. Young, 251–75. New York: Continuum, 2003.

Tappy, Ron, and P. Kyle McCarter, Jr., eds. *Literate Culture and Tenth-Century Canaan: The Tel Zayit Abecedary in Context*. Winona Lake, IN: Eisenbrauns, 2008.

Tappy, Ron, et al. "An Abecedary of the Mid-Tenth Century B.C.E. from the Judean Shephelah." *Bulletin of the American Schools of Oriental Research* 344 (2006): 5–46.

Thorion-Vardi, "The Use of the Tenses in the Zadokite Documents." *Revue de Qumran* 12 (1985–86): 65–88.

Tigay, Jeffrey. *Deuteronomy*. Jewish Publication Society Torah Commentary. Philadelphia: Jewish Publication Society, 1996.

———. "Israelite Religion: The Onomastic and Epigraphic Evidence." In *Ancient Israelite Religion: Essays in Honor of Frank Moore Cross*, edited by P. D. Miller, P. Hanson, and S. D. McBride, 157–94. Philadelphia: Fortress, 1987.

———. *You Shall Have No Other Gods: Israelite Religion in the Light of Hebrew Inscriptions*. Harvard Semitic Studies 31. Atlanta, GA: Scholars Press, 1986.

Titunik, Irwin R. "The Formal Method and the Sociological Method (M. M. Baxtin, N. Medvedev, V. N. Voloshinov) in Russian Theory and the Study of Literature." In *Marxism and the Philosophy of Language*, by V. N. Voloshinov, translated by L. Matejka and I. R. Titunik, 175–200. Cambridge, MA: Harvard University Press, 1973.

Torczyner, Harry. *Lachish I: The Lachish Letters*. Oxford, UK: Oxford University Press, 1938.

Torrey, Charles C. *Ezra Studies*. Chicago: University of Chicago, 1910.

———. *Leading Captivity Captive: "The Exile" as History and Ideology*. Journal for the Study of the Old Testament Supplement Series 278. Sheffield, UK: Sheffield Academic Press, 1998.

Toubouret-Keller, Andrée. "Language and Identity." In *Handbook of Sociolinguistics*, edited by F. Coulmas, 315–26. Oxford, UK: Blackwell, 1997.

Tov, Emmanuel. "Hebrew Biblical Manuscripts from the Judaean Desert: Their Contribution to Textual Criticism." *Journal of Jewish Studies* 39 (1988): 5–37.

———. "The Orthography and Language of the Hebrew Scrolls found at Qumran and the Origin of These Scrolls." *Textus* 13 (1986): 31–57.

———. "Reply to Dong-Hyuk Kim's Paper on 'Tov's Qumran Orthography.'" *Dead Sea Discoveries* 11 (2004): 359–60.

———. *Scribal Practices and Approaches Reflected in the Texts Found in the Judean Desert*. Studies on the Texts of the Desert of Judah 54. Leiden, Netherlands: Brill, 2004.

———. *Textual Criticism of the Hebrew Bible*. Minneapolis, MN: Fortress; Assen, Netherlands: Van Gorcum, 1992.

Trudgill, Peter. *Sociolinguistics: An Introduction to Language and Society*. 4th ed. New York: Penguin, 2001.

Ullendorff, Edward. "Is Biblical Hebrew a Language?" *Bulletin for the School for African and Oriental Studies* 2 (1971): 3–17. Reprinted in Ullendorff, *Is Biblical Hebrew a Language? Studies in Semitic Languages and Civilizations*. Wiesbaden, Germany: Harrassowitz, 1977.

Ulrich, Eugene. *The Dead Sea Scrolls and the Origins of the Bible*. Grand Rapids, MI: Eerdmans, 1999.

Unseth, Peter. "The Sociolinguistics of Script Choice: An Introduction." *International Journal for the Sociology of Language* 192 (2008): 1–4.

Vanderhooft, David. "*ʾel-mĕdînâ ûmĕdînâ kiktābāh*: Scribes and Scripts in Yehud and in Achaemenid Transeuphratene." In *Judah and the Judeans in the Achaemenid Period: Negotiating Identity in an International Context*, edited by O. Lipschits, G. Knoppers, and M. Oeming, 529–44. Winona Lake, IN: Eisenbrauns, 2011.

———. *The Neo-Babylonian Empire and Babylon in the Latter Prophets*. Harvard Semitic Monographs 59. Atlanta, GA: Scholars Press, 1999.

Vanderhooft, David, and Oded Lipschits. "A New Typology of the Yehud Stamp Impressions." *Tel Aviv* 34 (2007): 12–37.

Van de Sande, Axel. *Nouvelle perspective sur le système verbal de l'hébreu ancien*. Leuven, Belgium: Peeters, 2006.

Van Gelderen, E. *A History of the English Language*. Philadelphia: John Benjamins, 2006.

Voloshinov, Valentin N. *Marxism and the Philosophy of Language*. Translated by L. Metejka and I. Titunik. Cambridge, MA: Harvard University Press, 1986.

Von Dassow, Eva. "Canaanite in Cuneiform." *Journal of the American Oriental Society* 124 (2004): 641–74.

Van Soldt, Wilfred. "The Written Sources: The Syllabic Akkadian Texts." In *Handbook of Ugaritic Studies*, 28–45, edited by W. Watson and N. Wyatt. Leiden, Netherlands: Brill, 1999.

Waltke, Bruce, and Michael O'Connor. *An Introduction to Biblical Hebrew Syntax*. Winona Lake, IN: Eisenbrauns, 1990.

Webster, Noah. *An Essay on the Necessity, Advantages, and Practicality of Reforming the Mode of Spelling and of Rendering the Orthography of Words Correspondent to Pronunciation*. Boston, 1789.

Weidner, Ernst. "Jojachin, König von Juda." In *Mélanges Syriens offerts a M. René Dussaud*, 2:923–28. Paris: Geuthner, 1939.

Weinfeld, Moshe. *Deuteronomy and the Deuteronomic School*. Oxford, UK: Clarendon Press, 1972. Reprint, Winona Lake, IN: Eisenbrauns, 1992.

Weitzman, Steve. "Why Did the Qumran Community Write in Hebrew?" *Journal of the American Oriental Society* 119 (1999): 35–45.

Whitelam, Keith. *The Invention of Ancient Israel: The Silencing of Palestinian History*. London: Routledge, 1996.

Williamson, Hugh G. M. *Israel in the Book of Chronicles*. Cambridge, UK: Cambridge University Press, 1977.

———. *1 and 2 Chronicles*. Grand Rapids, MI: Eerdmans, 1982.

Wimmer, Stephan. "The Prince of Safit? A Late Bronze Hieratic Inscription from Tel es-Safi/Gath." *Zeitschrift des Deutschen Palästina-Vereins* 123 (2007): 37–48.

Woodhouse, Robert. "The Biblical Shibboleth Story in the Light of Late Egyptian Perceptions of Semitic Sibilants: Reconciling Divergent Views." *Journal of the American Oriental Society* 123 (2003): 271–90.

Woolard, Kathryn A. "Language Ideology as a Field of Inquiry." In *Language Ideologies: Practice and Theory*, edited by B. Schieffelin, K. Woolard, and P. Kroskrity, 3–47. Oxford Studies in Anthropological Linguistics 16. New York: Oxford University Press, 1998.

Woolard, Kathryn, and Bambi Schieffelin. "Language Ideology." *Annual Review of Anthropology* 23 (1994): 55–82.

Wright, George Ernest. *The Old Testament against Its Environment*. London: SCM Press, 1950.

Yadin, Yigael. *Bar-Kokhba*. New York: Random House, 1971.

Yadin, Yigael, and J. Naveh. *Masada I: The Aramaic and Hebrew Ostraca and Jar Inscriptions*. Jerusalem: Israel Exploration Society, 1989.

Yadin, Yigael, et al. *The Documents from the Bar Kokhba Period in the Cave of Letters*. Jerusalem: Israel Exploration Society, 2002.

Yeivin, Israel. *The Hebrew Language of Tradition as Reflected in the Babylonian Vocalization*. 2 vols. Jerusalem: Academy of the Hebrew Language, 1985. Hebrew.

———. *Introduction to the Tiberian Masorah*. Missoula, MT: Society of Biblical Literature, 1980.

Young, Ian. *Diversity in Pre-Exilic Hebrew*. Tübingen, Germany: Mohr, 1993.

———. "Israelite Literacy: Interpreting the Evidence, Part I." *Vetus Testamentum* 48 (1998): 239–53.

———. "Late Biblical Hebrew and the Qumran Pesher Habakkuk." *Journal of Hebrew Scriptures* 8, no. 25 (2008) [online journal].

Young, Ian, and Robert Rezetko. *Linguistic Dating of Biblical Texts: An Introduction to Approaches and Problems*. With the assistance of Martin Ehrensvärd. 2 vols. London: Equinox, 2008.

Zimmern, Heinrich. *Akkadische Fremdwörter als Beweis für babylonischen Kultureinfluss*. 2nd ed. Leipzig, Germany: Hinrichs, 1917.

Zorn, Jeffrey. "Mizpah: Newly Discovered Stratum Reveals Judah's Other Capital." *Biblical Archeology Review* 23, no. 5 (1997): 28–38, 66.

Index